EARLY
CONCERT - LIFE IN AMERICA
(1731 – 1800)

Da Capo Press Music Reprint Series

MUSIC EDITOR
BEA FRIEDLAND
Ph.D., City University of New York

EARLY
CONCERT - LIFE IN AMERICA
(1731 – 1800)

BY
O. G. SONNECK

DA CAPO PRESS · NEW YORK · 1978

Library of Congress Cataloging in Publication Data

Sonneck, Oscar George Theodore, 1873-1928.
   Early concert-life in America, 1731-1800.
   (Da Capo Press music reprint series)
   Reprint of the 1907 ed. published by Breitkopf &
Härtel, Leipzig.
   Includes bibliographical references.
   1. Music — United States — History and criticism.
I. Title.
[ML200.3.S6 1978]   780'.973   78-2580
ISBN 0-306-77591-3

This Da Capo Press edition of *Early Concert-Life in America* is an
unabridged republication of the first edition published in Leipzig in 1907.

Published by Da Capo Press, Inc.
A Subsidiary of Plenum Publishing Corporation
227 West 17th Street, New York, N.Y. 10011

Manufactured in the United States of America

EARLY
CONCERT-LIFE IN AMERICA

(1731—1800)

BY

O. G. SONNECK

LEIPZIG

BREITKOPF & HÄRTEL

1907

TO MY WIFE

PREFACE.

WITH this book I attempt to lay the historical foundations of one important side of our country's musical life. Intended as a source-book, it is addressed to those seriously interested in musical history and it is cast in a form peculiar to source-books, which necessarily resemble mosaics and — mosaics are not to everybody's taste. While I have taken pains to leave as little dust as possible on these pages, I fear that they lack that literary brilliancy which makes, at first reading, even a poor book attractive. Those sterner critics who will take issue with me on that score I beg to remember how very difficult a task it is to turn a virgin-forest into a garden.

On the other hand, as this work is addressed to the student more than to the amateur, his familiarity with the history of music in Europe was taken for granted. Therefore European conditions were discussed only where I disagreed with current doctrines, where a European background was necessary for the proper historical perspective, or, where danger-signals might be helpful. References to early opera in America were kept as brief as possible because I hope to complete a comprehensive essay on this subject before long. For the same reason, other topics, bearing indirectly on our early concert life, were kept in the background. Similarly, biographical and bibliographical data were included in so far only as they seemed called for or affected the biographical notes given in the index to my Bibliography of Early Secular American Music.

In order to preserve as much of the eighteenth century flavor as possible, names have been spelled as they appeared in my sources and only, when it would have been cruel to let the reader wrestle with the printer's devil, have I adopted the form now commonly used. Probably it will also prevent confusion if I remark that, as a rule and for obvious reasons, not the earliest announcements but those nearest to the date fixed for the concert have been quoted.

The data on concerts given in our country until 1750 have been published in form of a separate article in the New Music Review, 1906.

Washington, D. C., May 6, 1906.

O. G. Sonneck.

CONTENTS.

INTRODUCTION.

JOHN BANISTER is generally credited with having given the first public concert to which admission was gained by way of payment. After losing his place at the English court, he hired "over against the George Tavern in White Friars", London, a room with "a large raised box for the musitians, whose modesty required curtains", as Roger North puts it in his Memoirs, and advertised the first of his daily public afternoon-concerts for Dec. 30, 1672[1]). But it has always appeared rather incredible to me that the democratic idea of public concerts should have taken concrete form at so late a date. In view of the fact that about forty years only had elapsed since the discovery of opera when public opera was introduced at Venice in 1637, this sceptical attitude towards tradition will be pardoned if it is further remembered that concerts, in one form or the other, certainly antedated the birth of opera and became indispensible to the happiness of music-lovers during the seventeenth century.

Mr. Louis C. Elson is the possessor of the constitution, list of members, etc. in a latin manuscript volume pertaining to a musical club which existed, as the entries prove, at least from 1560 to 1588 presumably at Amsterdam, the members frequently joining with distinguished visitors in *consort*[2]). That this was not the earliest musical society on record, the term implying performances of music, in other words, concerts, goes without saying as in Bologna and Milan such existed under the venerable name of Accademia as early as 1482 and 1484 and rapidly increased there and elsewhere until in the seventeenth century some Italian cities possessed three or four[3]). In France, as Brenet pointed out in her admirable book on 'Les Concerts en France sous l'ancien régime', the poet Jean Antoine de Baïf and the musician Joachim Thibaut de Courville founded not later than 1567 the Académie de Baïf, receiving therefore *lettres patentes* in 1570 and though mixed literary-musical entertainments were offered to the members, yet

---

1) See Davey's History of English Music.
2) Described in the Musician, 1904, p. 464 though Mr. Elson did not take cognizance of the great importance of his find for the history of musical societies.
3) Grove, New ed., article Academia.

we may see in this academy the cradle of concerts at Paris. Nor did the provincial towns remain in the rear of the movement for very long as such academies, though their financial and material side escaped even the scrutinizing eye of Brenet, were frequent throughout France about 1625 and in Mersenne's time (1588—1648) *assemblées de concerts* evidently were a common occurrence.

In the German speaking countries such musical societies seem to have been of somewhat later origin, though the Cantorey Gesellschaften and their antipodes, the convivial gatherings at which the rollicking Quodlibets were sung, did much to pave the way for the Collegia Musica, the term originally being merely the latin for "eine musikalische Zusammenkunft" (Walther) and not implying an academic flavor. In Switzerland the first Collegium Musicum with weekly meetings has been traced by Nef to Zürich and to the year 1613, others soon following in other Swiss towns. A few years later, in 1616, Prague saw a similar club spring into existence; Philip Spitta has entertainingly written of the Musikalische Societät of 1617 at Mühlhausen, and so on until Germany, like France, was well supplied with musical societies whose members to their own and their guests' delight played and sang the music of their times, as becomes sensible amateurs, without pretensions to virtuosity, this probably being true even of the famous Collegium Musicum founded by Mathias Weckmann and "zween vornehme Liebhaber der Musik" at Hamburg in 1660[1]).

In England the movement appears to have set in not later than 1600, otherwise Dekker's line in 'A Knights Coniuring' of 1607

"To this consort roome resort none but the children of Phoebus (poets and musitions)"

would be incomprehensible. A few decades later, Pepys mentions in his diary a concert at 'The Mitre' in 1659—60 with no hint that concerts were still a novelty (Davey). This impression is strengthened by Roger North who describes the weekly meetings held in a tavern near St. Paul's

„Where there was a chamber organ that one Phillips played upon, and some shop keepers and foremen [apparently forming a musical club!] came weekly to sing in concert, and to hear and enjoy ale and tobacco, and after some time the company grew strong."

---

1) Not 1668 as generally stated. See Max Seiffert's 'Mathias Weckmann und das Collegium Musicum in Hamburg' (Sbde. d. IMG. 1900—1901, p. 76—127). This Collegium Musicum of 1660 is said to have been the first founded in Germany, but I am confident that others will be found to antedate it, once an exhaustive history of musical societies in Germany is attempted. Thus, for instance, Alfred Heuss recently drew attention to a remark in Mattheson's Ehrenpforte which would lead to infer that Jodocus Willichius founded one at Frankfurt a. d. Oder towards the end of the sixteenth century and it is also well known that such literary clubs as Harsdörfer's Hirten und Blumen Orden an der Pegnitz (1642) in Nürnberg resembled the Académie de Baïf in the combination of literary and musical interests.

Finally Anthony Wood who was at Oxford University in 1651 has left us a vivid account of the practice of chamber music for viols at Oxford where he went to a weekly meeting of musicians, amateurs and professionals, combining into a band of over sixten performers.

Of this weekly music meeting, Hawkins remarked in his History of Music, after enumerating the names of the "Noblemen", "Drs" (Doctors), "Masters" and "Strangers" who constituted it in 1665 that it

... was the first subscription concert of which any account is to be met with: indeed it seems to have been the only association of the sort in the kingdom; the reason of this might be, that the pretenders to the love of music were not then so numerous as they have been of late years. A concert was formerly a serious entertainment, at which such only as had a real and genuine affection for music assembled ...

Selected at random as these notes are, they suffice to prove that the idea of musical cooperation had gained root in Europe before the period with which this book occupies itself. Now the concerts given by the musical clubs whether they cultivated vocal or instrumental music or both, were public only in so far as the members chose to extend admission by way of invitation, the guests, as for instance in Switzerland, appreciating the courtesy with substantial souvenirs. Still less public were, of course, the concerts given by kings, princes and noblemen at their courts and palaces to the aristocratic world, but rumors of the splendour of Cromwell's State Concerts, for instance, or of the daily concerts and spectacles at Versailles must have spread into the masses and our innate desire for forbidden fruit certainly helped to drive a democratic wedge into the absolute exclusiveness of the music-loving aristocracy and the relative exclusiveness of the bourgeoisie as maintained in their musical clubs. The general public had to be content with the glowing accounts of domestics, musicians and privileged friends except on such fairly frequent and regular occasions when by order of the sovereign or the city-fathers the court-musicians, Stadtpfeifer and Ratsmusikanten would exhibit their skill in public. Thus entertainments partaking of the character of public concerts were not altogether missing in the daily life of a people, more passionately devoted to home-music of the best kind and on terms of closer social intimacy with the musicians than is now unfortunately the case[2]).

---

1) See Naylor Shakespeare and music, 1896, p. 12.
2) By the way, those who, a few years ago, hailed the socalled Verleger-Concerte at Leipzig as a novelty, will perhaps hear with regret that even this happy idea was anticipated in the sixteenth century. Says N. Yonge in the dedication of his collection 'Musica transalpina', 1588 to Gilbert Lord Talbot:
"... a great number of Gentlemen and Merchants of good accompt (as well of this realme as of foreign nations) have taken in good part such entertainments of pleasure as my poor abilitie was able to afford them both by the exercise of Musicke daily used in my house, and by furnishing them with Bookes of that kind yearly sent me out of Italy and other places."

However, public concerts proper in all probability claim an humbler origin. Had the gentleman *or* merchant of Shakespeare's time listened to or made others listen at the barbershop to the "stringed noise" of the lute or viol, to use Milton's words, until his turn came to busy the deft hand and gossiping tongue of the tonsorial artist, and did he then proceed for a bumper of ale to the taverns or "Musik Houses" of which there were many in the time of Charles II, as Hawkins says, he was almost sure to find there one or several ambulant musicians, the socalled "Waits", who, for a consideration, would strike up his favorite Pavana, Saltarello, Air or Jig. And if we remember that by far the majority of public concerts were still held at taverns at the end of the eighteenth century, it will not be considered a fantastic idea, I hope, to trace the sources of our public concert-life to the taverns and their fiddling parasites. From the custom to collect the fee after the *concert* from everybody present to an arrangement by which such thirsty souls, who desired to enjoy music in privacy, agreed to pay an equal share, in other words an embryonic form of obligatory admission-fee was but a short and logical step. Nor can I make myself believe that the idea of payment on a still more dignified and solid business basis, with its obligations, rights and advantages to both the performer and the audience, whether congregating in taverns or in the homes of music lovers, was either foreign to that age or remained so until John Banister's time. Indeed there are signs that it did not. If Mathias Weckmann's Collegium Musicum was "öffentlich, sowohl für fremde als einheimische Liebhaber ausgestattet" it is plausible that the fifty instrumentalists and singers forming the club and performing weekly in the refectory of the Dom charged admission in order to defray expenses and if Jacques de Gouy describes the *concerts spirituels* held before 1650 at the house of Pierre de Chabanceau de la Barre as the first given at Paris, though they were not, Brenet was justified in arguing that de Gouy's statement would be acceptable only if he meant concerts *publics et payants*.

Should after all, John Banister's innovation have consisted merely in this that he was the first to planfully make public concerts a regular and more dignified feature in the musical life of the city? Again it is Hawkins who allows us to draw this inference. To be sure, he seems over-anxious to credit Thomas Britton with the introduction of public concerts simply because the assistants and patrons of the small-coal man belonged to the upper classes (and Burney, of course, when copying his in many respects historically more important rival, was altogether too much of a historian for aristocrats to question the wisdom of such a course) yet Hawkins though reluctantly enough, felt obliged to write (v. 5, p. 1):

In the interim it is proposed to speak of those musical performances with which the people in general were entertained at places of public resort, distinguishing between such as were calculated for the recreation of the vulgar and those which for their elegance come under the denomination of concerts. The first of these were no other than the musical entertainments given to their people in Music Houses, already spoken of, the performers in which consisted of fiddlers and others, hired by the master of the house, such as in the night season were wont to parade the city and suburbs under the denomination of the Waits. The music of these men could scarcely be called a concert, for this obvious reason, that it had no variety of parts, nor commixture of different instruments: Half a dozen of fiddlers would scrape Sellenger's Round, or John come kiss me, or Old Simon the King with divisions, till themselves and their audience were tired, after which as many players on the hautboy would in the most harsh and discordant tones grate forth Green Sleeves, Yellow Stockings, Gillian of Craydon, or some such common dance-tune, and the people thought it fine music.

But a concert, properly so called, was a sober recreation; persons were drawn to it, not by an affectation of admiring what they could not taste, but by a genuine pleasure which they took in the entertainment. For the gratification of such the masters of music exerted their utmost endeavours and some of the greatest eminence among them were not above entertaining the public with musical performances, either at their own houses, or in more commodious, receiving for their own use the money paid on admission. And to these performances the lovers of music were invited by advertisement in the London Gazette ...

And then follows not only John Banister's advertisement of his concert on December 30, 1672 but also the announcements of his concerts in subsequent years and many others until 1698. Yet Hawkins sought to brush John Banister aside in favor of Thomas Britton! Whatever his reasons for this strange contradiction might have been, Banister's example was followed in 1678 by Britton, whose famous concerts in Clerkenwell lasted until 1714. Another concert room, independent of ale and tobacco, was opened about 1680 in Villiers Street at the York Buildings. If Mr. Davey says that the entertainments there became very fashionable he is probably mistaken as Roger North, evidently alluding to the same undertaking, asserts that the music masters finding that "money could be got that way" had the room built in Villiers Street but that their socalled *Music Meeting* failed for lack of proper management. It is also Roger North who says that about the time of Banister's venture a society of gentlemen of good esteem met "often for consort". Their room becoming crowded they took one in a tavern in Fleetstreet but, and this remark is interesting, disbanded when the taverner made a "pecuniary consort of it". However the tide was not to be stemmed and public concerts soon became a permanent, prominent and ever growing branch of concert-life in London with those of the Academy of Ancient Music (1710), the Castle Society (1724), and Mrs. Cornely's subscription concerts (1765), conducted by Abel and Bach, as principal stepping stones, quite apart from the *benefit* concerts given by Gluck, Quantz, and innumerable other virtuosos.

On the continent, the concert-life continued to center in the activity of the Collegia Musica, Académies and other more or less private organisations. Brenet tells us that about 1700 it had become quite customary for music teachers to give musicales at their homes "pour s'attirer pratique" and that in 1724 the monthly musicales, given since about 1720 by Crozat, the richest man in Paris, were combined with the 'Concert Italien' of Mad. de Prie on the subscription basis, the sixty members wittily being dubbed *gli Academici paganti*, but it remained for Philidor to introduce periodical concerts, in appearance and principle really public. This he did with his 'Concert Spirituel' of 1725, but it should be remembered that these concerts took place at the Académie Royale de Musique only on days of great religious festivals when operatic performances were prohibited and that they originally were subject to other curious strictures.

By this time Lübeck had enjoyed her unique 'Abendmusiken' on the five Sundays before Christmas for more than fifty years. Founded by Buxtehude in 1673 and blessed with the fruits of his genius these 'Abendmusiken', though perhaps not in theory, practically were public sacred concerts with admission fee. Later on, Telemann founded in 1713 the 'wöchentliches grosses Concert im Frauenstein' at Frankfort o/M., continued in 1723 by the 'Winter Concert' which formed the back bone of Frankfort's organized concert-life until the end of the century[1]). It was also Telemann who after his removal to Hamburg introduced similar subscription concerts about 1720 first in the Drillhaus and since 1722 at his home, performing principally his own vocal music of larger compass. Though Telemann retained for both his ventures the title of Collegium Musicum, the entertainments were really more public than private[2]). This was certainly the case with the weekly 'Musikalische Concerte' at Leipzig, the one under Joh. Seb. Bach and the other under Joh. Gottlieb Görner, the performers being recruited to a large extent amongst the students, for Mizler in his Neu-eröffnete Musikalische Bibliothek, 1739 says (I, 63) plainly enough:

"Die beiden öffentlichen Musikalischen Concerten, oder Zusammenkünfte, so hier wöchentlich gehalten werden, sind noch in beständigem Flor."

In Berlin and Vienna the democratic idea of public concerts was naturally slower in assuming permanent shape than in such cities as Frankfort, Hamburg or Leipzig and thus we notice that in Berlin the 'Akademie', the 'Assemblee', Agricola's Concert, and especially the 'Musikübende Gesellschaft' still retained about 1750 an air of exclusiveness and that their concerts were decidedly more private than public in character[3]). If furthermore Hanslick

---

1) Israel, Frankfurter Concert-Chronik von 1713—1780.
2) Sittard, Geschichte des Musik- u. Concertwesens in Hamburg. On the other hand the famous culinary-concerts given by Count Eckgh at Hamburg in 1700—1701 at which Reinh. Keiser conducted himself "mehr als ein Cavallier, denn als ein Musikus" were private. (See Mattheson.)
3) See Marpurg, Hist.-Krit. Beyträge, 1754/5, Entwurf einer ausführlichen Nachricht von der "Musikübenden Gesellschaft zu Berlin".

failed to trace public concerts at Vienna before 1740[1]), this failure certainly is significant enough, though, or rather because, Hanslick's statement is not correct. He overlooked Mattheson's ironical entry in the 'Musikalische Patriot' (p. 26):

"Meiner Correspondenten einer . . . meldete mir vor einiger Zeit aus Wien, dass daselbst ein gewisser netter Clavier Spieler, etc. ein Concert gehalten, wobey sich die Liebhaber so häufig eingestellet hatten, dass, nach geschlossener Rechnung, just 10½ gute Groschen von dem Maestro eingebüsset worden; anstatt, dass er vermuthet haette, einen guten Beutel voller Gulden davon zu streichen."

Consequently public concerts of the *benefit* type were actually given at Vienna at least as early as 1728 but they seem to have been sporadic. Nor does it appear from the pages containing the quotation that the fate of this particular *maestro* was exceptional in German cities. Indeed men like Mattheson seem to have cultivated a grudge against the virtuosos especially the Italian, who were rapidly forcing — and not always in a, manner legitimate or artistic — a new element into the musical life of their time. To have foreseen that the musical life of Europe was irrisistibly gliding into democratic channels by sheer force of the underlying current in general sociological conditions and by the equally strong trend towards disintegration in the evolution of musical forms and their vehicles of performance, in short the steadily crystallizing distinction between orchestral and chamber music with all the consequences, to have clearly foreseen this could not reasonably be expected of Mattheson and his contemporaries. However, without going too far into evolutional theories, this much appears from all contemporary and historical accounts to be certain: the public concert-life of German cities remained in an undeveloped condition for decades after John Banister's innovation had borne plentiful fruit in London. This fact is of great importance and carries with it obvious inferences if we wish to assume a proper and impartial attitude towards the early history of concert-life in the British Colonies of North America.

When reading the histories of music in America we almost gain the impression that the emigrants of the seventeenth century detested not so much the religious, political or economic atmosphere of Europe as the musical and we feel overawed by the constellation of mysterious motives prompting Providence to send to our shores out of all the millions who inhabited Europe just those few thousand beings who had no music in their souls. Now, the Puritans, the Pilgrims, the Irish, the Dutch, the Germans, the Swedes, the Cavaliers of Maryland and Virginia and the Huguenots of the South may have been zelots, adventurers, beggars, spendthrifts, fugitives from justice, convicts, but barbarians they certainly were not.

---

1) Hanslick, Geschichte des Concertwesens in Wien, 1869.

Until some historian displays the courage, the skill and the patience to unearth and collect the data pertaining to our musical life before 1700 all ponderous meditations on the subject will remain guesswork.   Possibly, even probably, music was at an extremely low ebb, but this would neither prove that the early settlers were hopelessly unmusical nor that they lacked interest in the art of 'sweet conchord'.   It was simply a matter of opportunity, for what inducements had a handful of people, spread over so vast an area, struggling for an existence, surrounded by virgin-forests, fighting the Red-man, and quarelling amongst themselves to offer to musicians?   We may rest assured that even Geoffrey Stafford, "lute and fiddle maker" by trade and ruffian by instinct, would have preferred more lucrative climes and gracefully declined the patronage of musical Governor Fletcher had he not been deported in 1691 to Massachusetts by order of this Majesty King William along with a batch of two hundred other Anglo-Saxon convicts[1]). In fact, as Mr. Elson pointed out[2]), the 'Observations made by the Curious in New England', printed at London in 1673, inform us that "in Boston there are no musicians by trade".   Of the *dilettanti* nothing is said, but that such existed in the Colonies, we know well enough from Sewall's diary and as the early settlers were not unlike other human beings in having voices, we may take it for granted that they used them not only in church, but at home, in the fields, in the taverns, exactly as they would have done in Europe and for the same kind of music as far as their memory or their supply of music books carried them.   That the latter, generally speaking, can not have been very large, goes without saying, for the emigrants of those days, even the well-to-do, had but vessels like the Mayflower — a wonderful box of Pandora though she must have been — at their disposal for the storage of household goods that were absolutely necessary.   This would also explain why so seldom musical instruments are mentioned in the inventories of those days.   They were to be found, however, in the homes of the wealthy merchants of the North and in the homes of the still more pleasure seeking aristocratic planters of the South.   Indeed, there can be little doubt that the nearest approach to a musical atmosphere in feeble imitation of European conditions was to be found in the South rather than in the North.   Still, we might call the period until about 1720 the primitive period in our musical history without fear of being convicted of hasty conclusions.

After 1720 we notice a steadily growing number of musicians who sought

---

1) See the amusing account of Geoffrey Stafford in Spillane's History of the American pianoforte, p. 14.
2) See his book on 'the National Music of America', p. 46.

their fortunes in the Colonies[1]), an increasing desire for organs, flutes, guitars, violins, harpsichords, the establishment of "singing schools", an improvement in church music, the signs of a budding music trade from ruled music paper to sonatas and concertos, the advent of music engravers, publishers and manufacturers of instruments, the tentative efforts to give English opera a home in America, the introduction of public concerts, in short the beginnings of what may properly be termed the formative period in our musical history, running from 1720 until about 1800. If I further maintain that during this period secular music developed more rapidly than sacred and soon became the more important of the two, a comparison between the history of our early sacred music, with which we have been fairly well acquainted, and this history of our early concert life — together with opera, the other main branch of secular music — will substantiate my theory contrary to popular axiom though it may be.

---

[1] In this connection a glimpse into Boston of "ye olden Time" may afford entertainment. Mr. Thomas Brattle, a wealthy Puritan and a man of artistic instincts, bequeathed in 1713 an imported organ to Brattle Square Church. It was promptly rejected for religious reasons and was then presented, in accordance with the will, to King's Chapel, the vestry procuring in a Mr. Price. the first organist as "the sober person to play skilfully thereon with a loud noise" as Mr. Brattle put it. The second organist was Mr. Edward Enstone, imported from England in 1714 at a salary of £ 30 yet" with dancing, music etc" it was thought it would answer (See Hist. of King's Chapel). Accordingly he filed on Feb. 21, 1714 a "petition for liberty of keeping a school as a Master of Music and a Dancing Master 'but it was disallowed by ye Sel. men." Not withstanding this refusal Mr. Enstone opened his school and the Select Men felt so chagrined by his impertinence that they promptly instructed in the following year the town-clerk to present "a complaint to Session." This the town-clerk probably did but evidently Mr. Enstone and not "ye Sel. men" carried the day for in 1716 Mr. Enstone inserted in the Boston News Letter on April 16—23 this instructive advertisement, a veritable historical document. "This is to give notice that there is lately sent over from London, a choice Collection of Musickal Instruments, consisting of Flageolets, Flutes, Haut-Boys, Bass-Viols, Violins, Bows, Strings, Reads for Haut-Boys, Books of Instructions for all these Instruments, Books of ruled Paper. To be Sold at the Dancing School of Mr. Enstone in Sudbury Street near the Orange Tree, Boston.
  NOTE. Any person may have all Instruments of Musick mended, or Virgenalls and Spinnets Strung and Tuned at a reasonable Rate, and likewise may be taught to Play on any of these Instruments above mention'd; dancing taught by a true and easier method than has been heretofore."
Mr. Enstone still appears to have resided at Boston in 1720 advertising himself as dancing master and keeper of a boarding house "where young Ladies may be accommodated with Boarding, and taught all sorts of Needle Work with Musick and Dancing, etc."

CHARLESTON[1]) AND THE SOUTH.

WHEN and where the first public concert took place in what are to-day the United States of North America would be difficult and useless to answer. Difficult, because the earliest concert recorded in our newspapers, diaries, documents, etc. by no means would imply it to have been the first; useless because the history of our concert life as concert-life could not reasonably be deducted from a stray concert without noticeable traces. Still, there is a good deal of fascination in unearthing *first* events and it must be admitted that chronology, too, imposes certain duties on the historian.

The earliest allusion to a public concert in our country of which I am aware dates back to 1731 but it would not surprise me to see still earlier references brought to light, now hidden in some neglected source of information. If theatrical performances, however primitive, seem to have been given at New York as early as 1702 including such of the 'Fool's Opera' — we are indebted to the autobiography of the adventurer and comedian Anthony Aston for the statement — and if between 1702 and 1730 other performances have been traced[2]), then we might hesitate in dating the first concert in our country as late as 1731.

Though this concert was advertised in the Weekly News Letter of Boston and though, therefore, Boston seems to have the right of precedence, I prefer to trace the earliest concerts given at Charleston, S. C., be it only to emphasize the fact that New England's share in the development of our early musical life has been unfairly and unduly overestimated to the disadvantage of the Middle Colonies and the South.

A few months only separate the concert given on Dec. 1731 at Boston

---

1) Population: 1790—16359; 1800—20473 inhabitants. With one or two exceptions all similar data on the population of the cities appearing in this book have been gleaned from the statistics on "Comparative population of thirty-two of the largest cities in the United States", as printed in the Seventh Census, 1850. It might also serve a useful purpose to remark here that Mr. B. Franklin Dexter has estimated the entire population in the American colonies at only 400 000 inhabitants in 1714, 1 200 000 in 1750, 2780000 in 1780 and 4 000 000 in 1790.

2) More about Mr. Daly's and Mr. McKee's discoveries will be said in a volume on 'Early opera in the United States'.

and the earliest — to my knowledge earliest — concert at Charleston, for we read in the South Carolina Gazette, Saturday April 8—15, 1732[1]):

"On Wednesday next will be a *Consort*[2]) of Musick at the Council Chamber, for the Benefit of Mr. Salter."

It will be seen presently that the good citizens of Charleston encouraged Mr. John Salter sufficiently to give further concerts during the following seasons. In the meantime concert second and third took place during the summer of 1732 and the respective advertisements contain a few additional details. We read in the same newspaper on June 24 — July 1:

"For the Benefit of Henry Campbell the 6th of this Month, at the Council Chamber, will be performed a Consort of Vocal and Instrumental Musick: To begin at 7 o' Clock.

N. B. Country Dances for Diversion of the Ladies[3])."

and on Saturday, Sept. 23—30:

"At the Council Chamber, on Friday the 6th of October next, will be a Consort of Vocal and Instrumental Musick. Tickets to be had at Mrs. Cook's and at Mrs. Saureau's House at 40 s. each.

N. B. To begin precisely at Six o'clock."

It is a pity that we are not informed of what the "Vocal and Instrumental Musick" consisted but this absence of detail by no means permits us to infer that the program was not worth mentioning for it should be remembered that in Europe, too, the custom prevailed to observe silence in the advertisements as to the program[4]). Then as now it was considered

---

1) T. Witmarch began to publish the S. C. Gaz. in Jan. 1732. As previous to this month concerts could not very well have been advertised in Charleston, it is very possible that concerts were given there before 1732. The inference is plain.

2) For the history of the obsolete term *consort* see James A. H. Murray's 'New English dictionary on historical principles, 1893'. From the partial similarity of meaning with the French *concert* and the Italian *concerto* it is clear how instead of this unfamiliar word the English word *consort*, meaning originally a number of people consorting together, was substituted in musical terminology for 1) several instruments or voices playing or singing together (Fleming, 1587) 2) singing or playing in harmony (Marlowe 1586) 3) "a company of Musitions together" (Bullokar, 1616) 4) a musical entertainment (Evelyn's Diary, 1617: "Sir Joseph ... gave us ... a handsome supper, and after supper a consort of music"). Not until well into the 18th century did the current form *concert* take the place of *consort*. For instance, Grassineau still defines in 1740 "Concerto, or Concert, *popularly a consort*, ..." and also W. Tansur in his 'New Musical Grammar', 1746 says: "Concert-Consort: A piece of musick in parts."

3) During the following years Henry Campbell appears in newspaper advertisements mainly as dancing master. He gave a number of balls at the Theatre in Queenstreet. From the fact that in Dec. 1750 a "Sarah Campbell, Dancing Mistress" inserted an advertisement it may be inferred that Henry Campbell had died in the meantime.

4) It should also be kept in mind that printed programs did not become customary outside of France, England and America until towards the end of the eighteenth century. Sittard traced such in Hamburg as far back as 1729, but Hamburg, in this and other respects, presents an exception to the rule (perhaps on account of vicinity to London) and we need but read what Hanslick had to say on printed programs in Vienna to find the above remarks corroborated. To further illustrate the point, I quote the following anecdote from Marpurg's 'Legende einiger Musikheiligen', 1786:

"Ein Liebhaber der Musik, der in Paris und London gewesen war, und die dortigen

sufficient to draw attention to the place of performance, name of the virtuoso or society, prices of tickets, date and hour of performance and the ticket agents. It might also be opportune to remark here that "Country dances for Diversion of the Ladies" after the concert were not a Colonial invention. Indeed it would have been a suicidal plan to thus insure a better attendance had not the same custom prevailed in Europe, for Colonial society would hardly have submitted to any innovation not sanctioned by London society.

In the absence of proof to the contrary we may argue that the Colonials were treated, in imitation of concerts given at London, to more or less skillful renditions of Corelli, Vivaldi, Purcell, Abaco, Händel, Geminiani and such other masters whose fame was firmly established in Europe and perhaps what Mattheson said in his Ehrenpforte of the programs played at the concerts of the Musikalische Akademie of Prague was true also of our earliest concerts:

"Der Anfang wurde mit einer Ouverture gemacht, hierauf wurden auch Concerte gespielt, und auch wechselweise darunter gesungen, oder Solo gehöret. Den Schluss aber machte eine starke Symphonie."

But to return to Mr. John Salter! For Wednesday, Oct. 25, 1732 he advertised for his benefit a concert in the South Carolina Gazette in the usual form with "a Ball after the Consort" and this concert is of some historical importance as it probably was the first to which our newspapers paid attention. Under the local news the Gazette printed on Sat. Oct. 21—28:

"Charlestown, Oct. 28.

On Wednesday Night there was a Concert for the Benefit of Mr. Salter, at which was a fine Appearance of good Company. A Ball was afterwards opened by the Lord Forester and Miss Hill."

May be it is mortifying to us musicians that this first musical criticism should have been a bit of society-news with special allusion to the *beau* of the town, Lord Forester, but did the New York papers of our own times subject us to less mortification when the first performance of Wagner's Parsifal at New York brought their society-editors into greater-prominence than the musical?

This benefit concert at the Council Chamber of Mr. Saltar, as the Gazette sometimes called him, was followed by others, in 1733 on Feb. 26 and April 2, in 1735 on Jan. 23; in 1737 on March 8; in 1738 on Jan. 17.[1])

---

musikalischen Einrichtungen kennete, kam in eine Stadt Deutschlands, wo ein ansehnliches Concert war. Weil er glaubte, dass es allhier eben so wie dort seyn würde, so fragte er beym Eingang im Concert den Herrn Director, ob er nicht so gefällig seyn wollte ihm den gedruckten Anschlag der aufzuführenden Tonstücke zu communicieren. 'Mein Herr, antwortete der Herr Director, ich weiss zur Zeit noch nicht, was wir heute machen werden, noch wer sich *solo* wird hören lassen."

1) See the corresponding numbers of the South Carolina Gazette.

when I lost track of this musician whose wife, by the way kept a boarding school for Young Ladies where John taught music. Other benefit "consorts of Vocal and Instrumental Musick" were given during these years for Mrs. Cook, the ticket-agent, in 1733 on Feb. 26, when "none but English and Scotch songs" were to he sung", in other words *the first song recital in our country*, and in 1737 on June 14[1]) for "the Widow and Children of the late Mr. Cook". This concert took place at the Play House in Queenstreet as did on Nov. 22 of the same year a benefit concert for a musician of quite an illustrious name. This and the naïve tenor of the announcement, in the South Carolina Gazette, Oct. 29—Nov. 5 will warrant a quotation:

"At the new theatre in Queenstreet on Tuesday the 22d instant being St. Cecilia's Day, will be performed a *Concert* of Vocal and Instrumental Musick, for the Benefit of Mr. *Theodore Pachelbel*, beginning precisely at 6 o'Clock in the Evening.

Tickets to be had at the House of the said Mr. Pachelbel, or at Mr. Shepheard's Vintner.

N. B. As this is the first time the said Mr. Pachelbel has attempted anything of this kind in a publick Manner in this Province, he thinks proper to give Notice that there will be sung a *Cantata* suitable to the Occasion."

Of Pachelbel's career nothing is known except that in February 1733, according to the church records of Trinity Church, Newport, R. I. "the Wardens procured the Services of Mr. Charles Theodore Parchelbel, of Boston (who was the first organist to assist in setting up the organ" presented by Bishop Berkeley[2]). From Newport he drifted in 1736 to New York and hence to Charleston.

Students of our early musical life will have surmised the reason for grouping the *benefit*-concerts together. The words "for the benefit" were usually added in the advertisements to distinguish such concerts from those given by amateurs with the assistance of professional musicians for their own amusement, in short, serial subscription concerts. Now, a number of concerts were advertised in the South Carolina Gazette that evidently were not intended for the benefit of any particular musician, the form of the advertisements being essentially the same as for the concert on Oct. 6, 1732. By way of general analogy, therefore, it might be argued that the first effort to establish a series of concerts at more or less regular intervals in Charleston, is to be dated 1732. This supposition certainly is strengthened by the following *N. B.*s to concert advertisements published on Jan. 20 and June 30, 1733:

"N. B. This will be the last Consort"
and

"N. B. This is the first time on the Subscription."

---

1) S. C. Gaz. May 21—28, 1737.
2) See Brooks, Olden Time Music, p. 52.

Hence it would seem as if the concert season opened in the summer and lasted until Spring! As far as I found them in the Gazette the dates were these: 1732, Oct. 6th, Dec. 5th (postponed from Nov. 21st "on account of the Council's sitting"); 1733, Feb. 5th, Juli 6th[1]); 1734, Feb. 19, March 19, May 14, Dec. 17th; 1735, Dec. 19.

For the following years until 1751 I have found no concerts announced except the benefit concerts for John Salter and Charles Theodore Pachelbel. This may be explained in different ways. Either it was not considered necessary to advertise concerts or none took place. The latter is the more plausible explanation. Why the interest in the concerts, at which John Salter probably was in prominence, died out, would be impossible to answer. Possibly the theatrical performances, including ballad operas, at the Court Room during 1735 and beginning with 1736 at the New theatre in Queen-street absorbed the interest of Charleston. Also the numerous balls held by the dancing masters Henry Holt, Henry Campbell and others may have been responsible for the fact. Indeed these dancing assemblies seem to have been the only notable public entertainments at Charleston from about 1740 to 1750. Nor did conditions change materially during the next ten years. Strange to say, though the number of musicians who settled at Charleston was steadily increasing during this decade, I have been able to unearth three concerts only, though this, of course, by no means implies that others were not given.

A Mr. Uhl advertised a concert for his benefit at Mr. Gordon's Great Room in Broadstreet for Nov. 29, 1751 and Frederick Grunzweig who came to Charleston in 1754 announced one for Jan. 30, 1755 but it "was put off on account of the bad Weather, 'till Thursday the 13th instant, Feb." Finally the Gazette announced on Oct. 11, 1760 that:

"at the house of Mr. John Gordon in Broad-Street on Wednesday the 29 of October (Instant) will be performed,
A *Concert* of Vocal and Instrumental Music. To conclude with a Ball. Tickets, at Five Shillings Sterling each to be had of Mr. Wallace at his Lodgings in Church Street or at Mr. John Gordon's in Broadstreet.

N. B. As the Gentlemen who are the best Performers, both in Town and Country, are so obliging as to assist Mr. Wallace on this Occasion, he makes no Doubt, but that it will be in his Power to give the greatest Satisfaction to those Ladies and Gentlemen who shall honor him with their Presence.
The Concert to begin precisely at Seven o'Clock in the Evening."

For some reason, however, Mr. Wallace could not give the satisfaction promised until Nov. 4th.

---

1) Others would probably have been advertised but unfortunately the file of the South Carolina Gazette as published by T. Whitmarch (in possession of the Charleston Library Society) stops with no. 86, Sept. 1st. L. Timothee's continuation began on Feb. 2, 1734 with No. I!

As Benjamin Yarnold who resided at Charleston as organist of St. Philip's from 1753 to 1764 and as Peter Valton of London succeeded him in the same year, Yarnold becoming organist of St. Mary's, it is possible that both these able musicians gave concerts but I failed to trace them. The next reference to a public concert after 1760 I found in the South Carolina Gazette for Sept. 7—14, 1765 when Mr. Thomas Pike who had arrived in Charleston in November of the previous year as dancing, fencing and music master inserted this amusing advertisement:

"On Wednesday the 25th instant, September, the Orange Garden, in Trade Street, will be opened for the Night only. when a *Concert of Vocal and Instrumental Musick* will be performed by Gentlemen of the place, for the entertainment of all lovers of harmony. Concerto on the French Horn and Bassoon by Mr. Pike.

A subscription is opened for the same, as none but subscribers will be admitted; nor will any be taken at the door. The subscription is two dollars for three tickets, to admit two ladies and a gentleman. — Subscriptions are taken in and tickets delivered by Thomas Pike, at the same place.

N. B. It is hoped no persons will be so indiscreet as to attempt climbing over the fences to the annoyance of the subscribers, as I give this public notice that I will prosecute any person so offending, to the utmost rigour of the law.

Thomas Pike."

A number of "unforeseen accidents" obliged Mr. Pike to twice postpone his concert which "for the better accomodation of the subscribers [was] moved from the Orange Garden to the Theatre in Queenstreet" on Oct. 16th[1]). From the program it would appear that Mr. Pike was assisted by other soloists and an orchestra.

PROGRAM.

Act I.

French Horn Concerto
2d Concerto of Stanley
Solo on the Violincello
5th Concerto of Stanley
Bassoon Concerto
Song
Ouverture in Scipio[2]).

Act II.

French Horn Concerto
Concerto on the Harpsichord
Trio
Bassoon Concerto
Song
French Horn Concerto of Hasse.

---

1) South Carolina Gazette, Sept. 28—Okt. 5, 1765. In August Mr. Pike advertised his desire to instruct ladies and gentlemen "very expeditiously on moderate terms in *Orchesography* (on the art of dancing by characters and demonstrative figures").
2) Probably from Haendel's opera.

A few weeks later, on Nov. 13th "Peter Valton's Concert" took place at the theatre under similar conditions and we are told in the Gazette of Oct. 19—Oct. 31 that "besides a variety of Concertos, Overtures, Solos etc. [there would be] two Songs, sung by Miss Wainwright and two by Miss Hallam who never appeared in public. — Likewise a concerto on the Harpsichord[1])."

Strange to say, just when the scarcity of musical data in the South Carolina Gazette could induce us to believe that music was at a very low ebb at Charleston, the contrary is true for in those years a society was founded which has existed for well-nigh 150 years though its musical character has changed into that of an exclusive *assembly* of Charleston's first families with hardly any serious musical ambitions. The very name proves that when the society was founded in 1762 the object was to organize the music lovers of the city into a serious musical club. I am alluding to the St. Cœcilia Society to which, and not to the Stoughton Musical Society of 1786, therefore belongs the honor of being our oldest musical society. Fortunately a copy of the printed "Rules" has been preserved and though they are dated 1773 we may take it for granted that they had been in force since the foundation of the society. They follow here as copied from the reprint in the South Carolina Historical and Genealogical Magazine, 1900, v. I, p. 223—227[2]):

"RULES of the St. Cœcilia Society: Agreed upon and finally confirmed, November 22d, 1773.

I.

The Society shall be called the *St. Cœcilia Society* and consist of one hundred and twenty members.

II.

There shall be annually four General Meetings of the Society, namely, on St. Cœcilia's Day, which shall be the Anniversary of the Society, and on the third Thursday in February, May and August, on which General Meetings the Members of the Society shall dine together.

On the anniversary, the Society shall break up at Five, and on the other General Meetings at Six o'clock in the afternoon; at which hours, the Steward shall call for and settle the bill. Every member shall be charged twenty shillings currency towards defraying the expence of the dinner; and in case of any deficiency, the same shall be paid by the members present at the said meetings.

III.

The Society, on their anniversary, shall elect, by ballot, a President, Vice President, Treasurer and Steward, and eleven other members, residents in Charlestown, who,

---

1) Evidently the people of Charleston were broad — minded enough to allow their organist to cooperate in concert with members of a very worldly profession, for both ladies were actresses.

2) The title of the excessively rare pamphlet (12⁰. 11 p; preserved at the South Carolina Historical Society, Charleston) reads: "Rules of the St. Cœcilia [!] Society Charleston, Printed for the Society by Robert Wells 1774."

with the fore-named officers, shall be constituted Managers for the current year. And in case any member, a resident in Charlestown, shall, upon his election, refuse to serve as officer or Manager of the Society, such person so refusing, if an officer, shall pay a fine of ten pounds currency; and the Society shall proceed to an other election in his or their room.

IV.

On the first Thursday in every month, there shall be a meeting of the managers, at six o'clock in the evening, from the first of October to the first of April; and at seven o'clock, from the first of April to the first of October.

In case of the death, resignation, or removal from Charlestown, of any of the managers, the remaining managers are empowered to supply the vacancy.

But in case of the death, resignation or removal from Charlestown, of any of the officers, the managers shall call an extraordinary meeting of the Society, giving at fortnight's notice thereof in all the weekly gazettes: And, on every other emergency, the same power is vested in them.

V.

The managers are empowered to fix the number and times of the *Concerts;* the anniversary only excepted, on the evening of which, a concert shall always be performed; also, to regulate every other matter relating thereto, as well as every other business of the Society, during the recess of the Society.

VI.

On every anniversary, each member shall pay, into the hands of the treasurer, for the use of the Society, the sum of twenty-five pounds currency.

Upon notice from the treasurer in writing, of his arrears due to the society, whether these arrears be for his annual subscription, his dinner expences, or any other fine incurred by him in the Society, any person neglecting or refusing to discharge the same, at the next general meeting of the Society, he shall no longer be deemed a member.

VII.

Any person desirous of becoming a member of the St. Cœcilia Society, shall signify the same by a letter, directed to the President of the society; and whenever a vacancy happens in the society, the members present, at their next general meeting, have power to elect, or reject, the candidate offering himself; which election, or rejection, shall be by ballot only; and the assent of two-thirds of the members present shall be necessary for the admission of such candidate. And every person, on his election, shall subscribe to rules of the Society, and pay to the treasurer, for the use of the Society, thirty-five pounds currency.

VIII.

Every member is allowed to introduce to the concert as many ladies as he thinks proper, who are to be admitted by tickets, signed by a member, and expressing the name of the lady to whom each ticket is presented.

No other person is to be admitted, except strangers, and they only by tickets, from a manager, signed and directed as before specified.

No boys are to be, on any account, admitted.

IX.

The treasurer shall immediately, upon his election into office, take charge of all the ready monies, bonds, securities, and other effects, belonging to the Society; and give bond to the president and vice-president to be accountable to them, or to the order of the president and managers, for the same, fire and other inevitable accidents excepted.

He is not, on any account, to pay, or lend at interest, any of the Society's monies but by order of the Society, or the order of the president, together with the approbation of the managers.

X.

At all meetings of the Society, not less than twenty-one members, and at all the meetings of the managers, not less than five members shall be a Quorum to transact business.

All matters, canvassed at any of those meetings, shall be determined by a majority of votes, the election of members only excepted, which, according to Rule VII, is to be determined by, at least, two thirds of the Society present at their general meetings.

The President, or in his absence, the vice-president, or, in case of the absence of both of them, a person chosen as chairman by the members present, shall keep the order and decorum of the Society.

Every member, speaking of business, shall adress himself immediately to the Chair.

XI.

At every general meeting, the Society shall proceed to business at eleven o'clock in the forenoon; and in case the president, vice-president, or treasurer, do not attend at the said hour, they shall each pay a fine, to the Society, of thirty-two shillings and six-pence currency; and every other member, residing in Charlestown, who does not attend at the said hour, shall pay a fine of ten shillings currency; unless the Society, to whose judgment all fines are to be referred, shall, at their next general meeting, see sufficient cause to remit the same.

None of the foregoing rules shall be altered, or any new ones enacted, until they have been proposed and agreed upon, at two general meetings of the Society."

Thus encircled with rules and regulations the St. Cœcilia Society formed until the end of the 18th and far into the 19th century the center of Charleston's musical life as far as it found expression in concerts. The number of concerts every year seems to have varied, as the concert-seasons opened and closed at irregular dates, but as a long as a season lasted the concerts took place fort-nightly and one of the by-laws called for a yearly concert on St. Cœcilia's Day, Nov. 22. The orchestra was formed partly of gentlemen-performers and partly of professional musicians, the latter being engaged by the season. We have ground to believe that the managers spared no expense in securing musicians capable of performing the best music of the period and as evidence of the enterprising spirit governing the society in those years I submit an interesting advertisement which the society sent as far as New York, Philadelphia and Boston for insertion! We read for instance in the Boston Evening Post, June 17, 1771:

"Charlestown, South Carolina, April 11th, 1771.

The *St. Cœcilia Society* give notice that they will engage with, and give suitable encouragement to musicians properly qualified to perform at their *Concert*, provided they apply on or before the first day of October next. — The performers they are in want of are, a first and second violin, two hautboys and a bassoon, whom they are willing to agree with for one, two or three years.

John Gordon, President
Thomas Ln. Smith, Vice President."

Under the circumstances it is not surprising that Charleston soon became attractive to musicians and consequently the number of benefit concerts, as defined, rapidly increased during the next decades.

The following pages deal only with these as concerts given by the St. Cœcilia Society go without saying[1]). But an exception to the rule must be made here. When the South Carolina Magazine reprinted the rules of the St. Cœcilia Society, it was claimed in a foot-note that "so far as has been discovered, the first mention of the St. Cecilia Society in print was made in the South Carolina Gazette for December 3rd 1772." This is not correct as the same paper published on Oct. 6—13, 1766 the following:

"The St. Cœcilia Concert will be open'd to the subscribers on Tuesday evening next, at 6 o'clock, at the house of Mr. Robert Dillon; before which time the subscribers are desired to send to the treasurer for their tickets of admittance, who is empowered to receive the subscription money.

By order of the President

Isaac Motte, Treasurer."

In the following year Anthony Labbé, a musician who still figures in the Charleston directory for 1797, advertised a concert for Jan. 29. Shortly afterwards a species of entertainments was introduced at Charleston during the summer months which shows how eagerly the Colonials were on the *quivive* of the latest London fashion.

I mean the 'Ridotto al fresco' opened in 1732 by Jonathan Tyers at the 'New Spring Gardens' in London, better known as 'Vauxhall Gardens'. To this freshair resort fashionable folk would flock during the summer evenings and listen to open-air concerts while partaking of refreshments. The entertainments became so popular that from 1736 on they were given every evening[2]). The fact that in 1745 Dr. Arne was engaged as composer illustrates how the managers sought to maintain a high musical standard. But gradually the entertainments turned into a sort of vaudeville with fireworks, etc. though concerts remained a feature. After having sunk lower and lower in character they were discontinued in 1859. Says Mr. W. H. Hadow in Grove's Dictionary:

"Vauxhall Gardens had a longer existence than any public gardens in England and assisted in maintaining a taste for music as a source of rational enjoyment, although they did little or nothing towards promoting its advancement."

---

1) It would also be rather difficult to say much about them as they generally were not mentioned in the papers. (The same by the way, is true also of concerts given by musical societies in Europe during the 18th century.) It is to be hoped that some day some member of this exclusive and uncommunicative society will take the public and the historians into his confidence and give us the history of the St. Cœcilia Society. Unfortunately, as I was informed through the friendly exertions of Miss Charlotte St. John Elliott, early records, minutes or reports of the society do not seem to exist.
2) As early as 1661 Evelyn speaks in his diary of "the New Spring Garden at Lambeth a pretty contrived plantation" as a place of public amusement, but the musical entertainments remained very primitive for decades.

The same author claims that the New Spring Gardens were opened for the first time under the name of 'Vauxhall Gardens' in 1786. This may be, but the popular name must have been 'Vauxhall Gardens' for many years previous, otherwise the entertainments, first imported from Italy, would not have enjoyed an international reputation under exactly this name. For instance, in Frankfort o. M. "eine Art von Vauxhall" was introduced during the Herbstmesse of 1771[1]) and at the Hague Ernst Sieber's 'Nieuw Vaux Hall op de Scheveningsche Weg' existed as early as 1749[2]).

At Charleston, Vauxhall concerts were introduced in 1767 by the enterprising Messrs. Bohrer, Morgan & Comp. The advertisements may tell the origin of the Charleston Vauxhall and incidentally remind us of the fact that only gradually have audiences been educated to keep silent during concerts. In those days quite the contrary was customary and Burney, for instance, demonstrated the impression made by the Haendel Commemoration of 1784 by remarking that stillness reigned whereas

"The best operas and concerts are accompanied with a buzz and murmur of conversation, equal to that of a tumultous crowd."

We read in the South Carolina Gazette, June 1—15, 1767:

"By particular desire of Gentlemen and Ladies. The managers of the *New Vauxhall Concert*, instead of having them three times, will perform only once a week, on every Thursday; to begin precisely at seven o'clock in the evening.
Tickets to be had at Mrs. Barkhouse's, Mr. Holliday's and Mr. Tuke's tavern, and at the Bar, at fifteen shillings each.
Tea and coffee is not included in the price of the ticket.
Bohrer, Morgan & Comp."

and on July 6—13:

"Advertisement Extraordinary.
On Thursday the 23d inst. will be exhibited at New Vauxhall *A Concert of Vocal and Instrumental Music*. To begin at eight o'clock in the evening, at a dollar a ticket, which may be had at the bar.
Between the parts of the concert, four or five pieces will be exhibited by a person who is confident very few in town ever saw, or can equal, his performances.
After which there will be a pantomime entertainment, then a ball.
Tea and coffee is included in the expence, till the person above mentioned begins.
This will positively be the only time of his performing, unless by the particular desire of a genteel company.
He finds himself obliged to request that silence may be observed during his performance."

Unless Messrs. Bohrer, Morgan & Comp. found it unnecessary to constantly draw public attention to their establishment it would seem that the undertaking enjoyed but a short existence, as no further reference to

---

1) Israel, op. cit.
2) Scheuleer's article on 'Haagsche somer concerten in de achtiende eeuw' (T. d. V. v. N. N. M., 1904).

the New Vauxhall concerts is to be found in the South Carolina Gazette. All the concerts advertised during the next years were given, with one exception, by Peter Valton[1]), but as in 1772 an 'Orphaeus Society' existed in Charleston[2]) it is probable that Charlestonians had occasion to enjoy other concerts besides these and those of the St. Cœcilia Society.

Though not stated, the fact that "tickets [were] to be had of Peter Valton" clearly indicates that the concert announced to take place at Mr. Robert Dillon's on March 24, 1768 was for his benefit. He further advertised a subscription concert for April 5, 1769 and "concerts of vocal and instrumental music ... at Mr. Pike's Assembly Room" for April 22, 1772 and Feb. 2, 1773. At the latter the first violin was played by "Mr. [Thomas] Hartley lately arrived" from Boston and "among other select pieces" was to be performed "a concerto on the harpsichord, by a lady, a pupil of Mr. Valton's". Now, as then, the best method of advertising one 's ability as a teacher!

In the meantime, on Nov. 27, 1772[3]) a concert had taken place the announcement of which finely illustrates by-gone methods of advertising:

"CONCERT, by Desire.

On Friday the 27th of November instant, at Pike's New Assembly Room, will be performed a Concert of Vocal and Instrumental Music.

The vocal part by a gentleman, who does it merely to oblige on this occasion.

The whole sum that may be raised on this occasion, to be laid out for a covered way and elegant portico next the street; thereby to enable ladies and gentlemen always to go to the new suite of rooms, without being incommodated by the weather.

N. B. As the expence to complete the same amounts to a considerable sum, it is hoped the ladies and gentlemen will not think a guinea for two tickets an extra demand."

In 1773 a few entertainments were given at Charleston which belong to the history of American vaudeville as well as to the history of our concert life. In January of this year, the "celebrated" Mr. Saunders came to town who appears to have been a formidable forerunner of our present-day magicians. It evidently occurred to a Mr. Humphreys, when he contemplated giving a concert, that the engagement of Mr. Saunders would be to his own advantage and he consequently inserted in the South Carolina Gazette of March 22, 1773 this announcement which presumably thrilled all connoisseurs of *leger de main:*

---

1) Peter Valton, besides being the organist of St. Philip's, dealt in "good and handsome new spinets" and other musical merchandise. He also, on Oct. 10, 1768 advertised "Proposals for printing by subscription Six Sonatas for the harpsichord or organ; with an accompaniment for a violin ... opera prima". Whether or not these sonatas left the press, I have been unable to ascertain.

2) That this was a musical society, appears from an advertisement signed "William Packrow, First musician" in the S. C. Gaz. April 9, 1772.

3) S. C. Gaz. Nov. 19, 1772.

"For the benefit of Mr. Humphreys on Wednesday the 31st of March instant the celebrated Mr. Saunders will, for that night only, exhibit his highest *dexterity* and *grand deception*, which have never yet been exhibited in this province, in Mr. Stotherd's Long Room behind the Beef Market. Among a number of other surprising performances, Mr. Saunders will let any number of ladies or gentlemen think of as many cards as they please, and the same will be found in a roasted leg of mutton, hot from the fire, which will be placed on the table . . .

After Act I an air to the French horn, by Mr. Humphreys.

After Act II Mr. Stotherd will play the French horn and guitar in concert.

After Act III a Song by Mr. Humphreys.

After Act IV a Song by Mr. Stotherd.

The whole to conclude with a duette by Mr. Humphreys and Mr. Stotherd, to the guitar.

The doors to be opened at six o'clock, and the performance will begin at seven.

No person to be admitted without a ticket, which may be had at the place of performance, and at the Coffee House. — Table seats one dollar each, and others twenty shillings.

N. B. Mr. Saunders, after the performance, will teach the spectators several amazing tricks on cards, etc. gratis.

*** Mr. Humphres will esteem it a particular favour of those ladies and gentlemen, who intend to favour him with their company, to apply some time before his benefit night, in order that he may have seats made proper for their reception."

A similar performance followed on April 29, during which Mr. Saunders had several new tricks — up his sleeves. Mr. Stotherd announced as his share in this joint *benefit:*

"After Act I
> Mr. Stotherd will sing the *Dust last* — a favourite cantata, accompanied with the guitar.

Act the 2d
> He will play the French horn and guitar in concert.

After the 3d
> A song by Mr. Humphreys.

After the 4th
> *The Lark Shrill Notes*, accompanied with the guitar by Mr. Stotherd.
> The whole to conclude with a Hunting song called *Away to the fields* — by Mr. Stotherd.

But back to more legitimate concerts! In the South Carolina Gazette, March 28, 1774:

"Mr. FRANCESCHINI having the permission of the Honourable the President, the Vice President, and members of the St. Cœcilia Society, and the assistance of the gentlemen performers, begs leave to acquaint the public, that on Tuesday the 12th day of April, at the New Theatre in Church Street will be performed a *Grand Concert* of Vocal and Instrumental Music for his benefit.

A solo and a concert on the violin by Mr. Franceschini, on the viol d'amour, Sonata on the harpsichord, etc. etc.

Tickets . . . at one dollar each.

N. B. After the concert proper music will be provided for dancing."

A few months later, a musician arrived at Charleston who subsequently became prominent in the musical life of New York and Boston, then calling himself, in distinction from his son, P. A. Van Hagen, sen. But in 1774 he advertised himself as "P. A. Van Hagen, jun., organist and director of the City's Concert in Rotterdam". The logical inference would be that there must have been active in Europe, presumably in Holland, a Van Hagen, sen., so that the Van Hagen family would be one of those in whom the musical profession was inherited from father to son, of which the Bach family furnishes the most famous example.

The correctness of the inference may easily be proven. The 'Journal zur Kunstgeschichte und zur allgemeinen Litteratur' contains in the second part an 'Entwurf eines Verzeichnisses der besten jetzt lebenden Tonkünstler in Europa'[1]). Under organists the entry is to be found (1776):

"Rotterdam. Herr von Hagen aus Hamburg, ein Schüler des grossen Geminiani".

This was probably the Peter Albrecht von Hagen who in 1740 appeared at Hamburg as violin virtuoso[2]). It is clear that he cannot have been identical with our P. A. Van Hagen, jun. The missing link is furnished by Burney who, in his famous book on the 'Present State of music in Germany, the Netherlands . . .', 1773 wrote under Rotterdam:

"M. Van Hagen, a German, who is the principal organist here, is likewise an excellent performer on the violin, of which he convinced me by playing one of his own solos. He was a scholar of Geminiani, and he not only plays, but writes very much in the style of that great master of harmony.

His daughter has a fine voice, and sings with much taste and expression. His the has been under Mr. Honaür [sic] at Paris."

It was evidently this son, a pupil of the composer and violinist Leonzi Honauer, who emigrated to Charleston where he proposed teaching organ, harpsichord, pianoforte, violin, violoncello, viola besides "The manner of composition to any that are inclined to be instructed therein". It is also characteristic of "Monsieur" Van Hagen that he did not insert his card before he had shown his abilities in a "Grand Concert of Vocal and Instrumental Music", announced in the South Carolina Gazette, Oct. 24, 1774 for Oct. 27th at Mr. Valk's Long Room for his own and the benefit of Signora Castella, possibly the professional name of Miss Van Hagen. This concert, too, was to be given "by permission of the St. Cœcilia Society", which can mean nothing more than that it enjoyed the patronage and assistance of the musical forces of the society for it is hardly credible that the St. Cœcilia possessed the power to veto concerts. Of the program we hear nothing and the only particulars in the advertisement were these:

"The vocal parts by Signora Castella, who will also perform several airs on the Harmonica or Musical Glasses[3]).

---

1) From J. W. Enschedé's article 'Nederlandsche musici in 1776' C. T. d. V. v. N. N. M. 1904, p. 292—294.
2) Sittard, op. cit.
3) Franklin's Armonica, just then very popular both in Europe and America.

The instrumental parts by Monsieur Van Hagen, Mr. Abercromby[1]), Mr. France-schini, and others."

This was the last benefit concert advertised before the War of the Revolution and during the war to my knowledge only three concerts took place, announced no longer in the South Carolina Gazette but — a glimpse into political history — in the *Royal* Gazette! The first was given by Signor Franceschini on March 14, 1781 and the second anonymously on Oct. 8th of the same year when there was to be "a concerto solo upon the harpsichord, by a lady, and solo upon the violin, etc. and a ball". As tickets were to be purchased also at Mr. Abercromby's possibly he was connected with the affair. The third concert, on May 24, 1782, was again for the benefit of Mr. Franceschini. He requested the

"honour of such of the ladies company as used to frequent the assemblies". He admitted "the gentlemen of the navy, army and the most respectable part of the town — at half a guinea each."

After the war the St. Cœcilia Society again began to flourish and matters musical at Charleston gradually resumed their former appearance. Yet a marked difference is noticeable. Before the war concerts had almost exclusively been given by itinerant or resident musicians. Now they found unwelcome competitors in the members of the theatrical companies, in a similar manner as the members of the Mingotti troupe for a while had paralized the chances of non-operatic musicians at Hamburg.

Thus the first concert after the war was given by an artist who, before our struggle for independence, had repeatedly won the hearts of the Colonials with her fine voice and method of singing and now was destined to soon enthuse the American public with her interpretative powers in the repertory of ballad-opera: Maria Storer, from 1787 on better known as Mrs. Henry. She had gone with Douglass' American Company to Jamaica when the first signs of war clouds appeared on the political horizon and she did not return until after the war. Then, when the comedians flocked back to the United States, she seems to have joined those who in the spring of 1785 opened a short season at the theatre in the City Exchange at Charleston, and she remained here until her appearance at New York in 1786[2]). Her benefit concert was advertised in the South Carolina Gazette, May 9 for May 17th but of the program and the assistant performers nothing is said. However, the concert did not take place for some reason or the other. This becomes evident from an advertisement of a concert

---

1) Mr. Abercromby combined the "profession of musick and dancing" and in 1775 "entered into partnership with Mr. Sodi, who, for many years, had the sole conduct of the dances at the Italian Opera in London".

2) These data will be of interest to readers of Seilhamer's 'History of the American Theatre'.

"at the City Tavern ... for the benefit of Miss Storer" for Oct. 12, 1785 when she assured the public that "every exertion will be used to render the concert worthy attention" and remarked that tickets of the 17th of May ult. will be admitted on the above nights" [sic].

If this concert was *post*-poned, an irregularity of quite are unusual nature happened to a concert with ball which had been announced for Oct. 27, 1785. It was *pre*-poned to Oct. 26th.

For the following year quite a few concerts are recorded but they were mostly theatrical performances under the disguise of concerts, the disguise being adopted to steer clear of the strong current against the theatre shortly after the war. The method adopted was this that "between the acts" or more correctly between the musical numbers such plays as the 'Spanish Friar', altered by Garrick from Dryden's tragi-comedy were performed. The "characters" were generally "expressed in the bills for the day" so that for all practical purposes the written or unwritten law was obeyed and at the same time theatre-goers were fully informed of histrionic details.

In this connection these sham-concerts are of particular importance. They show that Charleston now possessed a building well adapted for enter-tainments of every description as they were given in "Harmony Hall at Louisburgh without the city". A description, printed in the New York Independent Journal, August 5, 1786 reads:

"We hear from Charleston, S. C. that a principal merchant of that city and a Mr. Godwin, comedian, have leased a lot of land for five years and have erected a buil-ding, called Harmony Hall, for the purpose of music meetings, dancing and theatrical amusements. It is situated in a spacious garden in the suburbs, of the city. The boxes are 22 in number, with a key to each box. The pit is very large and the theatrum and orchestra elegant and commodious. It was opened with a grand concert *gratis* for the satisfaction of the principal inhabitants, who wished to see it previous to the first night's exhibition. The above building hast cost £ 500 ..."

Before the opening of Harmony Hall where Godwin's company performed until the spring of 1787, Joseph Lafar, a musician who seems to have estab-lished the first regular music shop at Charleston in 1786, gave a concert with ball for his benefit at the City Tavern on Feb. 14, 1786. Circumstantial evidence also points to him as the moving spirit of an interesting concert enterprise thus advertised in the Charleston Morning Post, Nov. 13, 1786:

"By Subscription.

A CONCERT AND ASSEMBLY. Every fortnight, to be held at Mr. Broeske's Long Room, No. 68, on the Bay. The first concert to be on Monday the 19th of No-vember.

Subscriptions taken in at Mr. Lafar's only, two doors from the corner of Church-street, in Traddstreet, when a place for the Concert and Assembly may be seen."

This first concert was postponed to Nov. 27. Though no more is said about the enterprise in the papers, it is hardly probable that the first concert remained the last. If not, then those music-lovers who frequented both these concerts and those of the St. Cœcilia Society certainly were treated to enough good music to satisfy the most thirsty melomaniacs.

For the years 1787 and 1788 I have been unable to trace concerts (independent of the St. Cœcilia Society!) and for the year 1789 only two entertainments deserving the name. On March 31, 1789 the South Carolina Gazette advertised:

"On Thursday evening, the second of April, at the Great Room; Traddstreet, (late William's Coffee House) will be performed, A CONCERT of Vocal and Instrumental Music. In part of which will be recited, a musical dialogue between *Thomas and Sally, Dorcas and Squire.* To begin at seven o'clock.

In order to prevent the place of performance from being crowded, a calculation has been made of the number which it will properly contain, and a proportionate number of tickets struck off, without one of which no person whatever can be admitted.

Tickets at three shillings each, to be had at Markland and M'Iver's Printing Office, no. 47 Bay, and at the place of performance."

The advertisement of the other concert is even more curious as it will strongly drive the point home to all familiar with Israel's Frankfurter Concert-Chronik how much our concert-life, though, of course, inferior in quality, had in common in outward appearance with that of Europe. The advertisement, in the South Carolina Gazette, April 28, 1789, runs:

"This Evening ... A DIVERTISSEMENT; Selections:
Il *Penseroso* — Jane Shore. Alicia.

Songs, Water parted from the Sea, Anna's urn. Selections. *L'Allegro* — Archer, Boniface, Foigard, Serub, Sullen, Mrs. Sullen, Dorinda, and Cherry. Songs: Come live with me and be my love; Which is the man?; Lud! don't keep teazing me so."

When Mr. Godwin in May 1787 "in consequence of a late act of legislature" saw himself compelled to "relinquish theatrical representations" he made the best of his embarrassing situation by delivering lectures at Harmony Hall[1]), besides teaching there music, fencing and dancing: But in 1790 he could not resist the temptation of again testing the limitations of the legislative act. Accordingly he advertised in the City Gazette, Jan. 7th:

"On Saturday evening [Jan. 9th] at the Lecture Room, late Harmony Hall, will be a Concert between the parts will be rehearsed (*gratis*) the musical piece of *Thomas and Sally.* To which will be added, a pantomime, called *Columbia,* or, Harlequin Shipwreck'd.

Maria's Evening Song to the Virgin, Miss Wall."

The idea of "rehearsing (*gratis*)" a ballad opera was certainly very ingenious and reminds us of the tricks adopted by the friends of the German naturalistic drama early in the nineties of the last century in order to avoid a conflict with the censor. Shortly afterwards, on Jan. 23, 1790, another

---

1) Charleston Morning Post, May 31, 1787; Feb. 22, 1787. Late in 1794 Harmony Hall changed its name into City Theatre.
2) City Gazette, June 10, 1791.

concert was given but again concert-music appears not to have been the real attraction for it was announced that "during the parts . . . the famous Saxon [would] have the honor to give a representation of a dance upon wire".

Of the few concerts of 1791 three had this in common that they were given for charity. The first took place on March 17 under the direction of the St. Cecilia Society "for the benefit of a numerous family in distress" and the second for the benefit of "Mr. Lafar, lately returned to this city" on June 16th. May be the concert on March 17 was also given for his benefit as after assuring the public "that the endeavors of the performers will be exercised in selecting those pieces best calculated to please the audience" Mr. Lafar remarked[1]):

Mr. Lafar, after a series of misfortunes, has been advised by some of his friends, to attempt this method to alleviate the distress of his family: it is the more pleasing to him, as it will afford an opportunity to a generous public to display those sentiments of philanthropy, for which they have always been conspicuous . . ."[2])

The third concert was to enable the commissioner of the orphanhouse who had already collected 800 l. for the purpose, to lay the foundation of the building. The price of admission was ten shillings and the concert was to be held at the City Hall on Oct. 20, under the auspices of the *Amateur Society*[3]), to which I have found no further allusion. A fourth concert may or may not have been given for charity, but this is of little interest compared with the source where the reference appears. George Washington was just then on his Southern trip and it is in his diary that we find under date of May 1791 this characteristic entry:

". . . went to a Concert at the Exchange at wch. there were at least 400 ladies the number & appearance of wch. exceeded anything of the kind I had ever seen."

Though the files of the City Gazette are complete for 1792 I failed to find references to concerts in this year, for the daily performances on the musical glasses together with Mr. Saunders' "exhibition of equilibrium" at M' Crady's assembly room can hardly be termed concerts. Then, from 1793 on to the end of the century, Charleston enjoyed a surprisingly vigorous musical life. During these years English opera flourished splendidly and from 1794 on until about 1796 French and Italian operas were introduced by a company of French comedians who had managed to escape the terrorists in St. Domingo. So it came that side by side with operas by Arne,

---

1) City Gazette, June 10, 1791.

2) Mr. Lafar seems to have met with sufficient encouragement to remain at Charleston for it appears from the papers that he opened a dancing assembly in 1791, translated French and English "grammatically and orthographically", copied music and reopened his music shop. He died at Charleston in 1797.

3) City Gazette, Oct. 11, 1791.

Atwood, Shield and others such by Rousseau, Grétry, Cimarosa, Paisiello were heard at Charleston. This influx of French musicians exercised an influence also upon the concert-life. Not alone did the singing members of the companies generally participate in the concerts but the French musicians together with those residing at Charleston and those who belonged to the orchestra in the English companies formed a phalanx sufficiently large and capable to render the "full pieces" of the current European concert repertory. Thus the revolutions in France and St. Domingo contributed to laying the foundation of our cosmopolitan musical life with all its advantages and drawbacks. It will be seen that Stamitz, Gossec, Haydn, Gyrowetz, Pleyel, Grétry, and other European celebrities, including Mozart and Gluck[1]) figured on the programs, and these programs together with those submitted in subsequent chapters will perhaps induce our program annotators who delight in dating first performances in our country of Haydn, Gluck and Mozart as late as 1850 and later, to be more cautious in the future.

It might be said that the concerts were only few in number but it should not be forgotten that there is a difference between concerts traced and concerts actually given. Moreover, it should constantly be kept in mind that the St. Cecilia Society[2]) with its concerts formed the real backbone of Charleston's concert life and that in 1794 another musical society, the Harmonic Society, appeared on the plan. The concerts of these societies were public only to a certain degree. Therefore they were not advertised, yet they were concerts and consequently the entertainments announced in the papers were additional to the regular subscription concerts of these societies. However, not the number of the benefit concerts is of importance but their general character.

The first concert of 1793 was given by the "professors and amateurs" on Feb. 19 for the benefit of the Orphan House, Mr. Williams "politely" offering them his assembly room and services free of all expenses "in order to promote so laudable an institution"[3]). Here is the

PLAN OF THE CONCERT.
Act 1st.

Grand Overture of	Haydn
Quartetto of	Pleyel
A song by Mr. Courtney	
Duetto, violin and clarinet, of	Michel
Sinfonie concertante of	Davaux

1) It should be remembered that Mozart figured none too prominently on concert programs before 1800 even at Vienna!
2) From 1790 on this form of the name prevailed.
3) City Gazette, Feb. 12 and 16, 1793.

ACT 2d.

Concerto grosso of .. .. Corelli
A French song, accompanied with guitar and violin
Concert, violin .. .. Giornovichi
Concerto, grand pianoforte, ... Hoffmeister
To conclude with a favorite
Sinfonie of the celebrated .. .. Pleyel."

This was followed on Dec. 17 at Williams' Coffee House by a concert for the benefit of "Messieurs Petit, Le Roy, Foucard and Villars, musicians, instructed by the most eminent professors in their line in Europe"[1]). The "Distribution" reads:

Grand Overture, music of .. .. Heyden
Clarinet Concerto, Mr. Foucard.
Quartetto (by Pleyel) Messrs Petit, Poition, Villars and Le Roy
A Song, by Mr. West, jun.
Violin Concerto and Marlborough, with the variations, by Mr.
 Duport, aged 13 years.
Overture of Carvane, music of .. .. Gretrie.

SECOND PART.

Grand Overture, music of .. .. Gretrie.
Clarinet quartetto, by an amateur
A Concertant symphony for two violins and tenor, by Messrs.
 Le Roy, Poition and Villars
A Song by Mr. West, jun.
Violin concerto, by Mr. Petit
 The concert will conclude with the Overture of Henry IVth.[2])

The most important concert of 1794 was the one held on March 6th under the patronage of the St. Cecilia Society at West & Bignall's Theatre "for the benefit of the distressed inhabitants of St. Domingo now in this city" with the following rather miscellaneous program[3]):

ACT 1st.

Sinfonie .. .. Pleyel
Song, Mr. Chambers
Quartett Violin .. .. Pleyel
Song, Mr. Clifford
Overture .. .. Gretrie

ACT 2d.

Grand Overture (la Chasse) .. .. Gossec
Song, Mr. West
Sonata Pianoforte, Rondo by Mrs. Sully
Duett, Mr. Chambers & Mrs. Chambers.

---

1) City Gazette, Dec. 12 and 14, 1793.
2) Probably the one by Martini.
3) City Gazette, March 6, 1794.

ACT 3d.

Grand Overture   .. ..   Haydn
Song, Mr. Chambers
Concerto Violin, by Mr. Petit   .. ..   Viotti
Glee, Mr. Chambers, Mrs. Chambers, and Mr. West.

AFTER THE CONCERT

A Double Allemande and Reel, by Mr. M. Sully, Mrs. Chambers
and Miss Sully.
A Grand Ballet, by Mons. Francesquy, Mons. Dainville, Mons.
Val and Madame Val.
The whole to conclude with Manly Feats of Activity by Mr.
M. Sully.
Boxes to be taken as usual. Tickets at 5 s each ... None but
the managers admitted on the stage."

Also a concert may be noted which Mr. Clifford, a member of West and
Bignall's company, advertised early in July. It seems that his benefit at
the theatre was not a "good benefit" on account of the inclemency of the
weather and Mr. Clifford who was terribly in debt proposed having a concert

"wherein he hopes for their patronage [of the ladies and gentlemen of Charleston]
that he may act like a man of principle and honor to those whom he may owe any
thing to, being desirous not to leave Charleston with a dishonourable name!"

Whether the concert, so oddly advertised, took place I did not ascertain.

For the year 1795 the data are somewhat more numerous and interesting.
The first was a "grand concert" given by Mr. Jacobus Pick on March 26th
at William's Concert Room with this program[1]):

ACT 1st.

Overture, composed by .. ..   Girovetz
Song, by Mrs. Pick
Quartetto .. ..   Pleyel
Concerto on the Clarinet, composed and performed by .. ..   Mr. Dubois[2])
Song, by Mr. J. West
Rondo .. ..   Pleyel

ACT 2d.

Sinfonie   .. ..   Haydn
Song, by Mrs. Pick
Concerto on the Violin, by Master Duport   .. ..   La Motte
Song, by Mr. J. West
Sonate on the Pianoforte, by Mr. Eckhard .. ..   Dussek
Duetto, by Mr. and Mrs. Pick
Pot Pourris on the Harmonia, by Mrs. Pick
Sinfonie   .. ..   Pleyel

Though a program like this did not consume much more than two
hours, as the symphonies of Haydn and his contemporaries are very much

---

1) City Gazette, March 26, 1795.
2) The advertisement reads "Mrs. Dubois", evidently a mistake.

shorter than those of Beethoven, not to mention Bruckner or Mahler, yet it is well known that our forefathers possessed wonderful endurance. (Beethoven's concerts at Vienna!) Furthermore it is claimed that the custom prevailed to advertise a whole symphony though frequently only one or two movements were really played. It is also interesting to note that the time had not yet come when a rigorous distinction was generally made between orchestral and chamber-music programs. This observation applies even more strongly to the program as inserted by Mr. J. West for his benefit concert at Williams' Assembly Room on April 16[1]):

Act 1st.

Sinfonie .. .. Haydn
Song, Mrs. Pick
Quartetto .. .. Daveaux
Song, J. West
Sonata, grand pianoforte, Mrs. Sully
Song, Mad. Placide
Rondo .. .. Pleyel

Act 2d.

Sinfonia .. .. Guenin
Song, J. West
Concerto Clarinetto, Mr. Dubois
Song, Mrs. Pick
Sonata, grand pianoforte, Mrs. Sully
Duetto, Mrs. Placide and J. West
Grand Sinfonie .. .. Pleyel

After the concert the music will attend as usual to accommodate any parties who wish to dance.

In the meantime, on April 9th in the City Gazette, "Citizen" Cornet announced that he had

"established in the house in Broadstreet, near Kingstreet, in which the baths were formerly kept, a *Vaux Hall*, after the Parisian manner, in which there will be dancing on every Saturday ... the orchestra will attend at American or French societies if required ..."

but evidently the establishment was not opened until late in October, for we read in the City Gazette, Oct. 22:

"Citizen Cornet has the honour to inform the public that the opening of Vaux Hall will be on Saturday next, the 24th instant, at 7 o'clock in the evening, at No. 44, Broadstreet, near King Street. There will be an excellent *Orchestra* of *French Music* a supper and refreshments. The price is two dollars for each gentleman, accompanied or not by ladies."

The Vaux Hall was closed on Oct. 31st on account of additions Citizen Cornet was making. They consisted in decorations by the "Citizen" Audin. But Citizen Cornet had not merely imbued the American spirit of enterprise.

---

1) City Gazette, April 15, 1795.

He still possessed the obliging qualities of his race. Thus he notified the public in December that

"when the night is unfavourable carriages will be sent to the ladies who might be prevented thereby from honouring the Hall with their presence"[1]).

Probably Mr. Le Roy did not belong to Cornet's "orchestra of French music" for otherwise he would have held his benefit concert at Vaux Hall instead of at Williams' coffee-house on Dec. 17th[2]). Be this, as it may, Mr. Le Roy "flattered himself with a hope that the judicious choice of the pieces [would] induce the ladies and gentlemen of this city to honour him with their presence".

Act 1st.

Symphonie .. .. Hayden
Song, by Mrs. Pownall
Concerto on the basse, by Mr. Le Roy Pleyel
Duett, by Mrs. Pownall and Mr. Bergman
La Chasse .. .. Stamitz[3])

Act 2d.

Symfonie .. .. Pleyel
Concerto, Pianoforte, Mr. De Villers .. Kotzeluch
French song, by Mr. Pownall
Concerto Violin, by Petit .. .. Jernovick
A Favorite solo, by Mrs. Pownall
Overture, the Battle of Ivry .. .. .. Martini

N. B. Between the acts, Mr. Le Roy will perform several pieces on the Spanish guitar ...
Silence is requested during the performance."

If this remarkable program allows us to form an adequate opinion of the musical taste of Charleston, those of the following year will afford an opportunity for offering a few useful historical remarks in a different direction. Mr. Le Roy had styled his concert and, historically speaking, justly so a "grand concert". So did Messrs. Petit and Villars, when they announced for their benefit at the City Theatre on March 21st[4]) the following:

"SELECTION.
Act 1st.

Grand Overture .. .. Haydn
Concerto, on the Clarinet, by Mr. Foucard .. .. Michel
Sonata, Piano Forte, by Mr. Devillers .. .. Pleyel
A Favorite song, by Mrs. Pownall
Concerto on the Violin, by Mr. Daguetty .. .. Yarnovick
Sinfonie concertante .. .. Pleyel

---

1) Cornet added to this advertisement (City Gazette, Dec. 12, 1795) that "he continues to repair and tune musical instruments and he has no objection to go to the country on this service when he may be required". No doubt but that his services were frequently required for these were still the days of the capricious harpsichord.

2) City Gazette, Dec. 16, 1795.

3) As a rule, unfortunately no distinction was made between Johann and Karl Stamitz. The 'La Chasse' symphony was by the latter.

4) Originally announced for March 3d.

Act 2d.

Overture in Samson .. .. Handel
Concerto on the Hautboy, by Mr. Graupner[1]) .. .. Fischer
A French song, by Mrs. Pownall
Concerto on the Pianoforte, by Mr. Devillers .. .. Bertoni
A Favorite song, by Mrs. Pownall
Concerto on the Violin, with the favorite rondo of Marlborough, by
    Mr. Petit .. .. Viotti
Grand Overture in Henry IV .. .. Martini

    N. B. The Piano Forte will be played on by Mr. Devillers, and not, as it has been announced by a mistake, by Mr. Villars, for whose benefit is the Concert.

    Silence is requested during the performance of the several pieces.

    The Concert to begin at 7 o'clock precisely. Seats in the boxes will be taken previously as usual: Tickets to be had at the Office of the City Treasurer, at 6 s. each.''

Quite different in character was the concert advertised in the following manner in the City Gazette March 21, 1796:

SACRED MUSIC.

Mrs. Pownall respectfully acquaints the public that agreeable to her engagement with Mr. Solle, previous to her coming to Charleston, she is entitled to his theatre, on Thursday the 24th instant. Religious subjects being best adapted to Passion Week, she has for that evening prepared a *Grand Concert Spirituale*, or Spiritual concert, consisting chiefly of overtures, songs and duets, selected from the most celebrated of Handel's oratorios: the Messiah, Judas Maccabeus, Esther, etc. etc. arranged as follows:

Act 1st.

Overture to the Messiah, with recitative 'Comfort ye my people,
    every valley shall be exalted', by Mrs. Pownall
Martini's Grand Overture to Henry the IVth.
Song from the Messiah, 'He was despised', to conclude with
    'But Thou did'st not leave his soul in hell', by Mrs. Pownall.
Duet, from Judas Maccabeus, 'From this dread scene, these adverse
    powers', by Mrs. Pownall and Miss C. Wrighten
Overture in Sampson .. .. Handel

Act 2d.

Overture, Occasional Oratorio .. .. Handel
Song from 'L'Allegro il Pensorosi' [!], 'Sweet bird', by Mrs. Pownall
    accompanied on the violin by Mons. Petit
Concerto Pianoforte, by Mr. De Villers
Song from the Messiah 'Rejoice greatly, O Daughter of Sion' by
    Mrs. Pownall
Concerto Clarinet, by Mons. Foucard
Song from the Messiah, 'He shall feed his flock like a shepherd', by
    Mrs. Pownall
Duet from Judas Maccabeus 'O lovely peace with plenty crown'd',
    by Mrs. Pownall and Miss Wrighten.
Overture to Esther .. .. Handel

    N. B. Silence is requested during the performance of the several pieces. The concert to begin at 7 o'clock precisely. Doors will be open at six. Tickets ... at 5 s each.''

---

    1) As Gottlieb Graupner became more prominent at Boston, more will be said of his career in a subsequent chapter. At Charleston Graupner was a member of the City theatre orchestra.

On March 24th the City Gazette informed the public that a "synopsis of the concert ... with the words of the anthems, songs etc." was for sale at the Columbian Herald Printing Office and that this synopsis would be necessary for every lady and gentleman as no bills were to be distributed in the house, thereby implying that the distribution of bills had been customary at previous concerts. Evidently Mrs. Pownall's[1]) idea, unusual for Charleston, of giving a Spiritual Concert met with public approbation as she gave" some additional sacred music and oratorio ... and several serious readings by [the actor] Mr. Chalmers" on March 26th[2]).

Still more important was a concert to which, by the way, perhaps for the first time in our country the title 'Musical Festival' was applied. The fact that Gluck's overture to Iphigénie en Aulide and Haydn's only Stabat Mater, composed probably in 1773 and over which Hasse grew so enthusiastic and Reichardt later on so critical, were performed and also the fact that the announcement contains some very interesting particulars as to the orchestral forces employed, certainly warrant a reprint of the advertisements relating to the occasion as they appeared in the City Gazette, April 18 and July 2.

"GRAND MUSICAL FESTIVAL.

For the benefit of Mr. Poiteaux, who informs the public that on or about the first of June next, will be performed at the Charleston Theatre, the celebrated *Stabat Mater* of Doctor Haydn, with a few selected pieces of instrumental music, as shall be more fully expressed in the bills of the concert.

The solos, duettes and chorusses and instrumental parts to be filled up by the most eminent professors and amateurs in town, who have all offered their assistance for this singular occasion. Besides the vocal parts, the orchestra shall be composed as follows: one organ, twelve violins, three basses, 5 tenors, six oboes, flutes and clarinets, two horns, one bassoon, and two pair kettle drums, in all 30[3]).

---

1) This great actress and singer was known in England as Mrs. Wrighten, of whom English critics said that she could not be equalled as *Lucy* in the Beggar's opera and Mr. Seilhamer claims that she was surpassed as a singer by Mrs. Billington and Mrs. Oldmixon only. She was also famous as Vauxhall singer. Mrs. Pownall came to America in 1792 as member of Hallam and Henry's company.

2) I wish to call the attention of readers not familiar with the historical vicissitudes of *Oratorio* to the fact that also in Europe it had become customary to apply the term to entertainments in which either an entire oratorio was performed or miscellaneous selections from such and that it was also quite customary to perform concerts, etc. between the acts or numbers. Compare, for instance, Hanslick's book on concerts in Vienna.

3) The modern, but as all sensible lovers of art hope, soon antiquated craze for enormous halls, enormous orchestras, enormous music, makes even those who should know better, too often forget that entirely different conditions prevailed during the eighteenth century. Indeed, the usual performances of 18th century music, the early Haydn included, are but caricatures with several dozen string instruments drowning the desperate struggles of two oboes, two flutes etc. for a hearing and the backbone of the whole, the harpischord, being cheerfully cut out of the body orchestral in favor of artificial trimming and stuffing for the further display of the string quartet. Yet it would be so easy to infuse style into these renditions if only the conductors would cast a glance into Quantz, Ph. Em. Bach and other writers or study the orchestra

The above hymn has met with great applause at the public and private concerts in London and as Mr. Poiteaux will spare no trouble, time or expences in getting it up, no doubt but the greatest success will attend the execution of it.

The Hymn and a translation of it shall also be published in future bills."

In addition to this we read in the City Gazette, July 2, 1796 further details:

Grand Overture (with a full orchestra of upwards of thirty performers) by Gluck in Iphigenie.

Chorus — Mrs. Pownall, Miss M. Wrighten, Miss C. Wrighten, Messrs. Douvillier, Bergman, Erimbert, Harris, J. West etc.

Solo — Mrs. Pownall
Chorus — as before
Solo — Mrs. Pownall
Solo — Mr. J. H. Harris
Solo — Mr. Bergman
Chorus — As before
Violin concerto of Jarnowick — Mr. Poitiaux

---

statistics as laid down in Marpurg's 'Historisch-kritische Beiträge', 1754—1757. There we find that the orchestra consisted at the court of Gotha of 15 instrumentalists, of Prince Henry of Prussia of 11, of Prince Carl of 17, of the Bishop of Breslau of 17, of Count Branicki of 19, of Rudolstadt of 27, of Anhalt of 16, of Salzburg of 32, of Berlin of 36 only! According to Laborde the opera orchestra at Paris numbered 47 persons in 1713 and 64 in 1778 but this was proverbially an enormous orchestra and it should not be overlooked that "tous les instruments comme tymbales, trombones, tambourins se remplissent par quelques' uns des 64 musiciens". According to Durey de Noinville not more than 36 instrumentalists were employed in the orchestra of the world-famous Concert Spirituel in 1751! The nearest approach to our modern orchestra (in balance rather than in size) was to be found at Mannheim. There the celebrated 'Churfürstlich Pfälzische Capell- und Kammermusik' consisted in 1756 (see Marpug) of 10 first, 10 second violinists, 2 flutists, 2 oboists, 4 'cellists, 2 double bass players, 2 bassoonists, 4 viola players, 4 horns, 2 organists, "annoch zwölf Trompeter und zwey Pauken".

To illustrate the expansive tendency I quote from Mizler's Musikalische Bibliothek, 1754 and Kunzen und Reichardt's Studien, 1793 the following specifications of the court-orchestra at Berlin. 1754: 12 violinists, 4 flutists, 3 oboists, 3 viola players, 5 'cellists, 1 lutenist [!], 3 "Clavierspieler und Compositeurs", 3 bassoonists, 2 "violons", 1791: 2 Capellmeister, 2 Concertmeister, 2 Clavecinisten, 1 harpist, 27 violinists, 6 viola players, 9 'cellists, 5 double-bass players, 4 flutists, 5 oboists, 3 clarinetists, 5 hornists, 5 bassoonists, 1 Serpante, 2 trumpeters, 4 trombonists, 1 kettle-drum player.

But the orchestras at Berlin and Paris were by no means typical. We know, for instance, that even in Beethoven's time, in 1784, the kurkoellnische Orchestra at Bonn numbered only 22 musicians and Koch says (under Besetzung) in his Musikalisches Lexikon, as late as 1802: "Man nimmt gemeiniglich an, dass z. E. mit acht Violinen, zwey Violen, zwey Violoncelle, und zwey Contraviolone verbunden werden, wenn die Stimmen verhältnissmässig besetzt seyn sollen", *i. e.* in proper proportion to the usual reed and brass instruments. If this was the average orchestra at the beginning of the nineteenth century, Rousseau, under *Concert*, defines the *minimum* generally accepted about 1768 as follows: "On ne se sert gueres du mot de *Concert* que pour une assemblée d'au moins sept ou huit musiciens, et, pour une musique à plusieurs parties".

Without pretending to have gone into this matter very deeply, I hope to have made it clear that orchestras like that employed at Charleston on the above mentioned occasion were quite respectable in size even if measured by European standards and this footnote will serve as a danger signal for all those who, because of unfamiliarity with the subject, are apt to believe themselves transported into ridiculously primitive conditions because our early American orchestras numbered *only* from ten to fifty performers!

Duetto — Mrs. Pownall and Mr. Douvilier
Solo — Mr. West
Chorus — As before
Solo — Mr. Erimbert
Solo — Mrs. Pownall
Grand chorus — As before
Martini's Grand Overture, with full orchestra, in Henry the IVth.

Mr. Poitiaux informs the public that every exertion has been made use of on his part, and by those Gentlemen who assist him, to render this night's entertainment one of the grandest ever known here; the piece having already been two months in rehearsal, promises great success in the execution.

Tickets for the boxes, pit or gallery five shillings each, to be had at Mr. Young's bookstore, at Mr. Bradford's music store and other usual places.

The Stabat, with a translation in English verse, by the Rev. Doctor Gallaher, of Charleston, will be given with the tickets.

The Concert will begin precisely at eight o'clock and finish a quarter after ten. The greatest silence is requested during the performance.

Leader of the concert, Mr. Petit.
Organist,   Mr. Devillers.

On August 1st, Mrs. Pownall was again advertised to sing at Williams's Long Room on August 4th for the last time in America, but on the morning of the concert she printed a card in the newspapers

"that from an unforeseen and unnatural change which has taken place in her family she is rendered totally incapable of appearing this evening; she, therefore, declines giving the entertainment at Williams's and requests those persons who have bought tickets to return them to her at Mr. Rogers's in Broadstreet and receive their money.

The unforeseen and unnatural event in Mrs. Pownall's family was the elopement of her daughter Caroline Wrighten with Alexander Placide, the pantomimist. The effect of the elopement upon Mrs. Pownall, says Mr. Seilhamer, was completely to prostrate her, the shock proving so severe that she died on the 11th of August, only eight days afterward, it was said, of a broken heart. Although this distinguished actress had made her London *debut* under the name of Mrs. Wrighten as early as 1770, she was, according to the obituary notices in the Charleston papers, only in her fortieth year at the time of her death.

The only benefit concert of the year 1797 I traced, was given on March 9th at Williams's Long Room for the benefit of Mrs. Lafar, "the widow and children of the late Mr. Joseph Lafar, musician"[1]) who had died in distressed circumstances. On this occasion Messrs. Petit, Foucard, Daguitty, Brunette, Villars, Devillers, Legat, Eckhard etc. as "instrumental principal performers" and Mrs. Placide and Mr. J. West as vocal, generously assisted in rendering the following program, interesting because a symphony by Mozart appears thereon though we are not told which of the thirty-four (?)

---

1) City Gazette, March 6, 1797.

written by the master, then still considered somewhat of a musical anar-
chist, was played.

PLAN OF THE CONCERT[1]).

Act 1st.

Overture in Iphigenie	Gluck
Song, Mrs. Placide	
Concerto, Mr. Devillers	Krumpholtz
Duet, Mr. West and Mrs. Placide	
Rondo	Pleyel

Act 2d.

Grand Simfonie	Mozart
Song, Mr. West	
Concerto Violin, Mr. Petit	Jarnovick
Song, Mr. West	
Simfonie	Massonneau.

In the City Gazette, Oct. 10, 1798 Mr. Edgar, like most of the persons
who gave concerts in those years, a member of the Charleston Theatre
company, announced for the same evening:

A CONCERT of Vocal & Instrumental Music, intermixed with Readings and
Recitations.

Part I.

Will be recited a piece, called The *Prodigal* ... by Mr. Waldron

Part II.

A Variety of *Singing*, with the friendly aid of some gentlemen of this city.

Part III.

Extracts from the late celebrated Oration of the Honourable H. W. Dessaus-
sure, Esq.

Part IV.

An Occasional epilogue, by Mr. Edgar.

Part V.

Will be recited ... Scenes ... from Mr. Murphy's Farce of *Three Weeks after
marriage*.

Shortly afterwards, on Nov. 8, 1798 was advertised for the same evening
for the benefit of Mrs. Grattan at Williams's Long Room a concert, which
really was a concert. The program reads:

Act 1st.

Sinfonia	Haydn
Clarinet Concerto, by Mr. Foucard	Michel
Bravura song	Sacchini
Solo Pianoforte (Mrs. Grattan)	Clementi

---

1) City Gazette, March 8, 1797.

ACT 2d.

Overture .. .. Vanhal
Quartetto, by Mr. Daguetti,[1]) .. .. Pleyel
French song, accompanied on the harp by Mrs. Grattan .. Milico
Violoncello concerto, by Mr. Dumarque, lately arrived from
 Philadelphia .. .. Dumarque
Hail Columbia .. .. Taylor[2])

On March 5th 1799[3]) the violoncellist Demarque, *alias* Dumarque gave a concert "composed of some of the first musicians of this city"..."at Williams's Coffee House, in the room occupied generally by the St. Cœcilia Society" with a program on which the "local" composers seem to have figured prominently:

ACT I.

Sinfonia .. .. Gerowitz
La Bataille de Trenton .. .. M. De Villers
Song (the Soldier tir'd etc.), Mrs. Grattan.
Concerto Clarinet Mr. Foucard
Rondo .. .. Pleyel

ACT II.

Sinfonia .. .. Haydn
Concerto Violin, Mr. Petit
Concerto Pianoforte, Mr. De Villiers
Concerto Violoncello, Mr. Demarque
To conclude with the celebrated song of Hail Columbia, by
 Mrs. Grattan.
  After which the ball will commence. The concert to begin precisely at 7 o'clock ...

"Weather permitting" Mr. Labatut, a clarinetist, announced for his benefit on Dec. 14, 1799 the following program:

PART I.

Grand simphonia .. .. Haydn
Quartetto, Flute .. .. Pleyel
Song, by Mrs. Placide
Duetto, Pianoforte by Mr. Eckhard & Son Pleyel
Concerto de clarinet .. .. Vanderhagen
Finale .. .. Haydn

PART II.

Grand overture .. .. Gyrowetz
Sonata, Pianoforte by Mr. Eckhard .. Cramer
Song, by Mrs. Placide
Simphonia concertante .. .. Daveaux
Quartetto, Clarinet, by Mr. Labatut.
Grand Simphonia .. .. Cimarosa

---

 1) He evidently was the *primarius*. His name was spelled in many different ways.
 2) Of course, this does not mean that Mr. Taylor was the composer of Hail Columbia but that be sang it, the audience possibly joining in the *chorus*.
 3) City Gazette, March 4, 1799.

In the same year a third attempt was made to establish a Vaux-Hall at Charleston. This time by the popular ballet-dancer Mons. Placide who inserted in the City Gazette, June 19:

VAUX HALL GARDENS, corner of Broad and Friend Streets.

Mr. Placide ... in consequence of the advice of his friends ... has established that extensive garden now in his possession as a Vaux Hall; where every kind of accommodation and refreshment will be given to those who wish to spend an agreeable evening.

The airy and healthful situation of the Garden; a Military Band, composed of musicians, masters in their profession; elegant illumination in the many avenues and arbours, the low price of admittance, and the particular attention that will be paid to the visitors — are considerations which induce him to think that he will be highly compensated by a generous public, for all the very great expences he has incurred by establishing this novelty in the summer amusements of the citizens of Charleston.

N. B. The Vaux Hall will open on Monday evening next and continue for the summer season two evenings in a week, viz, Monday and Thursday ... The band will play from eight to half past ten. Tickets of admittance, half a dollar ...

Though on the opening night "strawberry ice-cream for this night only" was to be had, the "concourse" of visitors was so great that not enough benches and other accommodations were to be found. In later advertisements the public was informed that no "persons of color" would be admitted and no absence checks would be given to those who might wish to retire before the Vaux-Hall was over. This last rule was modified in the second season in so far as "to prevent confusion gentlemen are requested, when they wish to go out, to leave something with the doorkeeper"! Such restrictions, however, did not interfere with the popularity of the resort and encouraged by public support Placide went to the expense of engaging the opera-singer Mr. Chambers, just returned from Europe, as *star*. Other vocalists were Mr. and Mrs. Marshall, Miss Sully, a pupil of Mr. Chambers, and Mrs. Placide. Occasionally fire-works were added and as "cold supper [was] prepared at a minute's warning, with additional refreshment" it goes without saying that Placide's Vaux-Hall became a very popular resort. The programs were announced regularly but it will be sufficient to quote the one for the opening night, June 23, 1799 as it is typical.

"At half past eight o'clock — 'Lovely Man' — Mrs. Marshall
At nine o'clock — 'Loose were her tresses seen' — Mrs. Marshall
At half past nine o'clock — 'Listen to the voice of love' — Mrs. Placide
At ten o'clock — 'Ah, why confine the tuneful bird' — Mrs. Marshall
At half past ten o'clock — Trio 'Sigh no more, ladies' — Mr. and Mrs. Marshal
    and Mrs. Placide.
The music to begin at 8 o'clock.

On special occasions Mr. Placide outdid himself to satisfy his guests. For instance on July 8, 1799 "a painting, representing the Independence of America, or the Fourth of July, painted by Mr. Belzous" was to be raffled and a feature of his Vauxhall, reminding us slightly of Bayreuth, was this that "a bell [would] ring five minutes previous to each of the songs". That Mr. Placide, — in print at least — had become a very patriotic American will be seen from a poetical effusion which he inserted in the City Gazette, July 3, 1799 in anticipation of good business on the glorious Fourth:

ODE TO VAUX HALL.

Ye Belles and Beaux, who take delight
In pastimes gay to spend the night,
To Vaux Hall Garden each repair
Were music soft and debonnaire,
With pleasing rapture fires the mind,
And dying murmurs to the wind;
Where the jet d'eau delights the eye,
Throwing its water to the sky;
While *Hail! Columbia!* from the band
Proclaims a free and happy land.

Apparently our poet monopolized the musical interests of Charleston for I found no concerts given in 1800 outside of Vaux-Hall except one and by a very curious coincidence it will be seen that both the first and the last concerts given at Charleston during the period here treated were for the benefit of two musicians bearing the same name: Salter. As the second Mr. Salter called himself in a concert advertisement in the Virginia Herald, Fredericksburg, Va., May 9, 1800 "organist, late from England" he probably was not a descendant of the Mr. John Salter to whom Charleston owed so much during the thirties. The second Mr. Salter appears to have been organist at New Haven, Conn. about 1798. He then drifted gradually to the South, giving concerts for instance at Trenton and Brunswick in 1798. At Charleston he then inserted the following pathetic announcement in the City Gazette, March 1, 1800:

To the humane and friendly.

Mr. *Salter* respectfully informs the ladies and gentlemen of this city that he has lately been afflicted with the loss of sight, which incapacitates him from following his profession as a teacher of music; and he is obliged to solicit the attention and favours of a generous and humane public, to enable him to support a wife and three young children.

With the assistance of the performers of the St. Cecilia Society, on Thursday next, the 4th of March, at the Concert Room in the Coffee House, he will give a *Concert* of Vocal and Instrumental Music in which he and his daughter will take a part.

Tickets, at one dollar.

These pages on early concerts at Charleston will have proved how indispensable a careful study of our old newspapers is if a half-way comprehensive insight into the history of early music in America is desired. Unfortunately the files of these old newspapers are very incomplete, but what is a still greater obstacle to individual research consists in this that they are so exasperatingly scattered through the different libraries of the East. In compiling data for a history of early music in America, one is almost compelled to check the scattered files as if the work was intended rather for a history of early American newspapers. I was able to submit some interesting information on concerts at Charleston because of the ex cellent condition of the Charlestonian papers as on file at the Charleston Library Society, but this file is exceptionally perfect. As soon as other Southern cities, prominent in those days, as Annapolis, Md. and Williamsburg, Va. are approached the obstacle mentioned is very depressing. The people of Maryland and Virginia were never inclined to be ascetic. They enjoyed the pleasures of life, they freely patronized dancing assemblies[1]) and theatrical performances, they loved music and yet concerts are not easily traced. In fact, I found only one advertised in the Maryland Gazette of Annapolis before 1760 and this was not given at Annapolis but at a place now insignificant, at Upper Marlborough. The "grand concert of music" was advertised on June 14 for June 28, 1753.

The perusal of the rather imperfect Maryland Gazette of Annapolis for the years 1760—1800, as on file at the Maryland Historical Society, the Library of Congress and Harvard University, does not yield much better results. But as several musicians may be traced at Annapolis and as several theatrical companies occasionally performed there with George Washington in the audience, the inference is reasonable that the few concerts traced by me were not the only ones given.

In Oct. 1774 George James L'Argeau, a specialist on the Musical Glasses, announced that he would perform on this instrument daily between the hours of 3 and 6 for half a dollar each. We also learn that he had opened a dancing and fencing school, a frequent combination in the formative period of our early musical life. Not until the year 1790 did I run across any entertainments, properly to be termed concerts. Then a Mrs. Sewell advertised on Dec. 16 for the same evening "her musical entertainment and ball ... at the ball-room" but not even the price of admission is mentioned. Two years later Raynor Taylor appeared at Annapolis. Being a musician of recognized attainments, as will be seen in subsequent chapters, he certainly felt out of place in these primitive musical surroundings. He had been appointed organist of St. Anne's in Oct. 1792 but from an advertisement that appeared in the Maryland Gazette, April 11, 1793 it would

---

1) In his 'Travels through the Middle Settlements of North America in 1759/60 ...' (1775) Burnaby, when describing the ladies of Virginia goes so far as to say that "they are *immoderately* fond of dancing ... Towards the close of the evening, when the company are pretty well tired with country dances, it is usual to dance jiggs, a practice originally borrowed, I am informed, from the negroes ..."

seem that those gentlemen who induced him to accept the position had preferred not "to pay the half year's subscription" due on his salary. Evidently the employment of a collector availed little. Under the circumstances, Raynor Taylor decided to leave Annapolis end of May, not without thanking publicly those families who had employed him as music teacher and requesting his debtors to make application for payment. During his short career at Annapolis he gave two entertainments or "Extravaganzas" of the *Olio* species, for which he was famous both in England and in America. The program of the first may follow here as announced in the Maryland Gazette Jan. 24, 1793, that of the second performance on Feb. 28 with his "burletta never performed, called The Old Woman of Eighty-Three" as *pièce de résistance* being very similar in character:

TAYLOR'S MUSICAL PERFORMANCE at the Assembly Room, Annapolis on Tuesday next the 28th of January will be performed an Entertainment in three parts.

PART I.

A Selection of Comic and pastoral songs. Consisting of 'Gay Strephon', a comic song, by Miss Huntley.
The 'Scornful lady; or I wonder at you', by Mr. Taylor.
'Amintor, or the Arcadian Shepherdess,' a pastoral, by Miss Huntley.
'Jockey and Moggy,, a comic song, by Mr. Taylor.
The 'Happy Shepherd and shepherdess', a pastoral duet, by Mr. Taylor and Miss. Huntley.

PART II.

A Dramatic proverb (performed in London with great applause) being a burletta, in one act, called

The GRAY MARE'S THE BEST HORSE.

Consisting of 'A Breakfast scene a month after marriage', a duet by Mr. Taylor and Miss Huntley.
The 'Mock wife in a violent passion' by Miss Huntley.
'A Father's advice to his son in law', 'Giles the countryman's grief for the loss of a scolding wife', the 'Happy Miller', by Mr. Taylor.
'Dame Pliant's obedience to her husband', by Miss Huntley.
The 'Obedient wife, determined to have her own way', a duet.
'New married couple reconciled', a duet.
Finale, 'All parties happy', a duet.

PART III.

A Mock Italian opera, called CAPOCCHIO AND DORINNA, dressed in character.
Signor Capocchio, an Italian singer and director of the opera, by Mr. Taylor.
Signora Dorinna, an Italian actress, by Miss Huntley.
Consisting of recitative, airs and duets.
Capocchio's application to Dorinna to engage her as a singer.
Capocchio requests Signora Dorinna to sing, her affectation there upon, and his admiration of her performance, a duet.
Cappocchio's 'Declaration of love to Dorinna', a song. by Mr. Taylor.
'A Description of an opera audience', a bravura song, by Miss Huntley.
Her very modest and reasonable demands for her performance, and Cappocchio's ready compliance.

Her engagement settled, a duet.
Each part to be preceded by a piece on the Grand Pianoforte, by Mr. Taylor.
The whole of the music original and composed by Mr. Taylor.
Tickets one dollar each . . .
Young ladies and gentlemen, under twelve years of age, may be accommodated
with tickets at half a dollar each. To begin at seven o'clock.

Besides Taylor's extravaganzas may be mentioned "a new species of entertainments" with which the actors Chalmers and Williamson "presented" the ladies and gentlemen of Annapolis in December 1797 at the Ball-Room. They were called

"The TABLET, or, just in time, consisting of readings, recitations and songs". The only item of interest about these affairs is that "particular care will be paid to keep the room warm".

Baltimore, though founded not very much later than Annapolis[1]), soon became the more important of the two cities. Her natural growth naturally carried with it a speedy development of musical life but not until after the War of the Revolution did this become noticeable. Then opera, concert-life, music trades and so forth began to flourish in proportion to the general prosperity of the city and for a while it looked as if Baltimore was destined to ultimately rival older cities like Philadelphia or Boston in musical matters.

Though sporadic concerts may have preceded it, one given in 1784 was the first to attract my attention. William Brown, the flutist of Philadelphia fame, announced the entertainment for his benefit in the Maryland Journal for Jan. 30th not without remarking that his "superior talents on the German flute gained much applause in Europe and this country"[2]). This concert consisted of vocal and instrumental music whereas for June 15, 1786 a concert of instrumental music only was to take place at Mr. Grant's. This was followed on September 28th by a concert of vocal and instrumental music with a ball at Mr. Page's Concert Room when a musician made his bow to the music lovers of Baltimore whose name is connected with the musical origin of 'Hail Columbia'. The fact that the concert for the benefit of Philip Phile, the violinist, took place at a place termed a Concert Room would lead us to infer that concerts were not uncommon in Baltimore, though now traced with difficulty. This supposition is strengthened by the announcement in the Maryland Journal Nov. 9, 1787 that.

"This evening, at the request of a number of gentlemen, promoters of the Baltimore dancing assemblies and *concerts for the season*, will be a concert at Mrs. Starck's new building."

---

1) First settled in 1662 Baltimore became a town in 1730. In 1752 B. had 200 inhabitants, in 1775—6000, in 1790—13500 and in 1800—26500.
2) During these years George James L'Argeau who settled at Baltimore about 1780 gave daily performances on the Musical glasses as he had done previously at Annapolis.

Finally, by turning to the files of the Maryland Gazette of 1786 the necessary evidence is gained, for the following advertisement on April 14, proves that subscription concerts were founded in 1786:

CONCERT.

It is proposed to establish a Musical Concert, by subscripton for three months certain or any time longer the subscribers may chuse, to be held at Mr. William Page's large room in Gaystreet, which room is extremely adapted for the purpose. There are already provided, several well-toned instruments and suitable music, with eight capital performers. — As every attention will be observed to conduct the performance in the most elegant and approved manner it is hoped that the proposal will meet with the approbation and encouragement of those ladies and gentlemen who are friends of the polite arts. — Subscription papers with the *Rules of the Society* are lodged in the hands of several gentlemen at Mr. Page's in Gaystreet, and Mr. Murphy's bookstore in Market Street[1]).

Whether these concerts were connected or not with subscription concerts evidently given in 1788 or early in 1789 by a Mr. Boyer would be difficult to ascertain. At any rate, on Friday April 3, 1789 through the medium of the Maryland Journal:

"The public are respectfully informed that there will be a concert performed on Thursday next, at Mr. John Starck's tavern. *Those ladies and gentlemen who have heretofore honoured Mr. Boyer with their subscriptions*, are in a particular manner requested to attend the same."

This concert was postponed "for a short time" and on April 14, Mr. Boyer announced that his next would be given "at Mr. Daniel Grant's Fountain Inn." A third (?) was advertised by Mr. Boyer on May 22 to take place "at Mr. John Starck's Indian Queen".

In November of the same year Ishmail Spicer opened his 'Singing school in the Court House ... for the improvement of church musick", or rather psalmody as his proposals were printed under this heading. Less than half a year afterwards, Mr. Spicer considered the progress made by his pupils sufficient to exhibit them in a concert of sacred music at the Protestant Episcopal Church "on the first Monday in May". As the advertisement appeared in the Maryland Journal, Friday, April 16, 1790 the date of performance was May 3. The money arising from the sale of tickets was to be left in the hands of Mr. James Calhoun "to be appropriated to such charitable and useful purposes as shall be approved of by ... a committee appointed for the purpose".

A few weeks later the musical public of Baltimore had occasion to enjoy a concert of quite a different character as will be seen from the program, thus advertised in the Maryland Journal, May 25:

---

1) William Murphy, it seems, was the first to circulate music in Baltimore. Advertisements to that effect appeared in 1785.

A GRAND CONCERT Vocal and Instrumental will be performed at Mr. Starck's rooms, at the sign of the Indian Queen in Market Street, on Friday evening, next the 28th instant, by a company of French musicians, lately arrived in this town. It will begin precisely at eight o'clock.

FIRST ACT.

1st. A Grand symphonia, in full orchestra.
2d. An opera song, by M. de Lisle, with its accompaniments.
3d. The Overture of the Two Grenadiers, a modern opera.
4th An Opera song, by Mrs. de Lisle.
5th Concerto de Faudo [Fodor?] by Mr. Emanuel.

SECOND ACT.

6th A Grand symphonia, in full orchestra.
7th A Favorite song, from the celebrated opera, Richard Cœur de Lion [by Grétry] by M. de Lisle.
8th An other favorite opera song, by Mrs. de Lisle.
9th A Duet for two voices, by M. and Mrs. de Lisle.
10th Solos on the violin, by M. Emanuel.

Tickets may be had at the bar of the Indian Queen at one dollar each. — No Person will be admitted without a ticket.

The performers in this concert take the liberty to intreat the protection and countenance of the ladies and gentlemen of this town. They have been induced to come to America by the deserved reputation which the inhabitants bear abroad of possessing a taste for the polite arts, and especially the music[1]). They therefore assure the public, that every possible exertion shall be made by them to gratify it; in the accomplishment of which, they shall deem their arrival in this part of the American empire, one the happiest events of their lives.

The same, exceedingly polite and flattering musicians reappeared in a similar concert on June 4, the program comprising among other numbers a "new quatuor" and songs from Grétry's opera Zemire and Azor. They then treated on June 12th the public of Baltimore to a performance of Pergolese's Serva Padrona under the title of "The Mistress and Maid. The music by the celebrated Italian *Pere Golaise*", the compositor evidently

---

1) This compliment was very flimsy. I believe to be familiar with most of the autobiographies, diaries, accounts of travels referring incidentally to music in America and certainly this "deserved reputation" could not very well be founded on such authors, as f. i. 'The American traveller', Anburey, De Beaujour, Boyle, de Crevecoeur, A. M. C. M., Davis, Kalm, Fontaine, Dunton, De Pontbigand, La Rochefoucauld-Liancourt, Smyth, Thomas, v. Bülow, Wiederhold, Burnaby, etc. On the contrary, these authors, if they ment oned music at all, had nothing favorable to say about their impressions. A few quotations will show what even friendly inclined foreigne·s had to say on the subject. Isaac Weld, for instance, wrote in his 'Travels through the States of North America', 1799: "... Their knowledge of music, indeed, is at a very low ebb". Johann David Schoepf in his 'Reise', Erlangen, 1788 maintained amongst other things that "die Musik war vor diesem letzten Kriege noch ganz in ihrer Kindheit ... Während des Kriegs und nach demselben aber, hat, durch die von den verschiedenen Truppen zurückgebliebenen Musikkundigen, sich der Geschmack weiter verbreitet und man hat nunmehro in den grössten Städten Conzerte ... [In Charleston] soll Geschmack an Musik, Mahlerei und schönen Wissenschaften überhaupt, schon lange her dort allgemeiner sein"! Perrin M. Du Lac in his 'Voyage' Paris 1805 delivers himself of this nonsense: "Les talens d'agrément, la musique, la peinture et la danse

endeavouring to put the unfamiliar name of the great Italian *maestro* into intelligible French!

Merely mentioning William Miller's concert and ball at Grant's Assembly Room on April 6, 1791 two concerts are on record, amongst the first given in our country by musical prodigies. In the Maryland Journal June 17, Mr. De Duport announced that:

"Master Louis De Duport's benefit night will be on Thursday the 30th instant, who will, by particular desire, play a solo concerto of Stamitz on the violin and several favorite airs with variations. — The ball will be conducted by Mr. De Duport, which his son Master Louis, will open with the Shepherd's character dance in dresses, and music adapted to each."

Evidently Master Louis filled the house for "by particular desire" he had another benefit at the Indian Queen on July 11th the program being in part:

1. A Duetto, composed by Mr. Breval, and performed by Master De Duport.
2. Solo concerto, composed by Mr. Jarnowick, and performed by Master De Duport.

Character Dances, composed by Mr. De Duport.
1. Le Sauvage in parliament.
2. Harlequin, an entertainment.

These dances will be performed with dresses suitable to each and the Sauvage pantomime will be redered more natural from the appearance of a forest.

The ball will be opened by eight young ladies who are to dance two Double minuets, and afterwards a Double cotillion will be performed by sixteen."

In the same year Alexander Reinagle[1]), the excellent harpsichordist, conductor and composer inserted the following proposals in the Maryland Journal, July 29 for a

y seroient encore ignorés, si quelques François n'en eussent, depuis quelques années, apporté le goût avec eux". The English Gentleman who translated the Marquis de Chastellux 'Travels in North America' took occasion to add to a few friendly lines in a footnote: "It is very certain that any person educated in Europe, and accustomed to the luxury of music and the fine arts, and to their enjoyment in the two capitals of France and England, must find a great void in these particulars in America. This the translator experienced during his residence in that country . . ." In Brissot de Warville's Nouveau voyage, 1788 the most characteristic passage is this: "Music, which their teachers formerly proscribed as a diabolic art, begins to make part of their education" and the best the Prince de Broglie had to say is that "some of them [the women in Boston] are pretty good musicians, and play agreeably on several instruments". These quotations will suffice to show what foreign travelers really thought of music in America. The trouble with all these accounts, however, is that their authors either visited our country during the war, when music naturally was at a standstill, or did not take the difference in size and population between our cities and London or Paris into consideration. In short they were good observers but poor historians. Still it would afford some entertaining reading, if I were to collect all these accounts into a separate essay.

1) Alexander Reinagle, was born in 1756 in Portsmouth, England and died in Baltimore, Sept. 21, 1809 leaving a melodramatic oratorio based on Milton's Paradise Lost unfinished. R., a pupil of Raynor Taylor, developed an astonishing activity as pianist, composer and manager. Perhaps his greatest importance lies in the history of opera.

SUBSCRIPTION CONCERT of Vocal and Instrumental Music (Under the direction of Mr. Reinagle) the vocal parts by Mrs. Gee.

Conditions.

1. That there shall be two concerts, the first to be held on Thursday the 11th of August, and the next on the Thursday following at Mr. Starck's Long Room.

2. That every subscriber pay three dollars at the time of subscribing.

3. That every subscriber will receive six tickets which will admit himself and two ladies to each of the concerts.

4. None but subscribers to be admitted.

After each concert there will be a ball ...

The program of the first concert escaped me. That of the second, on August 18, was printed in the Maryland Journal August 16 and was worthy of an artist like Reinagle.

PLAN OF THE CONCERT.
ACT I.

Overture of	Ditters
Hunting song 'Thro woodlands and Forests' ..	Mrs. Gee
Sonata, Pianoforte	Mr. Reinagle
Quartetto of Boccherini	Mr. Emanuel
Song 'As the Snow'	Mrs. Gee
Overture of	Bach[1])

ACT II.

Overture	Guglielmi
Ode to Delia	Mrs. Gee
Sonate, Pianoforte	Mr. Reinagle
Concerto, Violin	Mr. Emanuel
Two part song	Mr. Reinagle and Mrs. Gee
Finale	Pleyel.

A third concert, though probably not on the subscription, was offered under Reinagle's direction "the vocal parts by Mrs. Morris", the popular actress and ballad opera singer, on Oct. 18th. About a year later, Raynor Taylor arrived at Baltimore from London and calling himself "music professor, organist and teacher of music in general" announced his intention on Oct. 2, 1792:

"to perform a musical entertainment on a new plan, the whole of which will be entirely original, and his own composition. In the course of it many songs will be sung by his pupil, Miss Huntley, late of the theatre Royal, Covent Garden, a young lady, whose performance has been highly approved both in London and America."

The concert was then advertised for Oct. 17th. Mr. Taylor, in the course of this *olio*, was to play, as at Annapolis, "several pieces on the portable Grand Pianoforte "besides joining Miss Huntley in two sketches, " An Interlude, called 'The Ambitious Countryman' " and "A whimsical performance called the 'Flight of Fancy' ". Raynor Taylor's *vis comica* which had been a drawing card for Sadler's Wells, must have immediately found

---

1) Of course, the 'London' Bach.

favor with the people among whom he had cast his lot for he offered three further entertainments of the kind. The programs were different on each occasion. Miss Huntley was to sing "many favourite songs, in the serious, comic and pastoral style" and for the third concert "some gentlemen, performers on violins, etc. etc." kindly offered their assistance.

In 1793 a Mr. and Mrs. Vermonnet settled at Baltimore, opening a "Seminary for young ladies". Mr. Vermonnet apparently was not only a dancing but also a music master by profession for he advertised a concert at his house in Harrison Street for March 8, postponed from March 5th. That this was intended as one of a series we are allowed to infer from the N. B. to the announcement:

"N. B. If Mr. Vermonnet meets with encouragement from the public, be proposes giving a ball once a month, after the concerts."

Maybe Mr. Vermonnet like other Frenchmen whom the French Revolution drove to the United States became a professional musician only by force of circumstances. At any rate he did not hesitate to take part in a concert held on July 22, 1793 under the direction of Messrs. G. Kalkbrenner and W. Miller at the Exchange, for the benefit "of our distressed brethren, the French". As the price of admission was the usual, one dollar, probably the appeal of the managers to the "usual liberty and charity" of the ladies and gentlemen of Baltimore drew a large audience to a concert "solely intended for the benefit of the sons and daughters of distress".

However, the concert was postponed to July 24th for on July 23d in the Maryland Journal the managers inserted this attractive announcement:

A CONCERT TO-MORROW EVENING.

The public may be assured that the greatest efforts are making to render this entertainment grand, beyond any thing of the kind ever exhibited in Baltimore. In particular we beg leave to mention, having engaged Miss Buron, who has been singer to the Queen of France, and was obliged to leave that happy situation and fly to the West Indies, in the late disturbances in France and now once more is obliged to seek an asylum in these United States, being driven in a most distressed situation from Cape François. She now offers her cordial assistance to aid the benevolent design together with a number of respectable gentlemen amateurs, who will render this concert pleasing and universally satisfactory . . .

Young Misses to be admitted *gratis.*"

A few weeks later, on August 14th, Miss Buron appeared in a concert for her own benefit at Grant's New Assembly Room. Mr. Richard Curson and Mr. Buchanan managed the affair and "several gentlemen . . . promised to exert their vocal abilities at the concert". In the course of the entertainment Miss Buron had

"The pleasure of returning thanks to the liberal inhabitants of Baltimore, for their distinguished patronage, in an English song, composed and adapted for the occasion."

Again the amateur-musicians came to the rescue of some unfortunate refugees on Nov. 25 at Starck's Long Room with a concert for the benefit of a Mr. James Vogel, "lately arrived from St. Domingo; Mr. and Mrs. Demarque; and Mr. Beranger from Europe". The program reads:

FIRST PART

Overture	Pleyel
Song	Mrs. Demarque
Concerto on the violoncello	Mr. Demarque
Quatuor on the clarionet .. .. :.	Mr. Beranger
Sonata of Pleyel on the piano	Mr. Vogel
French song, accompanied on the lute	Mr. Beranger
End of the first part a Medley overture, arranged by	Mr. Reinagle.

SECOND PART.

Symphony of	Haydn
Song	Mrs. Demarque
Concerto on the clarionet	Mr. Beranger
Overture d'Iphigenie[1]) en Aulide, in quatuor for the piano, by Pleyel	Mr. Vogel
Solo on the violoncello, composed by Mr. Demarque	Mr. Demarque
Overture of Pleyel, by a gentleman.	
French song, accompanied on the lute	Mr. Beranger
To conclude with a Grand Medley, arranged by ..	Mr. Reinagle.

For the year 1794 I have been able to trace only one concert. It took place at Grant's Assembly Room on Nov. 27th after the New Theatre had closed its doors for the season. It was given for the benefit of a member of the company, Mrs. Demarque, wife of the violoncellist. The following program was rendered with Mr. Vogel as conductor:

FIRST PART.

1st. A grand Symphony of Pleyel, in full band.
2d. A grand Arietta, sung by a French lady.
3d. The Overture de Iphigenie, upon two forte piano, by Mr. Vogel and a young lady about 8 years old.
4th A quartetto of Pleyel, by an amateur.
5th A Concerto on the Violincelle [!] by Mr. De Marque.
6th A Duetto between a Forte Piano and harp, by Mr. Vogel and an amateur.

SECOND PART.

1st. Symphony concertante of Pleyel, by two amateurs.
2d. A Concerto of Pleyel, on the Forte Piano, by Mr. Vogel.
3d. A grand Arietta, sung by a French lady.
4th A Sonata on the harp, by a French amateur.
5th A grand Overture of Haydn, for two forte pianos, by Mr. Vogel and a young lady about 8 years old.
6th The Battle of Prague[2]), on the Forte Piano, by Mr. Vogel.
7th To conclude with a grand Overture of the Melomanie [3]).

---

1) Probably by Gluck.
2) Kotzwara.
3) Opera (1781) by Stanislaus Champein (1753—1830).

The time was now approaching when public opinion in America was equally divided for and against the terrorists of the French Revolution, until in 1798 an extreme antipathy against things French swept over our country owing to political friction. In 1795, however, public pity for the French refugees was still very strong and such pathetic appeals as for instance a Mrs. D'Hemard made when she advertised for Feb. 27th

"a small concert on the harp only, wherein she will execute several pieces of music and particular beautiful songs, with their variations."

were bound to soften the hearts and loosen the purse strings of a public accustomed to seeing in the newspapers side by side with English advertisements such in French. The lady found herself, as she said, forced to give a concert

"by the unhappy circumstances common to all the unfortunate French, to have recourse for the means of her sustenance to a talent which, in happier times, would have served only to embellish her education".

Because Mrs. D'Hemard was an amateur it does not follow that under normal political conditions her concert would have been an imposition, for we know from Burney and other sources that often the aristocratic amateurs of those days could hold their own against professional virtuosos and if Mrs. D'Hemard flattered herself in the Federal Gazette:

"to obtain the suffrages of the public, by the superiority of her talent over those who have performed on the same instrument in this country".

this was in all probability true, as harpists were then none too numerous in the United States.

As far as the musical life of our country was concerned, the French Revolution proved a blessing as besides the exiled amateurs a considerable number of able professionals settled in our country. They broadened, as will have been noticed, our musical horizon by acquainting Americans with many French works in a distinctively French interpretation. In the North, to be sure, the French element did not leave very visible traces but in Baltimore and in the South it almost predominated for several years. Apparently the intrusion of the French did not cause much professional jealousy for, as a rule, English, German and Italian musicians peacefully worked side by side, and perhaps more so than to-day when our musical life has lost little if anything of its cosmopolitan character. —

On July 14th, 1795 Louis Boullay, a violinist, who had just arrived at Baltimore gave a "grand" concert of vocal and instrumental music "the instrumental parts to be performed by Messrs. Boullay, Demarque, Daugel and Shetky etc.", these gentlemen evidently being the soloists. On July 15th[1]) Mr. Vogel, with the assistance of the "Musicians from the New Theatre,

1) Federal Intelligencer, July 14, 1795.

Philadelphia" gave also a "grand" concert, at Mr. Starck's with this program:

ACT FIRST.

Grand Symphony	Haydn
Sonata Piano Forte, with Scotch airs introduced	Mr. Vogel
Grand Arietta de L'Amant Jaloux[1]), by a lady just arrived in town.	
Concerto Violoncello, composed and to be performed by ..	Mr. Demarque
Imprisonment of the rulers of France	Mr. Vogel
Quartetto of Pleyel, by Messrs. Boullay, Daugel, Demarque and an amateur.	

ACT SECOND.

Grand Symphony	Pleyel
Sonata on the harp, an amateur.	
Grand Ariette de L'Amant Statue[2]), by a French lady.	
Concerto of Jarnovic for the violin	Mr. Boullay
Siege of Valenciennes	Mr. Vogel
Full Piece	Haydn

On Dec. 4th, Mr. Marshall and Mrs. Warrell gave a concert with ball at Mr. Bryden's Fountain Inn. Both were members of Wignell and Reinagle's company which played a summer-season at Baltimore in 1795. To the some company belonged the by far more famous Mrs. Oldmixon and Miss Broadhurst who announced a joint benefit concert for Dec. 9th. Originally the concert was to consist of both vocal and instrumental music but on the day of performance the ladies issued through the medium of the Maryland Journal the statement:

"That several persons of the band which they had engaged being obliged to leave Baltimore, some gentlemen have offered to accompany their vocal exertions, which as far as possible they will strive to render a compensation for the instrumental music, to be given.

CONCERT.

PART 1st.

Duet, 'Time has thinn'd my flowing hair', Miss Broadhurst and Mrs. Oldmixon.
Song, 'Tis not wealth', Miss Broadhurst.
Quartett.
Song 'Je ne scai quoi', Mrs. Oldmixon.
Duet 'Sweet content' (Dr. Arnold) Miss Broadhurst and Mrs. Oldmixon.

PART 2d.

Duet 'Turn fair Clara', Miss Broadhurst and Mrs. Oldmixon.
Song (by desire) 'Amidst illusions' Miss Broadhurst.
Sonata, Piano Forte, Mr. Vogel.
Song 'Sweet Echo', echoed by Miss Broadhurst, Mrs. Oldmixon.
Duet (by desire) 'The Way worn traveler', Miss Broadhurst and Mrs. Oldmixon.

₊ Two gentlemen have undertaken to regulate the ball.

---

1) Grétry.
2) Dalayrac.

On July 7, 1796 a concert was advertised in the Federal Gazette by an Italian musician in a manner to inspire suspicion rather than confidence in his abilities:

TO THE LOVERS OF MUSIC.

Signor Trisobio, an Italian professor of vocal music, who had the honor to be employed three years in the Royal Chapel by the queen of Portugal and who last winter sung in London before all the royal family, being now in this town, where he is to stay but for a few days, is determined to give a concert of vocal and instrumental music on Saturday next 9th inst. Therefore he respectfully informs all the ladies and gentlemen of Baltimore that he will execute several serious and comical Italian songs, composed by himself, and other pieces, of the most celebrated Italian authors. He will likewise sing some serious and comical French and English songs.

Between the songs, selected pieces of instrumental music will be executed by the best performers of this town. Mr. Vogel will execute on the forte piano a concerto of the famous Dussex [!], and one of his scholars, only seven years old, will play a sonata with two forte pianos.

Signor Trisobio hopes he will receive here the same approbation he met with in several European cities, and he will experience the effects of that goodness which characterizes the Americans.

The concert will be given at Mr. Bryden's Fountain Inn ...

Soon after Signor Filippo went to Charleston, S. C. He then moved to Philadelphia, advertised his 'Scuola del canto', struggled hard to make a living as singing teacher and died in extreme poverty at Philadelphia in 1798.

The program of the next concert which I was able to trace at Baltimore and which took place at the Old Theatre near the Wind Mill on July 13, 1796 was almost exclusively French in character

1st PART.

A Grand Overture of Haydn.
De la coquette volage, song, Miss Tiesseire [!].
The Siege of Gibraltar, on the piano, with accompaniments
of violin & horn .. .. Mr. S. Marc
Simphonie concertante of Viotti, Mrs. Yanda and Cha-
teaudun.
The Grand song of Renaud l'art[1]) Miss Teiseire [!].
Quatuor, on the French horn, M. Chailleau.
Sot potpourri, with variations, composed by M. Chateaudun.

2d. PART.

Grand Overture of L'aleyrac[2]).	
A Comic song	Mr. S. Marc
Grand sonata of Pleyel, on the piano	Mr. Vogel
Vole à nos voix, song	Miss Tieissier [!]
The little duo of French tunes, for two horns	Mr. Chailleau and L'Arnaud
La Canzonetta	Miss Teisseire [!]

To conclude with the President's March with the full band.

---

1) Renaud d'Ast, opera by Dalayrac.
2) Of course Nicolas d'Alayrac (Dalayrac) 1753—1809 is meant.

In June 1796, J. H. Schmidt "formerly organist to the cathedral of Schiedam in Holland" arrived in town from Charleston as teacher of music "on the various keyed instruments and the refined art of singing and accompanying songs". His ambition was to show his "abilities, politeness and patience, which are so necessary for a good teacher" and to "produce patent pianos superior to any in this place". Unfortunately just then Charleston was visited by a conflagration and Mr. Schmidt's superior patent pianos were mostly destroyed before they could be shipped to Baltimore. To alleviate his misfortunes Mr. Schmidt decided to test the "well known generosity of the inhabitants of Baltimore" by a concert on August 11 at Bryden's Fountain Inn where "he engaged the upper long room which is very airy and pleasant". After having received promise of assistance of some of the gentlemen musicians of the New Theatre and others, Mr. Schmidt advertised the program of the first act "The exact arrangement of the whole [to] be given in Thursday's papers". On Monday Aug. 8th the first *act* of the concert, which was postponed to Aug. 16th, consisted of a

> Grand simphony from Giernowycke [!].
> Song from Handel's Messiah on two new piano fortes of Hanston.
> A Duo by Messrs. Schmidt and S. Marc.
> Concerto on the violoncello.
> Simphony of Pleyel.

The last concert in 1796 that came to my notice took place at Gray's Gardens, a fashionable summer resort, on Sept. 12th. Though the program of this "grand medley concert" as printed in the Federal Gazette, promised a plentiful musical *menu*, the N. B.'s in the advertisements will probably attract as much attention as the names of Haydn, Bach, Wanhal, Pleyel, Kotzeluch, Rosetti, played "by the performers and band of the New theatre".

PART THE FIRST.

Overture	Haydn
Song 'And all for my pretty Brunette'	Mr. Darley, jun.
Symphony	Pleyel
Song 'I can't for I'm in haste'	Mrs. Warrell
Overture	Bach
Song 'Oh, none can love like an Irish man'	Mr. Marshall
Symphony	Vanhall
Song 'The General Lover'	Mr. Darley
Concerto on the clarinet	Mr. Wolfe
Comic song 'Courtship and matrimony'	Mr. Bates
Overture	Kozluck
A Favorite Scotch ballad	Mrs. Marshall

The President's March.

PART THE SECOND.

Irish song 'Oh dear, what can the matter be'	..	Mr. Marshall
Symphony	..	Rosette
A Hunting song	..	Mr. Darley
Neighbor Sly	..	Mr. Bates
Song 'Absence thou foe to love'	..	Mrs. Warrell
Glee 'How merrily we live'	..	Mr. Marshall, Mr. Darley and Mrs. Warrell

Catch — the cries of Durham.

The Marseilles Hymn.

Leader of the band, Mr. Gillingham[1].

The Gardens to open at five o'clock and the performance to commence precisely at 6.

A handsome collation will be provided. Admittance half a dollar.

N. B. To prevent inconvenience and imposition, Mr. Gray requests the public to take notice that all waiters who are employed by him, in the service of that evening will wear numbers, to distinguish them.

Ladies and gentlemen desirous of obtaining particular rooms, boxes or situations in the gardens are requested to send their servants in time to ascertain them.

A number of constables will attend to preserve order.

Taking the fact that I have been unable to trace any as a criterion[2], not many concerts were held during 1797 and also the remaining years of the century show a decided stagnation in the concert life of Baltimore though on the other hand the well supplied music stores of Joseph Carr and R. Shaw did much to acquaint the music lovers of the city with the current repertory. The first concert mentioned during 1798 brought the harpist Mrs. D'Hemard before the public with her daughter as star-attraction.

"Little Marianne, aged 6 years, who lately returned from Philadelphia, where she has given a Concert which excited the admiration of her hearers, so much so that she was looked upon as a phenomenon".

had occasion to show her "astonishing musical powers" at Bryden's Fountain Inn on May 4th in this following program:

1. Overture of Blaise and Babet[3] on the pianoforte, by   Miss Marianne
2. A Sonata followed by a Medley on the harp, by .. ..   Mrs. D'Hemard
3. The Battle of Prague[4] and the Cottage maid, executed and sung, accompanied by the piano, by .. ..   Miss Marianne
4. A Duo of the harp and piano, by   ..   Mrs. D'Hemard and Miss Marianne

---

1) George Gillingham, who had played in the orchestra at the Haendel Commemoration of 1784 was from all accounts a very able violinist. His career as leader extended far into the nineteenth century. A picture representing him in this capacity at the Park theatre, New York in 1827 is preserved at the New York Historical Society.

2) Messrs. Chalmers and Williamson presented their 'Tablet, or Just in time, readings, recitatives and songs' with which we are already familiar, in December. Besides songs these entertainments contained sonatas and overtures played on the pianoforte by Mr. Carr, jun.

3) Dezède.

4) Kotzwara's insipid piece enjoyed an unrivalled popularity until about 1850. It was cast aside in favor of 'the Maiden's Prayer'.

5. The variations on the harp.
6. An English and French air song, accompanied by the
   piano, by .. ..   Miss Marianne
7. A great Sonata of Pleyel on the piano, followed by 'the
   Little Sailor Boy, sung and accompanied on the piano,
   by .. ..   Miss Marianne
8. By the same, several entertaining variations of Pleyel
   and Haydn.
The concert will terminate by a ball.

A "whimsical entertainment" called "Fashionable variety with a Touch
at the times consisting of various descriptions, recitations, comic songs etc."
— evidently on the order of a *revue* — which the actor Mr. Bates gave on
May 8th may be mentioned in this connection as it helped to spread the
popularity of

"a new patriotic song, called Hail Columbia, accompanied with the President's
March, as now singing with unbounded applause at the theatre, Philadelphia."

A few weeks later, on June 20th, Mrs. Oldmixon, not being booked for a
performance at the theatre, gave a concert with readings at Bryden's Fountain Inn assisted by her collegue Mr. Harwood and Mr. Menel of the theatre
orchestra. The character of the entertainment may be inferred from the
program of a similar "grand concert of vocal and instrumental music in
three acts interspersed with readings and recitations, serious and comic"
as it took place "by authority" at the New Theatre on June 26th:

ACT I.

An occasional Address.
Overture .. ..   Hayden
Song .. ..   Mr. Marshall
Recitation 'The Water Bottle, or a Cure for a scold',
   a comic tale .. ..   Mr. Bernard
Song .. ..   Mrs. Warell
Concerto on the violin .. ..   Mr. Gillingham

ACT II.

Glee 'How merrily we live that soldiers be'.. ..   Mr. Marshall, Mr. Gilling-
                                                   ham, Mrs. Stuart, Mr.
                                                   Shaw, Mrs. Marshall
                                                   and Mrs. Warrell
Comic Reading 'The story of Johnny Gilpin'.. ..   Mr. Harwood
Grand symphony
Favorite Scot's ballad 'Auld Robin Gray' .. ..   Mrs. Marshall
Concerto on the violoncello .. ..   Mr. Menel
Comic catch 'the Cries of Durham'

ACT III.

Introductory symphony
Serious Reading 'A Monody on the death of the late
   favorite and much lamented performer, by ..   Mr. Wignell.

Glee 'Wind gentle ever-green'
    Comic song 'this life
    is like a country dance' .. .. Mr. Bernard
Catch. 'New patriotic Roundelay' and chorus .. Mr. Marshall, Mr. Hardinge
                                             Mr. Fox etc.

This was a *limited* concert as, in order to prevent inconveniences from the heat, the number of tickets was limited "on which account no person can be admitted without a ticket", a restriction easily explained if it be remembered that during the eighteenth century influential and popular gentlemen had access to the stage very much like Caucasian visitors have to-day to the Chinese Theatres in San Francisco. Though the Federal Gazette had advertised this grand concert "for one night only", apparently the demand for tickets was so great and the limited audience so well pleased that a "positively last night", entirely varied from the first, was given on June 28th under the title of "a grand musical selection". Dibdin's most popular songs were the feature and by desire a duet of Giornovichi on the violin and violoncello was performed by Mr. Gillingham and Mr. Menel.

As a 'Musical Society' existed at Baltimore in 1799, advertisements to the effect appearing in the papers, it may be surmised that it gave concerts, but, to my knowledge, they were not announced publicly. I found only two concerts advertised in the Federal Gazette for this year. The first, on the order of those of 1798, took place at the New Theatre on Jan. 22d for the benefit of the band. Though the program contained nothing of unusual interest, it is characteristic enough to follow here as a matter of historical record:

ACT 1ST.

Grand overture .. .. Haydn
Song .. .. Mr. Marshall
Trio (Wranizky) .. .. Mr. Hupfeldt
Song .. .. Daugel and Shetky
Sonata, Grand Piano Forte .. .. Mr. Reinagle
Song .. .. Mrs. Marshall
Concerto Clarinet .. .. Mr. Wolfe

ACT 2D.

Song .. .. Mr. Fox.
Quintetto (Pleyel) .. .. Messrs. Gillingham, Hupfeldt,
                                      Daugel, Brooke, and Shetky
Song .. .. Mrs. Warrell
Rondo, Clarinet (Michel) .. .. Mr. Wolfe
Reading 'Monsieur Tonson' .. .. Mr. Harwood
Concerto, Violin .. .. Mr. Gillingham
Full piece (Gerowetz)

The other concert was held at Bryden's Fountain Inn on April 26th for the benefit of Messrs. Dubois and Wolfe who presented these selections:

FIRST PART.

Overture to Henry to IVth or Bataille d'Ivry ..	Gretry[1])
Medley Trio, for a clarinet, violin, and lute	Messrs. Wolfe, Daugel and Dubois.
Sinfonia concertante for two clarinets, Messrs. Dubois and Wolfe	Pleyel
Rondo and March, to Henry IVth	Gretry

SECOND PART.

Sinfonie	Haydn
Quintetto (principal part by Mr. Hupfield)	Pleyel
Medley, familiar airs on the Piano Forte	Mr. Vogel
Concerto, Clarinet, Mr. Dubois	Michel

Merely mentioning the open air concerts in 1800 of the rival "gardens" of M. De Loubert and Mr. Mang, the latter known as Chatsworth Gardens [2]), this chapter on concerts in the South may be brought to an end with a few necessarily brief references to concerts outside of Charleston, Annapolis and Baltimore.

Whereas in the other Colonies, New England excepted, *high*-life was centralized in one city, Virginia could boast of several towns of almost equal importance and equal social attractions: Williamsburg, Richmond, Fredericksburg, Alexandria, to which may be added Norfolk and Petersburg. To these small but gay places the planters, with or without their ladies, would go to transact business, to attend the races, to frequent the theatres and dancing assemblies, in short to bring some variety into their by no means dull life on the plantations. Williamsburg seems to have been the center of attraction until after the war when the state house was removed to Richmond. This change in general conditions had its effect also on the musical life of Williamsburg, primitive though it was. Whereas concerts are not easily traced after the war, a few are on record for previous years. George Washington, for instance, entered in his ledger for April 2, 1765:

"By my Exps to hear the Armonica 3. 9".

and under April 10, 1767 "Ticket for the Concert"[3]). I have been unable to ascertain by whom these concerts were given. Perhaps by Francis Alberti whom we shall meet again in the next chapter and who, as he sold the tickets, seems to have been connected with a concert of instrumental

---

1) *Sic*, though the opera was by Martini.
2) As Mr. De Loubert had succeeded in procuring "the band of instrumental music, under the direction of Mr. Wormrath" previously engaged for Chatsworth Gardens Mr. Mang found himself obliged to advertise in the Federal Gazette June 4th that "any person capable of furnishing and leading a band, is invited to make an engagement for himself and other performers".
3) See Paul Leicester Ford's monograph on 'Washington and the Theatre' (Dunlap Soc. Publ. 1899).

music, given on May 19, 1769 at Hanovertown near Williamsburg at Mr. Tinsley's. The concert was to "consist of various instruments, by gentlemen of note, for their own amusement". It was requested in the Virginia Gazette, May 11 "by the ladies that the company may be governed by a becoming silence and decorum". A ball, "if agreeable to the company", the *if* being quite superfluous, was to follow.

The earliest allusion to concerts at Fredericksburg I have found is contained in a *card* in the Virginia Gazette, Richmond, Jan. 10, 1784. It was directed "to all lovers of music, vocal and instrumental, in Virginia or elsewhere" by the Harmonic Society of the town of Fredericksburg. This society apparently gave concerts at the Concert Room in the Market House on "the third Wednesday evening in each month" and was "peculiarly intended for benevolent purposes". Tickets for those who were neither members nor performers cost one dollar each and "the music of the evening always [consisted] of three acts, which affords a grand entertainment of four hours"! The society earnestly required the attendance of all gentlemen in the country who were performers on instruments, or who had valuable collections of music.

Though presumably occasional concerts were given in the meantime, I found none advertised until May 6, 1790 when the Virginia Herald inserted the following characteristic advertisement:

A *Concert*, Vocal and Instrumental (For the benefit of Mr. Kullin) to be held at Mr. Brownslow's brick building, formerly the stage office, in Fredericksburg, on Monday, the 10th of May, 1790. When will be performed, some of the best pieces of the most famous composers, in the execution of which several gentlemen of this place have offered their kind assistance.

Mr. Kullin will perform on the harpsichord, as also on a Piano Forte organized, just arrived in this town, which, by its excellence, far surpasses any key'd instrument ever seen here. Mr. Victor will also perform a solo on said instrument with accompanyment for the violin. Some of the new compositions for two performers on one harpsichord, will, in the course of the evening, be executed by Mr. Kullin and Mr. Victor. [1])

In the following year on Oct. 12th a concert with ball was held at Mrs. Hackley's under the direction of Mr. Emanuel. As the pieces to be performed were to be expressed in the bills, we are at a loss to ascertain the program unless it is preserved among the papers of some old Virginian family. On Nov. 4, 1797 a prodigy, already known to us, "proposed" for the same evening a concert at Mrs. Gatewood's Concert Room with the assistance of several gentlemen of Fredericksburg: poor little "Miss" Marianne D'Hemard, "only five years old, 8 months from Paris". Just on a visit to this

---

[1]) John Victor, teacher on the harpsichord, pianoforte, spinet and guitar, tuner and repairer moved from Port Royal to Fredericksburg in April 1789.

place from a triumphal tournée to Philadelphia, Baltimore, Alexandria and Richmond she showed her precocious talents

"in the Battle of Prague — Nicolai's Favorite Sonata opera 3d — Several pieces by Pleyel — Overture de Iphigenie, par Mr. Edelman, with a number of other pieces which have been the play things of the last six months of her life."

But Marianne was not the only child whose musical talents in those days were forced to alleviate the distressed circumstances of her parents. We remember the children of Mr. Salter playing for the benefit of their half blind father at Charleston and the same "musical family" endeavoured to entertain the" humane and friendly" of Fredericksburg with a "pleasing, innocent and scientific species of amusement" on May 10th, 1800.

Of concerts given at Petersburg I have been able to trace only the one for the benefit of Mrs. Sully and Mrs. Pick, advertised in the Virginia Gazette and Petersburg Intelligencer for June 25, 1795. As these musicians were not assisted by an orchestra their program necessarily partook of the character of the average benefit recital to which we have nowadays become accustomed.

PART 1.

A Grand Sonata of Pleyel's on the Piano Forte, accompanied on the violin — By Mrs. Sully and Mr. Pick.
A Favourite Song 'Whither my love' — By Mrs. Pick
A Favourite Scotch Reel, with variations — By Mrs. Sully.
The Favourite Duett of 'the Way worn traveller' — By Mr. and Mrs. Pick.
A Grand Sonata of Steibelt's, to conclude with the favorite Air of 'The Rose Tree' with variations — By Mrs. Sully.
The Marseilles Hymn, in English — By Mrs. Pick.

PART 2.

A Grand Sonata of Clementi's on the Piano Forte, accompanied on the violin — By Mrs. Sully and Mr. Pick.
A French Song — By Mr. Pick.
The Favourite Air of Lira Lira, with variations, from the Surrender of Calais[1]), — By Mrs. Sully.
An Italian Duet, sung by Mrs. Sully and Mr. Pick
The Favourite Air of Moggy Lauder, with variations on the Piano Forte — By Mrs. Sully.
The Hunting Song of Tally Ho! — By Mr. Pick.
Sonata on the Italian Harmonica, with several known airs.
To begin precisely at 7 o'clock. Tickets at 6 s. each . . .

It is safe to say that, whenever and wherever during the last quarter of the eighteenth century concerts of any importance were given in the small towns they generally were due to the enterprise of the musical members of theatrical companies just then performing at these places. This is also true of the several concerts held at Norfolk, Va. in 1796 and

---

1) Arnold.

1797. The programs may follow here as advertised in the American Gazette and in the Norfolk Herald. For October 7th, 1796 Messrs. Decker and Graupner announced a benefit concert to "their friends in Norfolk and Portsmouth" with these selections:

PART I.

A Grand Overture .. .. Stamitz
A Favorite Song 'The Poor little Negro' by Mr. Prigmore.
A Sonata on the Pianoforte, by Mr. Letuz.
Sweet Nightingale, by Mrs. Graupner, accompanied by Mr. Graupner
    on the hautboy
A Violin Duet (Pleyel) by Messrs. Decker and Graupner
Finale .. .. Le Duc

PART II.

Concerto on the hautboy, by Mr. Graupner.
Bright Chanticler, a favorite Hunting Song, by Mr. Prigmore.
A French Song, by Mons. Douvillier.
(By desire) Fisher's Rondo with variations on the hautboy, by Mr. Graupner.
A Favorite Song by Mrs. Graupner.
What is Love? a favorite Duet, by Mrs. Graupner and Mr. Prigmore
The Concert to conclude with the Federal Overture [1]).
To which will be added a Musical Entertainment, in two acts, called The Wedding Ring (not performed here these four years) . . .

On April 13, 1797 was performed at the Theatre

" . . .a selection of *Sacred Music* from the oratorio of the Messiah, etc. Composed by G. H. [!] Handel, under the direction of Mr. Shaw.

VOCAL PERFORMERS.

Mr. Bartlett — Mr. Shaw — Mr. Robbins — Mrs. Decker — Mrs. Shaw.

INSTRUMENTAL PERFORMERS.

Mr. Decker — Mr. Duval — Davezuc — Mr. D. Mard — Mr. Shaw — Mr. Robbins — and Mr. Letuz.

Two days later a "Divine Concert of vocal and instrumental music" was held at the Town Hall at which "the best performers in Norfolk" were to assist. The advertisement continues:

Several *Sacred Hymns,* Psalms, Songs, Trios and Quartets, will be sung by the French ladies and gentlemen who performed at the last concert.
A variety of *fine pieces of music* from the best composers will be played on the Forte Piano, Harp, Flute, Hautboy and Violin.
The *Stabat* from the music of the celebrated Italian composer Jacchiny [2]) will be sung in latin by three or four voices. To conclude with the Sacred Glee of *ó Filii, ó Filiae;* & Hallelugha [!] on the harp, bass and violin, sung in latin by four voices.

Owing to the inclemency of weather, this concert which seems to have been given in competition with the one of April 13th, was put off until

---

1) A very popular piece composed by Benjamin Carr of Philadelphia.
2) Evidently misprint for Sacchini.

April 20th. On April 17th, the Norfolk Herald printed the full program, certainly an odd one.

FIRST PART.

Overture. Gearnovicks Concertante.
Stabat, etc., a latin anthem. Music of the celebrated Sacchiny, by three voices.
French Air and Duet, music of the same.
Pot-pourri of Marshal, on the Forte Piano.
Sacred French Hymn, music by le Moine, by three voices.
Quartetto on the German flute, or hautboy.
French Air, music of Sacchini
Quartett of voices. Music of the same.

SECOND PART.

Overture from La Rosiere, music of Grétry
'The Nightingale in the Grove', a favorite French song, music of the same.
The Battle of Prague on the Forte Piano.
Duet of Voices, music of Grétry.
French Air. Music of Piccini
Concerto on the violin, by Mr. Duval
French Song, accompanied by the harp.
To conclude with the Sacred Glee of ô Filii, ô Filiae, & Hallelugah.

Of the concerts given at Richmond[1]), a few, beginning with the year 1795, came to my notice. The first, a so called "grand" concert and ball was held on July 2d at the Eagle Tavern by Mrs. Sully & Mrs. Pick of the theatrical company just then performing there and who apparently formed a sort of travelling *team* in this year. The program as announced in the Richmond and Manchester Advertiser was the same as performed at Petersburg on June 25th. On Feb. 17, 1797 the Virginia Argus printed proposals for a concert by subscription under the direction of R. Shaw, of the orchestra belonging to Wignell & Reinagle's company. Shaw, who shortly afterwards opened a music store at Baltimore seems to have been opposed to idleness for wherever the fortunes of the company carried him, he filled his leisure hours with music lessons. He also fully understood the advantages of advance-notices as he took occasion to remark in his proposals that

the greater part of the performers being at present in Petersburg, such persons as are desirous of promoting the concert, are requested to subscribe previous to Thursday evening the 23d inst. at which time the concert will be advertised, if a sufficient number of subscriptions are received to defray the expences — if not, the money will be returned to those who may have subscribed.

Sufficient subscriptions having been received, R. Shaw gave the concert on March 1st at the Eagle Tavern with a program remarkable for the unusually careful distinction between performers and composers:

---

1) Population: 1790—3761; 1800—5737 inhabitants.

PART I.

Overture .. ..
Song 'Primroses deck the bank's green side, by Mr. Bartlett   Linley
Sonata on the Grand Piano Forte, by Mr. Frobel .. ..   Pleyel
Song, 'Amidst the illusions', by Mrs. Shaw .. ..   Shield
Concerto, German flute, by Mr. Shaw .. ..   Devienne
Song, 'Twins of Latona', by Mr. Robins .. ..   Shield

PART II.

Song, 'Love sounds an alarm', by Mr. Bartlett .. .. ..   Handel
Quartetto, oboe, violin, viola & bass .. ..   Back
Song 'Loose were her tresses' by Mrs. Shaw .. .. ..   Giordani
Glee, 'Sigh no more ladies', by Messrs. Bartlett, Robins, Shaw, and Mrs. Shaw.
Symphony — Finale.
Between the first and second parts, the facetious history of John Gilpin will
be recited by Mr. Green.

Then on April 26, 1800 we again run across unfortunate Mr. Salter and his still more unfortunate children. The program, as printed in the Virginia Federalist, April 26th does not contribute anything to our knowledge of what was played in the United States of the 18th century and may be dismissed with the remark that the children played sonatas, airs, variations and so forth and sang songs in "character", for instance Master Salter one "in the character of an American sailor".

Concerts were also given at Alexandria, in those years, which practically means Washington[1]). One, advertised for April 30, 1793 "for the benefit of an unfortunate emigrant" was postponed to May 1st and again to May 4th. It must have been a very primitive affair to judge from a naïve passus in the advertisement in the Columbian Mirror, May 1st:

"By this unexpected delay, however, a considerable acquisition will be made to the music — the addition of a Thorough Bass upon the harpsichord, which will be performed by a lady, will render the entertainment much more pleasing and satisfactory, than anything of the kind heretofore experienced in this town."

Another quaint glimpse into by-gone times when the enjoyment of concerts was not facilitated for Alexandrians by street cars, is afforded by a notice in the Columbian Mirror on the day of performance:

"For the convenience of the ladies who mean to attend the concert this evening, a carriage is provided for their conveyance, going and returning; applications to be made to Mr. Jesse Simms — the Concert will not begin until the carriage is unemployed."

On June 27, 1795, at Mr. Abert's Room, postponed from June 25th, Mrs. D'Hemard entertained Alexandria on the pedal harp with sonatas, concertos, favorite airs with variations and songs accompanied by the harp. This concert enables us to form the acquaintance of a gentleman who apparently was considered a musical authority in Alexandria: Elisha C. Dick. Over his signature appeared this remarkable testimonial in the Columbian Mirror of June 23d:

---

1) The population of Washington in 1800 was 3210 inhabitants.

"I have heard Mrs. D'Hemard perform upon the harp, and presuming my testimony may, in some degree, contribute to promote the object of this lady, on the present occasion, I can venture to predict that the expectations of those who shall attend her performance will not be disappointed. — Mrs. D'Hemard's judgement, taste and execution upon the pedal harp are not, in my opinion, to be surpassed by any one."

It seems that others concurred in this opinion for Mrs. D'Hemard saw herself obliged to repeat her performance, "the last time of playing" taking place on July 7th.

On July 16th, Mrs. Sully and Mrs. Pick appeared in a concert the program of which was the same as in their entertainment at Richmond on July 2d and at Petersburg on June 25th, the fourth number only in both *acts* being changed to a song by Giordani, respectively the popular song 'Cottage Maid'. In the following year, on May 10th, a concert of vocal and instrumental music at the Presbyterian Church was advertised under the heading Sacred Harmony. The pieces were selected from Haendel, Addison, Madan, Alcock, Reed, Billings and others. As the psalmodist Alexander Rhea was connected with the church, presumably he gave the concert. In 1797, on Oct. 14th, Mrs. D'Hemard reappeared with her daughter "five years old". The program contained Marianne's repertory as executed in other towns which certainly was astonishing enough no matter how childish the performance must have been.

Merely mentioning a song recital interspersed with recitations offered to the public of Alexandria by Mrs. Oldmixon on June 28, 1798 I conclude the chapter on concerts in the South with three references which prove, at least, that Savannah, Ga. was not without concerts in the eighteenth century. Because only three concerts were traced by me, it should not be inferred that the musical life of Savannah was less developed than that of other Southern cities. The explanation of this scarcity of data is easy. The file of the Georgia Gazette at the Massachusetts Historical Society fully covers the years (April) 1763 to (May) 1770 but the last thirty years of the century are represented by a few stray numbers only at Harvard University and I was not able to extend my historical expedition as far South as Savannah, where a perusal of fuller files certainly would enable the student to prove that Savannah was just as musical as her rival cities of equal size: 5166 inhabitants in 1800.

Presumably the first advertisement of a concert at Savannah occurred in the Georgia Gazette, May 21, 1766 in the following form:

"For the benefit of Mr. John Stevens, junior, on Wednesday the 4th June next, being his Majesty's birthday, will be performed, at Mr. Lyon's Long Room in Savannah.

A Concert of Musik. After the concert musick will be provided for a ball Tea, Caffee, cards, etc. etc.

Thirty years later, on Sept. 15, 1796 a "grand" concert was given at the Filature. This was preceded by a concert on August 19, 1796 at the Assembly Room thus politely advertised in the Georgia Gazette Aug. 18th:

J. West's highest respects wait on the ladies and gentlemen of Savannah and its environs and humbly sollicits their patronage on this occasion and assures them nothing shall be wanting on his part to render this evening's entertainment worthy their attention.

Act I.

Symphonie	Bach
Song	Mr. J. West
Song	Mr. Sully
Song	Mr. Nelson
Hornpipe	Master Duport
Song	Mr. J. West
Song	Mr. J. West

La Fille a Simonette, composed (with variations) by Mr. Daguetty for two violins and bassoon, by Messrs. Daguetty, Duport and Brunette.

Act II.

The *Anacreontic Song*, consisting of songs, catches and glees

Anacreontic Song	Mr. J. West

Duetto, 'Time has not thinn'd my flowing hair'
Glee 'Drink to me only with thine eyes'
Catch 'Poor Thomas Day'
Duetto 'With my jug in one hand'
Duetto 'From night till morn'
Song, Mr. Sully, America, Commerce and Freedom

Act III.

Symphonie

Song	Mr. Nelson
Concerto on the violin	Master Duport
Song	Mr. J. West
French Dance	Master Duport
Song	Mr. J. West
Glee	Mr. Nelson, Mr. West and Mrs. West.

Grand Symphonie.

Probably data on early concerts at so musical a city like New Orleans would be welcome but I have been unable to ascertain such. Still, as Grace King says in her book on New Orleans (1895) that in 1791 among the first refugees from St. Domingo came a company of French comedians who hired a hall and gave regular performances for twenty years including opera and ballet, it goes without saying that concerts were not missing. Should a half-way complete file of Le Moniteur de la Louisianne, founded in 1794, be discovered, it would be easy enough to trace the beginnings of a concert life at New Orleans. However, too much should not be expected, as the city contained in 1800 only 8000 inhabitants, negroes included!

PHILADELPHIA[1].

GOTTLIEB MITTELBERGER in his 'Reise nach Pennsylvanien im Jahre 1750 und Rückreise nach Teutschland im Jahr 1754' (Stuttgart, 1756) says on p. 104:

Zu Zeiten führen einige Engelländer in Privat Häusern ein Concert auf dem Spinnet oder Klavicymbel auf.

Public concerts he does not mention, nor have I been able to trace such at Philadelphia before 1757 though the files of the American Weekly Mercury, the Pennsylvania Gazette and later weeklies are fairly complete from 1719 on. Granted that the Philadelphians, and especially the Quakers, were more inclined to reject worldly amusements than the Southerners and even the Puritans of New England, yet they were human and an atmosphere of refinement and culture pervaded Philadelphia . The fact, therefore, that in Charleston, New York and Boston concerts can be traced long before 1757 renders the introduction of concerts at Philadelphia at so late a date doubtful, not to say, incredible.

However, on Jan. 20, 1757 the Pennsylvania Gazette notified the public that

"By particular Desire

On Tuesday next, the 25th instant, at the Assembly Room in Lodge Alley will be performed a Concert of Music, under the direction of Mr. John Palma; to begin exactly at six o'clock.

Tickets to be had at the London Coffee House, at one Dollar each; and no person to be admitted without a ticket."

A second concert was announced for March 25th in the Pennsylvania Journal, March 24th. Though the Journal did not mention the musician for whose benefit the concert was given, we are able to trace him in a source which will appeal to all good Americans: George Washington's ledger. The father of our country made this entry in 1757:

"March 17th. By Mr. Palmas Tickets 52 S 6."

This was presumably the first, though by no means the last, concert attended by George Washington!

---

[1] Population: 1731—12000; 1790—42 520; 1800—69 403 inhabitants.

By contrasting musical events at Philadelphia before 1750 and after, I believe to have proved in my monograph on Francis Hopkinson[1]) that the musical life of Philadelphia suddenly began to develop with surprising speed. Music began to play a prominent part at Commencement and an Orpheus Club, evidently a musical society, is said to have existed as early as 1759. Music was cultivated more and more in the homes of the people, church music improved visibly, and English opera found a firm footing at Philadelphia through the medium of the (Old) American Company of Comedians. But, for some reason or the other, the concert life did not progress so rapidly. May be the musical gatherings at the homes of John Penn, Dr. Kuhn or Francis Hopkinson absorbed the interest of the amateurs. At any rate, public or half-public concerts remained comparatively few before the war, if we are allowed to trust the newspaper announcements. For instance, between 1757 and 1764 I have not found a single one advertised. Then, however, Francis Hopkinson and James Bremner and a few years later Giovanni Gualdo improved conditions energetically with the assistance of such amateurs as just mentioned and those musicians who had settled at Philadelphia.

When the subscriptions for the organ at St. Peter's Church had proved insufficient "for compleating the design" a concert was advertised for this purpose under the direction of James Bremner[2]). It was to take place at the Assembly Room in Lodge Alley on Feb. 21, 1764 and was the first concert I came across after the one given by John Palma in 1757 on whom George Washington spent the considerable amount of 52 Sh. 6. In the following year, on April 10th, Bremner arranged and conducted an entertainment which speaks well for his abilities and the standard of taste prevailing at Philadelphia.

---

1) 'Francis Hopkinson and James Lyon. Two Studies in Early American Music', Washington, D. C., 1905. In this work I have fully described the concert life at Philadelphia from 1760 to 1770 and therefore see myself compelled to indulge in self-quotation.

2) James Bremner, a relative of Robert Bremner, the Scotch music publisher, composer and editor, came to Philadelphia in 1763. In December of this year he opened a "music school .. at Mr. Glover Hunt's near the Coffee House in Market Street" where he taught "young ladies . . . the harpsichord, or guitar" and "young gentlemen . . . the violin, German flute, harpsichord, or guitar". Bremner possibly became organist at St. Peter's in 1763 but all we know for certain is that he held a similar position at Christ Church in 1767 and that he is spoken of in the vestry minutes in Dec. 1770 as "the late organist". After an absence of several years he is again spoken of (in the diary of James Allen) as organist of Christ Church in 1774. He died near or at Philadelphia "on the banks of the Schuylkill" in Sept. 1780. The most prominent of his pupils seems to have been Francis Hopkinson who possessed several compositions of his teacher. Those still extant are a 'Trumpet air' a 'Lesson', a 'March', 'Lady Coventry's minuet with variations', all for the harpsichord. He was also the author of 'Instructions for the sticcado pastorale, with a collection of airs', London, n. d. (Mentioned by Fétis).

The tenor of the advertisement is so interesting as to deserve to be copied in full. It appeared thus in the Pa. Gaz. on April 4, 1765:

College of Philadelphia, April 4, 1765.

For the Benefit of the Boys and Girls Charity School.

On Wednesday Evening next there will be a Performance of Solemn Music, vocal and instrumental, in the College Hall, under the Direction of Mr. BREMNER. The vocal Parts, chiefly by young Gentlemen educated in this Seminary, and the Words suited to the Place and Occasion, being paraphrased from the Prophets, and other Places of Scripture, upon the Plan of the musical performances in Cathedral's, etc. for public charities in England.

The *Chorus* and other sublime Passages of the *Music* will be accompanied by the *Organ*, and the Intervals filled up with a few Orations by some of the Students.

It is hoped that the Merit of the Performance as well as the Nature of the Charity, by which several Hundreds of destitute Youths for more than 15 years past, have at a great Expense received the Benefits of Education, and been rendered useful to the Community, will entitle this Design to a general Countenance.

The Hall will be properly illuminated and the Music so disposed, that the Galleries and the Body of the House will be equally advantageous for hearing. The Performance will begin precisely at Six o'Clock, and there will be no Admittance but by Ticket, and through the great South Door, which will be opened at Five. Any Persons desiring a printed Copy of the Words to be sung, may have the same gratis, on Delivery of their Tickets at the Door, and Care will be taken that the greatest Order be preserved.

Tickets, at one Dollar each, to be had of Mr. Kinnersly, Mr. Bremner, and Mr. Bradford, or by sending to any of the Trustees or Masters.

On April 18 the Pa. Gaz. reported that:

The whole was conducted with great Order and Decorum, to the Satisfaction of a polite and numerous Audience. Thirty Pounds was raised for the Benefit of the Charity Schools belonging to the said College.

The Persons who so desired received a printed copy of

THE PLAN OF A PERFORMANCE OF SOLEMN MUSICK;

to be in the Hall of the College of Philadelphia, on Wednesday Evening April 10th, 1765, for the Benefit of the Charity School.

ORATION.

ACT I.

Overture, Stamitz.

Air. Prov. iii. from ver. 13 to 17, and iv, 8
Richer far is Wisdom's Store,
Than from Mines of *Gold* can flow;
Brighter is her heavenly Lore,
Than the Ruby's proudest Glow.
Thrice happy he, whose youthful Mind
Seeks in her Courts his joyful find!

II

Her right Hand gives *length* of Days,
Honour in her Left she bears;
Pleasure waits on all her Ways
Peace in all her paths appears.
Around their Brows, who her embrace,
Her Hand a Wreathe divine shall place.
Sixth Concerto, Geminiani.

5*

ORATION.

ACT II.

Solo, on the Violin

Overture, Earl of Kelly

Air. Isaiah lv. 1. 2. John vii. 12

Parted from celestial Truth,
Science is but empty show;
Come to God in early youth;
Where the living Fountains flow!

Come and drink the waters *free;*
Why in fruitless Searches toil?
Wisdom's ever-blooming Tree
Loves to Spread in Virtue's Soil.

Second Overture, Martini

ORATION.

ACT III.

Overture in Artaxerxes; Arne.

Sonata on the Harpsichord.

Chorus Ps. XLVI. from ver. 1 to 5.

God is King! from Day to Day,
Let each tongue his Praise resound;
To each Land his Fame convey,
Tell it to the Heathen round

II.

Tell them; from those Gods to fly,
By their erring Lips ador'd.
He who made yon radiant Sky,
Thron'd in Glory, is the Lord.
Hallelujah! Let us sing:
God made the Skies; is King![1])

In the meantime, an effort had been made to introduce subscription concerts at Philadelphia. On January 12, 1764 the Pa. Gaz. printed the following advertisement:

Philadelphia, January 12, 1764.

On Thursday, the 19th instant, at the Assembly Room in Lodge Alley, will be performed a *Concert of Musick*, to be continued every Thursday, till the 24th of May, following.

No more than 70 Subscribers will be admitted, and each, on paying Three Pounds for the Season, to have one Lady's Ticket, to be disposed of every Concert Night, as he thinks proper. Subscriptions are taken in at Messrs. Rivington and Brown's Store, and by Mr. Bremner, at Mr. Glover Hunt's, in Market street, near the London Coffee House.

N. B. The Concert to begin precisely at 6 o'clock.

Unless James Bremner arranged these fortnightly subscription concerts the supposition is not unreasonable that Francis Hopkinson was the moving

---

1) Copied from a copy at the Library Co. of Philadelphia.

spirit of the enterprise. I base this on a letter which he wrote to his mother from Dublin on July 12, 1766. He said therein, when mentioning that he met a Mr. Flanagan: "he used to come sometimes to my concerts". At any rate it is safe to say that Hopkinson was connected with the Subscription Concert, if not as founder or manager at least as subscriber and performer.

It seems to have met with the favor of the subscribers, for a second season was thus advertised in the Pa. Journal on Nov. 1, 1764:

SUBSCRIPTION CONCERT, at the Assembly Room in Lodge Alley, begins on Thursday the 8th day of November next and to continue every other Thursday 'till the 14th of March following.

Each subscriber on paying Three Pounds to be intituled to two Ladies tickets for the season. Subscriptions are taken in at Messrs. Rivington and Brown's bookstore...

The Concert to begin precisely at Six o'Clock in the Evening.

The subscription concerts seem not to have been continued during the winter of 1765, at least I have found no information to that effect.

Unfortunately it became customary to advertise the date only of regular subscription concerts and not their programs, a habit which is easily explained. They were not absolutely public entertainments but accessible only, as a rule, to the subscribers, and therefore it was hardly necessary to publish the programs in the newspapers. Programs, in the majority of instances, as stated, are traceable only in the papers if a public concert was arranged for the benefit of individual professional musicians.

For these reasons we shall never know exactly—unless the programs are extant in some collection of early play bills and the like—what works were performed and who performed them at these concerts. If the programs were arranged by Francis Hopkinson, his fine library would furnish a clue to the character of the compositions played and we might argue that the subscribers had ample opportunity to become familiar with a "variety of the most celebrated pieces now in taste", as Stephen Forrage expressed himself when advertising a concert for Dec. 31, 1764 "for the benefit of Mr. Forrage and others, assistant performers at the Subscription Concert". On this occasion, by the way, Forrage appeared as one of the earliest virtuosos on Franklin's "famous Armonica, or Musical Glasses, so much admired for their great Sweetness and Delicacy of its tone".

The "Subscription Concerts" of which Francis Hopkinson seems to have been the manager probably were not interspersed with choral music, but would best be classified, to use a modern term, as soirées of chamber-music. The works which called for the largest number of performers certainly were the Concerti Grossi, concertos for several solo-instruments with orchestra-accompaniment. To play these, not more than a dozen musicians were required, and this number could easily have been recruited amongst the gentlemen-amateurs and professionalmusicians of Philadelphia. Extracting the names and their specialty from the newspaper advertisements we might form the following idea of the orchestra:

Francis Hopkinson would preside at the harpsichord. The strings would be represented by James Bremner, Stephen Forrage, John Schneider, Governor John Penn[1]) and two or three other amateurs. When occasion called for it, John Schneider would play the French horn, Ernst Barnard, George D'Eissenburg or, if he still resided at Philadelphia, John Stadler the German flute; and that oboists were to be had in the Quaker City was shown in my monograph on Francis Hopkinson.

Amusingly primitive as all this may seem to readers not historically trained, it was a beginning, and the seventy subscribers certainly enjoyed the music as much if not more than hundreds and thousands of those who fill a modern concert-hall and listen attentively to music much of which, though now considered immortal, will be forgotten as have been forgotten the compositions by such gifted men as Valentini, Corelli, Pugnani, Stanley, Geminiani, etc., played by Hopkinson, his friends and the "Assistant Performers".

That Francis Hopkinson's part in laying the foundations of a concert life at Philadelphia has not been exaggerated may be inferred from the fact that during the two years of his sojourn in England and though James Bremner was residing at Philadelphia, no concerts are to be traced there, that is to say in 1766 and 1767. Indeed the concert life continued to be at a very low ebb until late in 1769 when we again notice an upwards tendency, due mostly to

"John Gualdo, Wine Merchant from Italy, but late from London ... [who] opened a store in Walnut Street, between Second and Front Streets ... in August 1767."

To judge by the papers, this Gualdo, who reminds us of Viotti in his double capacity of musician and wine merchant, was quite a character. He "adapted and composed music for every kind of instrument"; sold instruments; kept a servant boy, who, at a moment's notice, copied any desired fashionable piece of music, and taught ladies and gentlemen how to play on the violin, German flute, guitar and mandolin, etc. In October 1769 Gualdo intended "to sett off for Europe ... to transact some particular and advantageous business for himself and other gentlemen of this town". He therefore begged "the favour of every person indebted to him, to make a speedy payment and in so doing, they will enable him to discharge his own debts before he leaves America, for which part of the world every free

---

1) John Penn, Lieutenant-Governor of Pennsylvania, friend of Francis Hopkinson, and amateur musician, was born in London 1729 and died in Bucks County, Pa., in 1795.

man in his right senses, should have an everlasting regard, for reasons before now quoted by gentlemen more learned than the subscriber". For reasons best known to himself and his debtors, Gualdo preferred not to set off to Europe, as will be seen.

The first concert given by John, or more correctly, as he was an Italian, Giovanni Gualdo, was announced in the Pa. Journal Nov. 9, 1769, in the following manner:

> At the Assembly Room, on next Thursday, (being the sixteenth of November) will be performed a *Grand Concert of Vocal and Instrumental Musick;* with Solos played on different instruments: the concert to be directed by Mr. Gualdo, after the Italian method[1]).

1) Apparently this method was a novelty for Philadelphia but exactly what Gualdo meant by "directed after the Italian method", I am not prepared to say. Emil Vogel's remarkable essay, 'Zur Geschichte des Taktschlagens' (Peters Jahrbuch, 1898) is commonly considered the best contribution to the history of conducting, but shortly after its publication Mr. Walter Unger, a friend of mine and pupil of Adolf Sandberger, selected for his doctor thesis the same subject because he noticed that Vogel's pioneer essay did not cover the ground fully and I remember having copied at Mr. Unger's request certain passages from books in the library of the Liceo Musicale of Bologna which he claimed would shed new light on the matter. However, as Mr. Unger's thesis does not seem to have been finished or published we have to depend on Emil Vogel as the best authority. The crucial point in the history of conducting appears to be the problem of the baton. The chironomy of the middle ages knew conducting by gestures only but audible conducting either by hitting the music stand with the right hand or with a paper roll is traceable as early as the tenth century. This latter method gradually became universal for church music and vocal music in general. A baton (longer than the ordinary paper roll) was occasionally used for larger bodies of performers as for instance at a banquet given by Cardinal Graf Helfenstein in 1564 with 50 vocalists and 80 instrumentalists when the conductor held a "gülden Stecken in der Hand".

Operas were conducted differently, in Italy from the cembalo with gestures and in France by beating time on the floor with a massive stick (in Lulli's time) and later on by marking time with the violin bow, this prerogative of the leader becoming customary for all orchestral music in France, England and Germany during the second half of the eighteenth century. In Germany, Vogel asserts, a paper roll was used during the first half of the eighteenth century not only for vocal but also for orchestral music. All these methods were more or less audible and not until about 1800 did the energetic appeals for continuous, inaudible conducting bear fruit. The modern baton, says Vogel, was first introduced in Germany in 1801 by Landgraf Ludwig von Hessen in Darmstadt who then began to conduct with baton and music stand with score before him. This method gained foot every where else very much later, 1812 in Vienna, 1817 in Dresden and in Leipzig not until 1835.

All this seems plausible enough and yet, after having hunted for references to conducting in olden times, I cannot suppress, the opinion — and I found myself in accord with W. H. Henderson — that several points call for further investigation. It is certainly not the place here to discuss the matter fully and I therefore merely submit two references which go to show that Vogel's theory of the vicissitudes of the baton are not wholly correct. In Johann Beerens 'Musicalische Discurse', 1719 we find this "Von dem modo oder Art und Manier zu tactieren".

> "An etlichen Orten haben die Organisten ein höltzern Gestelle und in demselben einen höltzernen Arm diesen treten sie mit dem Fuss auf und nieder dabey ich mich dann fast krank lachen müssen. Andere tappen mit dem Fuss wider den Boden, dass er pufft ... Andere tactiren mit dem Kopfe ... Andere nehmen zusammengerolltes Papier in die Fäuste und vergleichen sich also mit denen Kriegs Generalen ... Etliche führen den Tact mit einer, etliche mit beyden Händen ... *Andere gebrauchen sich eines langen Steckens oder Stragels*, ohne Zweifel vermittelst desselben die unachtsamen Jungen auf den Schädel zu schmeissen."

Tickets at a Dollar a piece to be had of the Waiter at the London Coffee House, and at Mr. Gualdo's in Front-street, near the Bank-meeting. To begin exactly at half an hour after Six o'clock.

N. B. Hand Bills will be printed mentioning what pieces shall be performed in the two acts. The evening to be ended with a ball (if agreeable to the Company) without further Expense.

As the Pa. Journal printed the program on the day of performance we are not a great loss if none of the printed hand-bills are extant:

ACT I.

Overture composed by the Earl of Kelly.
'Vain is beauty, gaudy flower,' by Miss Hallam.
Trio composed by Mr. Gualdo, first violin by Master Billy Crumpto.
'The Spinning Wheel,' by Miss Storer.
A German flute Concert, with Solos, composed by Mr. Gualdo.
A new Symphony after the present taste, composed by Mr. Gualdo.

From Nef's 'Collegia Musica', I quote the following passus in the anonymous satire 'Die Reise nach dem Konzerte' Basel 1755:

"Aber es war ... einer mit einem dünnen Stecklein welcher damit in der Luft ob sich und nid sich schlug und still machte."

Consequently the baton was known both in Germany and Switzerland before 1800. In England 'beating time' cannot have been abolished altogether about 1780, for otherwise the anecdote in the Musical Memoirs of Parke (who assisted) would be without a point. He narrates that when Dr. Hayes of Oxford and Dr. Miller of Doncaster came to town to give their gratuitous assistance as conductors by *beating time* at the Handel Commemoration of 1784 they were "set down" by Cramer, the leader, who gave the signal for the beginning by tapping the bow. This was quite in keeping with what Jackson says in his 'Present state of music in London', 1791:

"Instrumental music .. [is] carried to so great a perfection in London, by the consummate skill of the performers, that any attempt to beat the time would be justly considered as entirely needless."

But what I miss particularly in Vogel's essay in order to explain Gualdo's remarks, is a clear reference to the method of "directing" orchestras *outside* of the theatre in Italy about 1750 and later, and in England, which would mean also in America, about 1750 and earlier. If what Mattheson says in his Critica Musica, 1722, applies also to the next decades, namely: "In den Italienischen Orchestern wird kein Tact geschlagen", then we may argue that the custom of *leading* an orchestra originated in Italy and spread from there about 1750 to other countries where the function of conducting the orchestra lay either in the hands of the cembalist or of a real conductor. It is further more inconceivable to me that the use of a baton in orchestral music should have suddenly sprung into existence about 1800 and the authors quoted seem to contradict any such theory. Perhaps after an exhaustive treatment of this *per se* very irrevelant problem the solution will suggest itself that a baton rather than the unwieldy paper roll was used by the cembalist and remained in use in orchestral music until temporarily superseded by the violin bow of the leader. With the growth of the orchestras and with the gradual and absolute abolishment of the cembalo the conductor naturally stepped on the raised platform, baton in hand, from beginning to end of the piece, with the score in front of him.

Finally, to gain an idea of just how the conducting was done by the cembalist, we need but watch the pianist in the modern vaudeville-orchestras (undoubtedly the direct, though perhaps illegitimate descendants of the 18th century orchestra), especially in Italy, where he will first mark time with the baton and often enough with the hideous noise of yore, then lay it aside for a while, then take it up again at a change of tempo or for some other reason, and so on throughout the performance, but using merely his hand for the necessary gestures only when he finds it inconvenient to pick up the baton.

Act II.

A new Violin concerto with solos, composed by Mr. Gualdo.
A Song by Mr. Wools.
A Sonata upon the Harpsichord, by Mr. Curtz.
Solo upon the Clarinet, by Mr. Hoffmann, junior.
A Song by Miss Hallam.
Solo upon the Mandolino, by Mr. Gualdo.[1]
Overture, composed by the Earl of Kelly.

Truly a program worth noticing, especially as it shows Gualdo in his capacity as composer. His works not being extant, we have no right to express an opinion concerning their merits. At any rate, Gualdo himself seems to have been very much in favor of his music if he ventured to devote an entire evening more or less to his own works; and I doubt not that this concert of November 16, 1769, was the first "composers'-concert" given in our country.

The affair was clearly for Gualdo's own benefit, since the Subscription Concerts did not begin until November 30. On this day we read in the Pa. Gaz.:

To the Philo Musical Ladies and Gentlemen.

This evening will be performed the first Concert by Subscription, at Mr. Davenport's in Third Street. The Vocal Music by Messieurs Handel, Arne, Giardini, Jackson, Stanley and others. The Instrumental Music by Messieurs Geminiani, Barbella, Campioni, Zanetti, Pellegrino, Abel, Bach, Gualdo, the Earl of Kelly and others.

Tickets for one Night, at f ve shillings a Piece to be had of the Waiter of the London Coffee House, and at Mr. Davenport's. No admittance will be given without the Tickets, nor Money received at the Concert room. To begin at Six o'Clock.

N. B. In the best Part of the Room Chairs will be placed for the Ladies and Benches for the Gentlemen.

Gualdo is moving here in exceptionally good company. If all the Subscription Concerts were of the same standard then we moderns are not justified in haughtily smiling down on Gualdo and his assistant performers, for a glimpse into musical dictionaries will show that most of the composers named were by no means mediocrities. But what counts more than this, they were contemporaries of Gualdo, Hopkinson, and Penn, and just as modern in those days as are now Brahms, Wagner, Tschaikowsky, Richard Strauss, Debussy. Consequently the ready appreciation of foreign novelties by the American public is an inheritance of Colonial times and not the result of German immigration during the nineteenth century[2].

---

1) Gualdo seems to have had a predilection for this instrument. The Library of Congress, for instance, possesses some manuscript trios of his in this curious combination: 'Six easy evening entertainments for two mandolins or two violins with a thorough bass for the harpsichord or violoncello'. The British Museum possesses in print his op. 2, 'Six Sonates for 2 German flutes with a thorough bass' on which he is called Giov. Gualdo da Vandero.

2) The Bach mentioned was not Johann Sebastian but his son Johann Christian,

The next concert under Gualdo's direction which I was able to trace is instructive, as its program discloses the fact that none of the orchestral instruments employed in Europe for concert purposes were missing at Philadelphia, not even the Clarinet, at that time by far less common than to-day.

We read in the Pa. Chronicle, Oct. 1—8, 1770:

To the Public.

By particular desire, on Friday, (being the 12th October) a concert of music will be directed by Mr. Gualdo, in which the following pieces will be performed in two acts.

Act I.

Overture with Violins, German Flutes, French Horns, etc.—
Concerto with Solos for two German Flutes—Quartetto—
Trio—Solo upon the Clarinet—Symphony—
Solo upon the Violin.

Act II.

Overture—Concerto upon the German Flute—Solo upon the Harpsichord—Quartetto—
Solo upon the Mandolin—Symphony.

N. B. Tickets at a Dollar a Piece, to be had at Mr. Gualdo's in Norris Alley, and at the Waiter of the London Coffee House.—To begin at half an Hour after six in the Evening.

In the Pa. Journal November 8, 1770, a similar concert was advertised "two days after Christmas", with the remark that

at the request of several Gentlemen and Ladies, Mr. Gualdo, after the Concert, will have the room put in order for a Ball, likewise there will be a genteel Refreshment laid out in the upper room for those Ladies and Gentlemen who shall chuse to Dance, or remain to see the Ball. For the Ball he has composed six new minuets, with proper cadence for dancing, and he flatters himself will be favourably received.

Tickets at Ten Shillings a piece . . .

N. B. If any Gentleman or Lady should chuse to go away after the concert, the Porter will return Half a Crown to each Person.

I doubt very much whether many persons took advantage of this *N. B.*, for from all we know of the Colonial dames and cavaliers they would rather have missed the German flute concertos and symphonies than Gualdo's "six new minuets with proper cadence for dancing".

One month later, on Jan. 24, 1771, Gualdo advertised another concert, to take place on Feb. 8. This was probably the last concert which he conducted for his benefit. He announced on Aug. 22d his intention to direct a "Concert of Music at the Assembly Room", on the eighteenth of October "the day after the races" but cruel Nemesis interfered. By the seventeenth of this month

Sigr. Gualdo lies in Chains in one of the Cells of the Pennsylva. Hospital,

---

1735—1783 who settled in England, which fact procured him the name of the "London" or "English Bach". Once celebrated, his works are now underrated.

as Francis Hopkinson wrote in a letter to John Penn and melancholically he added:

poor Butho [1]) was kill'd a few Weeks ago by a Fall from his House.—Except Forage and myself I don't know a single Votary the Goddess hath in this large city.

The contradiction, with all due respect for contemporary evidence, is apparent. Could Sigr. Gualdo announce a concert for the eighteenth of October, unless there were sufficient votaries of the Goddess to play and sing at her altar? At any rate, hardly had John Penn received his friend's lines when the Pa. Gaz. on Nov. 28th, 1771, printed the following advertisement which certainly goes to show that the outlook was not quite so gloomy as the Father of American Composers would have us believe.

By Permission and Particular Desire.
For the benefit of Mr. John M'Lean (Instructor of the German Flute) will be performed at the Assembly Room in Lodge Alley, CONCERT OF MUSIC (Vocal and Instrumental) to begin precisely at Six o'Clock in the Evening on Thursday the fifth of December.

The Concert will consist of two Acts, commencing and ending with favourite Overtures, performed by a full Band of Music, with Trumpets, Kettle Drums, and every Instrument that can be introduced with Propriety. The Performance will be interspersed with the most pleasing and select Pieces, composed by approved Authors; a Solo will be played on the German Flute by John M'Lean; and the whole will conclude with an Overture composed (for the Occasion) by Philip Roth, Master of the Band belonging to his Majesty's Royal Regiment of North British Fusileers.

Several Gentlemen, who wish to encourage and reward Merit, have suggested this public Amusement, and have designed to honour with their Protection the Person for whose Benefit it is intended; one Instance of their condescending goodness, he will ever gratefully acknowledge, in consenting, it should be Known, they have been pleased to offer their Assistance in the Performance, which every possible Means will be used to render agreeable and entertaining to the Company, for whose further Satisfaction, it is also proposed, that after the Concert there shall be a Ball; on this account the Music will begin early, and as soon as the 2d. Act is finished the usual Arrangement will be made for dancing.

N. B. The Tickets for the Concert may be had at the different Printing Offices in this city, at the Bar of the Coffee House and at Messieurs Duff and Jacob's Taverns in Second and Third Streets. Price 7 *s* 6.

In July and August of the following year, Philadelphians had occasion to enjoy a series of 'Lectures on Heads' with singing and other entertainments, the sixth of which was given on Aug. 18th for the benefit of the hospital. A few days later, on August 24th, a concert was given by a Mr. Smith who sang a selection of the last and "most approved" songs at Vauxhall and Ranelagh, as f. i. 'Rule Britannia', 'As late' I wander'd o'er the plains', 'Sweet Willy', 'O! Young Jockey', 'Infancy, the cruel tyrant', 'The Echoing horn', 'Adieu, thou lovely youth', 'Come, come my dear girl', 'God

---

1) In his reply (Cavendish Square June 26, 1772) John Penn wrote sympathetically: "I am very sorry for the fate of poor Butho. I believe he was an honest fellow though he often occasioned much discord in our small concerts". Poor Butho!

save the King'. This popular program, strange to say, was rendered at the State House and to make things more attractive

"The State House [was to be] grandly illuminated, and the performance [concluded] with a superb and elegant firework under the direction of Mr. Dumont who has had the honour to perform in London and divers places of this continent, with great satisfaction . . .

To prevent confusion, it is humbly hoped, no one will take it amiss their not being admitted without a ticket which may be had for the Concert and Fireworks, at seven shillings and six pence, and the Fireworks only two shillings and six pence each, at the bar of the London Coffee House."

Gradually the political problems that were to lead to the Declaration of Independence began to absorb all public interest. It is therefore not surprising that very few musicians only cared to give concerts, the expenses of which possibly would not have left anything for their *benefit*. In fact, not until several ladies and gentlemen desired Signor Sodi "to shew his talents as master" do we run across another concert. It was thus advertised in the Pennsylvania Journal, June 15, 1774:

GRAND CONCERT & BALL, at the Assembly Room in Lodge Alley, on Friday the 17th of June, 1774, for the benefit of Signior *Sodi*, first dancing master of the Opera in Paris and London, in which Mr. Vidal who has been a musician of the Chambers of the King of Portugal will play on divers instruments of music.[1])

FIRST ACT.

1. A Symphony. 2. Mr. Vidal will play a Sonetta on the Guitare Italian, with the violin. 3. A Symphony. 4. Mr. Vidal will play a duetto on the mandolino, accompanied with the violin. 5. First Act will finish with a march composed by Mr. Vidal.

SECOND ACT.

1. A Symphony. 2. Mr. Vidal will play a capriccio on the guitar. 3. A Symphony. 4. Mr. Vidal will play a solo on the psaltery, and a minuet imitating the echo. 5. Second act will end with another march composed by Mr. Vidal.

After the concert, Signior Sodi will dance a louvre and a minuet with Miss Sodi; then a new Philadelphia cotillion composed by Signior Sodi. Miss Sodi will also dance a rigadoon and minuet with Mr. Hulett [of New Jork]. A new cotillion; then the allemande by Miss Sodi and Mr. Hulett; also Signior Sodi will danse a jigg, afterwards Mr. Hulett will dance a hornpipe and to finish with a ball for the company.

Signior Sodi added his intention to open a dancing school and Mr. Vidal acquainted the public that he wished to dispose of "a parcel of fine trinkets and jewels in the newest fashion, with a variety of diamond rings, and a great quantity of instrumental strings".

In view of such advertisements there can be little doubt of a temporary retrograde movement in Philadelphia's musical life during the years preceding the war. This observation is further borne out by an advertisement which "Mr. Victor, musician to her late Royal Highness the Princess of Wales,

---

1) Possibly he was identical with the guitarist B. Vidal mentioned by Fétis and Eitner.

and Organist at St. George's London" inserted in the Pennsylvania Packet, Oct. 17, 1774. After acquainting "the musical gentry in general" that he gave instructions on the harpsichord, forte piano, violin, German flute, etc. and especially" in the thorough bass both in theory and practice", Mr. H. B. Victor[1]) took occasion to remark that he

"intended to give a concert, and to perform on his new musical instruments, but is obliged to postpone it for want of able hands; the one he calls *Tromba doppio con tympana*, on which he plays the first and second trumpet and a pair of annexed kettle drums with the feet, all at once; the other is called *Cymbaline d'amour*, which resembles the musical glasses played by harpsichord keys, never subject to come out of tune, both of his own invention."

How far away is this from the legitimate concerts given by Bremner, Hopkinson and Gualdo in the sixties! Still, such freakish entertainments have their *raison d'être,* and if, as Brenet tells us, Marie Leczinska, wife of Louis XV, and her courtiers enjoyed the charlataneries of Jacque Loeillet immensely who, like the amazingly clever and exceedingly artistic Leopoldo Fregoli of our own time, would act and sing the parts of an entire opera cast with lightning changes of costume and appearance, then the Colonials really cannot be censured if they applauded Victor's antics on the Tromba doppio con tympana.

Soon afterwards our struggle for independence began. Our people continued to enjoy and cultivate music in the privacy of their homes, so far as the vicissitudes of war allowed it and more than one captive Hessian officer, as we know from diaries, ingratiated himself by lending a musical hand. But music in public ceased to flourish.

Many "gentlemen performers" were on the field of honor and those who were not would hardly have dared in such times to spend their money on opera or concerts. In the first place, the women, often more patriotic and more sensible than the men, would have objected and in the second place they then would not have had the excuse of over-taxation when expecting George Washington to vanquish a formidable foe with an ill-clad, ill-fed and ill-trained army. Even if Congress had not recommended in October, 1778 that the several States pass laws to prevent theatrical entertainments "and such other diversions as are productive of idleness"[2]), I doubt whether the people themselves would have encouraged concerts, though a sufficient number of musicians remained in Philadelphia to have performed at public concerts if such had been desired. For instance, in 1779 "Brother Proctor's band of music" assisted in the "celebration of St. John,

---

1) From an other newspaper advertisement we learn that H. B. Victor was a German who emigrated to London in 1759. He remained at Philadelphia at least until 1778.

2) Louis C. Madeira, Annals of music in Philadelphia, 1896, p. 33.

the Evangelist's Day by the Society of Free and Accepted Masons" and in the following year, during Commencement at the University of Pennsylvania, also a band of musicians figured prominently. But this was towards the end of the war and, on the whole, it may safely be said that our public music consisted in those years of that of the fife and drum and of such songs as 'Yankee Doodle', 'God save the thirteen states', Billing's forceful hymn 'Chester' and Hopkinson's satirical ballad 'Battle of the Kegs' sung to the tune of 'Annie Laurie'.

Of course, while Lord Howe's victorious army held Philadelphia, the city resounded of songs of quite a different nature and Philadelphia became a kind of *petite Paris*. Said Captain Johann Heinrichs of the Hessian Jäger Corps in his letter-book under date of Philad. January 18, 1778:

".... Assemblies, concerts, comedies, clubs, and the like make us forget there is any war, save that is it a capital joke[1])."

and beautiful, gossip-loving Miss Rebecca Franks enthusiastically wrote in a letter (Sept. 1777) to her friend Mrs. Paca:

"Oh! how I wich Mr. P. would let you come in for a week or two. I know you are as fond of a gay-life as myself. You'd have an opportunity of raking as much as you choose, either at Plays, Ball, Concerts or Assemblies. I've been but three evenings alone since we moved to town ..."

This gay-life of the British and Tories of Philadelphia reached its climax in the splendours of Major André's 'Mischianza' in 1778. Immediately afterwards they found to their sorrow that the war was not a capital joke. Hurriedly they evacuated Philadelphia and had Miss Rebecca not followed the flag of her choice, she would now have been alone most of her evenings, for life at Philadelphia would have been very monotous indeed for a young lady of her temperament. The only entertainment of any pretensions, which the Americans would have offered her, once Philadelphia again came into our possession, was Francis Hopkinson's patriotic 'oratorial entertainment '*Temple of Minerva*', performed in semi-operatic style at an "elegant concert" which Lucerne, the minister of France, gave on Dec. 11, 1781 in honor of Generals Washington, Greene, "and a very polite circle of gentlemen and ladies".

On such rare state occasions only did the end of the war bring any entertainments resembling concerts, but immediately after the war the concert-life of Philadelphia seemed to awaken as from a lethargic stupor. The first event of importance was the establishment in 1783 of the fortnightly 'City Concert' and John Bentley, afterwards leader in the orchestra of the Old American Company, who founded them deserves to be considered

---

1) In 'Extracts' from his letter-books. 1778—1780. as translated by Julius F. Sachse in the Pa. Mag. of Hist, v. XXII.

one of the most important figures in the musical history of Philadelphia.

As the second concert was to be on November 11th, the first must have taken place late in October. The subscriptions were limited for want of room as will be seen from the advertisement of the second concert in the Pennsylvania Packet, November 6th:

CITY CONCERT.

The subscribers will please to take notice that the next concert will be on Tuesday the 11th instant, at the Lodge Room. As a number of gentlemen expressed a desire of subscription, whose subscriptions Mr. Bentley could not receive till he had ascertained the number the room would hold: he now informs them that the subscription is open for 25 more subscribers, after which it will be finally closed. Tickets for non-subscribers may be had at 10 *s* each . . . .

The dates of the other concerts fell on Nov. 25, Dec. 9, Dec. 23, 1783; Jan. 6, Jan. 28, Feb. 17, March 2, March 16, April 2, 1784 (the last), in all eleven. The programs do not seem to have been printed in the newspapers, not even the soloists being mentioned except when Signora Mazzanti, whom Boston had already heard before the war, was announced as the vocal soloist for the fifth. However, it goes without saying that John Bentley engaged the best musicians to be had in the city and that he performed music in keeping with the refined taste of such men as Francis Hopkinson and Thomas Jefferson.

If Bentley, as he expressed himself, had been hampered during the first season by "the peculiar circumstances of the time" he seems to have overcome the difficulties when announcing the second series in this instructive advertisement in the Pennsylvania Packet, Sept. 9, 1784:

CITY CONCERT.

Mr. Bentley once more submits his proposals to the public, for a Subscription Concert, to be continued during the six winter months. Having considerably enlarged his plan, in compliance with the general wish, and having obtained a reinforcement of vocal as well as instrumental performers, he flatters himself that he shall be able to furnish a more elegant and perfect entertainment than it was possible (from the peculiar circumstances of the time) to procure during the last winter. The liberal indulgence which was then shewn to a first attempt, obstructed by many difficulties, the rising taste for music, and its improved state in Philadelphia, are objects that must constantly excite Mr. Bentley's attention to whatever can increase the public satisfaction, or entitle him to a continuance of their favour and applause.

Proposals.

1st. That there shall be a Concert once in two weeks commencing in October: each concert to conclude at half past nine in the evening, after which rooms will be opened to Dancing and Cards.

2d. That every subscriber shall be entitled to tickets for two ladies, besides his own admittance.

3d. That each Subscriber pay two guineas and a half.

4th. That officers of the army and strangers (only) shall be admitted on paying 10 *s.* each.

The room, last season, having been found cold, proper care will be taken to prevent it this season, by placing stoves in different parts, in which the first will be placed in the early part of the day.

The first concert of the series was given on Nov. 2d and the City Concert then proceeded regularly until April 26th except that by the desire of the majority of subscribers the first December concert was deferred until the twenty-first "being in the same week with the Assembly", the one announced for Feb. 1st to Feb. 4th "on account of the inclemency of the weather" and the one for March 1st to March 3d in order not to conflict with" the laudable undertaking for the benefit of the poor at the theatre". Unfortunately we are again at a loss to know John Bentley's repertory. We learn only that in the first concert "some favourite catches and glees" were introduced and in the concert on Feb. 4, 1785 "several favourite airs, by an amateur and a young lady (being her first appearance in public)" also that on March 17th was performed "a grand medley in which [was] introduced the favourite song of Alieen Aroon with some other favourite airs and Auld Robin Gray". This medley was repeated on April 16th, the concert concluding with a "glee and chorus from the opera of the Castle of Andalusia" by Samuel Arnold.

During the winter of 1785/86 the City Concert was discontinued, probably owing to a three-cornered quarrel between Henri Capron[1]), William Brown and John Bentley, the leading musicians of the enterprise but when Alexander Reinagle arrived at Philadelphia in 1786, he immediately, by virtue of his superior talent and individuality, assumed control of the musical affairs of the city. Evidently he brought about a reconciliation between Capron and Brown — Bentley had gone to New York — for on October 18th the Pennsylvania Journal printed the proposals to the effect that twelve fortnightly concerts should be given commencing on Oct. 19th. The conditions as to admission were somewhat similar to those of Bentley, the subscription being fixed at two guineas instead of two and a half and the admission of strangers to one dollar each. The proposals were signed by H. Capron, A. Reinagle, W. Brown and A. Juhan who assured the public of their "greatest endeavours ... to render every performance agreeable and satisfactory to the lovers of music", that "a new orchestra is erected and the greatest care will be taken to make the room agreeable". The first concert was announced for October 19th at the City Tavern and at last we are in position to form an opinion, and a very favorable opinion it will

---

1) He probably was identical with the "able violinist one and of the best pupils of Gaviniés" who, according to Fétis, performed at the Concert Spirituel in 1768. Fétis and Eitner mention several of his published works. Of these the Library of Congress possesses 'Six sonates à violon seule et basse', op. 1.

be, of the music performed at these concerts as the programs were regularly announced in the papers. The "Plans" follow here with their respective dates.

FIRST CONCERT, OCT. 19, 1786.

Act I.

Favorite Symphonie	Vanhall
Song, Mr. Capron	Gretrey
Sonata, Piano Forte	Haydn and Reinagle

Act II.

Concerto Flute	Windling
A Favorite Rondo	
Solo Violoncello	Tilliere

Act III.

Concerto Violin	Cramer
New Symphony	Haydn
Miscellaneous Concerto	
Glee	

SECOND CONCERT, NOV. 1st.

Act I.

Overture	Toeschi
Song, Mr. Reinagle from the Duenna[1])	
Concerto Flute	Stamitz

Act II.

Concerto Violin	Fiorillo
Symphony	Lachnith
Sonata Piano Forte	Reinagle

Act III.

Concerto 2d	Corelli
Duett, Violin and Violoncello	Breval
By particular desire, the Miscellaneous Concerto.	

THIRD CONCERT, NOV. 16th.

Act I.

Overture	Vanhall
Duett, Violin and Violoncello	Breval
Concerto	Corelli

Act II.

Concerto Violin	Pesch
Symphonie	Stamitz
Sonata Piano Forte and Violin	Reinagle

Act III.

Quartett	Kammel
Concerto Flute	Eichner
Symphony	Haydn

---

1) Opera by Linley.

FOURTH CONCERT, NOV. 30th.
Act I.
Overture (with flute obligato) .. .. Haydn
Song, Mr. Reinagle .. .. Baily
Solo, Violin .. .. Juhan

Act II.
Concerto Flute .. .. Brown
Symphony .. .. Andrie
Solo Violoncello with familiar airs .. .. Capron

Act III.
Double concerto, Flute and violin .. .. Davaux
Favorite Rondo .. .. Martini
Sonata Piano Forte .. .. Reinagle
Symphony

FIFTH CONCERT, DEC. 14th.
Act I.
Overture .. .. Van Hall
Song .. .. Reinagle
Solo, Violoncello .. .. Tillier

Act II.
The favorite Overture of Rosina [1])
Concerto Flute .. .. Mezger
Sonata Piano Forte .. .. Mozart

Act III.
Symphonia .. .. Haydn
Song
Concerto Violin .. .. Fiorillo

SIXTH CONCERT, DEC. 28th.
Act I.
Overture .. .. Lord Kelly
Song .. .. Reinagle
Solo Violin .. .. Heimberger

Act II.
Overture .. .. Lachnith
Sonata Piano Forte .. .. Haydn
Song (by request) .. .. Du Poids de la Vienesse

Act III.
Concerto Violoncello .. .. Capron
Overture of Rosina
Concerto Flute .. .. Fialla

SEVENTH CONCERT, JAN. 11, 1787.
Act I.
Overture .. .. Ld. Kelly
Song .. .. Gretry
Quartetto flute .. .. Schmitbaws
                                            [Schmittbauer]

---

1) Shield.

Act II.

Overture	Vanhall
Concerto Violin	Borghi
Quartetto	Davaux

Act III.

Sonata Piano Forte	Prati

Solo violoncello by Lesire
Overture of Rosina.[1])

EIGHTH CONCERT, JAN. 25th.

Act I.

Overture	Bach
Song (newly composed)	Reinagle
Concerto Violoncello	Trickler

Act II.

Overture	Haydn
Sonata (English guitar and song)	Capron
Quartett	Kammel

Act III.

Concerto Flute	Stamitz
Sonata Piano Forte	Haydn
Sonata Violin	Heimberger
Finale	Vanhall

NINTH CONCERT, FEB. 8th.

Act I.

Grand Overture (performed at the Musical Fund, London)	Haydn
Song	Reinagle
Sonata, Guitar	Capron

Act II.

Overture	Bach
Solo Violin	Juhan
Duetto Piano Forte and Violin	Reinagle

Act III.

Duetto Violoncello and Violin	Capron
Concerto Flute	Brown

Overture to the opera Rose et Colas [2])

TENTH CONCERT, FEB. 23d.

Act I.

The Grand Overture	Haydn
Song	Reinagle
Concerto Violin	Borghi

Act II.

Sonata, Piano Forte	Reinagle
New Solo, Flute	Brown
Overture	Bach

---

1) Shield.
2) Monsigny.

6*

Act III.

Solo Violoncello	Tilliere
Favorite Quartett	Kammell
Overture	Toeschi

ELEVENTH CONCERT, MARCH 8th.

Act I.

Symphonie	Rosette
Song	Reinagle
Concerto Violin	Giornovichi

Act II.

Concerto Piano Forte	Bach
Duet Violin and Violoncello	Vachon
Overture	Vanhall

Act III.

Overture	Stamitz
Rondo Flute	Vanhall
Overture of the Poor Soldier	Shield

TWELFTH AND LAST CONCERT, MARCH 22d.

Act I.

The Grand Overture	Haydn
Song	Giordani
Quartett (Violoncello obligato)	Daveaux

Act II.

Overture of Artaxerxes [1])	
Concerto Violin	Giornovichi
Sonata Guittar (by request)	Capron

Act III.

Concerto Flute	Brown
Concerto Piano Forte	Schroeter
Overture	Haydn

This fortrightly City Concert at the City Tavern was continued during the next winter under the management of Brown and Reinagle with this difference that the concerts were no longer supplemented by balls, at least not officially. But by far more significant is the fact that tickets were now for sale at 7 s. 6 d. for the individual concerts, this evidently meaning that they were now entirely public. The "Plans" of the concerts, which like most others usually began at seven o'clock, were these.

FIRST CONCERT, NOV. 22, 1787.

Act I.

Grand Symphony	Haydn
Song	Sarti
Concerto Violoncello	Trickler

---

1) Arne.

Act II.

Sonata Pianoforte .. .. Reinagle
Song by Mrs. Hyde
Concerto Flute.. .. .. K. Prussia [King of Prussia!]

Act III.

Solo Violin .. .. Vanhall
Song (The Soldier tir'd of war's alarms) .. .. Mrs. Hyde
Finale .. .. Gossec

SECOND CONCERT, DECEMBER 6th.

Act I.

Overture .. .. Stamitz
Song .. .. Mrs. Hyde
Concerto and Flute .. .. Daveaux

Act II.

Sonata Piano Forte .. .. Prati
Solo Violoncello .. .. Handel
Quartetto .. .. Stamitz

Act III.

Concerto Flute .. .. Brown
Song (Tally Ho) .. .. Mrs. Hyde
Finale .. .. Guglielmi

THIRD CONCERT, DEC. 20th.

Act I.

Symphonie 15th .. .. Stamitz
Song
Quartett .. .. Stamitz

Act II.

Trio, Piano Forte, Violin and Violoncello .. .. Haydn
Solo Violoncello .. .. Schetky
Overture .. .. Abel, Opera 14.

Act III.

Concerto Flute .. .. Brown
Solo Violin .. .. Reinagle
Overture, Rosina . .. . Shield

FOURTH CONCERT, JAN. 3, 1788.

Act I.

Overture first .. .. Stamitz
Song
Concerto Flute .. .. Brown

Act II.

Trio, Piano Forte, Flute und Violoncello .. .. Schroeter
Song .. .. Gretry
Concerto .. .. Corelli

Act III.

Overture .. .. Abel
Solo Violoncello .. .. Schetky
Symphony .. .. Bach

FIFTH CONCERT, JAN. 17th.

Act I.

The Grand Symphony	Haydn
Song	Sarti
Concerto Violoncello	Brown

Act II.

Sonata Piano Forte	Schroeter
Song	
Double Concerto Flute and Violin	Daveaux

Act III.

Concerto Flute	Brown
Solo Violin	Reinagle
Symphony	Gossec

SIXTH CONCERT, JAN. 31th.

Overture	Stamitz
Song	
Sonata Guitar	Capron

Act II.

Sonata Piano Forte	Reinagle
Song	Gretry
Concerto Flute	Brown

Act III.

Concerto	Stanley
Concerto Violoncello	Capron
Overture	Stamitz

SEVENTH CONCERT, FEB. 14th.

Act I.

Overture	Gossec
Song	
Quartett	Stamitz

Act II.

Sonata Piano Forte	Reinagle
Concerto Violoncello	Capron
Overture	Andree

Act III.

Concerto	Stanley
Rondo Flute of	Fisher and Brown
Symphonie	Lachnitt

EIGHTH CONCERT, FEB. 28th.

Act I.

Overture 1st	Stamitz
Song	Gretry
Quartett	Stamitz

Act II.

Sonata Piano Forte of Garth and Rondo	Brown
Solo Violoncello	Schetky
Favorite Symphonie	Vanhall

ACT III.

Concerto .. .. Stanley
Quartett Flute
Symphonie 2d .. .. Stamitz

NINTH CONCERT, MARCH 13th.

ACT I.

Overture .. .. Abel
Song
Quartett Violoncello .. .. Davaux

ACT II.

Overture .. .. Abel
Song
Concerto Flute

ACT III.

Concerto Piano Forte .. .. Schroeter
Miscellaneous Concerto.

Apparently the City Concert was then discontinued as no further reference to it is made until the attempted revival in 1792 when on Oct. 31st, Bache's General Advertiser printed the following:

CITY CONCERT of Vocal and Instrumental Music under the direction of Messrs. Reinagle, Moller & Capron. The principal vocal part by Mrs. Hodgkinson. The public are respectfully informed the first concert will be held on Saturday the 18th day of November at Oeller's Hotel in Chestnutstreet. The directors flatter themselves that from the engagements they have made with the several performers of eminence, and the arrangements of the music, the concerts will meet with the approbation of the public.

Subscriptions are received by Mr. Oellers at his hotel...

It is a curious fact that, whenever an artistic undertaking does not find root, some sympathetic enthusiast will step forward and in a lengthy dissertation on the powers and beneficial influence of art gently urge the public to save such a meritorious enterprise from its doom. Generally the public reads the appeal with pleasure, feels ashamed for a day or two and then relapses into its *dolce far niente*. In the case of the City Concert one of the subscribers after the third concert either could no longer resist the temptation to expound his views on music in general and on concerts in particular or he felt dissatisfied with the support given an enterprise in which he was interested being a subscriber. As a curious specimen of eighteenth century phraseology and esthetics his entreaties as published in the Federal Gazette, Dec. 24, 1792 will not fail to arouse some interest in this connection. If the City Concert was not continued in the winter of 1793 this was probably less due to public indifference than to the after-effects of the terrible yellow fever epidemic which raged at Philadelphia during the year 1793:

ON THE CITY CONCERTS.

Of all the amusements offered to the public there are none that surpass in value those now under consideration — whether reference be had to present pleasure, or to future profit — whatever improvement can be expected from the sight of polished and agreeable companies, or from the comtemplation of beautiful and interesting objects, combined with melody of sound — or whatever good effects can be produced on the temper of familiar and domestic life; from the lenient and assuasive balm of music and harmony, are here to be perfectly enjoyed, without crowds, without late-hours, or many other inconveniences frequently experienced at public places. To be pleased at a concert, you have only to sit down and to hear.[1])

One bench supports you and one joy unites — there is no struggle for precedency, or for place, nor any necessity of pre-engaging a box or a partner; you are not martialled out in regular files for a dance, nor enjoined a strict order of figure or succession. The mind vacant admits of deep and copious draughts of pure and intellectual pleasure, calculated justly to allay and to soften the ruggedness incident, even, to the necessary pursuits and avocations of life.

In such situations, the musick should be smooth and affecting, the songs artless and rural, borrowed chiefly from scenes of country life; so the rich man may feel a species of delight in transporting himself a moment from the splendours that usually surround him, to scenes of tranquil and unambitious ease; and the poor man consoles himself to think that some of the most flattering views of life are to be drawn from the situation of those who, like himself, are treading only the humbler walks of life.

It is said that in England Royalty is sometimes pleased to retire from the palace and the throne to the humbler amusements of the cottage in order to enjoy alternately the highest pleasures permitted to mankind, to be found perhaps in either case, tho' chiefly in the latter.

Just eulogiumns are due to Messrs. Reinagle, Moller and Capron, for the public spirit and the shining talents with which they have distinguished the arrangements of their concerts, but it is a great accession to the pleasure that other performers thrown on the hospitality of the country by the distresses of a neighbouring island, are also encouraged and supported and are making an amusement move frequent that before returned but too seldom.

From such circumstances may be expected a gradual improvement in the national taste and a greater fondness for one of the most delectable pleasures permitted to mortality — while it is hoped none will be offended at the preference given to this entertainment since it is certain no other stands in equal need of public commendation and favour to support and continue it.

A Subscriber.

The eight programs which show a somewhat stronger leaning towards chamber music than those of the preceding series were these.

FIRST CONCERT, DEC. 1, 1792 (postponed from Nov. 18th).

Act I.

Grand Overture of Haydn, called la Reine de France
Song .. .. Mrs. Hodgkinson
Quartetto composed by Mr. Gehot
Concerto Violoncello .. .. Mr. Capron
    (Composed by the celebrated Duport)
Sinfonia .. .. Bach

---

1) A sound bit of advice which the public unfortunately will never learn to heed. The public in its wild desire to know "how to listen to music" usually forgets "to sit down and hear"!

Act II.

Quartetto .. .. Mssrs. Reinagle,
Gehot, Moller and Capron.
Song .. .. Mrs. Hodgkinson
Sonata Piano Forte .. .. Mr. Moller [1])
Double Concerto, Clarinet and Bassoon .. .. Messrs. Wolf and
Youngblut
Overture .. .. Reinagle

The concert will begin exactly at 7 o'clock; tickets for admission
of strangers 7 *s* 6 each to be had of Mr. Oellers at his Hotel.

SECOND CONCERT, DEC. 15th.

Act I.

Overture .. .. Mr. Moller
Song .. .. Mrs. Hodgkinson
Quartetto Flute .. .. _.. .. Mr. Young
Concerto Bassoon .. .. Mr. Youngblut

Act II.

Overture .. .. Bach
Concerto Violin .. .. Gehot
Song .. .. Mrs. Hodgkinson
Sonata Piano Forte .. .. Mr. Reinagle
Concerto Violoncello
Finale .. .. Haydn

Between the first and second act the favourite glee of 'Sigh no more
ladies' will be performed by Mr. and Mrs. Hodgkinson, etc.

THIRD CONCERT, DEC. 29th.

Act I.

Grand Overture of Haydn, called La Reine de France
Quartetto of Pleyel .. .. Messrs. Gehot [2]), Rei-
nagle, Moller and
Capron
Song .. .. Mrs. Hodgkinson
Concerto, Violoncello .. .. Mr. Capron

Act II.

Overture, expressive of the four different nations, viz.
French, English, Italian and German.

Duetti, arranged for the Piano Forte and Clarinet by
Mr. Moller .. .. Miss Moller and
Mr. Wolf.
Song .. .. Mrs. Hodgkinson
Finale .. .. Roeser

---

1) Our John Christopher Moller probably was identical with the "Moeller, J. . .
C. . ." of whose works several are mentioned by Eitner.

2) The printer insisted on calling him Jehot, but his name was Jean Gehot.

FOURTH CONCERT, JAN. 12, 1793.
Act I.

Grand overture	Stamitz
Quartetto on the French Horn	Pelissier [1])
Song	Mrs. Hodgkinson
Concerto German Flute	Mr. Young
Sinfonia	Stamitz

Act II.

Overture	Vanhall
Song	Mrs. Hodgkinson
Concerto Clarinet	Mr. Wolff
Sonata Grand Piano Forte	Miss Moller
Concerto Violoncello	Mr. Capron
Finale	Stamitz

FIFTH CONCERT, JAN. 26.
Act I.

Grand Overture	Kozeluch
Song	Miss Moller
Quartetto	Mr. Reinagle
Concerto Violoncello	Mr. Capron
Sinfonia	Abel

Act II.

Overture	Stamitz
Song	Mr. Capron
Sonata Piano Forte	Miss Moller
Quartetto Young	Mr. Young
Finale	Haydn

SIXTH CONCERT, FEB. 9th.
Act I.

Overture	Martini
Song	Mr. Chambers
Quartetto (Pleyel) Messrs. Reinagle, Gehot, Moller and Capron	
Concerto Bassoon	Youngblut
Song	Mr. Chambers

Act II.

Overture	Mr. Ditters
Song	Mr. Chambers
Sonata Piano Forte	Mr. Reinagle
Concerto Violoncello	Mr. Capron
Song	Mr. Chambers
Finale	Stamitz

SEVENTH CONCERT, MARCH 2d.
Act I.

Overture 1st	Cambini
Quartetto German Flute	Mr. Young
Song	Mr. Capron
Concerto Bassoon	Mr. Youngblut
Sinfonia	Stamitz

---

1) More will be said about Victor Pelissier in the chapter on New York. Possibly identical with the Pelissier of whom the Cons. Nat. at Paris possesses 'Amusements variés avec accomp. de musette'.

Act II.

Overture 2d	Cambini
Duetto	Miss Moller & Mr. Capron
Quartetto	Messrs. Reinagle, Capron
Sonata Piano Forte	Gehot and Moller
Solo, Violoncello	Mr. Moller
Solo, Violoncello	Mr. Capron
Finale	Haydn

EIGHTH AND LAST CONCERT, for the benefit of Miss Moller, March 31st, postponed from March 16th.

Act I.

Overture	Boccherini
Concerto Flute	Mr. Young
Quartetto	Pleyel
Solo Violoncello	Mr. Capron
Sinfonia	Stamitz

Act II.

Overture	Abel
Miscellaneous Quartett	Mr. Reinagle
Concerto Piano Forte	Mr. Moller
Finale	Abel [1])

In view of programs like these, I believe, the customary good natured or ill-natured smile worn by historians when stumbling accidentally across an isolated eighteenth century program in our country will have to be cancelled once for ever. Though several of the composers who figured on these programs have since passed into (perhaps unmerited) oblivion, they were prominent masters in those days and names like Haydn, Grétry, Bach and Mozart are still household names in every musical community. If the arrangement of the 'Plans' seems a trifle checkered at times to us moderns who fail to find the same or worse faults in the programs of our own time, we should not forget that the City Concerts ran on strictly European lines and contained no oddities which could not easily be duplicated by quoting European programs. Further more if, for instance, Mr. Maderia writes[2]):

"Besides the real music, there is always a plentiful display of 'overtures' and 'concertos' by the local geniuses. Among the Juhans, Reinagles, and Brown, there is scant room for a Haydn"

this opinion falls little short of being absurd. Then as now soloists were in demand and the only difference lies in this that we now pay, or presume to pay, as much attention to the composer of a concerto as to the

---

1) Presumably Reinagle followed the custom of playing the first movement of a symphony as 'Overture', which was in keeping with the form of a first symphony movement and the last as 'Finale', as the last movements were generally so called unless bearing the title of Rondo. Of course, this should not be construed to mean that no real Overtures were performed!

2) Annals of music in Philadelphia, p. 37.

virtuoso performing it. In those days the performer of a concerto usually was his own composer. Hence a distinction between the two usually could not be made. But even when performing a concerto by some other composer-virtuoso it was not considered necessary to mention the composer because concertos were admittedly looked upon more or less as vehicles for the exhibition of skill and nothing better. This remark applies to Capron Brown, Gehot and other virtuosos, who, however, while guilty of the offense of composing, as are ninety nine out of a hundred musicians, succumbed to the temptation very much less oftener than Mr. Madeira seems to infer. If therefore "Concerto Flute—Brown" not necessarily means and probably does not mean that Brown played a concerto of his, then such arguments as those proffered by Mr. Madeira must be severely rebuked in the interest of fair and accurate historical criticism.

But supposing for the sake of argument that the local geniuses like the Juhans, Reinagles and Browns did freely intersperse the programs with their own compositions, does it therefore really follow that their concertos and overtures were void of merit? Did Mr. Madeira study them or did he ever see a copy of them? In view of the fact that only the most indifferent and unimportant compositions of these men have been preserved in America, such historical slaughter is not only hasty, but unfair and woefully unscientific. Even if their best works were less than mediocre, the fact (consult for instance Hanslick's book on concerts at Vienna) would still have to be taken into consideration that concert-givers everywhere in Europe habitually filled an entire evening with their own compositions which, only too often, were still more mediocre than their skill in performing them. Indeed, the American public was decidedly less often subjected to such cruelty than that of Europe. Finally, a glance at the programs of the City Concerts will show that only one "local genius" figured prominently on them: Alexander Reinagle. But as a few of his sonatas, preserved at the Library of Congress[1]) in autograph, prove him to have possessed unquestionable taste and talent as a composer, it is difficult to understand why he should not have acquainted the subscribers to the City Concert with his works even if, as was often enough the case, a symphony by Haydn figured on the same program. If with such arguments, which betray the incapability of projecting one's-self into changing (and unchanged) conditions — the *sine qua non* of the historian — if with such arguments facts and data are to be grouped and cemented into a historical structure, then we may just as well frown on the musical life of our own time and close

---

1) It may serve a purpose to remark that the Library of Congress also now possesses works by Capron and Gehot, printed in Europe and Rondos by Brown printed in America.

the book of history with a cynical smile. Rather than to fight such wind-mills, the harmless question may be asked of those historians who delight in anachronistic arguments, how many American cities of fifty thousand inhabitants there are to-day with orchestral subscription concerts such as Philadelphia and other smaller cities enjoyed more than a century ago?

The query would be still more pointed, if an enterprise for which a Mr. Duplessis who kept an "English school for young gentlemen only" in Market Street was responsible, had been favored with success. The little I have been able to find concerning his enterprise is this. On Feb. 22, 1786 there appeared in the Freeman's Journal an advertisement to the effect that there was

"to be let for Balls, Concerts etc. a convenient and completely ornamented Hall, 45 feet long, 21 feet wide, and 13 feet high from the floor to the ceiling, communicating to Market Street and Church alley."

This hall was rented by Mr. Duplessis who on June 9th, in the Pennsylvania Packet, under the heading 'Vocal and Instrumental Music' informed his friends and the public in general that he proposed opening in his new room in Church Alley:

A CONCERT of Vocal and Instrumental Music, such as Sonatas, Symphonies, select and favorite songs, etc. etc. The price of subscription tickets will be six dollars; and each ticket shall admit one gentleman and a lady to fourteen concerts the first of which will be on Saturday Evening, the 17th instant, precisely at 8 o'clock, and continue every Saturday until the 16th day of September.. . Tickets at 3 s 9 for ⌐ single person each day . . .

How many of these fourteen concerts were given is difficult to say. In fact it is possible to read between the lines of an advertisement on June 22d that Mr. Duplessis found himself obliged to abandon the enterprise. He notified the public that the Concert of "harmonial music" intended for June 17th was unavoidably postponed to June 24th and that it would be continued agreeably to former advertisements "provided there be a sufficient number of subscribers to defray the expenses".

If this and the more successful City Concert was a professional undertaking, Philadelphia also temporarily possessed entertainments continued on the older plan of amateur concerts. Whether the "New Concert" which began by subscription at the Lodge Room in Lodge Alley on Dec. 2, 1783[1]) independently of the City Concert but to which I found no further reference belonged to that class is not quite clear. However, an 'Amateur Concert' existed at Philadelphia during the season of 1786/87. The concerts took place at "Henry Epple's house [a tavern] in Racestreet" but beyond such notices as for instance that "the eighth concert is postponed on account of Mr. Wm. Brown's benefit" to Feb. 16, 1787[2]) the newspapers had very

1) Pennsylvania Packet, Dec. 2, 1783.
2) Pa. Packet, Feb. 15, 1787.

little to say about the enterprise, a fact quite in keeping with the character
of the 'Amateur Concert'. On Oct. 17, 1787 the subscribers were requested
to meet on the 19th "in order to chuse managers and a treasurer for the
ensuing winter". The first concert of this season of 1787/88 took place
on Oct. 30th and as the announcement was headed 'Musical Club' it might
be inferred that the Amateur Concert thrived under the auspices of a musical
society by that name. It was continued also during the next season when
ten concerts were given from Oct. 1788 to March 1789. By the fact that
occasionally prominent professionals advertised their benefit concerts under
the heading of 'Amateur Concert', another pendant to European customs
is furnished where virtuosos would perform *gratis* at the 'Amateur Concerts',
'Liebhaber Konzerte' or whatever their name was in the different countries.
Having thus levied a time honored tribute from the virtuoso, the organisation would then condescend to assist him in a benefit concert given under
its auspices. The underlying idea was that subscribers to the organization
would reward courtesy with courtesy but only too often did the virtuoso
see himself disappointed in his expectation of reciprocity. A concert with
ball on this plan was given between the sixth and seventh 'Amateur Concert'
by Philip Phile on Jan. 29, 1789. The program as printed in the Pennsylvania Packet, Jan. 26th will show that it resembled the programs as had
been played at the City Concert, to which probably the Amateur Concert
became the successor in public favor during those years:

FIRST ACT.

Grand Overture .. .. Vanhall
Sonata Piano Forte .. .. Reinagle
A Song
Concerto Violino .. .. Phile
Rondo Flauto solo

SECOND ACT.

Grand Overture .. .. Haydn
A Song
Concerto Clarinetto .. .. Wolf
Solo Violino .. .. Phile
Grand Overture .. .. Martini

The Amateur Concerts were continued until the season of 1790/91 when
they seem to have met with the fate of everything human. A few years
later, in the spring of 1794, an effort was made to combine both the professional and Amateur Concert. We read in Dunlop's American Daily
Advertiser in March:

"By Subscription. AN AMATEURS AND PROFESSIONAL CONCERT. Under
the direction of Messrs. Reinagle, Gillingham, Menel and Carr, at Mr. Oeller's Hotel,
Chestnutstreet, for six weeks, to be held weekly.

For the 2d, 4th, 6th concert each subscriber will be entitled to two tickets, for
the admission of ladies, and on the last concert night will be given a ball. Subscriptions

at five dollars, will be received at Carr & Co.'s Musical Repository, No. 122 Market-street, and at Mr. Oeller's Hotel.

Visitors can only be admitted by the introduction of a subscriber, for whom tickets may be had on the day of performance at the Musical Repository.

N. B. The Concerts will commence in the course of a fortnight.

However, the first concert was not held until April 8th. Of the programs of the series I found the following:

FIRST CONCERT, APRIL 8th, 1794.

ACT THE FIRST.

Overture	Haydn
Glee — 'Adieu to the village delights'	Baildon
Quartetto	Pleyel
Song — Carr — 'Sembianze amabili'	Bianchi
Concerto Violino	Mr. Gillingham

ACT THE SECOND.

Song, Mr. Carr 'Primroses deck'	Linley
Concerto Violoncello	Mr. Menel
Glee 'Come live with me'	Webbe
Concerto Clarinet	Mr. Henry
Full piece	Haydn

SECOND CONCERT, APRIL 15th.

ACT THE FIRST.

Overture	Haydn
Glee 'Awake Eolian lyre'	Dandby
Quartetto	Pleyel
Song — Mr. Carr — 'The ling'ring pangs'	Horace [Storace]
Concerto Oboe	Mr. Shaw

ACT THE SECOND.

Overture to Otho	Handel
Glee 'When Arthur first'	Calcott
Concerto Violoncello	Mr. De Marque
Song, Mr. Carr, 'Dear gentle Kate'	Hook
Overture for wind instruments	Panutge
Full piece	Haydn

THIRD CONCERT, APRIL 22d.

ACT THE FIRST.

New Overture	Pleyel
Glee 'Here in cool grot'	Mornington
Concertante by Messrs. Gillingham, Stuart, Shaw and Menel	Pleyel
Song — Mr. Carr — 'Mansion of peace'	Webb
Concerto Violin	Mr. Gillingham

ACT THE SECOND.

Concerto flute	Mr. Young
Song — Mr. Carr — 'Come, come thou Goddess' ..	Handel
Concerto Clarinet	Mr. Henry
Glee 'Sigh no more, ladies'	Stevens
Full piece	Haydn

Subscriptions at four dollars for the remaining nights.

FOURTH CONCERT, APRIL 29th.

ACT THE FIRST.

Overture	Stamitz
Glee	
Duet for violin and violoncello by Mr. Gillingham and Menel	Jarnovick
Song, Mr. Carr	
Concerto Violoncello	Mr. Menel

ACT THE SECOND.

New Overture	Haydn
Cantata — Mr. Carr .. .. —	Webbe
Concerto Clarinet	Mr. Henry
Glee	Mornington
Full piece	Haydn

This was the first and last season of the Amateurs *and* Professional Concert and with one exception also the last attempt at a series of subscription concerts during the century. With this exception is linked the name of a lady-musician, known to us from her career in the South and who also was identified with the foundation of a 'Linen & Muslin Warehouse' at Philadelphia in 1797. As Mrs. Grattan informed the public that "the second *Ladies Concert*" was to be held on Jan. 3, 1797 at Mr. Oellers' Hotel, obviously the first took place in December 1796. Of the first season of the 'Ladies Concert' hardly anything is known beyond what is contained in the announcement of the second concert in the Philadelphia Gazette, Jan. 3, 1797:

MRS. GRATTAN respectfully informs the ladies and gentlemen of the city that the second Ladies Concert will be on Thursday next, the 3d of January, at Mr. Oellers Hotel.

ACT 1st.

Grand Sinfonie	Haydn
'Holy Lord', Mrs. Grattan	Handel
Concerto Violin	Gillingham
Trio & chorus, Siege of Belgrade	Storace

ACT 2d.

Concerto in B, Mrs. Grattan	Dussek
'Ah, non sai', Mrs. Grattan	Sarti
Quartett	Pleyel
Grand Chorus, Pirates	Storace

The Concert will begin at half past six, and at half past eight the music will attend for the ball.

Mrs. Grattan begs leave to inform the ladies and gentlemen that the subscription book is at her house, No. 39 North Sixth Street, for the reception of those names who wish to honor her with their demands.

A subscription for eight nights, sixteen dollars, including a gentleman & lady's ticket, both transferable. Half subscription 8 dollars, including one ticket. Single ticket, two dollars.

Mrs. Grattan takes the liberty of requesting the subscribers to send for their tickets any day after Thursday the 15th December, at No. 39, North South Street. Single tickets to be had the day of the concert only, at the Bar of Mr. Oellers's Hotel.

Mrs. Grattan ventured on a second but more modest season in Dec. 1797. Probably because concerts alone did not pay, she announced her intention in Porcupine's Gazette, Nov. 29th of having "four concerts and balls during the winter". Subscribers' tickets were not transferable. Single tickets were to cost two dollars and season tickets six dollars. The concerts again began at half past six and

"the band to attend for the ball at eight. The expence of which Mrs. Grattan engages to discharge. The Concerts will begin as soon as the band arrives from New York".

This probably means that Mrs. Grattan was not on friendly terms with Messrs. Wignell and Reinagle and preferred to engage instead of their theatre orchestra that of their rivals, the Old American Company of Comedians.

Mrs. Grattan found herself obliged to devote her energies almost exclusively to chamber and vocal music. In fact on Dec. 16, 1797 she

"respectfully informs the ladies and gentlemen of the city that her first concert of *Vocal Music*" will be held on December 21st at Mr. Richardet's, the caterer.

The program reads:

ACT I.

Quartette .. .. Pleyel
Song 'Angels everbright' .. .. Handel
Glee (Messrs. Carr, Darley, jun. and Hill) 'The Mariners'
Song, Mr. Carr, 'The Primroses'
Duett, Mrs. Grattan and Mr. Carr .. .. Paisiello
Scotch glee. Mrs. Grattan, Messrs. Carr, Darley and Hill.

ACT II.

Concerto, Piano Forte, (by a young lady) .. .. .. Viotti
Song, Mrs. Grattan .. .. Sacchini
Glee, Messrs. Carr, Darley, jun., and Hill .. .. Jackson
Duet, Mrs. Grattan and Mr. Carr, 'Time has not thin'd'
Song, Mr. Darley, jun.
Quartette, Mrs. Grattan, Messrs. Carr, Darley and Hill.

Apparently the condition that subscribers' tickets should not be transferable not meeting with public approval, Mrs. Grattan made a compromise by stipulating that

"any subscriber on paying his subscription, will have a right to demand tickets for the unmarried part of his family, which tickets will admit them every night during the season."

In the announcement of her second concert, Jan. 2, 1798, our first lady manager incidentally took occasion to solicit the support and patronage of a generous public by remarking that "necessity obliges her to make this effort for the maintenance of her infant family". The program announced reads:

ACT 1st.

Sinfonia	Pleyel
Song, Mrs. Grattan, words from Shakespeare. Music by a lady.	
Quartette. Messieurs Gillingham, Hupfield, Daugel and Menel with a solo for Mr. Gillingham	Haydn
Song, Mrs. Grattan	Cimarosa
Concerto, Piano Forte by a young lady	Krumpholtz

ACT IId.

Concerto Clarinet	Mr. Wolf
Song, Mrs. Grattan	Sacchini
Sinfonia	Pichl

After which the band attended for the ball. This feature appealed to the charitable instincts of the public by far more than the concert and Mrs. Grattan after finding already in December "that the plan of her Concert is misconceived" and informing the public "that it is the same as the City Assembly" was sensible enough to strike colors on Jan. 25, 1798 and "respectfully informs the ladies and gentlemen of the city that agreeable to the wish of Mrs. Grattan's subscribers, on Tuesday next [Jan. 30] she gives "a ball with refreshments, instead of a Concert at Mr. Richardet's . . .".

Still, she cannot have submitted to the dancing enthusiasts altogether for on Feb. 28th the American Daily Advertiser, probably very much to Mrs. Grattan's benefit, announced that

"The President and his family honor the Ladies Concert with their presence this evening."

If it be asked why towards the end of the century subscription-concerts seem to have lost their hold on the public, several explanations may be advanced. In the first place, Wignell and Reinagle, when opening their New Theatre in 1793, gave predominance to opera. This departure must have absorbed a good deal of the musical interest of Philadelphia and it is a common observation that in smaller cities where opera becomes the feature of the musical life an *organized* concert-life suffers in proportion. Then the virtuosos found it more to their advantage to give benefit concerts independently of the traditional mutual-insurance policy and the more numerous the occasional concerts became the less necessity there was for a series of subscription concerts. Finally, concert-goers need a season of rest. They will frequent concerts in winter time if they are allowed to recuperate from the strain on their music nerves in the summer. But, if they are led into the temptation of dissipating musically during the summer *al fresco*, they are apt to take their vacation in winter. This was the case at Philadelphia where summer-concerts became a feature during the last decade of the eighteenth century.

The first to attempt something of the kind appears to have been Mr.

Vincent M. Pelosi, proprietor of the Pennsylvania Coffee House, who in May 1786 announced

that by the desire of several gentlemen, he has proposed for the summer-season to open a Concert of Harmonial Music, which will consist of the following instruments, viz.

Two clarinets
Two French horns
Two bassoons
One flute [1])

To begin the first Thursday of June and to continue every Thursday following, till the last Thursday of September. The orchestra will open at eight o'clock in the evening, and continue open until eleven, which shall play different and various airs, chosen from the most celebrated authors.

A few years later, in 1789, George and Robert Gray, proprietors of the popular "Gray's Gardens" in the suburbs of Philadelphia, followed suit. They gave weekly concerts from May to October. Thursday was concert-day and the concerts began at four o'clock and concluded "precisely" at nine. "A handsome stage wagon mounted on steel springs with two good horses" ran twice a day between the city and the ferry for the accommodation of passengers. On the last night of the season, October 14th, the band was "considerably" increased and the "vocal part" was executed by a Mr. Wolfe but the *clou* of the evening's entertainment consisted in the illumination of "the fall of water at the mill . . . more splendidly than upon any former occasion — the music playing opposite to the fall" — in the "Federal Temple".

Messrs. Gray publicly returned their sincere acknowledgments for the encouragement they had met with in "an undertaking, so new in America", at least as they thought, and they promised to improve the entertainment the next season. This second season began on May 8, 1790 with the illumination of the "transparent painting of the illustrious President of the United States, executed by Mr. Wright". On the fourth of July, the entertainment, as soon became customary, partook of a patriotic character with odes, songs and duets" in honour of the glorious event". That the managers well understood how to cater to the curious may be seen from the fact that they engaged for Sept. 2d "The son of Mr. D. Duport, not ten years of age, who has performed before the Royal Family in France" and who was to play two violin solos. On the whole, the music offered at these open-air concerts was of a rather high standard. For instance, the program for Oct. 16th, 1790 reads:

---

1) Again I must refer to Hanslick and others if the wrong idea is entertained that this *band* was ridiculously small.

PART I.

Grand Overture	Haydn
Symphonie	Stamitz
Grand Overture	Schmitt
A Song	Wolff
Violin Concert	Schultz
Symphonie	Lachnit

PART II.

Overture	Martini
Flute Concert	Phile
Song	Wolff
Clarinet Concert	A. Wolff
Symphonie	Abel
Harmony music	Phile

In view of such programs it is not surprising that Messrs. Gray's efforts were appreciated by music lovers and at least one had the courage of conviction to express himself accordingly in the Pennsylvania Packet. He had this to say "On the Gardens of the Messrs. Gray":

Being well persuaded that great numbers of our fellow citizens acknowledge with great esteem the merits of the Messrs. Gray, by procuring them in their delightful gardens, a gratification which all the luxuries of a wealthy city could not bestow; and being myself an enthusiastic admirer of the heartfelt charms of nature — I step forward to declare our sentiments on this subject.

In every situation of life amusements are necessary to recreate our minds and bodies after toil and anxious cares... Genuine music is also a very commendable recreation, for it expresses and animates the sublime and pathetic affections of the mind. Its powers are so great, as in a high degree to influence the national character. This has been the opinion of great legislators. From my own observations on different nations and on divers classes, in the same country, I can affirm that popular songs and favourite tunes are good indications of the people's character.

... Those who have not yet this season visited the gardens of Messrs. Gray, will be pleased with some account of the late improvements. Several trees, shrubs and flowers have been added to the grounds. A beautiful orchestra is built over the door of the main building; from which the sweet notes of music flow with ease through the waving groves, and over the placid meanders of Schuylkill. The band is composed of 9 or 10 instruments. The vocal part is made up of two male and as many female voices, which perform well a variety of sentimental songs. On the front of this orchestra is a painting of Handel, the celebrated musician, done by Mr. Witman, a young artist and native of Reading..."

For how many summers these concerts were continued I do not know, but I am under the impression that music ceased to be a noteworthy feature at Gray's Gardens in 1793.

That a demand was *in the air* for summer-concerts about 1790 is borne out by the fact that a few weeks after Messrs. Gray had added music to the attractions of their resort, George Esterley, proprietor of 'Harrowgate', advertised under the catch-line "Vauxhall Harrowgate" similar weekly concerts with illuminations, etc. They were to begin on Saturday, August 29, 1789, "the vocal parts by a lady from Europe who has performed in all the operas in the theatres Royal of Dublin and Edinburgh". Though Mr. Esterley considered

"the rural situation and many natural beauties of Harrowgate ... so well known"

that he deemed a particular description unnecessary, yet he thought it worth while to remark that

"it is decorated with Summer houses, arbors, seats, etc. and a large new house, consisting of a number of rooms for large and small parties. The Mineral springs, shower and plunging baths are in best order. A good and plentiful table with liquors of the best quality; tea, coffee, fruit, etc... furnished on the shortest notice ..."

The lady engaged for the "vocal parts" was Mrs. Rankin but if her fame was great, her duties at Harrowgate were light. At least, if she was not supposed to give innumerable encores in addition to the one solitary song in every "part" of the concert as announced in the programs, f. i. on Sept. 19th, 'Blythe Sandy', 'Had I a heart for falsehood train'd', 'The lark's shrill notes', and 'Tally Ho'. The orchestral and concerted numbers at Harrowgate consisted of such works as overtures by Abel, "full pieces" by Fischer and others, concertos and 'Martini's march'.

The concerts at Harrowgate continued regularly every season, at least until 1796 for on Aug. 3, 1796, Claypole's Daily Advertiser printed a poetical effusion "On Harrowgate. Written by Miss C. P. a young lady of sixteen before she left the Garden", of which a few lines may follow here as a warning to other young ladies of sixteen:

> "Nature and art combine, with graceful ease,
> To elevate the mind, and please the eye;
> There shrubs, and flowers, and interwoven trees,
> And streams are seen, which murmur gently by.
> The shady walks and artificial aisles,
> And music whisp'ring thro' the verdant leaves,
> The heart of every painful care beguiles,
> And peace, and pleasure every object breathes."

A few weeks later, on Sept. 30th, Messrs. Bates and Darley of the New Theatre informed the public that they had leased "the manor house and grounds of Bush Hill (The property of William Hamilton Esq.)" and purposed opening them by subscription in the following spring "for the general accommodation and amusement of the public under the name of Pennsylvania Gardens and Hotel" with concerts during the summer months "after the manner of the public gardens of Paris, Vauxhall, London etc." The resort was actually opened on June 16, 1797 under the name of Bush Hill or Pennsylvania Tea Gardens, but an unlucky star seems to have hovered over the enterprise as already in December 1797 the partnership between William Bates and William Darley was dissolved by mutual consent. May be the fear of a second yellow fever epidemic was partly responsible for the failure but as long as the concerts lasted they certainly must have been

quite enjoyable to judge from the "cast" as published in Porcupine's Gazette,
June 15, 1797:

> "Vocal performers — Messrs. Darley, sen.; Darley jun.; Bates, and Miss
> Broadhurst.
> Instrumental — Messrs. Hopefield [Hupfield] Wolfe, Mucke, Homann, Brooke,
> Shetky, Petit, Oznabluth [!], Morel, De Clary, etc. —
> Organist, Mr. B. Carr."

Possibly it was Benjamin Carr's organ playing at these concerts which
induced John Mearns of the 'Centre House Tavern and Gardens' to add
in 1799 "to the entertainment which his house afforded ... at a very great
expense ... a Grand organ of the first power and tone, which [was to] be
played every Monday, Wednesday, and Friday evening during the summer".
It was John Mearns' ambition to produce his organ to an admiring assembly
on the Fourth of July, but he was disappointed "in getting his organ fixed"
and instead engaged "a complete band of Martial Music", which was
decidedly more in keeping with what his forerunners in the business used
to offer on Independence Day. In the following year Mr. Mearns further
imitated them by making concerts a regular feature at the Centre House
Gardens but the programs, as those of the first decade of the nineteenth
century generally, were rather "popular" in character. The program for
the Fourth of July, 1800 with which these remarks on summer-concerts
at Philadelphia may be closed, will illustrate this convincingly:

Act I

A Grand March.	
Overture	Graff
Song 'Louisa'	Mrs. M'Donald
Favourite Air with variations	Pleyel
St. Bride's Bells	Mr. Hedderly

Act II

Duetto (Clarinets)	Pleyel
Song 'Two bunches a Penny, Primroses'	M. Donald
Grand Symphony	Buck [Bach?]
President's March (Musical Bells)	Hedderly
Song 'The Caledonian Laddie'	Mrs. M'Donald

To conclude with a variety of pleasing airs and occasional songs. In the course
of the evening will be exhibited a representation of General Washington.

It will have been noticed that the concerts so far described were predominantly devoted to instrumental music and that vocal music was represented
only by some airs, popular songs, duets, glees or the like. The reason for
this is not far to seek. Concerts of choral music require trained choruses
but of these Philadelphia could not boast until a few years after the war.
Of course, there were the socalled singing schools of olden times which
provided the churches of the city with a nucleus of ladies and gentlemen
fairly well grounded in church music, but from congregational and choir

singing, that is to say, from the usual psalms, hymns and anthems to cantatas, oratorios and secular choral works of larger compass is a wide step
and this step was impossible in America without choral societies. Now and
then men like William Tuckey of New York sought to overcome the obstacles to the cultivation of choral music but their efforts were frustrated
by general conditions which allowed choral music outside of the churches
and their appendices the singing schools, to be cultivated only timidly.
That this situation was not to the taste of the more ambitious singing
teachers and choir masters goes without saying but few only possessed,
in addition to the ambition and possibly the talent of doing things, the
less common faculty to analize conditions, to organize, and to know just
how to do things.

Among these very few men Andrew Adgate, whose career at Philadelphia came to an untimely end during the yellow fever epidemic of 1793,
certainly held a very conspicuous position as *P. U. A.*, President of the
Uranian Academy, as he proudly added to his name on title pages of his
publications. Adgate saw, and the historian must agree with him, that
for the time being the cultivation of choral music in general at Philadelphia
would closely have to be associated with a planful cultivation of church
music. Hence he founded early in 1784 by subscription 'The Institution
for the Encouragement of Church Music', also called in the newspapers
'Institution for promoting the knowledge of psalmody'. Properly a detailed history of this institution belongs to the history of church music and
to the history of musical instruction in our country, but as "public singings"
formed a feature of the institution its career must also be outlined in a
history of our early concert-life.

As stated, Andrew Adgate founded his institution in 1784. From the
beginning it "survived on public bounty", a rather bold and optimistic
point of departure, it must be confessed. When on April 1, 1785 "the trustees
of the Institution for promoting the knowledge of psalmody, having per-
ceived great inconveniences arising from an indiscriminate assemblage of
persons at the public singings" directed that admission tickets be prepared
for the subscribers, the affairs of the institution must have looked to out-
siders either very flourishing or very confused. Those who suspected the
latter were nearer the truth as on June 1st the trustees agreed to declare
the institution dissolved, the funds being exhausted. But Andrew Adgate's
resources evidently were not yet exhausted for on the very same day he
drew a wider "Plan of Mr. Adgate's Institution for diffusing more generally
the knowledge of Vocal Music" by establishing a Free School to this effect.
The plan met with the approval of several influential people and in the
Pennsylvania Gazette, Oct. 19th, signed Oct. 1st but headed "Philadelphia,

June 1, 1785" Adgate published his bold plan, of which the third para-
graph is perhaps the most important in this connection:

PLAN of Mr. Adgate's Institution for diffusing more generally the knowledge
of Vocal Music.

I.   That persons of every denomination desirous of acquiring the knowledge of
Vocal Music, on application to Mr. Adgate, and agreeing to observe the regulations
of the institution shall be admitted without discrimination, and taught *gratis.*

II.   That in order to carry into effect this liberal design, subscriptions at eight
dollars be received and such other methods adopted as the board of trustees, here after
to be named, may devise.

III.   That in compliment to the contributors of eight dollars, or more, the pupils
of this institution unite in giving twelve *vocal concerts* between the present time and
the first of June, 1786.

IV.   That subscribers of eight dollars be entitled to three tickets, which shall admit
one gentleman and two ladies, and subscribers of double the sum, to double the number
of tickets.

V.   That as soon as a competent number of subscribers shall have entered their
names, a meeting of the subscribers shall be called, in order to choose three persons
as trustees, who shall to the best of their judgment appropriate the monies which
have been or may be subscribed, and make such further regulations for the better
government of the above-mentioned institution as to them may seem necessary.

Oct. 1, 1785.

It is hereby made known, that as the above recited Plan has met with great encouragement — that the subscribers thereto have elected trustees, and that under
their patronage Mr. Adgate has commenced his instructions, at the University, to a
respectable number of pupils.

It is the object of the subscribers to establish a *Free School* for the spreading
the knowledge of *Vocal Music;* the trustees therefore invite every person who wishes
to be possessed of this knowledge to apply to Mr. Adgate at Mr. Conelly's in Second
Street, a little way North of Chestnutstreet, that his name may be entered as one
of the school, and his instructions commence, for which there will not be required of
him even the smallest compensation.

The more there are who make this application, and the sooner they make it, the
more acceptable will it be to the trustees and teacher."

The institution soon, in fact already in 1785, became known as the
'Uranian Society' and as such it figured until reorganized in 1787 when
the name 'Uranian Academy of Philadelphia' was adopted. In some respects the new plan as published in the Pennsylvania Mercury, March 30,
1787 is very much wider than the first and in others narrower. For instance,
whereas it provides for the instruction of three hundred pupils free of expense in three different schools, the number of public concerts was reduced
to "at least" one annual concert the proceeds of which were to be turned
into an accumulating fund. The management lays in the hands of 12 trustees
and "at least" twenty patrons, among whom we notice such prominent
men as Benjamin Rush and Francis Hopkinson. Even at the beginning
of the twentieth century the plan of the Uranian Academy will afford
interesting reading as it embodies ideas which only gradually have been
universally accepted and probably the document is the earliest on record

in our country wherein the necessity and advantage of making music "form a part in every system of education" is clearly pointed out:

PLAN OF THE URANIAN ACADEMY proposed to be established at Philadelphia, for the purpose of improving Church Music; — and intended to be opened on the third Wednesday of September, 1787.

Solemn music appears to have been used, from remote ages, in the worship of Deity. It was early introduced into Christian societies; and, in most churches, it still composes a part of divine worship. That such music may have its full effect, it should be regularly and decently performed. But 'tis an art which, like every other, demands time and pains to acquire; and of which, very few can obtain even a tolerable knowledge without the aid of a teacher. — Nevertheless, for the most part, people have satisfied themselves with learning so much of it as they could catch in the very act of performance in the churches.

It would seem that music should either be banished from places of worship, or performed in such a manner as to engage our attention and animate us in the celebrating the praises of the Deity. To improve church music effectually, and render it generally useful and agreeable, it seems necessary that it should form a part in every system of education; for children can no more sing than read correctly, without being taught. In conformity, therefore, to these ideas, it is proposed

I. That an institution, for the express purpose of teaching church music, be established at which three hundred pupils may, and, if so many apply for admission, shall be taught annually free of every expense.

II. That the name of this institution be, the *Uranian Academy of Philadelphia.*

III. That no applicant be refused admission into their academy on account of his religion or country; it is open and equally free to every denomination.

IV. That, for the convenience of the scholars, three places of instruction be established, namely, one in some central part of the city, one near to or in the Northern Liberties, and one near to or in the district of Southwark.

V. That, in order to give durable efficacy to the institution an accumulating fund be formed, on which no draught shall be made, until the annual income thereof be equal to the whole expense of annually instructing three hundred scholars, being the complement proposed in the first article.

VI. That to commence the formation of this fund, a grand concert be performed some time in the present spring; and afterwards for the purpose of increasing the fund that at least one such concert be performed in every succeeding year.

VII. That, with the same view, subscriptions be received from those who are disposed to encourage the establishment of this institution; and, that every subscriber of eight dollars, or more, be entitled to a vote at the election of trustees and patrons.

VIII. That, to give permanency to the good effects expected from this institution and that the funds thereof may have greater security in their management, the trustees shall apply to the legislature for an act of incorporation.

IX. That the academy be managed by 12 trustees who, for the 1st year, may assume the trust; but afterwards be annually elected by the subscribers.

X. That besides the trustees, there be, at least, twenty patrons of the institution, to be elected in like manner as the trustees, and to act with them as visitors, at the quarterly examinations of the scholars, and as managers at the annual concerts; and in general, to countenance and support the design.

XI. That the principal of the academy and his assistants be appointed and their salaries fixed by the trustees.

Having attentively weighed the reasons for establishing an institution for the purpose of improving church music, we are of opinion that it will be a beneficial influence on society and gradually effect an important and most agreeable change in that part of public worship.

Actuated, therefore, by a conviction of its utility, we give it our fullest approbation, and cheerfully undertake the trust and patronage of the institution during its minority, and to act as managers, in its behalf, at the first proposed Uranian Concert.

The concert will be performed on Thursday the 12th of April, at the Reformed German Church, in Race-street; a more particular account of which will be communicated to the public previous to the day. It has been estimated that the church will conveniently accommodate twelve hundred persons, exclusive of the performers; that number of tickets therefore will be struck off, and no more. Checks for the tickets, at 7 *s* 6 *d* each may now be had of Mr. Young, at the Southwest corner of Second and Church-streets, and of all the managers. A few days before the performance, the checks must be returned upon which the tickets will be delivered in exchange for them.

If the Uranian Academy did not flourish after 1787 as expected by the managers, certainly sensible theories like those embodied in their plan were not responsible for the partial failure. Probably many citizens in addition to the patrons and trustees were willing to subscribe to Adgate's reformatory ideas but Philadelphia was not yet ripe for their application on the bold and broad lines suggested. A further obstacle to a lasting success possibly was encountered in the proverbial professional jealousy among musicians. In this case the stumbling block was Alexander Juhan and it will be seen that he and others, for reasons professional and personal, simply refused to play under Adgate whose abilities were confined, as he said, "to the humble province of Solfa teaching". Gradually Andrew Adgate saw his energies reduced to their natural limits, that is to say, to the management and training of an efficient church choir.

As far as the concert life of Philadelphia is concerned, his Institution deserves lasting credit for he introduced choral concerts in Philadelphia and the fact that about the time of his death and for several years afterwards choral music was cultivated very timidly only, makes his enterprise all the more conspicuous.

His concerts were given in the hall of the University of Pennsylvania. Until June, 1785 they went by the name of 'Mr. Adgate's vocal music', then as 'Mr. Adgate's Vocal Concerts' and in 1787 they were styled 'Uranian Concerts', thus conforming to the official name of the institution. How many were given until June 1785 we do not know, but as on April 5, 1785 "several anthems and pieces of music [were to] be sung which have not been performed at any of the former public exhibitions" a certain regularity might be inferred. Beginning with April 5th, they were to be on the first

Tuesday evening of every month. Owing to the exhaustion of the funds, as announced by the trustees, this series came to an end on Wednesday, June 1, 1785. The programs were not printed in the newspapers and the only pertinent information is to be gleaned from the announcement of the concert on May 3d:

"After a number of pieces (among which will be a Te Deum and several, not heretofore performed): the exhibition will close with the celebrated anthem from sundry scriptures."

In accordance with Adgate's Plan of June 1st, published on Oct. 19th, the new series of twelve "vocal" concerts began on that evening and was carried through successfully, the last being held on June 7, 1786. At the "opening exhibition" were performed as *pièces de résistance* Billings' "The Rose of Sharon, which is an American composition in a style peculiar to itself: — and the celebrated anthem from sundry Scriptures 'Arise, arise, for the light is come and the glory of the Lord is risen upon thee, etc.' " If, with the exception of the program of the twelfth concert, none were printed in the papers this was due probably to the progressive idea, uncommon in the United States and still more so in Europe, of delivering a "syllabus" with the tickets[1]). To further accommodate strangers and "persons differently circumstanced"; subscriptions were received either for the whole course or a single evening and if it rained or snowed the concerts were "put off till the next fair evening". The program of the twelfth and last concert was thus announced in the Pennsylvania Evening Herald, June 3, 1786.

MR. ADGATE'S LAST CONCERT, consisting of vocal and instrumental music, will be performed at the University, on Wednesday evening the 7th of June, beginning at 8 o'clock. The pieces will, principally, be those exhibited at the late *Grand Concert*.

ORDER
PART I
1. An Anthem from the 118th Psalm
2. Easter
3. The Voice of Time
4. An Anthem from the 150th Psalm
5. An Anthem from the 122d Psalm

PART II
1. Instrumental only.
2. Washington
3. The Rose of Sharon
4. Jehovah reigns — from the 97th Psalm
5. Sundry Scriptures: 'Arise, shine, for my Light is come', etc. (Greatly celebrated)

---

1) A system still prevailing in the United States and so strikingly different from that of Germany where generally the concert-goers are supposed to pay for the program.

For some reason, however, this program was changed to the following [1]) :

1. Martini's celebrated Overture
2. An Anthem from the 18th Psalm
3. An Anthem from the 97th Psalm
4. A Violin Concerto by Mr. Juhan
5. An Anthem from the 150th Psalm
6. An Anthem from the 122d Psalm
7. The Rose of Sharon
8. A Flute Concerto by Mr. Brown
9. Hallelujah Chorus.

This was practically the same program as performed at the "Grand Concert" on May 4th. Properly this musical festival, as we may call it, belongs to the occasional benefit concerts, not yet considered, but as it was given under the auspices of the Uranian Society, a detailed narrative follows here in order to show what the society was capable of doing under Andrew Adgate energetic leadership.

On April 20, 1786 the Pennsylvania Packet drew public attention to the forthcoming event for which "the lovers of music, without distinction have generously volunteered in this service". Then on April 27th and on May 1st full particulars were published which, I believe, should be reprinted here in view of the singular historical importance of this truly "grand" concert:

A GRAND CONCERT OF SACRED MUSIC for the benefit of the Pennsylvania Hospital, Philadelphia Dispensary, and the Poor, for whom there has, hitherto, been no regular provision made — will be performed at the Reformed German Church in Race Street, on Thursday, the 4th of May. The doors will be opened at half an hour after nine o'clock in the morning, but not sooner, and the music will begin, precisely at eleven o'clock, after which no person can be admitted.

ORDER AND WORDS OF THE MUSIC

I. Martini's Overture.
II. An Anthem from the 150th Psalm
   "Let the shrill trumpet's war like voice
   Make rocks and hills rebound . . ."
III. An Anthem from the 18th Psalm by the Rev. James Lyon.
   "The Lord descended from above . . ."
IV. Flute Concerto by Mr. Brown
V. The Voice of Time
   'Hark! hark! Times hastes away' . . .
VI. An Anthem from the 97th Psalm, by Mr. Tuckey
   'Jehovah reigns, let all the earth
   In his just government rejoice . . .'
VII. A Violin Concerto by Mr. Juhan
VIII. An Anthem from the 122d Psalm by A. Williams.
   'I was glad, when they said unto me . . .'
IX. An Anthem, from the 2d of Solomon's Song, by Mr. Billings.
   'I am the Rose of Sharon, and the lily of the vallies . . .'

---

1) Pa. Journal, June 7, 1786.

X. Hallelujah Chorus from the Messiah, Handel
'Hallelujah — (often repeated) — For the God omnipotent reigneth,
Hallelujah, etc . . .'

Tickets at five shillings each are to be had of Mr. Young, at the Southwest corner
of Second and Chestnutstreets, and of all the managers. To prevent confusion, care
has been taken that the number of tickets struck off, should not exceed the number
of persons who, by estimation, can be accommodated at the place proposed. Correspondent to this idea, all who apply for tickets will have a right to be supplied, 'till the
whole number prepared is exhausted, after which it will be out of the power of the
managers to furnish more. And upon the same principle, on the morning of the exhibition, the persons supplied with tickets, as they successively offer themselves, will be
introduced to their seats. Indeed it is the desire, and will be the endeavour, of the
managers, to have the whole of this business conducted with that decency and dignity,
which its nature and design seem to require.

To administer some relief to him whose hope is like a shadow, to raise up him
who is bowed down with sorrow, and to shew that the fine Arts may and ought to sub-
serve the purposes of humanity are, we believe, the views with which the performers
have voluntarily, offered their service on this occasion. Under a full conviction of
their motives being such, and as the highest proof of our approbation, we have, chearfully, complied with their request and agreed to act as

MANAGERS.

For the Hospital	Trustees of the Musical Institution
Reynold Keen	George Nelson
Nathaniel Falconer	Azariah Horton
William Hall	Joseph Kerr
For the Dispensary	From the Trustees of the University
William White	Francis Hopkinson
Henry Hill	Of the Reformed German Church
Samuel Miles	Casper Wynberg.

Historically speaking, this concert belonged to the most ambitious
artistic events which our country had witnessed during its relatively short
musical life. It is one of the few concerts that attracted the attention of
historians, but blinded by prejudice or being hampered in their judgment
by the rather naïve impression as if such undertakings were possible without
a logical evolution of conditions, they have referred to it as they would to
a solitary palmtree in a desert. Such a standpoint is, of course, just as
untenable as would be the notion that such "feasts of harmony" with a
chorus of 230 and an orchestra of 50 were daily occurrences in the musical
life of by-gone generations. The public of Philadelphia, though accustomed
to noteworthy musical entertainments, was fully aware of the unusual
scope of Andrew Adgate's festival and quite in keeping with this attitude
was the attention which it found in the channels of public opinion. The
professional music critic, to be sure, had not yet made his appearance and
in our newspapers as in those of Europe, concerts were treated rather indifferently by the editors. On this special occasion, however, the editor
of the Pennsylvania Packet was so deeply impressed with the boldness,
magnitude and success of the charitable enterprise that, contrary to all

traditions, he reviewed the concert at length and with a minuteness foreshadowing the future of musical criticism. The report not only reveals the deep impression made by the concert but incidentally throws light upon its history and therefore must be considered a noteworthy historical document. It was thus published in the Pennsylvania Packet — and this is also an interesting side-light on the methods of journalism of yore — not immediately after the concert but on May 30th:

"Philadelphia, May 30.

On Thursday, the 4th of May, at the Reformed German Church, in Race Street, was performed a *Grand Concert* of Vocal and Instrumental Music, in the presence of a numerous and polite audience. The whole *Band* consisted of 230 vocal and 50 instrumental performers;[1]) which, we are fully justified in pronouncing, was the most complete, both with respect to number and accuracy of execution, ever, on any occasion, combined in this city, and, perhaps, throughout America.

The first idea of this concert was suggested to the trustees of the Musical Institution by the *Commemoration of Handel* in London and the *Sacred Concert* in Boston. It was planned in January last, and a series of preparatory measures pursued till its accomplishment. The morning, which had been previously announced in the public papers for this exhibition, having arrived, the doors of the church were opened punctually at the time proposed, the audience were successively conducted to their seats, and the performers took their several stations, the whole of which was done without noise or the least apparent confusion. At 11 o'clock the doors were shut, and, after a *dead silence* of about 5 minutes, this *feast of harmony* began with Martini's famous overture, which was performed with such a propriety of expression that, could the author himself have been present, he would not have thought his composition disgraced, or, the ideas he intended to convey, misunderstood. —

Then followed a succession of celebrated anthems, which were performed with a precision and effort sufficient to enforce powers of harmony on the most untutored ears. Between the anthems the force of the band was interrupted and contrasted by

---

1) A chorus of two hundred and thirty voices was enormous for a city of Philadelphia's size considering the fact that a chorus of about 275 voices only was employed during the Haendel Commemoration in Westminster Abbey May 26-29; June 3 and 5, 1784. It is also interesting to note that the proportion between orchestra and chorus at Philadelphia was about the same as is nowadays inflicted on us at Haendel festivals whereas in London in 1784 about 250 instrumentalists (among them of musicians who subsequently left their mark on music in America, Gillingham, Reinagle, Gehot, Pick, Phillips, Mallet, R. Shaw) sat in the orchestra according to the list given in Burney's account. Originally — and this would have been the other extreme — an orchestra of 400 performers had been planned as "it was determined to employ every species of instrument that was capable of producing grand effects in a great orchestra and spacious building". With naïve pride Burney added that only one general rehearsal for each day's performance was held "an indisputable proof of the high state of cultivation to which practical music is at present arrived in this country".

This and all similar Handel Commemorations may safely be put down as monstrosities and we need but read the diplomatic letter of Count Benincasa in which he communicated to Burney some requested statistics on the monstre-performances in the conservatories of Venice, to see that not every lover of music was overly impressed by the bigness of the affair. Finally it is interesting to compare the forces orchestral and vocal massed in honor of Haendel at London with those who performed the Messiah in the Domkirche Berlin, May 19, 1786. On this occasion, as we know from Hiller's 'Nachricht' the orchestra mustered besides the conductors 78 violins, 19 violas, 12 oboes, 12 flutes, 8 horns, 6 trumpets, 4 bassoons and two pairs of kettledrums, in all 141 performers, against a chorus of a trifle more than 100 voices.

two solo concertos. The first by Mr. Brown whose power over the German flute has astonished Americans, and would give additional grace to any royal band in Europe; the second which was a violin concerto, by Mr. Juhan, who not only displayed the most promising talents, but a taste and execution which did him present honor and gave acknowledged satisfaction.

The whole concluded with the exertions of the full band in the performance of that most sublime of all musical compositions, the grand chorus in the Messiah, by the celebrated Handel, to these words 'Hallelujah! for the Lord God omnipotent reigneth', etc.

To the skill and attention of Mr. Adgate, in training and instructing the voices, and of Mr. Juhan, in arranging and leading the instruments, may be attributed that forcible and uniform effect so manifestly produced throughout the exhibition. The general, and, for any thing known to the contrary, *unanimous* approbation of the audience, concided that this rational and exalted entertainment interested, and, as it were, swallowed up the attention of both hearers and performers and had, therefore, its full effect on the feelings of both.

The decorum and method observed in conducting the whole harmonized with the precision and order necessary to the perfection of a musical performance. No interruption from within, no disturbance from without, prevented the full enjoyment of this *Grand Concert*. — The measures which had been judiciously planned, and which were so punctually executed by those who had undertaken that duty, effectually prevented every disagreeable circumstance, which otherwise, by creating inconvenience and uneasiness, might have occurred to mar the entertainment.

Nearly one thousand tickets were sold; at two thirds of a dollar each, and the nett proceeds, after deducting for necessary expenses, have been delivered to the managers of the Pennsylvania Hospital, Philadelphia Dispensary and Overseers of the Poor, to be applied by them for the use of said institutions and unprovided poor.

The managers and overseers of these charitable establishments (who were not concerned in conducting the concert) as well wishers to humanity, return their sincere thanks to every person who had any share in this act of benevolence; — to the trustees of the Musical Institution, who laid the foundations of this benefaction, and established so uniform a system, as carried on the face of it a full conviction of the practicability of what was intended; — to Mr. Adgate and Mr. Juhan, whose abilities enabled them to foresee and provide against every difficulty, and to move this complicated machinery, as though it had been one entire piece, either in solemn and majestic dignity, or quick and animating measure, so as to produce in the result, such ideas of admiration and sublimity as nothing but itself could excite; — to the ladies and gentlemen in general, who, as performers, volunteered in this service, arising, thereby, superior to all local prejudices, and showing how easy it is to distinguish between an action that is truly commendable and the contrary; — to the pupils of the Musical Institution who have given such an incontestible proof of their proficiency in this pleasing art; — to the managers of the concert, who have shown, by example, how easy it is to conduct an exhibition of this kind with perfect order and decency; — and particularly Reformed German Congregation, who with such prompt chearfulness and perfect unanimity, lent their church in the *Cause of Humanity.*

If we were to trust this silvertongued report, nothing occurred to throw a discordant note into the arrangement and management of this Grand Concert, but there never yet was a musical festival without friction and Philadelphia's May Festival of 1786 offers no exception to the rule. Musicians *will* quarrel and it is a seven day's wonder if two musicians called upon to co-operate and share alike in the honors do not afterwards give vent to fits of professional jealousy. In this instance, the culprits were the very men to whom the Pennsylvania Packet attributed the artistic success of the concert, but it must be said in fairness to Andrew Adgate that Alexander Juhan was the aggressor.

In accordance with the "Plan", the promoters of the Uranian Academy made the necessary preparations for their first proposed Uranian Concert, and fixed the date for April 12, 1787. Probably because it became known that he was not willing to co-operate, Alexander Juhan took occasion to send to the Pennsylvania Packet on April 5th a letter stating his reasons and in which he left no doubt of as to his professional contempt for Adgate. Said he:

As every man who depends upon the public patronage is responsible to the public for his conduct, and cannot, in any degree, oppose their wishes and pleasure, without essentially counteracting his own interests, the subscriber thinks it his duty to state the reasons that have induced him to decline any part in the concert, intended to be performed at the Reformed Church, in Race-street, the 12th instant.

The applause of some who perhaps have more regarded his desire to please than his power and the encouragement of others, who, thinking they discerned some talents, meant to excite a professional emulation, have certainly sofar elevated the subscriber in his own opinion that he rates himself superior to the instruction of a person, who, with little knowledge in the theory, is confined in the practice of music to the humble province of Solfa. The subscriber candidly acknowledges therefore, that one reason for his declining to attend at the approaching concert, arises because the direction of the performance is confided to a gentleman whose abilities, however great in most respects, he deems very inadequate to a task, upon the execution of which, not only the combined force and harmony of the band, but likewise the skill and reputation of every individual must considerably depend.

Another, and a very forcible reason for the subscriber's conduct upon this occasion, is the neglect of consulting the principal performers as to the pieces of music, and the arrangement of the band. Those who are in the habit of public performance will select such pieces as (either for their intrinsic merit or the superior dexterity with which they can be executed) are most calculated to communicate pleasure and to command applause. It would surely therefore have improved the general effect of the entertainment, and could not have been considered as a very extraordinary indulgence, had those who were best able to determine upon the respective powers of the performers, been invited to select the music and to suggest what could be attempted with the greatest probability of success.

There were other motives of a more personal nature that operated with the subscriber. In consequence of his attention to the rehearsals of the last grand concert in May 1786, he had unavoidably suspended his attention to his scholars, which exposed him to some reproach and to a considerable pecuniary loss; — and in consequence of his exertions on the day of public performance, he was attacked by a violent fever, which confined him for several weeks to his bed.

Upon the whole, the subscriber hopes that as he could not consistently with his reputation, his interest or his health, engage in the concert under the direction of Mr. Adgate, the public will determine that he has most wantonly sacrificed to those considerations, the honor of contributing to their entertainment, but will still regard him as their

Most grateful and
Most devoted servant

Juhan.

Had this ill-timed and ill-mannered attack, so characteristic of a virtuoso and illustrating the struggle in those days for supremacy between the conductor and leader, contained the whole truth, it might have had a detrimental effect upon the concert, but Adgate immediately replied in a dignified tone and by referring to witnesses of a certain conversation with Juhan, he probably turned the tables against his opponent. He had this to say from his standpoint on April 7th in the Packet:

Mess'rs Dunlap & Claypoole,

Before the Plan of the Uranian Academy was drawn and before one step was taken toward carrying the intended concert into effect, three months ago, at least, I mentioned to Mr. Juhan that I had it in view to establish an institution, at which the poor might be instructed in church music, free of expense; and, as the first measure to be taken toward accomplishing this, to have a concert performed, similar to that of the 4th of May last. I introduced the subject that I might have the opportunity of consulting him thereon and engaging him as a principal in carrying the concert into effect. His answer to my proposition, as offered to him in general, was immediate and inequivocal! — *"We have agreed not to play any more for the poor."* This peremptory declaration, at the very introduction of the business, foreclosed effectually all consultation. I believed Mr. Juhan, and, in consequence, took my measures, independently of him, as well as I was able. Several persons were present when this conversation happened and recollect that the answer was as here related. I have taken notice of Mr. Juhan's publication, merely to state this fact, relative to *consultation*, just as it occurred: — he had an undoubted right to be the sole judge of what would contribute most essentially to his *interest* and *health*.

Andrew Adgate.

In the meantime, on May 30th, the Pennsylvania Mercury had printed in full the Plan of the Uranian Academy, signed by all the managers and trustees and it is delightful to see how seriously these gentlemen took a task which to-day would cause the managers of a similar festival little worry. Perhaps Adgate and the many prominent gentlemen whom he had interested in his project also considered it proper to imitate the managerial details of the Handel Commemoration of 1784 as closely as circumstances would permit. At any rate they set forth rules and regulations enough to overawe any audience as to their managerial problems. To us their methods may seem amusing but they are also instructive as they show how things were done in those days and that they were done very much in the same manner as to-day, even if with business-methods a trifle more complicated.

Some instructions were contained in the 'Plan of the Uranian Academy'. On April 9th, the Pennsylvania Packet further announced that with each ticket would go

"a Syllabus, containing the order and words of the pieces to be performed . . . the tickets which remain, after satisfying the checks may likewise be had of Mr. Young and of all the managers."

Finally on April 11th, in the Pennsylvania Herald:

"for the information of those who propose to attend it, the following particulars are made known:

I. That the church has four doors: — two, fronting Race Street: and two, opposite to them, on the south side of the church.

II. That the Eastermost door on Race Street (or that nearest to Third Street) is for the admission of *performers* only; and that the three other doors of the church are for the admission of the audience.

III. That no persons of any age whatever, can be admitted without a ticket.

IV. That the tickets, presented at each door, will be received by two managers, appointed for that purpose, and the persons who present them, conducted to their seats agreeably to their own choice.

V. That no tickets will be sold or money received at the door.

VI. That the doors will be opened, precisely at half after 9 o'clock in the morning; and shut, precisely at 11 o'clock: immediately after which the entertainment will begin."

Though these six paragraphes permit of some speculation, especially whether the door remained shut or not to late-comers, whether all persons were conducted by the volunteer ushers to their seats really agreeably to their own choice, and so forth, the audience, once seated with syllabus in hand, probably was good-natured enough to forget personal grievances when at 11 o'clock on April 12, 1787 the Rev. Dr. Andrews, President of the Uranian Academy, arose to open the First Uranian Concert with a prayer. Then followed a program, interesting in several ways. Though copies of the printed syllabus are still preserved, one for instance at the Library of Congress, it is only fair to reprint it here from the Pennsylvania Packet, April 9th, in appreciation of the great services rendered by the press to the promoters of the concert.

SYLLABUS

		AUTHORS
I.	Martini's celebrated Overture	
II.	Jehovah reigns: an anthem from 97th Psalm	Tuckey
III.	Te Deum laudamus	Arnold
IV.	Violin Concerto	By Mr. Phile of NewYork
V.	I heard a great Voice: an Anthem from Rev. XIV	Billings
VI.	Vital Spark: an Anthem on Mr. Pope's ode 'The dying Christian to his soul'	Billings
VII.	Overture in Artaxerxes	Arne
VIII.	Friendship thou charmer of the mind: From Watt's Lyric Poems	Lyon
IX.	The Rose of Sharon: an Anthem from 2d of Canticles	Billings
X.	Flute Concerto	By the Chevalier DuPonceau
XI.	Sundry Scriptures: an Anthem on the Nativity of Christ	Williams
XII.	The Hallelujah chorus: on the extent and duration of Christ's Government (from the Messiah)	Handel

At first glance this program may seem not only drawn-out but too miscellaneous, on the order of the so called "oratorio", but quite apart from the fact that many European programs of the time, for instance those of the Handel Commemoration, and far into the nineteenth century showed a similar *tutti frutti* tendency and that it is therefore uncritical to sneer at this particular program as has been done, it possesses one very strong feature of redemption and indeed the one which has been ridiculed. Nobody, in his right senses, will claim that William Billings and James Lyon were masters or even composers with a satisfactory knowledge of musical grammar (though for many of their errors the engravers are to be held responsible and not they), but they represented native art and native art will never develop, mature and flourish unless encouraged as a matter of principle. To-day, it often seems a matter of principle with conductors to push American music into the background on the not always convincing presumption that it amounts to nothing if compared with (frequently questionable) European importations. It is a lamentable fact that our representative composers, granting that of late years a sudden change to the better is noticeable, do not meet with the same encouragement as in the eighteenth century though they have ceased to be crude amateurs and possess, if nothing else, a technical skill equal to that of their European competitors.

Whereas, in its mixture of American and European elements, the program of 1787 presents nothing unusual for that period, the fact that the syllabus was followed for the benefit of the public by a curious kind of "Remarks" was perhaps unprecedented. When the idea gained root to add to programs for the benefit of audiences commentaries descriptive of the works to be played has not been settled but, as was said, the "Remarks" following the syllabus for the First Uranian Concert on April 12, 1787, appear to be the earliest example of annotated programs in America. In an embryonic form, of course, for the naïve commentary, as quoted below, is as far from the concise notes of a Henry Edward Krehbiel as from the encyclopaedic, sharp-witted annotations of Philip Hale, though, on the other hand, it is just as acceptable as the over-technical descriptions to which the modern music-lover frequently is exposed. The Packet treated its readers to "Remarks" on all the numbers presented but whereas, for instance, James Lyon's Hymn to Friendship was deemed worthy only of a few general hints like "A cheerful air", "Very plaintive", "Lively" this amusing yet serious tribute of respect was payed to

The HALLELUJAH CHORUS from the Messiah. By Handel.
(Introduced by three bars of Instrumental Music)

	Remarks
Hallelujah:	(Repeated often)
For the Lord God omnipotent reigneth:	[*Here the voices unite*]
Hallelujah: (several times)	
For the Lord God, etc.	[*By the Counter*, Tenor and Bass]

8*

Hallelujah: (several times)
    For the Lord God, etc.

> [1*st, by the treble; 2d by the tenor and bass, and then by the counter and tenor, whilst the other parts, through the whole of this passage, are repeating Hall. in every variety.*

The kingdom of this world, is become
    the kingdom of our Lord, and of his Christ
And he shall reign for ever, etc.
King of king, and Lord of lords:

> [Chorus]
> [A beautiful fugue]
> [By the Treble and Counter in long notes; whilst the tenor and Bass repeat 'for ever and ever, Hal.' in quick notes with intervals]

King of king, and Lord of lords:

> [Two or three times in very low notes; by the Treble: whilst the Counter, Tenor and Bass are repeating, 'for ever and ever, Hal.' often, in quick notes, with intervals: *The effect is wonderful.*

And he shall reign for ever and ever (often)
King of King, and Lord of lords:

> [Several times: the harmony very full]

And he shall reign, for ever and ever, Hal.

> [often: the last Hal. very slow]

Nowadays we expect to read an instructive and fairly unbiased review even of the heaviest program within twenty-four hours after the performance. In olden times journalism moved more slowly and it made little difference to the public when they received the news as long as they received it in somewhat stilted and grandiloquent language. To this rule the Pennsylvania Packet offered no exception. Not until April 23 was the First Uranian Concert reviewed and then in such a manner as happens now only if the sporting-editor of a provincial paper is suddenly detailed to turn a few handsome but non-committal sentences on a concert at which he felt utterly out of place. This "will strike every considerate mind with peculiar force" when reading what the Packet had to report on said April 23d:

Philadelphia, April 23.

On Thursday the 12th instant, was performed at the German Reformed Church in Race street, the *Uranian Concert.* — It was opened with an excellent prayer, well suited to the occasion, by the Rev. Dr. Andrews. The pieces being chiefly *Sacred Music,* and the object of the whole being 'the founding of an institution for improving such music throughout all the churches 'the propriety of consecrating the design in this manner, will strike every considerate mind with peculiar force.

The Entertainment began precisely at 11 o'clock in the forenoon, and continued about two hours. The audience and performers, together, consisted of 650 persons, who will ever be considered as the original *Benefactors and Founders of the Uranian Academy.*

To go thro' the comparative excellence of the pieces and merits of the performers is certainly unnecessary; — for if the general opinion of those who were present on the occasion, may be relied on, the whole of the performance taken together, was more complete and perfect in its execution, and the effect more decidedly pleasing than anything of the kind, ever exhibited in this city."

To have entertained only 650 "benefactors" minus the performers, instead of 1200, as evidently anticipated, must have been disappointing to the managers of the Uranian Academy. However, they were not disheartened as they advertised their second Uranian Concert, presumably a repetition of the first, for April 31st, but beyond the fact that it was postponed to May 7th[1]), that it was to take place at the University Hall at precisely eight o'clock, all references to the concert escaped me.

The next annual concert for the benefit of the Uranian Academy was given on April 30, 1788[2]). The advertisement, though not mentioning the program, is of some interest as it shows the beginning of a managerial detail which, in a modified form, became a universal custom. The innovation consisted in this that "red tickets", at a quarter of a dollar each "admitted the bearer" to the east wing of the gallery in the hall, opposite the performers, and the "black" at one eighth of a dollar to the lower part of the house. Of real historical importance is the fact that, according to this advertisement, Andrew Adgate's Plan was actually carried out, at least to a certain extent, as "the Uranian Academy was opened in Lodge Alley" on April 2, 1787. The twelve trustees and twenty-four patrons, in order to stimulate public interest, solemnly announced that they "on this and on future occasions, [would] countenance the *young performers, by attending their exhibitions in procession*".

Did some future occasion present itself to the thirty-six gentlemen for fulfilment of their pledge? I have been unable to ascertain this as the name of the 'Uranian Academy' disappears from the papers; the advertisement excepted in which Adgate notified the public that he had copyrighted in 1790 in the District of Pennsylvania his 'Rudiments of Music', styling himself on the title-page *P. U. A.*, evidently, President Uranian Academy. However, the institution continued to exist for a number of years. We know this from Scharf and Westcott's History of Philadelphia where it is claimed in a comprehensive but not always reliable chapter on 'Musicians and Musical Societies' that the "Uranian Society ... continued its meetings until after 1800", at the 'Uranian Rooms', corner of third and Market Streets. In the same voluminous work a "hall of the Uranian Society, South Fourth Street" is mentioned for the year 1805. Consequently the Uranian Academy or Uranian Society, whatever the name finally might have been, remained active for more than a decade after Adgate's death

1) Pa. Packet, May 3, 1787.
2) Pa. Journal, April 30, 1788.

but presumably it had more or less narrowed down to its natural field of activity, the training of one or more particular choirs. Indeed it will be seen presently how "Mr. Adgate's Choir" assisted at a concert in 1790.

Without doubt Andrew Adgate, whose ambitious career came to an end in 1793 during the yellow fever epidemic, was an acknowledged leader in the movement for vocal music and especially in 1788 his services were repeatedly required. For instance, the Independent Gazetteer, on August 5, 1788 in a report of the Commencement Exercises at the University of Pennsylvania, July 30th expressed the university's great obligations to Mr. Adgate for conducting the "sublime musical selections vocal and instrumental", "to the gentlemen who assisted him, *but particularly to the young ladies*".

Adgate was also in charge of the music at a curious entertainment advertised in the Pennsylvania Journal, April 2, 1788 in the following manner:

> On Saturday, the 5th of April, in the Hall of the University, Mr. Ely's school will have a public exhibition, consisting of *Vocal Music. Introductory* address. A variety of declamatory pieces and dialogues. The *Messiah*, a sacred poem, to be spoken by twenty boys, in white robes, who will all speak in unison. The whole will be interspersed with vocal music, suitable to the occasion, and close with the favorite anthem, the *Rose of Sharon*.
>
> The Music in the gallery will be under the direction of Mr. Adgate. Ladies and gentlemen, who will be so kind as to favor this infant exhibition with their notice, may procure a syllabus (containing the order in which the pieces are to be delivered) of Mr. Ely, in Fifth street, the fifth door above Cherry alley, between Arch and Race streets. The exercises will begin at three o'clock in the afternoon.
>
> N. B. The syllabus shown at the door, will admit the bearer without which, admittance cannot consistently be granted.[1])

The "Rose of Sharon' was, of course, by Billings whose predominating influence was just beginning to wane, at least, outside of the church. This is easily understood. About 1790 the influx of skilled European musicians, destined to revolutionize our musical life mainly to lts advantage but in certain respects also to its disadvantage, widened into an ever broadening stream. That such men as Reinagle, Hewitt, Carr, Taylor who brought with them an intimate knowledge of the best music of their age, did not take friendly to the crudities of Billings and our other early church composers goes without saying and as they now began to shape the destinies of our concert-life naturally a change in the vocal numbers on the programs soon made itself felt. This change is dimly perceptible in a program as announced in the Pennsylvania Packet, July 14, 1790:

---

1) Mr. John Ely's school probably was a private school, but in the next year (see Pa. Packet, Oct. 31) he advertised under the head of 'Psalmody' that he had opened a 'Singing School in the Schoolhouse adjoining to Archstreet church, which he "proposed to continue four evenings in the week until the first of May". The school was "intended solely for the improvement of church music" and "such tunes only" were to be taught as were "most approved by the different churches" in the city.

For a Benevolent Purpose.

A Grand CONCERT OF SACRED MUSIC, is intended to be performed at the Coffee House in Fourth Street this evening; the 14th of July 1790. To begin precisely at Seven o'clock.

PART I.

1. Grand Overture
2. Solo — Comfort ye, comfort ye, my people, etc. from the Messiah — By Mrs. Henry.
3. Chorus — Te Deum etc. from Arnold — By Mr. Adgate's choir.
4. Solo Anthem — O Lord! whose mercies numberless, etc. By Mr. Blagrove.
5. Solemn Concerto
6. Rejoice greatly, O Daughter of Zion, etc. from the Messiah — By Mrs. Henry.
7. Chorus — I was glad, etc. from Williams — By Mr. Adgate's choir.

PART II.

1. Overture
2. Solo — Pious orgies, pious Airs — By Mr. Blagrove.
3. Chorus — Arise, shine etc., from Williams — Mr. Adgate's choir.
4. Solo Anthem — Acquaint thyself with God, etc. from Dr. Green — By Mr. Blagrove.
5. Solemn Concerto.
6. Solo — I know that my Redeemer liveth, etc. from the Messiah — By Mrs. Henry.
7. Grand Hallelujah chorus, from the Messiah — By Mr. Adgate's choir.

Tickets for admission to be had at Mr. William Prichard's book-store, in Market Street — One Dollar each.

Strange to say, though announced as late as the day of performance to take place at the Coffee House, the concert really was given in the hall of Pennsylvania University. It would be interesting to know the method used to acquaint the subscribers of this change in time enough to avoid confusion, disturbance and disruffled temper.

If we may trust the criticism as it appeared on July 15th in the Federal Gazette, the concert must have been so superlatively wonderful that the "souls soared upon the wings of melody to its kindred skies". It is clear that such fascinating sentences never could have been penned by a professional critic, bred to stern economy of space and praise, and indeed it was not, unless the Pennsylvania Packet which printed literally the same enthusiastic rhapsody enjoyed a joint-ownership of this anonymous critical genius with the Federal Gazette. More likely, and quite in keeping with the habit depending upon a 'Brutus', 'Flavius', 'Censor' among their readers for political editorials, the papers simply published a report offered by some prominent music lover among their subscribers. For the benefit of such critics who will welcome an opportunity for replenishing their outworn vocabulary, the criticism of our anonymous who well might have signed himself 'Caecilius', 'Stentor' or 'Philomusicus' follows here in full:

GRAND CONCERT OF SACRED MUSIC. Performed yesterday evening in the College Hall.

In vain might we attempt to express the pleasing emotions which we experienced on this delightful occasion. The most glowing language would but debate the subject.

The refined feelings of a large and respectable audience can alone do justice to the merits of the performers. Never were the charms of vocal and instrumental music more happily united. The soul, attuned to harmony, forgot for a moment its earthly fetters, and soared upon the wings of melody to its kindred skies. The "heaven struck" imagination was transported far beyond the limits of mortality, by the *Grand Overture* with which the oratorio commenced: nor was it suffered to flag during the evening; on the contrary, it received fresh inspiration from every succeeding part of the performance, and winged its way to regions still more exalted till the sublime *Hallelujah Chorus* closed the enchantment.

Were we acquainted with any language which could paint the transports of the music enraptured soul, how grateful would be the task to convey to others an adequate idea of the delightful sensations which thrilled through every bosom, and smiled serene on every countenance! How happy should we be to descend to particulars, and to pay a due tribute of applause to those, whose musical skill and benevolent dispositions contributed to furnish such an exquisite feast.

Never in our opinion, were the vocal powers of Mrs. Henry displayed to better advantage. That lady has long attracted the admirations and esteem of the public. Her fascinating voice has long afforded delight to the friends of music and the drama. She has now given a pleasing proof of her excellence in *Sacred Music*. She has also evinced a generous disposition by coming forward on this humane occasion. Such nobleness of sentiment, such benevolence of mind, must endear her still further to the discerning and grateful citizens of Philadelphia.

Of Mr. Blagrove what shall we say? How express the delightful sensations which his beautiful anthems excited in every breast? How describe the judicious exertions of his excellent voice? — We dare not attempt it.

Too much praise cannot be given to M. Adgate and his choir for their exertions on this occasion. The whole of their part was well performed; the Hallelujah Chorus in particular was truly sublime.

The band consisted of about 20 private gentlemen to whose musical skill we were indebted for much of the magnificence and grandeur of the entertainment. We cannot conclude without paying a compliment to the judicious taste and benevolence of our citizens who countenanced this delightful undertaking, from the noblest of motives, *a benevolent regard towards merit in distress.*

Hardly had the waves of raptures passed through our amateur-critic's breast when an 'Oratorio of Sacred Music' given at the College Hall for the benefit of 'Holy Trinity Church' at 7 o'clock P. M. September 22, 1790 might have tempted him to express the same pleasing emotions which he experienced on July 14th. The program was of the usual "oratorio" order and together with the cosmopolitan character of the performers will be noticed the fact that Adgate had found a rival in the person of Mr. Heim:

PART I

1. Grand Overture
2. Chorus: 'Worthy is the lamb' . . . by Mr. Heim's Choir.
3. Solo on the Clarinett. By Mr. Wolff
4. Solo — 'As pants the heart for cooling streams' by a young lady.
5. A Sonata on the Piano Forte. By Mr. Reinagle.
6. A Solo — 'O Deus, ego amo te' — By Madame de L'Isle
7. Chorus — 'O thou to whom all creatures bow'. The Solos by a young lady, with a Hallelujah Chorus: By Mr. Heim's choir.

Part II

1. Overture
2. Chorus — 'So angels sing'. By Mr. Heim's choir.
3. Solemn Concerto.
4. Solo — 'Jesu dulcis memoria". By Madame de l'Isle.
5. A Concerto: By Mons. Emanuel.
6. Te Deum, including two solos, the first by Mons. de l'Isle, the other by Madame de l'Isle.

This concert was followed on November 2d[1]), by a "Vocal Concert at the Hall of the College" at which instead of charging admission "a collection [was] received after the concert for defraying the contingent expenses" and then the Pennsylvania Packet announced on November 16th the first of a *series of six subscription-"oratorios"!* It was again intended for the benefit of the Holy Trinity Church and took place on November 19th at the College Hall. The program reads:

PART I

1. Grand Overture
2. Chorus 'Glory to God in the highest' — By Mr. Heim's Choir.
3. Solo on the clarinet — By Mr. Wolff
4. Solo, 'To God the mighty Lord' — By a young lady.
5. A Quartetto Violino.
6. Solo, 'Comfort ye my people' — By a young lady.
7. Chorus 'Grateful notes and numbers bring' — the solo by a young lady and chorus by Mr. Heim's choir.

PART II

1. Overture
2. Chorus, 'Lift up your hands' — By Mr. Heim's choir.
3. A Sonata on the Forte Piano — By Miss Moller, not ten years of age.
4. Duetto 'Gott is mein Lied' — By a young lady and gentleman.
5. Solo, Violoncello — By an Amateur.
9. Chorus, 'Let all the lands with shouts of joy'. Solo by a young lady, and the chorus by Mr. Heim's choir, with a grand Hallelujah Chorus.

Subscription for six concerts, will be received by Mr. James Oellers, at two dollars, for which every subscriber shall receive six tickets of admission.

Tickets of admission to be had at Mr. James Oellers, Front street. Price one half dollar each, to nonsubscribers.

Unfortunately the dates and programs of the subsequent concerts have escaped me, for it does not seem plausible that the "vocal and instrumental music" following the afternoon service on the "Anniversary of the opening of the Holy Trinity Church", November 28, 1790 formed part of the series[2]).

With these subscription concerts the promising movement for choral concerts came to a sudden end. Though I made it a point to copy from the newspaper every reference to music, I found no choral concerts advertised during the last decade of the eighteenth century. Possibly such

---

1) Pa. Packet, Nov. 2, 1790.
2) Pa. Packet, Nov. 27, 1790.

were announced[1]) and merely escaped my attention, yet they must have been exceedingly few. It would seem therefore, that the anthems, sacred cantatas and the like were again, and perhaps justly, relegated to the "Singing Schools" and the church whence they had barely emerged into a more public light. Perhaps, also, we have to seek the historical explanation for the strange combination of devotional and concert-elements in the American church music of to-day in this source. A hundred years may work a multitude of stilistic changes but it takes more than a century to break traditional habits. On the other hand, the reasons for the sudden collapse of the movement for choral concerts are not far to seek. The virtuoso had commenced to assert his charms and where it is a question between a bravoura-aria and a chorus, the public rarely hesitates to side with the virtuoso. Only in countries or cities with a well-balanced, mature concert-life or where opera does not reign supreme will this observation be found to lack truth. About 1790 the musical life of Philadelphia was neither well-balanced nor beyond formative conditions, and in addition to this opera, English opera, of course, with a slight ingredient of French and Italian operas, was steadily gaining in power. Indeed to such an extent that the entire concert-life lay more or less in the hands of singers and instrumentalists, connected with Wignell and Reinagle's 'New Theatre', founded in 1793. With a man like Zelter at the helm it might have been possible to form and keep alive a choral society in spite of all natural obstacles and thereby lay solid foundations for a general interest in choral music at a comparatively early period, but this task was quite beyond the powers of an Andrew Adgate, however energetic he was, and hence the fascinations of virtuosity and opera of necessity were allowed to retard for many years the growth of an organized cultivation of choral music without which the musical life of no community can be said to be well-balanced. That a faint conception of all this was dormant in some persons may be taken for granted and possibly when Silas Dinsmoor in the announcement[2] of the opening of his Singing School[2]) scorned those who "chuse to pay their devotions in the Temple of Comus rather than in the House of God", he also voiced the sentiments of those who regretted the incoming tide of opera not so much on moral grounds but in the interest of choral music[3]).

---

1) For instance, Jacob Hilzheimer narrates in his diary that George Washington "with his lady" was present at a concert in the Lutheran Church on January 8, 1791. Possibly the concert was announced in one of the papers not examined by me.

2) Dunlap's Daily American Advertiser, Dec. 18, 1793.

3) If Scharf and Westcott in their History of Philadelphia 1884, v. 3, p. 2291, in writing of musical societies at Philadelphia claim that "the oldest was the Harmonic Society, which existed some time previous to the present century and continued to the year 1802 or 1803" they contradict themselves flatly as they say in the same

In addition to all the concerts so far unearthed, the end of the Revolutionary War saw an immediate revival of the 'Benefit' concerts, that is to say, concerts given at the risk and for the benefit of particular musicians. Who the first was to appeal to the public is, of course, very immaterial but as a matter of record it may be remarked that unless it was his "last" concert, of which the flutist William Brown spoke in October 1783, it probably was James Juhan, the self-styled inventor of the "Great North American Forte Piano" who had lately come to Philadelphia[1]). He presented a "variety of new and modern pieces of music, executed on various instruments" at a concert of vocal and instrumental music at the French Academy in Lodge Alley on August 6, 1783.

Then William Brown, who "having been prevailed on by several gentlemen to continue his stay in Philadelphia and being inclined to gratify them" offered in the Pennsylvania Packet, October 14, 1783 proposals for two subscription-concerts under his direction at the City Tavern on October 16th and 28th. The details of the announcement are curious enough to be quoted in full. Especially the idea of issuing tickets of different color deserves attention as it shows the beginning of a managerial detail in our country soon imitated by the Uranian Academy and since generally adopted:

"One subscription paper will be left at the said tavern, and another sent about the city, to either of which gentlemen may subscribe to, as conveniency or inclination may lead. The price to subscribers will be as in his last, viz. half a guinea to each person for the two concerts, who are to be furnished with red tickets so as to answer for both evenings.

Tickets for admittance to nonsubscribers will be signed in black, the price of which to be one dollar and a half for each concert. To render the entertainment more agreeable, Mr. Brown proposes that exclusive of the overtures, solos, lessons etc. there be some harmony music, the performance of which at his last concert having given such general satisfaction. — He further proposes to perform some well-known and approved Scotch airs, etc. with variations.

In 1784 William Brown was the first to go before the public with a benefit concert at the Lodge Room. It was announced for Feb. 5th but was postponed to February 19th[3]). Of the program nothing is said except that he proposed "(for that night only) to play several favorite airs with variations" an attraction imported from Europe where it was the vogue. Shortly

---

work in v. 2, p. 1088: "About 1802 the Harmonic Society was founded . . . for the study of sacred music. A clergyman, the Rev. Andrew Law was chiefly concerned in promoting the organisation . . . this association aspired to concert and usually give at least one in each year . . . This association was in existence as late as 1817". The Rev. Andrew Law is, of course, identical with Andrew Law, the psalmodist, whose erratic career would be well worth a monograph.

1) Pa. Journal, June 25, 1783.
2) Pa. Gazette, July 31, 1783.
3) Pa. Packet, Jan. 24, Feb. 12, 1784.

afterwards, William Brown must have gone to Charleston for on July 3d, having "lately arrived from Charleston" he announced in the Pennsylvania Packet a concert for July 9th to be followed by a ball. Tickets, at 10 s each, were "to admit a gentlemen and lady", a custom so eloquently centering in European advertisements around the *chapeau* whose place, at least in our country, is now taken by the matronly *chaperon*. Mr. Brown must have played the German flute to the delight of the gentlemen of Philadelphia to whose worldly attainments a proficiency on this instrument was considered just as essential as in medieval times for kings and noblemen a proficiency on the harp, or during the Renaissance the ability to sing a part *prima vista*, — evidently so, for he felt sure enough of an additional 'benefit' on September 16th. He also played a "double concerto for the violin and flute" at a concert given under similar conditions on March 23, 1784[1]) at the Lodge Room for the benefit of Philip Phile, whose fame rests nowadays on his problematic authorship of the 'President's March' which was to give life in 1798 to Joseph Hopkinson's, 'Hail Columbia'. Finally a concert, of course with ball, was given on April 6th[2]) "for the benefit of Mr. Juhan", leaving it open to doubt whether it was James or "Alexander Juhan, junior, Master of Music" who in December 1783 had lately arrived in Philadelphia[3]). The program consisted "of the most favourite music, and particularly a concerto on the flute, by a gentleman, a scholar of Mr. Brown".

In 1785, Mr. Brown, who seems to have been of a somewhat wandering disposition, was again the first on the plan. "Intending for Europe early in the spring" he thanked the citizens of Philadelphia "for every countenance and civility heretofore shown him" and "being solicited and encouraged by some of his particular friends" he announced his intention to have "one" concert before his departure. He "appointed" Feb. 8th as the date of this his "last" concert at the Lodge Room, which, in keeping with the proverbial, latent meaning of farewell affairs, by no means was to be his last appearance[4]). However, Mr. Brown, of whose benefit concerts Henri Capron soon was to remark that they invariably "opened a scene of considerable profit' assured

"the generous public that nothing will be wanting on his part to render the evening's entertainment as agreeable as may be wished having, as well to give a greater variety, as to please those who are not fond of overture music, selected and composed some pantomime music, which will consist of a variety of Scottish and other airs; with varia-

1) Pa. Packet, March 18, 1784.
2) Pa. Packet, April 1, 1784.
3) Pa. Packet, Dec. 23, 1783.
4) Pa. Packet, Feb. 2, 1785.

tions, etc. interspersed in a pleasing style; and to close the whole with the celebrated symphony of Martini, commonly called the Battle of Debarrie."

This compromise shows Mr. Brown to have possessed keen business instincts and those among our American musicians who enjoy the reputation of being business men first, second and third and then artists, may look to him as their legitimate forerunner. Indeed, Mr. Brown was accused by Mr. Capron to have gone so far as to recommend an application for payment at private concerts, an attitude nowadays considered perfectly proper but in those days entirely unprofessional. But what was this quarrel between Brown and Capron, — a worthy pendant to that between Juhan and Adgate? The answer may be found in an open letter addressed to the public by Capron in self-defense against certain malicious insinuations in the Pennsylvania Journal, Feb. 12, 1785. Though long, it unrolls such a delightful *Kulturbild* as to prove interesting reading:

TO THE PUBLIC

Mr. Capron being informed that the motives maliciously assigned for his absenting himself from Mr. Brown's benefit concert, may operate to his prejudice; and being solicitous on all occasions to evince the highest respect for the public, he begs leave to observe that he would chearfully have contributed his abilities to the entertainment of the evening, had Mr. Brown condescended to make the request.

Whatever insinuations, therefore, may have been introduced upon this occasion, Mr. Capron cannot but ascribe to the same spirit, which induced Mr. Brown to recommend an application for payment at private concerts (a conduct which he did not himself adopt, though he professed the introduction) that so he might create an interest with the public, by drawing an invidious comparison, and placing men for whom he avowed friendship and esteem, in an unmerited and disadvantageous light. In truth, Mr. Capron has acquitted himself of every obligation to Mr. Brown, and from the circumstances of that gentleman's conduct, he could never be again induced to enter into an intercourse of favours; but in order to the gratification of the public. The sincerity of his disposition in this respect, whatever may be Mr. Brown's superiority in abilities, he is confident cannot be surpassed; and surely it is sufficient triumph (without the aid of any dishonourable artifice) that every concert for the benefit of that Gentleman, opens a scene of considerable profit, while the only opportunity which the public has had to assist Mr. Capron, scarcely supplied the means to defray his expenses.

Upon the whole, Mr. Capron confides in the general candour, that considering his situation as a stranger, — as one, who, without deriving any pecuniary advantage, has punctually contributed to the winter's amusement, and as a performer desirous of, and indeed needing the patronage of the public, it will not be imputed to him as an offence that either through the pride or subtility of Mr. Brown's conduct, he was deprived of the honour of attending at that Gentleman's concert.

Though proverbially the devil is never quite so black as painted, Mr. Brown really seems to have had a malicious tongue and apparently did not enjoy an enviable reputation among his fellow-musicians. Not enough with Capron's attack, immediately below John Bentley, the manager of the City Concert, addressed a *card*, as such effusions were called, to Mr. Brown leaving nothing to be desired in candid condemnation of his character. This gentleman's unsavory character hardly interests posterity, whereas a reprint of

Bentley's *card* seems warranted for the valuable information it conveys
on the conduct of concerts and the professional etiquette of those days:

MR. BROWN.

Sir,

As the public prejudice, however excited, is of importance to one who depends
upon public favour, I deem it a duty I owe to myself, as well as to those whose generous
patronage has supported me in my professional pursuits, to counteract the insidious
attack you have made upon my character and interest; and by stating a few questions
relative to our connection in general, but particularly respecting my conduct at your
benefit concert, I trust it will fully appear that I have not only acquitted myself with
liberality to you, but likewise with the respect and gratitude which I have ever felt
for the public.

And first, Sir, allow me to enquire, whether, at any time, you desired my assistance
at your concert; nay, whether by refusing the loan of the harpsichord usually lent, you
did not give me room to suppose it was neither wished nor expected?

That you raised an opinion in the public that I occasioned the absence of two
performers, is certain; but as the truth is contrary to that opinion, I must request you
to declare the grounds upon which so indivious an insinuation was founded? The gentlemen alluded to, for reasons which I had no right to control, objected to any further
correspondence with Mr. Brown, upon the footing of favour. They had already acquitted themselves of their obligation to perform for his benefit, and as they are volunteers
at the City Concert, surely it would have been indelicate in me to have persuaded them
to any unprofitable trouble; or upon the idea of their living in my house, to have intruded
(contrary to their private feelings and disposition) any services you might require.

The situation of these gentlemen, as boarding and logding with me without any
charge or expence, might perhaps have induced you to think that any wish of mine
upon the occasion would have prevailed with them: But here let me recall to your
remembrance your own conduct upon our first acquaintance. Did you not live free
of every expence in my house for the whole of the last winter, and some months after
the concerts were closed? Did this induce you to perform without a premium or even
to consult my interest upon occasions which did not interfere with your own? No, Sir.
You were supported at my cost; your demand of three pounds for every night's performance was paid; and not withstanding this conduct on my part, you were ungrateful enough to traduce me in private, and to attempt my ruin with a most respectable
character, whose friendship I had essentially experienced. — Upon this case, I may
safely trust to the candor of the public for my satisfaction; and to your own feelings
(if you are not insensible to shame) for your punishment.

(A true copy)   John Bentley

To. Mr. Brown, at Mr. Dietrich's,
    Tobacconist, in Thirdstreet.

To give this sublime outburst of indignation a ridiculous sequel, shortly
afterwards, on March 15th in the Pennsylvania Journal, Mr. Capron — to
use his own words — a stranger in the country, ignorant of its language
and known but to few of its inhabitants, confiding in the hospitality of the
public disposition for that encouragement which he could not desire from
the assiduity of private friendship, or the advantages of popular reputation,
presented his respects to the public and solicited their attendance on March 29
at a concert of vocal and instrumental music to include a variety of familiar
airs, Scotch and English and a collection of Pantomime music never yet

performed in Philadelphia. To render the entertainment complete he intended to collect every assistance that might be necessary — including the *diabolus in musica* William Brown! And thereby hangs another tale, for on March 23d Mr. Capron respectfully informed the public that "on account of Mr. Brown's departure to Baltimore" he found himself obliged to defer his concert until April 12th. Poor Capron! For reasons unknown, not only was his benefit further postponed to April 19th but this evening turned out "so unfavourable that even his best friends could not attend the performance". In this calamity the ladies present "whose interest however extensive" did "not affect him more than the honor of their patronage" came to his rescue. They generously desired that another concert should be announced and Capron with the sincerest sentiments of gratitude fixed the date of this extra-benefit for May 3d when, posterity hopes, neither the absence of William Brown, nor the inclemency of the weather interfered with Capron's prospects. After that his star was steadily ascending and as far as Mr. Brown is concerned the fact that Francis Hopkinson accepted in 1787 the dedication of his 'Three Rondos' would permit the inference that the gentlemen of the world were more interested in his musicianship than in his character as exposed by Capron and Bentley.

The first benefit concert of 1786 was given on January 10th at the City Tavern by Mr. Juhan, either James or Alexander, and it was to consist "of the most favorite music"[1]). At the same place, for a dollar a ticket, which was fast becoming the usual price of admission, the troublesome William Brown entertained his clientele end of February with a concert for which, as he said, he "spared no pains, as well with respect to himself as to such other performers, so as to render the entertainment agreeable"[2]). This was followed by a concert for the benefit of either James or Alexander Juhan at Mr. Duplessis's New Room in Church Alley on April 25th[3]). The program consisted of the following "most favorite music":

FIRST PART.

Simphonie	Stamitz
Double Concerto Flute & Violin	Davaux
Quartetto	Cambini
Concerto Forte piano	Smith

SECOND PART.

Symphonia	Vanhal
Concerto Flute	Brown
Duetto Fortepiano	Smith
Concerto Violin	Borghi

1) Pa. Packet, Jan. 4, 1786.
2) Pa. Packet, Feb. 22, 1786.
3) Pa. Packet, April 22, 1786.

Shortly afterwards, on May 11th, postponed from May 9th, William Brown again assembled his friends at the City Tavern to listen to a concert of „instrumental music" consisting of such select compositions as he flattered himself, would not fail to please those who might honor him with their company[1]). The next concert, on Sept. 21st at the City Tavern seems to have been for the benefit of Henri Capron "lately returned from Charleston". Assisted by some of the ablest masters, as he remarked in the flowery announcement[2]), apparently composed with care and love by one of his English speaking friends, he rendered the following pieces.

PART FIRST

Overture to the Deserter[3])	
Song	Reinagle
Concerto Violoncello	Mr. Capron
Simphonia	
Concerto Violin	Mr. Juhan

PART SECOND

Overture to La Belle Arsiène[4])	
Sonata Pianoforte	Mr. Reinagle
Simphonia	
Concerto Flute	Mr. Brown
A Glee	

If this program had a decidedly French flavor, that of Alexander Reinagle's benefit concert at the City Tavern on Oct. 12th[5]) brought Haydn to the foreground, now irreverently often dubbed *Papa* Haydn but whose music in by-gone days when Stamitz and Abel still held the field must have sounded quite revolutionary and radical:

ACT I

Overture	of Haydn
Song	Mr. Reinagle
Concerto Violoncello	Mr. Capron

ACT II

Sonata Piano Forte	Mr. Reinagle
Concerto Flute	Mr. Brown
Concerto	of Corelli

ACT III

Sonata Piano Forte	Mr. Reinagle
Concerto Violin	Mr. Juhan
Overture	of Haydn
Trio and Glee	

---

1) Pa. Packet, May 8 and 9, 1786.
2) Pa. Journal, Sept. 10, 1786.
3) Probably by Dibdin.
4) Monsigny.
5) Pa. Journal, Oct. 7, 1786.

If Reinagle on this and other occasions more than probably was responsible for the pieces standing opposite his name, it is not quite clear, as was previously remarked, whether his comrades played concertos of their own. All of them may be traced as composers and it is therefore at least possible that they treated the audience to their own music, which may or may not have been of value. On the other hand, the custom prevailing to bestow a generous silence on the composers of works destined to show off the dexterity of virtuosos, it is also at least possible that they played concertos not their own. The fact that the program reads "Concerto of Corelli" need cause no apprehension in accepting this theory, for this evidently was a *concerto grosso*. In all likelihood the occasions when our early soloists would and would not appear as interpreters of their own works were about equally divided.

If the program of William Brown's benefit concert on February 13, 1787[1]) had not been an exception to the rule of not clearly indicating the composers of concertos, sonatas etc. it would go far to prove that Brown, Capron, Juhan and others were in the habit of performing their own works. It reads:

ACT I

Новая Overture, La Chasse   .. .. Stamitz
Song .. .. Reinagle
Concerto Flute .. .. Brown

ACT II

Sonata Piano Forte (La Chasse) .. .. Campioni
Canzonett .. .. Jackson
Concerto Violin .. .. Daveaux

ACT III

Duetto Violin and Violoncello   .. .. Cambini
Rondo Flute   .. .. Brown
Miscellaneous Concerto.
Overture Rosina[2]), by particular desire.

Possibly the printed programs, if such were issued, gave fuller details as to this interesting and for the bibliography of American music important point, but it stands to reason that the programs were generally printed in the newspapers in lieu of separate programs. Indeed, in countries where the custom still prevails to charge a fee for programs, many economical persons may still be seen at concerts with programs clipped from the newspapers.

When announcing his benefit concerts Henri Capron never failed to address the public in terms of the most abject and polite gratitude but when he respectfully solicited the attendance of his friends on March 6th at the

---

1) Pa. Packet. February 12, 1787.
2) Shield.

City Tavern he went a step farther in a direction which shows that though
he did not possess the *savoir faire* of his antagonist William Brown, he at
least knew how to advertise. Though these pages do not deal with a history
of musical instruction in our country, yet the appendix to Capron's program
is so quaint that a quotation may serve to alleviate the monotony of this
chronological narrative. Certainly the idea of demonstrating his abilities
as guitarist *ad oculos* of those who might have been attracted by his terms
was quite clever:

PLAN OF THE CONCERT

Act I
Symphonie .. .. Stamitz
Song .. .. Reinagle
Concerto Violoncello .. .. Capron

Act II
Grand Symphonie .. .. Vanhall
Concerto Violin .. .. Cramer
Sonata Guittare .. .. Capron
Overture, Rose et Colas[1])

Act III
Concerto Flute .. .. Fiolla
Sonata Piano Forte .. .. Reinagle
Overture .. .. Stamitz.

Mr. Capron respectfully informs the public that he instructs ladies and gentlemen
in the art of singing and of playing on the Spanish and English guitars, recording the
most approved method of the first masters in Europe.

His terms are one guinea for eight lessons, and one guinea entrance — the entrance
to be dispensed with if the person applying to him has received previous instructions
from another master. At two lessons per week he engages to perfect any person, possessing a tolerable ear, in the space of six months.

The guitar, from the late improvement which it has received, being so portable
and so easily kept in order, is now considered not only as a desirable but as a fashionable
instrument . . .

Two of the remaining concerts of the year 1787 were both given for the
benefit of Mr. Juhan which again would leave the puzzle open whether it
was James or Alexander unless the argument seems more plausible that
only one Juhan still resided at Philadelphia as otherwise the announcements
would have made some distinction between the two. In that case, the
chances are in favor of the younger Juhan, Alexander, easily traced in subsequent years whereas James disappears from the musical horizon. The
concerts were to be given at the City Tavern on May 29th and April 10th[2])
dates following each other so closely that the suspicion of identity is allayed
only by characteristic differences in the programs. The "plan" of the first
concert is of actual importance because it shows the introduction in our

1) Monsigny. .
2) Pa. Packet, May 23 and April 4, 1787.

country of the comparatively new idea of pianoforte music *à quatre mains:*

Act I

A new Overture	Reinagle
Concerto Flute	Brown
Song	Sarti
Overture	Haydn

Act II

Sonata Piano Forte of Haydn	Mr. Juhan & Mr. Reinagle
Concerto Violoncello	Capron
Solo Violin	Juhan
The Grand Overture	Martini

Tickets at 7 *s* 6 each to be had at the City Tavern, and of Mr. Juhan', — at Mr. Capron's in Morris Alley.

It may be taken for granted that Mr. Juhan and his associates on this occasion exerted themselves to the best of their abilities as no less an illustrious person than George Washington sat among their audience. We know this from Washington's diary; an entry appearing there on May 29th to the effect that he "accompanied Mrs. Morris to the benefit concert of a Mr. Juhan". The program of Juhan's second concert reads:

Act 1st.

Grand Overture	Martini
Song	Reinagle
Solo Violin (newly composed)	Juhan

Act 2d.

Overture to the Deserter[1])	
Concerto Flute	Brown
Sonata Piano Forte	Reinagle
Concerto Violoncello	Capron

Act 3d.

Concerto Violin	Cramer
Sonata Guittar	Capron
(By desire) the Overture to Rosina[2])	

Three weeks later, on June 12th, Alexander Reinagle had a benefit[3]). Presumably he was above the petty professional jealousies of musicians not quite his equals. Still it must have been gratifying to him that George Washington attended his concert[4]), as he had that of Juhan. If, as we have reasons to believe, he gave harpsichord lessons to Nelly Custis, Washington's adopted daughter, it was only natural that the "General" should thus show his appreciation of her teacher who appears to have had something

---

1) Either Dibdin or Monsigny.
2) Shield.
3) Pa. Packet, June 4, 1787.
4) See Washington's diary.

in common with Washington in dignified behaviour and appearance. The program offered certainly was very "modern" and if Reinagle played one of his sonatas now preserved in autograph at the Library of Congress, George Washington, providing he was more musical than he claimed to be, cannot have failed to observe that Reinagle was not only a good teacher but also a composer of merit:

ACT I

Overture	Bach
Concerto Violoncello	Capron
Song	Sarti

ACT II

Overture	André
Concerto Violin	Fiorillo
Concerto Flute	Brown

ACT III

Overture (La Buona Figliuola)	Piccini
Sonata Pianoforte	Reinagle
A new Overture (in which is introduced a Scotch Strathspey)	Reinagle

All these benefit concerts, as well as the only two I have traced for 1788 and 1789 began at 7 o'clock P. M. which seems to have come to be considered the desirable hour for entertainments in those days and a passing remark might well be made here that it still was customary, as in Europe, to have tickets for sale at the residence of the musician to be benefited, at taverns and bookstores. The programs of these two concerts, though I doubt them to have been the only ones given, show an inclination towards the music of the altogether too prolific composer Wanhal. The first was announced for the benefit of Mr. Rehine, a singer, for Nov. 25, 1788 but was postponed on account of the inclement weather to November 28th[1]) when Mr. Rehine did little more than fill in the intermissions between the instrumental numbers unless he expected to give *encores*, then less frequent and less vulgarly insisted upon than nowadays:

ACT I

Overture	by Mr. Stamitz
Song 'The Lover's petition	Mr. Rehine
Solo Violino	Mr. Phile
Song 'No t'was neither shape nor feature'	Mr. Harper
Quartet	Mr. Daveaux
Song 'O gentle maid'	Mr. Rehine
Sinfonia	Mr. Stamitz

---

1) Independent Gazetteer, Nov. 15 and 16, 1788.

Act II

Sinfonia	Mr. Vanhall
Song, 'Mary's Dream'	Mr. Rehine
Concert Clarinetto	Mr. Wolf
Hunting Song	Mr. Harper
Quartet	Mr. Kammel
Song 'Ma chère amie'	Mr. Rehine
Sinfonia	Mr. Kammel

The concert of 1789 took place on April 16th (postponed from the fourteenth on account of one of the principal performers being sick), for the benefit of the violinist Mr. Schultz at Henry Epple's, the fashionable *traiteur*[1]). The program to which Mr. Rehine contributed the "vocal parts" was advertised in this rather flimsy style:

Act I

Overture of Artaxerxes[2])	
Song	Rehine
Sonata Pianoforte	
Violino Concerto	

Act II

Symphonia, from Hall	Mr. Rehine
Song	
Quartetto	
Flute Concert	
Symphonia from Hall	

Of course, this mysterious "from Hall" was a misprint rather than an anglicized form of Van Hall and in a subsequent advertisement Mr. Schultz hastened to rectify the mistake.

Merely mentioning Philip Phile's concert on March 18, 1790 and that of Mr. Schultz on April 8th I hasten to a few concerts strikingly different in their programs from previous entertainments. So far the musical life of Philadelphia was distinctly English in character but now the French element made itself more and more felt. It goes without saying that this shifting of appearances was due to the French Revolution which drove a surprising number of refugees to our country and especially to the Middle and Southern states. The first sign of the new era came when "a company of French musicians lately arrived" announced their intention to give a "Grand concert of vocal and instrumental music" on July 29th[3]) at the City Tavern with this decidedly French program:

----

1) Pa. Packet, April 11 and 14, 1789.
2) Arne.
3) Pa. Packet, July 27, 1790.

FIRST ACT.

1. A Grand Symphonia, in full orchestra.
2. Mr. De Lisle[1]) will sing an arietta in counter tenor, from Ariane[2]), from the Grand Opera, at Paris.
3. Mrs. De Lisle will sing an arietta with several variations (de bravoure) from the fair Arsène — 'Est-il un sort plus glorieux'.
4. A Concerto of St. George, by Mr. Emanuel.
5. A Grand Symphonia in full orchestra.

SECOND ACT.

6. Mr. De Lisle will sing the arietta 'Le roy passoit' from the Deserter, music of Monciny [!].
7. Mrs. De Lisle will sing an arietta with several variations (de bravoure) from the Infant of Zamora[3]).
8. Mr. Emanuel will play several airs and that of Marlborough, [!] with variations.
9. Mr. and Mrs. De Lisle will sing the song of the False Magie in two parts, music of Grétry.
10. The concert will end with a grand symphonia in full orchestra.

₊ Mr. Reinagle and the members of the Amateur's Concert, will assist in the above.

If the performers declared that they "had been induced to come to America by the deserved reputation which the inhabitants bear abroad of possessing a taste for the polite arts, and especially for music" and that they deemed "their arrival in this part of the American empire, one of the happiest events of their lives", we know that this flattering ruse was rather thin and cannot have deceived readers familiar with the reports of French travelers who certainly did not contribute much to this musical reputation, supposedly a stronger inducement for emigration than the sequels of July 14th, 1789. Be this, as it may, the company apparently derived some benefit from their first concert as they gave two more on Sept. 3d, postponed from August 30th[4]) and September 29th. For the second concert, this program was selected:

ACT THE FIRST

1. A Grand Symphony
2. The Ariet of Lord Atkinson in Azemia[5]) 'Ciel! O! Ciel, quand ta rigueur': Sung by Mr. De l'Isle.
3. A Concerto of Fodor: by Mr. Emanuel.
4. The favourite Air 'La fauvette avec ses petits' in Zemira and Azor[6]), sung by Mad. De Lisle.
5. A Concerto: Symphony of Davaux, on the violin; by Mr. Emanuel and a son of Mr. D. Duport (a youth not yet ten years old).
6. The Ariet 'Sans chiens & sans boulette' from Rose et Colas, sung by Mr. De Lisle.
7. Gluck's Ouverture of Iphigénie en Aulide.

---

1) Also spelled Delisle, de l'Isle, the latter form probably being correct.
2) Probably by Edelmann, 1782.
3) Paisiello-Framéry, 1789.
4) Pa. Packet, August 28 and Sept. 3, 1790.
5) Dalayrac.
6) Grétry.

ACT THE SECOND

1. A full chorus Symphony.
2. The famous Air of Richard Coeur de Lion[1]);

O! Richard, O! mon Roi
L'univers t'abandonne!
Sur la terre il n'est donc que moi
Qui s'interesse à ta personne, etc.

Sung by Mr. De Lisle. (This celebrated air being played occasionally at a convivial meeting of the Body Guards of his Most Christian Majesty, worked so much upon their feelings as made them trample under foot their National Cockades, and nearly occasioned a counter revolution in France.)
3. A Concerto of De la Motte, by M. D. Duport, junior.
4. The Italian air, 'Vole à nos bois': Sung by Mad. De Lisle.
5. Several favorite tunes with variations will be performed by Mr. Emanuel and Mr. D. Duport junior.
6. Mr. and Mrs. De l'Isle will sing a duet.
7. The Overture of the French opera, Les Deux Tuteurs[2]).

The program of their third and last concert, held at the home of the dancing-master Sicard in Church Alley, reads:

ACT I

1. The Overture to a French opera called Les Deux Tuteurs.
2. An Arietta of Zémire and Azor — 'Le malheur me rend intrépide', to be sung by Mrs. Delisle.
3. A Concert on the Clarionet.
4. An Arietta from a French opera 'L'Amant jaloux'[3]). By Mrs. Delisle.
5. A new Concerto of Jarnovic by Mr. Emanuel.
6. A grand Symphony in full orchestra.

ACT II

7. Overture of Iphigénie, a grand French opera[4]).
8. An Arietta from a French opera (Le Silvain) 'Je sais braver le coup du sort'. By Mr. Delisle.
9. An Arietta from La Fausse Magie[5]) 'Comme au éclair' by Mr. Delisle.
10. Several airs with variations, and Marlborough. By Mr. Emanuel.
11. A Duo from Le Silvani, Grétry's music. By Mrs. and Mr. Delisle.
12. A grand Symphony in full orchestra.

Undoubtedly the music-lovers of Philadelphia profited by the performances of these and other Frenchmen but it must also be said that the programs with their operatic selections established a vicious precedent and only the good taste of men like Reinagle, who reigned supreme in matters musical, could stem temporarily the tide towards concerts that really were opera-anthologies in concert garb, a hybrid form of entertainment still

---

1) Grétry.
2) Dalayrac.
3) Grétry.
4) Probably Gluck.
5) Grétry. It will have been noticed with what care the company selected ariettes reminding the audience *nolens volens* of their misfortunes.

more or less in vogue in our own times, so boastful otherwise of esthetic enlightment. Furthermore the last decade of the eighteenth century with its influx of voluntary or involuntary adventurers brought into our musical life a sensational element of which it previously had been relatively free. Among other things, that esthetic abortion, the precocious child — with all due respect for a genius like Mozart who was a prodigy, something totally different! — was beginning to haunt the concert rooms and surely if, in accordance with European customs, Mr. D. Duport advertised his son "not 10 years of age, who has performed before the Royal Family in France" there were esthetic undercurrents at work which must have made men like Francis Hopkinson sigh for Colonial Times. "Not ten years of age" however, seems to have been the proper age of these socalled prodigies for this was also the drawing card for Miss Lucy Moller's concert on Dec. 3, 1790[1]) at which she played "a concerto on the grand pianoforte as also *the* [!] Sonata of the famous Haydn" and, being a wonder-child, she, of course, had performed in London "with the greatest applause and exceeded any child of her age". Under these circumstances it is probable that she derived a greater benefit from her concert than did a masterly musician like Alexander Reinagle from his on Dec. 29th[2]) of which, unfortunately I do not possess the program.

Though in all likelihood benefit concerts were given in 1791, I was not in a position to trace them. In 1792, Mrs. Kenna, who belonged to the theatrical company just then performing in the section of Philadelphia called Northern Liberties, held a concert of vocal and instrumental music at Oeller's Assembly Room on May 8th[3]). The program was of prodigious length and curiously interspersed with recitations:

The entertainment to open with an
Overture .. .. Smith
After which Mrs. Kenna will give
    A Dissertation on Hearts. Part First — The Heart of a Honest Soldier — The Heart of a captain — The Heart of a miser — A sound and upright heart.
Symphony .. .. Stamitz
Sonata Pianoforte .. .. Miss Moller
    Part Second — The Heart of a milliner and the Heart of a amiable woman.
Symphony .. .. Abell
Song 'Sweet Passion of Love' .. .. Mrs. Kenna
Overture .. .. Van Hall
    After which Mrs. Kenna will make a comparative view, showing the difference of Queen Elizabeth's Days and the Modes and Fashions of the Present Times.

1) Pa. Packet, Dec. 1, 1790.
2) Pa. Packet, Dec. 29. 1790.
3) Federal Gazette, May 8, 1792.

Symphony	Kammel
Song 'Water parted, etc.'	Mrs. Kenna
Symphony	Abell
Cherokee Chief's Death Song	Mrs. Kenna
Symphony	Stamitz

To conclude with
> *Satan's Address to the Sun*, from Milton's Paradise Lost, by
> Mrs. Kenna (which she had the honor of delivering before the
> Literati of Trinity College, Dublin)

Finale	Haydn

A fortnight later, on May 29th[1]), Joseph Cézar, "a pupil of the celebrated
Signor Viotti and first violin of the theatre in Cape François" gave a concert
at the College Hall of "the most applauded musical pieces in Europe".
Instead of mentioning their titles he continued by saying:

"Many amateurs of the first eminence being so kind as to honor him with their
patronage, will perform and amongst the great variety of pieces, which shall be per-
formed, the following are presented to the notice of the public.
By Mr. Cassignard, amateur, several pieces of his composition on the guitar.
By Mr. Pelissier, first French horn of the theatre in Cape François, a qua-
tuor of his composition.
By an amateur, a sonata on the harp.
The whole to be concluded by a grand simphony.

This concert, interesting because of the first appearance of such a skilful
musician as Victor Pelissier at Philadelphia, must have been somewhat of
a success, for Joseph Cézar "with a view of showing his gratitude etc. and
to give them and the public an additional proof of his anxiety to deserve
their encouragement", gave with the assistance of "many amateurs and
eminent professors of music" a second concert "at Mr. O'Ellers Hotel" —
even German names may be made to look Irish — on June 16th[2]) with
this program:

Overture

A grand Symphony in full chorus

ACT I

1. Pleyel's Quatuor. By an amateur, Messrs. Relein, Pelissier and Jos. Cezar.
2. Concerto of Signior Mestrino on the violin, by an amateur.
3. A Sonata and Marlborough's variations on the harp, by Mons. Salomon who
taught to play on that instrument in Paris.
4. A Song with music on the guitar. By Monsieur Cassignard, Professor of guitar.

ACT II

1. Fodor's Sonata with various tunes, By Jos. Cezar.
2. A Solo on the Clarinet, By Mr. Wolf.
3. An Arietta and a new Marlborough's song with music on the harp. By Mr.
Relein.
4. A concerto Symphony of Viotti. By an amateur and Jos. Cézar; and the whole
to conclude with a simphony of Heyden [!] in full chorus.

---

1) Federal Gazette, May 29, 1792.
2) Federal Gazette, June 15, 1792.

Next we notice a "grand" concert on Nov. 8th[1]) at Henry Epple's, evidently for the benefit of Mrs. Hodgkinson, with this program:

The vocal parts by Mrs. Hodgkinson. Leader of the band, Mr. Gehot, who will lead at the City Concert.

Act I

Grand Overture	Bichl
Quartetto	Pleyl
Song	Mrs. Hodgkinson
Concerto Pianoforte	Moller
Quartetto Clarinet	Wolf
Sinfonia	Bach

Act II

Overture of the Deserter[2])	
Concerto Violin	Gehot
Song	Mrs. Hodgkinson
Concerto Violoncello	Capron
Finale	Vanhal

The last concert of 1792 was "the French Concert" advertised for Dec. 22d[3]) but as Mrs. Pownall and Mrs. Chambers, two of the soloists, were on duty at the theatre on that evening the French musicians saw themselves obliged to postpone it to Dec. 24th when it would positively take place "as on that evening there will be no performance at the theatre". An illustration as to what extent the concert-life of Philadelphia had become dependent on opera and opera stars!

The benefit season of 1793 opened at Oeller's Hotel on Jan. 5th on behalf of the French musicians "the vocal part by Mrs. Pownall and Mr. Chambers". The "plan" certainly was varied enough to suit all tastes:

Act I.

Grand Symphonia.
Sonata on the harp, by Mr. Salomon
Song, Mrs. Pownall, accompanied on the harp by Mr. Salomon
Concerto on the violin, by Mr. Boullay
Sonata on the Pianoforte, accompanied by the violin, Messrs. Guenin and Petit
Song (Handel) by Mr. Chambers
Quartetto, with variations, Messrs. Petit, Boullay, Pilisie [Pelissier] and a Gentleman

Act II.

Overture from the grand opera of Chimene[4])
Solo on the French horn, Mr. Pelisie
Song (by particular desire) 'The lark's shrill notes', Mrs. Pownall
Concerto on the violin, Mr. Petit.
A Medley on the Pianoforte, Mr. Guenin
Duet, by Mrs. Pownall and Mr. Chambers
To conclude with a Grand Chaconne, composed by the celebrated Floquets.

---

1) Federal Gazette, Nov. 5, 1792.   2) Probably Monsigny.
3) Federal Gazette, Dec. 22, 1792.   4) Sacchini.

Only a few days later, on Jan. 15th[1]) Mrs. Pownall and Mr. Chambers gave their own joint benefit. They had selected as program in

ACT I

Grand Overture.
Quartetto (Petit) with variations for the clarinet   Mr. Foucard
Song (in French) .. ..   Mrs. Pownall
Concerto for the Violin .. ..   Mr. Boullay
Song .. ..   Mr. Chambers
Grand Chacone (composed by L'Breton)
Duet .. ..   Mrs. Pownall and Mr. Chambers.

ACT II

Grand Symphonia
Song (3d time by particular desire)   .. .. ..   Mrs. Pownall
Concerto for the Violin .. ..   Mr. Petit
Song .. ..   Mr. Chambers
Sonata (Pianoforte, accompanied on the violin) Messrs. Guenin and Petit
Song .. ..   Mrs. Pownall
Grand Chaconne (composed by Floquet).
Duet — Mess. Pownall and Mr. Chambers.

During the evening, though not mentioned, Mrs. Pownall must have delivered an "Address in behalf of the French musicians" for it was advertised in Dunlap's American Daily Advertiser on March 26th as

"This day published and sold at E. Story's office in Fourthstreet . . . printed on writing paper and new type, containing 30 pages (price 15 d) . . . . delivered on her Benefit Concert Night, at Oeller's Hotel to a very crowded audience . . . To which are added, Pastoral songs, written by herself at an early period of life . . ."

This address certainly would prove not only pathetic but interesting reading, but unfortunately no copy has come to my notice.

For Jan. 19th two concerts were announced, one for Mrs. Hodgkinson, the other again for the French musicians, but John Hodgkinson hearing of "ungenerous" insinuations that he had selected this evening "with an intent to throw the French gentlemen out of their usual routine", protested and assured the public that he had engaged the hall at Oeller's without knowing of the French concert, had selected Saturday evening because Saturday was the best suited for concerts etc. and, as was quite true, not being in immediate necessity as were the French exiles, he wound up by saying that his wife's concert would be postponed to Jan. 21th[2]). The French musicians, thus having the field to themselves, entertained the public with a program largely identical with the one of their first concert. Two main numbers, however, were new, Grétry's overture to 'La Caravane

1) Federal Gazette, Jan. 11, 1793.
2) Dunlap's Daily American Advertiser, Jan. 17, 1793.

du Caire' and an "overture from Olide, opera of Iphigenia" whatever this might stand for [1]).

If the printer's devil took such liberties with, as we suspect, master Gluck's Iphigénie en Aulide, he displayed still more originality in transforming the title of an Italian song sung by Mrs. Hodgkinson at her song recital on Jan. 21th, announced so as to leave no doubt of the unimportance of instrumental numbers when stars like Mr. and Mrs. Hodgkinson made their bow to the public:

SONGS

(By desire) Primroses deck the banks green side
(Bravura) Cease gay seducers
(By desire) Kate of Aberdeen
(Italian) I now te mer, bel idol mio

In the course of the evening Mr. Hodgkinson will read Collin's Ode on the passions, the Three warnings, and Foote's celebrated Prologue on the Impossibility of pleasing everybody.

John Hodgkinson also deviated from traditional methods by having the tickets for sale at his lodgings only, with the exclusion of the different inns, book and music-stores.

Whether benefit concerts were given during the fall of 1793 I do not know and I therefore hasten to a species of entertainments which Raynor Taylor introduced in Philadelphia on Jan. 18, 1794 [2]) after having, as we know, *toured* the South with them. On said evening was performed:

AN ODE TO THE NEW YEAR]

With a variety of other pieces, consisting of songs, duets and trios, pastoral, serious and comic, entirely original, by Miss Huntley, and other young ladies and Mr. Taylor, by whom the whole of the music is composed — who will accompany the songs on the grand pianoforte and perform some extempore pieces on that instrument.

Finding, as he said on Jan. 28th, that several families, who intended to be present, were prevented by indisposition and other circumstances, Raynor Taylor — the date is not mentioned — gave

another performance with the assistance of Miss Huntley and an other young lady, called an *Olio* which will be similar in its nature, but different with respect to the particular pieces, those comprehending the first two parts being entirely new, and, among others, will consist of the following subjects: — The Poor female ballad singer, a pathetic song; Hunting song; Algerine captive; Sailor's song; Ding Dong Bell, or the Honeymoon expired, being the courtship and wedding of Ralph and Fan; Character of smart Dolly, a laughing song; Rustic courtship, or the unsuccessful love of poor Thomas, a crying song with duet, trio etc. and for the 3d part, by desire, will be repeated, the Ode to the New Year. Each part will be preceded by a piece on the Grand Pianoforte.

---

1) Dunlap's Daily Am. Adv. Jan. 17, 1793. Merely to throw sidelights, it may be recorded that the French gentlemen in anticipation of a modern custom, requested "such ladies and gentlemen as might be pleased to have music performed at their houses, to enquire for them". It is pretty safe to say that the prizes paid now and then even by "Bob" Morrison were in about in the same proportion as his millions to those of a Rockefeller.   2) Dunlap's Daily Am. Advertiser, Jan. 11, 1794.

The only other benefit concert I came across for 1794 was given on Nov. 29th. It was remarkable in two directions. First for a really interesting program and then for the pitiful manner of announcement. Truly the horrors of the black insurrection in St. Domingo are brought home to us when we read that the concert was to take place

for the benefit of a person who has fallen from the most independent affluent situation (if the annual receipt of 20 000 l. may be called so) to the most abject state of distress, in consequence of the massacre at Fort Dauphin, in the island of St. Domingo.
Conscious of the humanity of the citizens of America, he feels it unnecessary to rouse their sensibility by a more minute detail of his former and present situation, particularly as they are well known to several respectable characters in their city. He will only remark that a few years-nay, months since, it would have been difficult to persuade him that he should be reduced to the necessity of making this application to the humanity of a generous public, or that he should have recourse to that art which, in his earlier days, had been taught him merely as an accomplishment, in order to procure the necessaries of life for himself and family. He can assure the lovers of music that they will be amply gratified, as the selection has been carefully made, and will be executed with judgment.

PLAN OF THE CONCERT.

Act I

1. Overture, representing the Battle of Ivry, in grand orchestra[1])
2. Concerto on the Clarinet, by Mr. Henri
3. An English Air, by Mrs. Pownall
4. Concerto on the Violin, composed by Signior Viotti, by Monsieur Collet
5. Concerto on the Harp, by a lady
6. Overture, composed by Pleyel, in grand orchestra

Act II

1. Ouverture, composed by Haydn
2. A Quartetto, composed by Pleyel, by Monsieur Collet
3. Two airs in harmony, by eight wind-instruments
4. A French Ariette, by Mrs. Pownall
5. A Concerto on the Pianoforte by Krumpholtz, by Monsieur Gerin
6. Overture of the opera of Samatico Burlato[2]) in grand orchestra

On Jan. 20, 1795[3]) a Mr. Mechtler gave a concert for his benefit in the announcement of which we find as second number "a concerto de riots for the violin", whatever this might mean. Here is the whole program containing not less than three concertos, two symphonies and a "great" overture:

Act I

A great Overture d'Haydn
A Concerto de riots for the violin, by Mr. Collet
A Concerto of Kozeluch for the Pianoforte by Mr. Mechtler
A Symphony of Pleyel

---

1) Martini.
2) Fanatico Burlato by Cimarosa.
3) American Daily Adv. Jan. 16, 1795.

ACT II

A Symphony of Mr. ——
A Concerto, arranged and executed by Mr. Demarque
Petits airs variées for the harp
A Full piece.

Following this, Messrs. Guenin and Menel had a benefit at Oeller's Hotel on March 3d[1]) the "vocal parts" by the famous Mrs. Oldmixon over whom, many years later, Parker grew so enthusiastic. Again the program is noticeable for the predominance of concertos:

ACT I

A Grand Symphony
A Symphony concertante for two clarinets, by Messrs. Beranger and Lullier
A Concerto on the Violoncello, by Mr. Menel
A Concerto on the Pianoforte, by Mr. Guenin
A Song by Mrs. Oldmixon

ACT II

A Grand Symphony
A Concerto on the Violin, by Mr. Gillingham
A Favourite Song, by Mrs. Oldmixon
A Medley on the Pianoforte, by Mr. Guenin
A Full piece.

A few weeks later, on April 7th[2]), Mr. Collet presented for his benefit this rather formidable program:

ACT I

Symphony of Haydn
Quartetto of Pleyel, by Messrs. Gillingham, Collet, Thibaut and Menel.
Concerto of Signor Fodor, on the violin, by Mr. Collet
Concerto on the Fortepiano, by Mr. Guenin
Overture of the Two Guardians

ACT II

Overture du Barbier de Seville del Signior Paisiello
Concerto on the Violoncello, by Mr. Menel
Symphony of Krumpholz on the harp, by Mr. Mechtler
Duette of Jarnowick for the violoncello, by Messrs. Collet and Menel
A Full Piece

All these concerts of vocal and instrumental music were of a rather miscellaneous character and John Christopher Moller frankly acknowledged this tendency by calling the "grand" concert to be held at Oeller's Hotel on May 5th (postponed from April 14th)[3]) a "miscellaneous" concert. Now, Moller was a specialist on the Armonica, then no longer quite so fashionable as twenty years previous and he readily seized the opportunity to "introduce that instrument ... of which the late Dr. Franklin was the inventor" and, said Mr. Moller

---

1) Daily American Adv., March 3, 1795.
2) Philadelphia Gazette, April 1, 1795.
3) Philadelphia Gazette, April 3 and May 1, 1795.

"This instrument since so much improved in Europe by the first artists[1]) is, in point of tone and sweet harmony, second to none and in performance of modulation from which it derives its name, not excelled by any other."

This the audience had an occasion to judge for themselves as Moller introduced it on the program not only as a solo but also as an ensemble instrument.

Act I

Overture	Haydn
Song, arranged for the Harmonica by	Moller
Quintetto	Pleyel
Concerto Violin	Gillingham
Full Piece	Pleyel

Act II

Overture	Pleyel
Quartetto, Harmonica, 2 tenors, and violoncello by	Moller
· Concerto Violoncello	Manell [Menel]
Fantasia Pianoforte	Moller
Finale	Haydn

This miscellaneous concert was followed on July 2d[2]) by the still more "miscellaneous entertainment" for the benefit of Mrs. Oldmixon. It was to consist of

"Readings by Messrs. Chalmers and Harwood, Songs, Duets, Catches and Glees, by Mrs. Oldmixon, Miss Broadhurst, Mrs. Darley, Mr. Marshall, Mr. Shaw, Mr. Gillingham, Mr. Darley, Mr. Darley, jun. etc.
A Concerto on the Violoncello by Mr. Menel
Other interesting music. Leader of the band, Mr. Gillingham".

Apparently this sort of entertainment at which almost all the principal members of Wignell and Reinagle's New Theatre company assisted, pleased the public as several other similar affairs rapidly followed, for instance on July 20th and July 22d by Mr. Bates

"by way of an evening lounge, a species of entertainment . . . called Fashionable Variety, or, a Touch at the Times . . ."

If this fashionable variety was not intended as a concert, the "miscellaneous entertainment of readings and music" for the benefit of Miss Broadhurst on July 8[3]) had at least the appearance of a glee-concert:

Part. I. Overture Pleyel — Glee 'Come all noble souls' (Dr. Roger's) Miss Broadhurst, Mrs. Oldmixon, Mr. Darley, Mr. Marshall, Mr. Gillingham and Mr. Shaw — Duet 'The Way worn traveller', Miss Broadhurst, and Mrs. Oldmixon — 'Recitation, Mr. Moreton. Catch 'Mr. Spanker', accompanied on the violin by Mr. Gillingham, Miss Broadhurst — Catch 'The Cries of Durham', by desire, Mr. Darley, Mr. Marshall, Mr. Shaw, Mr. Gillingham, and Mr. Darley, jun. — Full piece, Haydn. Leader of the band, Mr. Gillingham. Conductor. Mr. Reinagle.

---

1) Röllig, Klein, Wagner, etc., and in America by Francis Hopkinson.
2) American Daily Adv. June 30, 1795.
3) American Daily Adv., July 8, 1795.

The program of the last concert of 1795, for the benefit of Mr. Gautier, at Oeller's Hotel on Dec. 1st[1]) is in so far noticeable, as pains were taken to distinguish in the concerto-numbers the composers from the performers:

1st Act.

The famous Overture of Demophon[2])
Jarnovick's concerto on the violin, performed by   Mr. Collet
A Sonata of Pleyel, on the Pianoforte, by   ..   Mrs. Sully
An Allegretto of Paisiello
A Concerto of the Clarinet, composed and exe-
cuted by   .. ..   Mr. Gautier

2d Act.

The Overture of Rose et Colas[3])
A Concerto of Vanhall, performed on the Piano-
forte by .. ..   Mrs. Sully
A Song by .. ..   Madame Larne
Concert on the Clarinet, composed by Mr. Lefevre
and executed by   .. ..   Mr. Gautier

The first benefit concert in 1796 was also the most important, at least historically. It was to be for Raynor Taylor's benefit who also conducted, that is to say, presided at the harpsichord and "held" the "vocal parts" with Miss Huntley at Oeller's Hotel on April 21[4]). A "band of the most eminent instrumental performers" had been engaged, presumably supplemented, as was customary, in the string group by amateurs. Now the importance of the announcement of this particular concert lies in the fact that it gave the composition of the band as follows:

First violin and leader of the band.. .. ..   Mr. Gillingham
Principal violoncellos .. ..   Mr. Menel
Double bass   .. ..   Mr. Demarque
Principal hautboy .. ..   Mr. Shaw
Tenor   .. ..   Mr. Berenger
Bassoon and trumpet .. ..   Mr. Priest
Horns   .. ..   Messrs. Grey and Homman
Violins .. ..   Messrs. Dongel[5]), Bouchony,
                                      Stewart and Shetky.

This was the *concertino*, the *ripieno*, of course, not being mentioned. Consequently the band was the full band of the times, clarinets missing, though to be had, simply because the program did not necessarily call for them. That Mr. Priest held both the principal bassoon and trumpet parts, may seem odd, but if he was supposed to do so, it must have been possible and this exchange of instruments was not at all unusual in those days.

---

1) American Daily Adv., Nov. 30, 1795.
2) Cherubini.
3) Monsigny.
4) Philadelphia Gazette, April 9 and 18, 1796.   5) Daugel.

Therefore the band contained thirteen "eminent" performers as principals
to which the *seconds* should be added and also a number of amateurs for
the *ripieno* strings and possibly for the flutes it such were needed. With
this orchestra, dwarfish if compared with modern monstre orchestras but
not dwarfish if compared with the average orchestra of that age, Raynor
Taylor executed a program consisting half of Haendelian music and half of
his own:

PART I

Overture.
Duet 'Fair Aurora', Artaxerxes — Miss Huntley and R. Taylor	Arne
Song 'To-morrow'	Taylor
Overture, Samson	Handel
Trumpet song, Miss Huntley (Trumpet by Mr. Priest)	Taylor
Concerto Hautboy	Mr. Shaw
Duet 'O lovely Peace' Miss Huntley and R. Taylor	Handel
March, Judas Maccabäus'	Handel

PART II

New Overture.
Song 'Amyntor', Miss Huntley	Taylor
Concerto Violin, Mr. Gillingham	,,
Song 'I wonder at you', Taylor	,,
Divertimento	,,
Cantata 'The Nightingale', Miss Huntley, Bird accompaniment on the flageolet by Mr. Shaw	,,
Finale, 'Spring', or 'Mirth and Innocent festivity', Miss Huntley and R. Taylor	,,

It is to be regretted that we possess no contemporary report of the impression made by Taylor's compositions on a public conversant with the
"modern" repertory of that period. The more so, as these more pretentious
works of his are lost and only a few insignificant songs remain which really
do not permit of gauging his talents as a composer. It is also a fact that
exceedingly few other American concert-programs mention his name and
perhaps the neglect of his works was the reason why Raynor Taylor risked
a concert consisting mainly of his own works.

The next concert, at least as far as I found it — a *reservatio mentalis*
which the reader is requested to constantly keep in mind — was a concert,
of course a *grand* concert, of vocal and instrumental music for the benefit
of Mrs. Sully and Mr. Gaultier at Oeller's Hotel on April 26th[1]) with this
rather miscellaneous program:

1st ACT

A celebrated Overture of Demophon[2])
    'The Soldier tired' by Mrs. Oldmixon
A Sonata of Pleyel, on the Pianoforte, by Mrs. Sully
    'Auld Robin Gray', by Mr. Marshall, composed by Mr. Reeve.

---

1) Philadelphia Gazette, April 25, 1796.
2) Probably either Cherubini or Vogel.

A favorite Scotch air, with variations on the pianoforte, by Mrs. Sully
'The Galley slave', by Mrs. Marshall
A Concerto on the Clarinet, composed by Mr. Gaultier and performed by himself.

2d ACT.

A grand Overture of Iphigenie in Aulide[1])
'Amid a thousand sighing silvains', by Mrs. Marshall — Hook.
A Concerto of Harman on the pianoforte, Mr. Sully
A Song, composed by Giordani, by Mrs. Oldmixon
'Tis beauty commands me', by Mr. Marshall
A Concerto on the clarinet, composed by Mr. Lefevre, and performed by Mr. Gaultier.

Then on July 5th[2]), Mr. Louis Boullay "hoped for the patronage" of his friends and "all amateurs of music". As a special attraction he offered "the whole orchestra of the New Theatre and several of the lovers of music", which bears out what was said of the band for Raynor Taylor's benefit. Boullay presented in

ACT I

Grand Overture	Haydn
Song	Miss Solomon
Concerto Clarinet	Mr. Wolf
Sea Song by Shield	Mr. Marshall
Quintette of Ponto [Punto] executed by Mr. Rosier, accompanied by Mr. Boullay, Mr. Beranger, Mr. Homen and Mr. De Marque	
Grand Symphony	Haydn

ACT II

Symphonie	Haydn
New Song with accompaniments on the clarinet, Mr. Wolf	Mrs. Marshall
Concerto on the Violin	Mr. Boullay
New Song	Mrs. Warrell
Concerto on the Violin	Mr. De Marque
Bravoura Song, with variations on the violin composed by Mr. Boullay	Mr. Darley
A humorous vocal parody on Shakespeare's Seven ages, Mr. Bates	
To conclude with a grand finale	Gluck.

To avoid confusion, it may be remarked that this appears to have been his final program, Punto's quintet having being substituted for the comic song 'John loves Jean and Jean loves John' as announced in previous advertisements.

The remaining years of the century brought a very noticeable decrease in the number of benefit concerts for the reasons mentioned. This is particularly true of the year 1797. We notice towards the end of the year a series

1) Probably Gluck.
2) Philadelphia Gazette, June 15, 1796.

of readings and recitations, called 'the Tablet, or Just in time', given with the assistance of Benjamin Carr, who played overtures, sonatas and potpourris, by Messrs. Chalmers and Williamson who sang such songs as 'Jacky and the Cow', 'The tar of all weathers' and 'Nancy, or the Sailor's journal' but of legitimate concerts very few only seem to have taken place. At any rate, I found only the one given on Jan. 9th[1]) at Oeller's Hotel for the benefit of Mr. Guenin with this rather indifferent program, the first and last number excepted:

ACT THE 1st.

A grand Overture, composed by Haydn
A Song, by Mrs. Warrell
A Symphony concertante, by Mr. Gillingham and Mr. Menel
A Song by Mrs. Warrell
A Concerto on the piano, by Mr. Guenin.

ACT THE 2d.

A concerto on the violoncello, by Mr. Menel
A Medley on the piano, by Mr. Guenin
A Concerto on the Violin, by Mr. Gillingham
A Song by Mrs. Warrell
And the celebrated Overture of Iphigenie[2]).

By March, 1798 little Susanne D'Hemard having, as we know, "been the admiration of the principal cities on the continent" where "her execution of the most difficult pieces of music, for judgment, taste and decision" were considered "uncommon" arrived in Philadelphia and immediately her mother or who ever managed her concerts, announced a benefit for this young lady "aged 6 years" for March 19th[3]) at Oeller's Great Room:

ACT I

1. A Symphony, accompanied by a grand orchestra of .. .. Heyden
2. Overture of Blaise et Babie [!][4]) on the piano by Miss D'Hemard
3. Lucy, a ballad .. .. Mrs. Grattan
4. Concerto on the Clarinet .. .. Mr. Dubois
5. Favorite Sonata of Nicholais [!] on the piano Miss D'Hemard
6. Ah! Nonai (Tachini) [!] .. .. Mrs. Grattan

ACT II

1. Overture with a grand orchestra .. .. .. Pleyel
2. Ballad by Heyden .. .. Mrs. Grattan
3. Battle of Prague on the piano .. .. Miss D'Hemard
4. The Trios of Rousseau, executed by Messrs. Yanda, Collet and Boucheny
5. Pantiro (Tachini) .. .. Mrs. Grattan

1) Philadelphia Gazette, Jan. 9, 1797.
2) Probably Gluck.
3) Porcupine's Gazette, March 12, 1798.
4) Blaise et Babette, opera by Dezède.

10*

6. Several Airs, with variations by Pleyel on the
   the piano, and several other favorite airs in
   French and English .. .. Miss D'Hemard
7. The Concert will be concluded with several
   much admired airs on the French horn and
   clarinet by .. .. Messrs. Coliot [Collet] and Dubois.

It is interesting to note that about the very year when 'Hail Columbia'
was written and when the estrangement between the United States and
France had reached so acute a stage that George Washington offered to
emerge from Mount Vernon and again become the first in war as he had
been in times of peace, almost all the benefit concerts were given by French
emigrants.   May-be they could rely only on the support of music-lovers
among the Anti-Federalists and probably they did not reep such harvests
as five or six years previous when the French refugees were received with
open arms, still, it is remarkable that they could dare appeal to a public
which partly had learned to hate the very sight of a Frenchman.   That
this same public entertained less passionate sentiments against artists, a
cosmopolitan folk after all, is very plausible since these concerts were given
with orchestras and necessarily entailed expenses not easily covered by
thin audiences.   Just when the excitement ran highest, Mr. Dubois offered
a benefit concert, on April 24th[1]) and presumably the fact did jar on the
sentiments of those narrow-minded people who love to carry politics
into art.

ACT I

Symphony	Haydn
Symphonie concertante for two clarinets —Pleyel—	Messrs. Dubois and Beranger
Song 'While successful proves the gale'	Mr. Marshall
Concerto Violoncello — Duport	Mr. Menel
Song 'Fragrant chaplete' [!] — Salieri	Mrs. Marshall

ACT II

Overture to Alexis and Justine	Grétry
Concerto Pianoforte — Pleyel	Mr. Guenin
Song 'This beauty commands me, my heart must obey'	Mr. Marshall
Concerto Clarinet — Michel	Mr. Dubois
Song 'Amidst the illusions' — Shield	Mrs. Marshall
To conclude with Kotzwara's 'Battle of Prague', arranged for a full band by	Schetky

Strikingly different in character was the program of the very popular
singer Miss Broadhurst on her benefit night at Oeller's Hotel, December 11th:

---

1) Porcupine's Gazette, April 21, 1798.
2) Porcupine's Gazette, Dec. 1, 1798.

Act I

Overture	
Song 'Ellen arise'	Miss Broadhurst
Quartette	
Song	Mr. Darley
Duet — Violin and clarinet	Messrs. Collet et Dubois
Italian [song] — i non piange [!]..	Miss Broadhurst

Part II

Overture	
Song "The new somebody", composed by B. Carr	Miss Broadhurst
Sonata, Pianoforte	Mr. B. Carr
Song	Mr. Darley
Concerto Clarinet	Mr. Dubois
New song 'The Flower girl'	Miss Broadhurst
Glee, three voices, 'Sigh no more ladies'.	

For 1799 I traced only three benefit concerts but all three show the strange fascination which in those days Kotzwara's insipid 'Battle of Prague' in the orchestral arrangement by Schetky must have exercised upon the public, a popularity, however, shared temporarily by Chateaudieu's Medley overture with the President's March (a reminder of 'Hail Columbia') as ingredient. The three programs though they did not enlarge the repertory may follow as a matter of record.

Mr. Dubois offered on February 26, 1799[1]) at Oeller's Hotel in

1st Part

Overture of Iphigenie	Gluck
Song	Mr. Marshall
Concerto Flute, Devienne	Mr. Declang
Song	Mrs. Marshall
Concerto Violin	Mr. Gillingham

2d Part

Medley Overture, with variations, in which is introduced the favourite air of the President's March	Mr. Chateaudieu
Grand ariette from L'Amant Statue[2]), arranged for two clarinets, two French horns and two bassoons. The principal part executed by	Mr. Dubois
Concerto Pianoforte	Mr. Guenin
Song	Mrs. Marshall
Concerto Clarinet, Michel	Mr. Dubois
To conclude with the Battle of Prague arranged for a full band by	Shetky

The music will be conducted by Mr. Gillingham. After the Concert a Grand Ball.

Then came Mr. Louis Boullay on March 25th[3]) with his "Grand concert vocal & instrumental" and it is very doubtful whether any other paper

1) Bache's Aurora, February 19, 1799.
2) Dalayrac.
3 Bache's Aurora, March 2, 12, 15, 1799. The concert was postponed from March 12 to March 16 and then to March 25 "on account of the performance at the theatre".

except Bache's Aurora would have dared to insert, as was done, Boullay's original announcement in French[1]), though party feelings for and against France no longer ran as high as in 1798. Mr. Boullay "a l'honneur de prevenir les amateurs de musique que son concert est fixé pour le 12 Mars prochain", we read but, as if to off set any indignant criticism, immediately below the appeal is translated into English and the program, too, is given in English!

Overture
A Song 'The Galley slave', by a young lady six
    years old[2])
Duett, by Messrs. Boullay and Dubois .. ..   Michel
Concerto (violin) by Mr. Boullay .. .. Giarnowick
Medley overture, in which is introduced the
    favorite air of the President's March .. .. Mr. Chateaudun[3])
Song, by Miss Corry .. .. Storace
Variations on the violin .. .. Mr. Boullay
Ariette
Concerto Clarinet, Mr. Dubois .. .. Michel
Full piece, Battle of Prague .. .. Schetky

It will have been noticed that during the last years of the eighteenth century gradually more care was taken to distinguish the composers from the performers. "The band, late of the New Theatre", however, when announcing a benefit at Oeller's Hotel for April 11th[4]) somewhat relapsed into the former habit of not making the distinction, a habit so unmindful of historians and bibliographers:

FIRST PART

Overture to Henry IV[5])
Symphony concertante for two clarinets —
    Messrs. Dubois and Wolfe — .. .. .. Pleyel
Canzonet 'My mother bids me', accompanied by
    Mr. Guenin on the Pianoforte .. .. .. Miss Broadhurst
Concerto Violin — Giarnowick .. .. .. Mr. Collet

SECOND PART.

Medley Overture .. .. Mr. Chateaudun
Concerto Pianoforte .. .. Mr. Guenin
Song 'Spirit of the Blest', accompanied on the
    Clarinet by Mr. Wolfe .. .. Miss Broadhurst
Concerto Clarinet .. .. Mr. Dubois
To conclude with the Battle of Prague. Arranged
    for a full band by .. .. Schetky
  ... The ball to commence immediately after the concert.

---

1) About 1790 it was quite customary, especially in Maryland, to insert advertisements in French.
2) If this was Miss D'Hemard, the young lady began surprisingly early to hide her age.
3) The name is spelled in different ways, and it is difficult to ascertain the correct spelling. I incline to Chateaudieu.
4) Bache's Aurora, April 9, 1799.
5) Martini.

The nineteenth century possibly was ushered in by Miss Broadhurst's benefit concert at the City Tavern on April 3, 1800[1]) with a bewildering array of vocal talent. The program was in keeping, being perhaps the most miscellaneous ever offered to the public of Philadelphia:

PART FIRST.

Overture	Haydn
Glee, 3 voices, 'Ask why a blush'	Taylor
Duet 'How sweet is the morning' (Carr)	Mr. Carr and Miss Broadhurst
Song 'When war begins' (Shield)	Mr. Darley
Recitation 'Mrs. Thrale's three warnings'..	Mr. Bernard
Song 'Primroses deck' (Linley)	Mr. Warrel
Concerto Violin	Mr. Gillingham
Song 'Let me wander etc. or let the merry bells'	Miss Broadhurst
Chorus 'And you and old come forth to play'	Handel

PART SECOND

Overture, Circe and Ulisses	Taylor
Song 'Pity then my tortured heart' (Giordani)	Miss Oldmixon
Duet 'Together let us range' (Dr. Boyce)	Mr. Taylor and Miss Broadhurst
Recitation. A dramatic vision of the court of Thespia	Mr. Bernard
Song 'The spirits of the blest' (Carr)	Miss Broadhurst
Sonata Pianoforte	Mr. Reinagle
Comic song 'I wonder at you' (Taylor) ..	Mr. Taylor
Comic glee 'Wives and husbands'	Hook.

Finally may be mentioned Mrs. M'Donald's benefit at the 'Centre House Gardens' on August 11th[2]). The program arouses interest merely for the fact that it allowed an ample display of "martial music", that is to say of so called band music which gradually and owing to general conditions grew on the average American as no other instrumental combination could and the stimulating, educational influence of which should not be underestimated in a future comprehensive history of music in America:

PART I.

Overture	by Pleyel
Duet 'How sweet in the Woodlands', Mrs. M'Donald and Mr. Devis (for that night only)	
Martial music by the band	
Song 'Be quiet, for I'm in haste'	Mrs. M'Donald
Overture	Bache [!]
Song 'Lash'd to the helm'	Mr. Devis
Overture	Arne

---

1) General Advertiser, March 31, 1800.
2) General Advertiser, Aug. 11, 1800.

PART II.

Overture	Haydn
Song 'Two bunches a penny, primroses ..	Mrs. M'Donald
Martial music, by the band	
Song 'Saturday night at sea'	Mr. Devis
Comic song (for that night only)	Mr. Rowson
Martial music by the band	
Duet 'Rise, Cynthia rise'	Mrs. M'Donald and Mr. Devis.

To complete the record of concerts given at Philadelphia before the nineteenth century we must retrace our steps to the years immediately following the war when the concert life of the Quaker City seemed full of promises subsequently not quite fulfilled. It was the period when theatrical performances were under ban of law. Pennsylvania, by adopting a recommendation of Congress in 1778, had probited them altogether and this law remained in force until 1789 when, thanks to the energetic propaganda of the Dramatic Association founded in January 1789, it was repealed[1]).

To pass such a narrow-minded law is easy enough but to enforce it is quite a different matter, especially if distasteful to a powerful minority. Consequently when Mr. Henry and Mr. Hallam, first separate and then in partnership, attempted a revival of the American Company of Comedians after the war, they found a strong support in this minority who feared no ruin of public morals from the theatre. Of course, the managers could not openly oppose the law but this law, like all laws, had its loop-holes and hence they found no difficulty in evading it. It was merely a matter of disguise and to the frequenters of the theatre it made precious little difference whether plays were announced as 'Lectures, moral and entertaining', 'Lectures being ... entertainments of representation and harmony', as 'Spectaculum vitae' or what not as long as the legislaters were duped. How the managers gradually felt their way until they boldly came out with regular theatrical performances under the most ludicrous disguises concerns us in this volume in so far only as their efforts contributed to the development of a concert life at Philadelphia.

From the beginning of this amusing crusade against the Philistines the 'Lectures', etc. "were properly diversified with music, scenery, and other decorations"[2]), and from this to the use of such an innocent looking title as 'Concerts' was but a short step. That music has charms to soothe the savage breast even of lawmakers, Messrs. Hallam and Henry experienced when their performances of operas as operas did not worry the watchful eye of the authorities and they, as wise men, preferred to call their theatre

---

1) For further particulars see the second volume of George O. Seilhamer's monumental History of the American Theatre, 1896.

2) Pa. Packet, April 10, 1784.

located in the Southwark, an Opera House. Thus it came to pass that the popular plays of the time were given at an Opera House incidental to concerts. One example will suffice to illustrate how ingeniously and amusingly the trick was turned. For instance, we find in the Pennsylvania Journal, June 21, 1788 this announcement:

OPERA HOUSE, SOUTHWARK.

On Monday the 23d of June, will be presented a *Concert*, between the parts of which will be delivered (gratis). A Comic Lecture in five parts, on the disadvantage of Improper Education exemplified in the *History of Tony Lulmkin*.

It seems that some persons interpreted the gratis very much to their own advantage for the managers on September 17 took occasion to remark that

"the ... lectures will be delivered (gratis) paying only for admission to a *Concert*".

That these concerts were merely sham-concerts goes without saying and it is even doubtful whether more pieces were played than when music was merely used to lessen the *ennui* of the audience between the acts. The whole arrangement simply resolved itself into this that the "Zwischenakts-musik", so absurdly dear to Americans, was promoted to the official *raison d'être* of the entertainments with the plays ostensibly as incidental, generous supplements. As a rule, this undoubtedly was true, but occasionally the music appears to have assumed the scope of a real concert. Again one program will be sufficient to illustrate the point. On January 13th, the Pennsylvania Packet announced for the same evening.

A CONCERT OF MUSIC.

Vocal and instrumental: Between the several parts of the concert will be delivered, *Lectures*, Moral and entertaining

FIRST ACT

Symphony	Kammel
Rondeau	Mr. Phile
Prologue and Lectures	

SECOND ACT.

Song	Mr. Wools
Lecture	
Song	Mr. Harper
Overture	Ditters
Fisher's minuet, Clarinet	Mr. Wolfe

The whole to conclude with a grand pantomimical finale in two acts, called *Robinson Crusoe.*

It may be doubted if these sham-concerts contributed perceptibly to the development of Philadelphia's concert life. This certainly was not the object of the managers who, as soon as the repeal of the anti-theatre law became effective, immediately threw off the disguise and discontinued the practice of giving concerts at the theatre. It never seems to have entered their mind that this practice might be made profitable in imitation of the custom then and still prevailing in European countries. In fact, not until 1793 were concerts again given at a theatre and then merely as a matter of expedience and necessity, though, of course, no longer in evasion of pedantic laws.

Differences had arisen in 1791 between Hallam and Henry, the managers of the Old American Company and Thomas Wignell. This actor then interested moneyed people in plans for a 'New Theatre' to be built in Chestnut-street with the result that a stock company was formed with Wignell and Alexander Reinagle as artistic managers. The erection of the house proceeded rapidly. It was "allowed by judges to be, in elegance and convenience equal to most and superior to many in Europe" and it was "computed that it would, with perfect convenience, hold 2000 people, or about 600 pounds"[1]). Naturally, expectations ran high and the stockholders, as stockholders will do, became impatient especially after they had received in January, 1793[2]) an opportunity to see the not quite completed interior modelled after the theatre Royal at Bath. Presumably because these gentlemen were so anxious to see their investments bring substantial returns at the earliest possible date, Alexander Reinagle decided to open the New Theatre with a series of three public concerts with the band and such members of the company as were already available. These concerts took place on February 2, 4 and 7, 1793. The programs of the first and last will show them to have been somewhat on the order of what we call to-day popular concerts, though the contemporary announcements styled them "grand". The Plan of the Concert on February 2d was this:[3])

ACT I

New Overture	Mr. Reinagle
Song 'On by the spur of valeur'	Mr. Chambers
Concerto Violin	Mr. Boullay
Song 'Kiss me now or never'	Mrs. Morris
Quartetto des petits airs Messrs. Petit, Boullay, Mallet	and Gehot
Song 'Poor Tom Bowling'	Mr. Harper
Sonata Piano	Mr. Reinagle
Glee 'Sigh no more ladies'	Messrs. Chambers, Harper and Reinagle.

ACT II

Grand Overture	Haydn
Italian Song	Mr. Mallet
Sonata, Pianoforte	Mr. Guenin
Song 'My Poll and my partner Joe'	Mr. Harper

---

1) Federal Gazette, Jan. 29, 1793.
2) Federal Gazette, Jan. 28, 1793.
3) Dunlap's Daily American Advertiser, Jan. 2 and 7, 1793 and Federal Gazette, Feb. 2, 1793.

Sonata, Harp	Mr. Salomon
Song, 'A Smile from the girl of my heart'	Mr. Chambers
Sinfonia concertante	Messrs. Petit and Boullay

ACT III

Sinfonia	Stamitz
Song 'Blythe Collin'	Mrs. Morris
Concerto Violin	Mr. Petit
Song 'Cottage Boy'	Mr. Chambers
Glee 'How merrily we live' ..	Messrs. Chambers, Harper and Reinagle

Between the first and second act, a Dance, in the character of Harlequin, by Master Duport. To conclude with a *Grand Dance*, called 'La Noble, or Henry the Fourth, by Master Duport.

The doors to be opened at 6, and the performance to begin precisely at 7 o'clock. Places to be taken and tickets to be had at the theatre every day from 10 till 5 o'clock. Boxes 7 *s* 6. Pit 5 *s*. 7¹/₂. Gallery 3 *s* 9.

For Februar 7th the program read:

ACT I.

Grand Overture	Haydn
Song	Mr. Chambers
Concerto Violin	Master Duport
Duetto, for two voices	Mrs. Morris and Mr. Reinagle
Hunting song 'While over the mountain's brow'	Mr. Harper
Sonata Pianoforte	Mr. Reinagle
Glee 'Lightly tread, 'tis hallow'd ground'	Messrs. Chambers, Harper and Reinagle.

ACT II.

Quartetto (Pleyel)	Messrs. Petit, Boullay, Mallet and Gehot
Duetto, 'From Morn till night'	Messrs. Chambers and Reinagle
Concerto Clarinet	Mr. Foucard
Song 'Poor Tom Bowling'	Mr. Harper, Chambers and Reinagle

ACT III.

Overture	Mr. Reinagle
Song 'Wives and sweet hearts' ..	Mr. Harper
Concerto Violin ˜..	Mr. Petit
Song 'The Traveller benighted'	Mrs. Morris
Finale	Stamitz

It would have been surprising, had the opening of the New Theatre passed without receiving attention from the press and Mr. Seilhamer was mistaken if he claimed this to have been the case. As a matter of fact, the Federal Gazette printed on Feb. 4, 1793 a detailed description of the theatre and then added this rather primitive criticism of the concert:

Last Saturday evening it was first opened to the public with a grand Concert of vocal and instrumental music and notwithstanding the inclemency of the evening, a large number of citizens appeared in every part of the house — the boxes exhibited a blaze of beauty — the pit was a display of respectable jugdes and the gallery was filled with orderly, well disposed citizens whose decency of behaviour deserves the greatest applause.

Mr. Reinagle introduced the evening's entertainment with a charming overture on the harpsichord[1]) — after which Mr. Chambers' 'On by the spur of valeur', 'Sigh no more ladies' and 'the Cottage boy etc.' gave great satisfaction. Messrs. Boulay, Mallet and Guenin's performances on the violin were exquisite and Mr. Saloman's Sonata on the harp gave infinite pleasure. But of all others that part of the entertainment, wherein Mrs. Morris' abilities in 'Kiss me now or never' and Master Duport's dancing came in, seemed to afford the most attractingly delightful sensations. — Indeed upon the whole, this theatre may be esteemed a place of the most rational amusement that have ever been exhibited to the attention and protection of the public in these United States.

After these concerts the theatre remained closed until re-opened on February 17, 1794 with a performance of Shield's opera 'Castle of Andalusia' and Mrs. Cowley's comedy 'Who's the dupe'.

The musical life of Pennsylvania outside of Philadelphia was exceedingly primitive and remained so, far into the nineteenth century. To be sure, in the Swedish and German settlements church music made part of the service and these settlers, as a matter of course, brought their nursery songs, folk songs, fiddles, German flutes etc. with them, in short musical instincts and interests, but all this did not go far towards creating a musical life and a few stray concerts, as for instance that "held in the Swedish Church on Darbyroad, six miles from the city" on Oct. 9, 1788[2]) consisting of vocal and instrumental music "with an oration on Civic Liberty" or the three concerts given during the summer of 1794 by a "small but select" band with the singers Darley and Miss Broadhurst as soloists at Lancaster, are not of much account[3]). It would particularly be out of place in tracing secular music to examine that exotic musical weed reared by Conrad Beissel and his associate mystics at the Ephrata cloister. It was a curiosity at its best and exercised no influence on the development of music in Pennsylvania.

Only in one settlement outside of Philadelphia flourished anything like a musical life and there the love of music was so deeply rooted as to make the town in course of time the center of the American Bach cult. When founding Bethlehem in 1741 the Moravian Brethren brought with them

---

1) Of course, Reinagle conducted this overture from the harpsichord, a procedure which our amateur-critic seems to have considered a solo.

2) Federal Gazette, Oct. 7, 1788.

3) See 'Travels in the United States of America, commencing in the year 1793, and ending in 1797 . . . by William Priest, musician late of the theatres Philadelphia, Baltimore and Boston', London .1802. (This scarce book, by the way, deals with a general description of America and contains next to nothing of interest to the musical historian.) Perhaps I have underestimated the musical importance of Lancaster in those days, for it is a fact that a music dealer by the name of Hutter had a sufficient demand for German music to enter into business relations with Breitkopf & Haertel of Leipzig as early as 1799 or 1800. Thus the famous firm invaded America more than a century ago as a perusal of their archives, courteously undertaken at my request, proved to their and my surprise.

from Germany a natural love of music and this love has ever since remained
an inheritance jealously guarded by both sexes. The settlement soon became famous for its musical athmosphere. Franklin, Washington, Samuel
Adams and other prominent men of Colonial Times when visiting Bethlehem
were deeply impressed by this musical athmosphere and their diaries and
letters vividly testify to this impression. But whereas in Philadelphia,
Charleston, New York and Boston the musical life was mainly an offspring
from English conditions, the German influence predominated in this and
other Moravian settlements. Furthermore, while the fame of Bethlehem's
music soon spread, her musical life never exercised a noteworthy influence
beyond her own bounderies. Within however, music brought joy and con-
tentment to young and old, music dwelled in the houses, in the church and
in the fields among the toilers, in short was essential to the daily life of
these sturdy people. This cannot be doubted if one reads Rufus A. Grider's
'Historical Notes on music in Bethlehem, Pennsylvania. From 1741 to
1871' (Philadelphia, 1873). Unfortunately this valuable book, possibly for
lack of authentic documents and traditions, rapidly passes over the more
secular aspect of the musical life of Bethlehem during the eighteenth century.
However, we are told that shortly after the foundation, and before 1750,
a Collegium Musicum was formed which existed for many years. Though
the members of the Collegium assisted in the weekly serenades ending oddily
enough in the graveyard with the improvised singing of hymn-tunes, it goes
without saying that the club, if it deserved its name at all, cultivated secular
music at least as much as sacred and if the orchestral parts to works by
Alberti and others as preserved in the library of the Philharmonie Society
originally belonged to the Collegium Musicum we need no further corroboration of this opinion. The very name would imply, by way of analogy with
conditions in Germany, informal gatherings of the active and associate
members of the club at regular intervals when they would form or deepen
acquaintance with orchestral, concerted or solo chamber music. In short,
amateur-concerts without pretensions as to perfect rendition but covering
a wide range of the best music of the age[1].

---

1) It would be interesting to know if the orchestra at Bethlehem was composed
of both sexes as at Herrnhut, where, as Busby says in his 'Concert room and orchestra
anecdotes', 1825, in the band of 40 or 50 persons the ladies played the violin, violoncello, flute and other instruments as well as the men, from whom, however, they sat
strictly separated!

NEW YORK [1].

In tracing the beginning of a concert-life in New York, the historian is compelled to again call attention to the scarcity of sources and hence to the limited reliability of his statements. Though William Bradford's New York Gazette appeared in 1725, the first eight years of this paper are practically of no assistance to us as only very few numbers have been preserved. We would rather miss a few numbers after Zenger's New York Weekly Journal appeared in November 1733 than be helpless for the years 1725 to 1733 for, even if no *consorts* were given before 1725 the non-existence (for all practical purposes) of the Gazette during those years would leave it open to doubt whether the first concert announced in the existing files was really the first. This concert took place in 1736 unless earlier advertisements escaped my attention, a sin of omission for which no person who has handled our old newspapers, will condemn me too severely. Still, the concert announced in 1736 cannot have been the first as becomes apparent from a poem printed among the *local* news of the Gazette, December 24—31, 1733:

> *Written at a Concert* of Music where there was a great Number of Ladies.
> Music has Power to melt the Soul:
> By Beauty Nature's sway'd
> Each can the Universe controul
> Without the other's Aid:
> But here together both appear
> And Force united try
> *Music* inchants the listning Ear
> And *Beauty* charms the Eye.
> What cruelty these Powers to join!
> These transports who can beat!
> Oh! Let the Sound be less divine
> Or look, ye Nymphs, less fair. [!]

The name of the musician for whose benefit the concert of 1736 was advertised is familiar to the reader: Charles Theodore Pachelbel who by the year 1737 drifted as far South as Charleston. He advertised in the

---

[1] Population: 1731—8628; 1773—21876; 1790—33131; 1800—60489 inhabitants

New York Gazette, Jan. 6—13, 1736 and in the Weekly Journal on "Monday", Jan. 12th:

> On Wednesday the 21. of January Instant there will be a *Consort* of Musick, Vocal and Instrumental for the Benefit of Mr. Pachelbell, the Harpsichord Part performed by himself. The Songs, Violins and German Flutes by private Hands.
> The Consort will begin precisely at 6 o'clock in the House of Robert Todd, Vintner. Tickets to be had at the Coffee House and at Mr. Tood's at 4 Shillings.

He used almost literally the same form of advertisement in the Weekly Journal, March 8, 1736 for a concert on the following day. Either Mr. Pachelbel believed in mental economy or he found himself obliged to postpone the January concert.

Strange to say, there occurs a gap of about eight years between these two concerts and the next. This may be explained in three different ways. Either others escaped me, or none were given, or they were given but the newspapers had not yet come to be considered an equally effective advertising medium as the street-crier or the house-to-house distribution of irresistible broadsides. At any rate, 1 did not trace a further concert until the New York Weekly Post Boy announced on Dec. 31, 1744 a concert of vocal and instrumental music for the benefit of Mr. John Rice, the organist of Trinity Church[1]), on Wednesday, Jan. 2, 1745 at Robert Todd's house. Tickets at five shillings each were to be had at *both* coffee-houses — evidently New York was fast becoming a metropolis — and the concert was to begin at the rather unusual hour of five o'clock. Of the program nothing is said.

Then came another long gap of five years, when a Mr. Quin gave a concert on Oct. 19, 1749[2]), at the Court Room of the City Hall. Again several years elapsed without any of the musicians who permanently or temporarily settled at New York appearing to have risked a benefit. Then Charles Love, the harpsichordist in Hallam's theatrical company which came to New York in 1753 and whose wife was prominent as ballad opera singer in the same company, advertised a concert during the summer. The entertainment, however, did not take place until the following January as appears from an advertisement in the New York Mercury 1754:

> For the benefit of Mr. Charles Love, at the New Exchange Ball Room, on Thursday the 24th instant, will be a *Concert* of vocal and instrumental Musick. To which will be added several select pieces on the hautboy, by Mr. Love. After the concert will be a *Ball*. Tickets at 5 s each, to be head of Mr. Love; at the King's Arms; and at Parker's and Gaine's printing office. Tickets given out last summer by Mr. Love, will be taken

---

1) In Mr. Morgan Dix' 'History of the Parish of Trinity Church', 1898—1906 we read that on Nov. 6, 1744 it was "voted to pay Colonel Moore the five guineas advanced to Mr. John Rice to come over here as organist, also to pay the passage of the said John Rice from London to this place". Subsequently, in 1753, John Rice appears as organist of Trinity Church in Boston.
2) It was advertised in the Weekly Post Boy, Oct. 2, 1749 for Oct. 12th, but was postponed.

that night. Mr. Love hopes that gentlemen and ladies will favour him with their good company.

The next to appear on the New York concert stage was a musician of unquestionable ability and who during the next twenty years did much to raise the standard of church music in New York: William Tuckey. As the inscription on his tombstone in the burial grounds of Christ Church, Philadelphia reads[1]):

"To the memory of. Mr. William Tuckey who was born in Sommersetshire in England and died September 14th, 1781 in the 73d year of his age."

it follows that Tuckey was born about 1708. That he held the position of Vicar Choral in the cathedral of Bristol and the clerkship of a parish in the same city before he came to New York appears from the first advertisement referring to Tuckey in the New York papers. It is so characteristic that I cannot refrain from quoting it as printed in the New York Mercury, March 11, 1754:

WILLIAM TUCKEY, Singing Master, desires to inform all lovers of *Psalmody* that in order to encourage and amend the singing in publick congregations in this city, all persons may be taught by him on very reasonable terms. As a great expectation of encouragement in this way, was the only motive which induced him to leave the cathedral of *Bristol*, where of he was for several years a vicar choral, and clerk of a parish also in the said city, places of considerable profit and on an establishment both for life; and not meeting with the encouragment he expected, is resolved to teach here no longer than one year more, which may be depended on: And as there is no person in this country duly qualified in the musical way, who has made a practice of teaching but himself, not only in church musick, in all its branches, viz. Services, Anthems, Chaunts, Responses and Psalms, according to the English, Dutch, French or Italian method; but also in the knowledge of a thorough base, and composing musick in parts both vocal and instrumental; management of musick for concerts, etc. he humbly hopes, through this information, to meet with better encouragement, or at least to establish the singing of parochial Psalms on a better and perfecter foundation than it hath been for some time past. He will undertake to compose or set to musick any piece on any subject, divine or moral, either in prose or verse, and adapt the musick according to the sense of the subject, for either a single voice, two, three, four or more voices, and for any sort of instruments, with or without a thorough base, for the organ, harpsichord, or spinnet, on application to him, and a moderate satisfaction. Specimens of his composing may be seen at any time, by any gentlemen or ladies, who desire it, and understand musick, he having several pieces for three, four or more voices, accompanied with almost all sorts of instruments, and his own composition.

The exact date of William Tuckey's arrival at New York is unknown but as on Jan. 31, 1753 it was

"ordered that William Tuckey (who is appointed by the Rector to officiate as Clerk jointly with Mr. Eldridge till further order) be allowed the annual salary of twenty-five pounds from the first of this month"[2]).

---

1) Edwart L. Clark, Record of the inscriptions on the tablets and gravestones in the burial grounds of Christ Church, Philadelphia, 1864, p. 34.
2) See Dix, *op. cit.*, I, p. 154 etc.

it may be surmised that he arrived during January 1753, provision also having been made by the vestry for the transportation of his wife and children who were to follow him.

Though Trinity Church possessed an organ and though church music had been cultivated for some time past in the parish, the conditions were primitive, principally owing to the absence of a really well trained choir. Now a Charity School had been founded in 1739 in close connection with Trinity Church and Tuckey was quick to see his opportunity. He evidently soon after his arrival impressed the vestry with the necessity of teaching the charity-children vocal music if the standard of music in the church was effectively to be raised. Accordingly it was voted on March 16, 1753 that he was to have the use of the Charity School room and also of the vestry room two nights of the week "for the teaching of his singing scholars". The wisdom of this decision soon became apparent and Mr. Dix, the historian of Trinity Church, asserts that Tuckey's conscientious and experienced efforts gradually gave to the church a choir of which the parish felt proud and which became noted even outside of New York. The statement is all the more interesting as in 1756 Tuckey was summarily discharged from the office of parish clerk in consequence of his "refusal to officiate in time of Divine Service". However, if thereafter his name disappears from the vestry minutes, he continued to act as musical instructor in the service of the parish. Mr. Dix merely admits this as a possibility but on the basis of subsequent events we must agree with Mr. Krehbiel who maintains that "his connection with the music of the church and its chapels lasted much longer than 1756"[1]).

These few remarks may serve as an introduction to his announcement in the New York Weekly Post Boy, December 15, 1755 of a benefit concert in conjunction with William Cobham, musician and dealer in "bear skins, spotted ermin, white and yellow flannels . . ."[2]).

For the benefit of Messrs. Cobham and Tuckey, at the New Exchange on Monday the 29 instant; will be a *Concert* of Vocal and Instrumental musick. Among a variety of select pieces, both vocal and instrumental, will be performed, the celebrated dialogue between *Damon and Chloe*, compos'd by Mr. Arne. A two part Song, in Praise of a Soldier, by the late famous Mr. Henry Purcell. An *Ode on Masonry* never perform'd in this country, nor ever in England but once in publick. And a Solo on the German flute, by Mr. Cobham.

Tickets to be had of Mr. Cobham, in Hanover Square; of Mr. Tuckey near Mr.

---

1) Henry Edward Krehbiel in an article on "Music in Trinity Church", N. J. Tribune, July 26, 1903. This article, based on material furnished by Dr. H. H. Messiter, who spent a long time in preparing a history of music in Trinity Church, is one of a splendid series of articles on 'Early church music in New York', N. Y. Tribune (Sundays) Middle of June to middle of October, 1903.

2) N. Y. Mercury, Oct. 23, 1758.

Willet's, at the New York Arms; and at the King's Arms; and at the new Printing
Office in Beaver Street at 5 *s* each.

To begin precisely at six o'clock. After the concert there will be a *Ball* for the
ladies.

The same announcement appeared in the New York Mercury, December 8th, but in program form and with this additional notice:

As it is conjectured that there will be a very full house, the managers of the concert humbly request the ladies and gentlemen who are pleased to favour them with
their company that they would be pleased to apply for their tickets in time that the
company may be as agreeable to them as possible.

Unquestionably the Ode on Masonry was a composition by William
Tuckey and unless it suffered too severely in the neighborhood of Arne and
Purcell, it may be conjectured that it, too, pleased the audience immensely.

In the following year the concert-goers of New York were called upon
to listen to good music "for the benefit of a poor widow". We read in the
New York Mercury, March 8, 1756:

On Thursday the 18th instant, will be open'd at the City Hall in the City of New
York, a *New Organ*, made by Gilfert Ash, where will be performed, a *Concert* of Vocal
and Instrumental Musick. In which, among a variety of other selected pieces, will
be introduced a song, in praise of musick, particularly of an organ; and another favourite
song, called 'The Sword that's drawn in Virtue's cause, both compos'd by Mr. Handel.
An *Organ Concerto*, compos'd by Sigr. Giovanni Adolfo Hasse.

It's hoped, lovers of harmony and charitable designs, will freely promote this
undertaking; thereby making their recreations the means of purchasing blessings to
themselves, and administring comfort to the afflicted heart, and relief to the distressed.

Tickets at five shilling each, to be had at Mr. Cobham's ... and at Mr. Ash's,
joining Mr. Willet's in Wallstreet; who continues the business of organ building by
whom gentlemen and ladies may be furnished with that noble instrument, in a convenient time after it is bespoke.

This appeal to the lovers of harmony and charitable designs was made
stronger by bringing the heart softening influence of — very bad — poetry
into action. On March 15th the Post Boy with the ever obliging courtesy
of the newspaper editor published the following communication:

Sir,

Please give the following lines a place in to-morrow's paper, to oblige Yours, A
Friend.

> Sure Music's powerful Charms can never plead!
> The cause of Poverty — and not succeed,
> While that to snatch the Friendless from Despair,
> To glad the Widow, and relieve her Care,
> To guard the Orphan, and its Intrest save,
> Are Actions just, commendable and brave:
> Then may each feeling Heart, whom Affl'ence bless
> Its Labours crown (next Thursday) with Success.
> *Musicus.*

Sure, music's powerful charms, the cause of poverty, a new organ by a
fellow citizen and an organ concerto by the famous 'caro Sassone' were attractions enough to crown the labours of the musici with success on that
memorable Thursday.

Unless the concerts enumerated were really only sporadic efforts, the very silence of the papers should, to repeat it, make us suspicious and I, for one, am inclined to doubt that the papers recorded all the concerts given. If actually during the years 1750 to 1754 no concerts took place, this may possibly be explained by the fact that just then several serious attempts were made by the companies of Thomas Kean, Robert Upton and William Hallam successively to interest New York in theatrical performances. As they included favorite ballad operas like the Beggar's Opera and the Devil to Play, possibly the interest in opera temporarily absorbed that in concerts, a phenomenon not unprecedented in the annals of music. The same explanation may hold for the short theatrical season of 1758—1759 but it does not carry much weight for the years 1755 to 1758 or 1759 to 1760. If, after all, only a few stray concerts were given in public at New York during those years, New Yorkers may find consolation in the fact that even in larger and more musical European cities with incomparably greater musical opportunities, public concerts were none too numerous.

After the concert of March 18, 1756, probably the first given at New York for charity, the newspapers again fail to offer clues until 1760 when we hear of the first subscription-concert. The advertisement, in the New York Gazette, Jan. 14, 1760, reads:

This is to give notice that the Subscription Concert will be opened on Thursday next, the 15th instant, at Mr. Willet's Assembly Room, in the Broad Way.

N. B. Those gentlemen that intend to subscribe to the said concert, are desired to send their names to Messrs. Dienval[1]) and Hulett[2]) who will wait on them with tickets, for the season.

It is to be regretted that the newspapers contain no further reference to this enterprise. I even failed to ascertain whether it was continued during the following year. If so, then the following characteristic announcement of a "publick and weekly concert of musick" in the New York Gazette, May 24, 1762 would prove that this was the third season. The fact that the concerts of 1762 were managed by Messrs. Leonard[3]) and Dienval need cause no apprehension as during the following seasons Mr. Hulett again appears to have been at the helm. The announcement reads:

This is to give notice to all gentlemen and ladies, lovers and encouragers of musick, that on Thursday next being the 27th instant, will be opened by Messrs. Leonard and

---

1) Alexander V. Dienval probably was first mentioned in New York papers in 1759 when he gave "notice that the violin and German flute are taught in the space of two or three months each" (Ben Akiba!). In November 1759 he, W. C. Hulett and the watchmaker-musician Procter opened a kind of music school where these instruments and the harpsichord were taught daily "from twelve till eight in the Evening".

2) William C. Hulett, actor, dancing and music master came to America in 1752 as violin player in Hallam's American Company.

3) Jacob Leonard is first mentioned at New York in December 1755 as dancing-master.

Dienval, Musick Masters of this City at Mr. Burner's Room, near the Battery *A publick and weekly Concert of Musick*, where any ladies and gentlemen will be admitted, at four shillings a ticket, which are to be had at the house of Mr. V. Dienval at the Upper End of Broadstreet near the Old City Hall and opposite the Watch House; where he continues to teach the violin, German Flute, hautboy, French horn, bass violin, tenor violin, etc. in the newest and best method . . .

The "concert for the season" was again "opened at Crawley's new Room" in November 1762 and after the first night (a Tuesday) was to be continued on every Thursday evening succeeding the Dancing Assembly[1]). Possibly the year 1763 also had its concert for the season. Certainly subscription concerts were given during the winter 1764—1765 as in a card "to the subscribers to the musical concert the managers and gentlemen performers considering that the sale of tickets may be attended with very disagreeable consequences, have therefore proposed the following regulations. That each subscriber be occasionally supplied by the managers — to be given by them only to gentlemen strangers". This regulation was, of course, directed against the indiscriminate sale of tickets to undesirable characters and the managers desired in this way to prevent disgraceful acts of rowdyism as on a certain occasion in those years at the theatre when eggs were thrown from the gallery into the pit and on the stage. Such indecent behaviour was exceptional but it was a common occurence the world over to disturb public entertainments by what the Italians wittily call "la musica dei palchi", the chatter and laughter of the box holders and indeed of the whole audience. Enough anecdotes are current to illustrate the point and it took considerable time to break this time honored, vicious habit. Amongst those who by their protests contributed towards that end was an *A. B.* who communicated a vigorous card to the New York Post Boy on December 27, 1764, apparently with the consent of the managers and gentlemen performers. The rather long but very entertaining document reads:

To the Printer.
Sir, you will oblige a great number of your friends and constant readers, if you will be kind enough to insert the enclosed in your next Thursday's paper.
Yours *A. B.*

It is a very just observation that a gentleman is to be known by his politeness — this qualification, wherever it is to be found, convinces us that it's possessor has seen the world and has had his manners formed by a good education. — The polite man is always received with pleasure, while the contrary character, tho' under every advantage of a gay appearance, never fail to strike with the disagreeable emotions of contempt and disgust.

I am led into this short reflection by a circumstance, I can scarcely think of without indignation. What I mean is the strange behaviour at the Concert, of a certain set of males and females to whom, out of mere complaisance to their appearance, I will give the soft appellation of gentlemen and ladies. — I am a dear lover of muisc and can't bear to be disturbed in my enjoyment of an entertainment so polite and agreeable. — How

---

1) N. Y. Mercury, November 8, 1762.

great then is my disappointment and vexation, when instead of a modest and becoming silence nothing is heard during the whole performance, but laughing and talking very loud, squawling, overturning the benches, etc. — Behaviour more suited to a *broglio* than a musical entertainment.

What is meant by so ill — timed an interruption — I know not; for tho' it may be true that to *Kick up a riot*, is a liberal amusement, and particularly adapted to *some* ladies, as it serves to attract the eyes of the other sex I am notwithstanding, pretty certain there might be a more proper place than the concert room found out for that purpose, for I cannot conceive that either the audience, or the gentlemen performers an under any obligations to bear those impertinencies — and I have an authority to assure those offenders against decency that if they don't resolve to behave better for the future; the managers and performers will be forced, either to leave all the performance or be reduced to the disagreeable necessity of insisting on their absenting themselves from a place where they do nothing but give offence; or if all this will not cure the complaint, there are some thoughts of hiring the adjacent room for the convenience of such whose conduct will not bear the eye of the public. —

It is presumed what I have wrote will not be taken amiss by the persons hinted at — it is not their *persons* but their *follies* which are become obnoxious. — While we are entering into laudable schemes for our improvement in the acts of oeconomy in private life, a hint for the better regulation of our conduct in public, cannot be unacceptable. — It may at least tend to guard us from those improprieties, which very deservedly expose us to the ridicule of every sensible stranger. This is the only end proposed by

X. Y. Z.

References to the subscription concerts of 1765, though such were probably given, escaped me and of those during the winter of 1766 nothing was said except that they began after several postponements on Dec. 18 at Mr. Burn's Assembly Room and that "a subscription book was opened at Mr. Hulett's, dancing master, who will wait on any gentleman, on notice given"[1]. Equally meagre are the allusions to the season of 1767. The New York Journal merely mentioned on Feb. 12, 1767 that the concerts would begin on that day and continue during the season exactly at half past six o'clock. Finally on Nov. 26, 1767, in the New York Post Boy, Mr. Hulett acquainted his friends that there would be no public concert that winter and that instead music would "be in waiting for those gentlemen and ladies that chuse country dances after the concert". Thus the enterprise died a natural death and not until December 10, 1773 was the Subscription Concert revived at Mr. Hull's Assembly Room. For Dec. 4th "in order that the whole may be conducted to the satisfaction of every subscriber" a meeting was called "to adjust the necessary matters" with a rehearsal to follow. It was then decided to give the first concert on Friday, October 10th and afterwards fortnightly on Thursdays[2]. As the subscriptions were to be taken in at Hulett's we may surmise that he managed the entertainment. "By desire" the concert of January 4, 1774 was to be followed "for that night only" by a ball and it is pretty certain that on this

1) N. Y. Journal, Nov. 20; Dec, 4, Dec. 18, 1766.
2) N. D. Journal, Dec. 2 and 16; N. Y. Gazetteer, Dec. 9, 1773.

occasion the *steps* Mr. Hulett taught and which William Dunlap when writing
his History of the American Theatre many years afterwards still remembered,
were very much in evidence. It is also pleasant to record as a glimpse into
by-gone times that the concert of February 17th was deferred until the
following Monday "on account of a public breakfast, given by the gentlemen
who compose the Society of the Friendly Brothers". As the subscription
concert began at half past six in the evening, this breakfast must have
been a rather lengthy affair if it could interfere with the concert, or shall
we be indiscreet enough to suspect that the gentlemen performers who
attended the breakfast might not have been, after their convivial performance, quite in a condition to tune their fiddles and read the music?

After that the concerts seem to have continued regularly until the second April concert was postponed from April 24th to April 28th; "that
night allowed to be a public concert for the use of Signiora Mazzanti, Mr.
Zedwitz and Mr. Hulett"[1]). The announcement then reads — and a quotation is necessary because it refers to the existence of a musical society in
New York at so early a date:

"On which evening the Gentlemen of the *Harmonic Society* have been pleased to
promise their assistance and Signiora Mazzanti will sing several English and Italian
songs. After the concert proper music will be ready to wait upon such ladies and gentlemen, as may chose to dance. Tickets at a dollar each, to be had of Mr. Rivington
and Hulett.

The subscribers will please to observe that to make amends for these interruptions
in the regular succession of the Subscription Concert, there will be after the above
advertised night, a concert weekly on Thursdays evenings."

The idea of giving open-air concerts during the summer gained root at
New York relatively early. The initiative belonged to a gentleman of the
euphonious but common name John Jones. As he himself gave the history
and a description of his enterprise, it is only fair to Mr. Jones to let him
have the floor. On June 3, 1765 he announced in the New York Mercury:

At the request of several gentlemen and ladies John Jones begs leave thus to acquaint the public in general that *Renelagh* [!] *Garden*[2]) will be open'd on Thursday
next (during the summer season) with a *Concert of Musick,* (if the weather will permit)
and to begin precisely at six in the evening and will continue till nine; the whole to be
conducted by Messrs. Leonard and Hullett. After the concert a small firework will
be play'd off, which will continue 'till ten: the whole to be managed with the utmost
regularity. As it is the first attempt of the kind ever known in those parts, he therefore hopes it will merit the applause of the gentlemen and ladies who will please to
favour him with their company.

Tickets for admittance to be had on Thursday next, Price 2 *S* 6 each.

N. B. Breakfasting from six in the morning 'till ten ... Notice will be given in
this paper every week, of the continuance of this concert, and of the particulars.

---

1) N. D. Journal, April 14, 1774.
2) The famous Ranelagh (House and) Gardens of London were opened in 1742
and ceased to exist in 1803. The performances there were somewhat of the same character as at Vauxhall Gardens.

These summer concerts lasted four years and then on March 6, 1769 Anthony Rutgers, Jun. advertised in the New York Mercury that there were "to be let the house and about 18 acres of ground belonging to the subscriber, known by the name of Ranelagh Gardens". Why the undertaking, which seems to have been well supported by the public, collapsed is difficult to tell. Perhaps "the indisposition of Mr. Jones", on account of which the concert of vocal and instrumental music on July 28, 1768 was deferred, had resulted in his death. However, as long as they lasted, these Ranelagh Garden concerts with fireworks contributed much to the enjoyment of the New Yorkers who, as Mr. Jones proudly claimed, judged his place "without exception to be far the most rural retreat near the city", "notwithstanding the artful insinuations of some ill-minded people to the contrary"[1]). As if his feelings were wounded, Mr. Jones in this announcement enumerated as special attractions — and his enumeration would have pleased even a past master in the art of enumeration as Peter Cornelius' immortal barber Abul Hassan Ali Ebe Becar:

"drawing rooms neatly fitted up; the very best of wine and other liquors, mead, filabubs, etc. with gammon, tongues, alamode beef, tarts, cakes, etc. and on notice given, dinners or other large entertainments, elegantly provided as usual: strict regularity at all times observed, and every accommodation studied to render this undertaking highly agreeable and satisfactory, in grateful return for the many favours conferred on the publick's obedient and very humble servant

John Jones."

As Mr. John Jones fully believed in the advantages of advertising we may gain a fairly correct idea of the Ranelagh Garden Concert. The entrance fee was 2 s. but "during the scarcity of cash" in 1766 he decided at the request of his friends that the tickets should pass at the bar for one shilling, which were accounted for as so much cash paid for anything the possessor was pleased to call for[2]). The concerts usually began at 8 o'clock in the evening but occasionally at seven and in 1768 Mr. Jones saw his way clear to hold them twice a week[3]). He made it a rule that on a "bad" evening the entertainment would be postponed to the following[4]). That music really was, at least in theory, the main feature is emphasized by the fact that the "genteel" fireworks were displayed between the "acts" of the concert and not *vice versa*. Unfortunately no full program seems to have been announced but we know that a "complete band of music" was engaged[5]). The solo-numbers consisted of pieces played by Mr. Leonard and others and the "vocal parts", a phrase of the day with which we have

---

1) N. Y. Mercury, June 30, 1766 and Aug. 26 1765.
2) N. Y. Gazette, Sept. 1, 1766.
3) N. Y. Mercury, Sept. 2, 1765, June 30, 1766.
4) N. Y. Gazette, July 20, 1766.
5) N. Y. Mercury, June 30, 1766.

become familiar, were held by a Mr. Jackson in 1765, by "a young lady who never performed in public before" in 1767 and after the return of the American Company in the following and last season by such popular actor-singers as Mr. Wools and Miss Wainwright who occasionally joined in duets as for instance on June 11, 1768. Only once is the title of a particular piece mentioned, when on July 4, 1768 Miss Wainwright was to sing by "particular desire" 'Thro the wood laddie'.

It is not surprising that Mr. John Jones' undertaking, launched under the alluring name of Ranelagh Gardens, met with competition. In 1766 Mr. Edward Bardin, proprietor of the "King's Arms Garden in the Broadway" then, of course, still in the "Fields", as New York's outskirts were called, endeavoured to wrest laurels from him. This gentleman "open'd" a concert of music, three times a week. He flattered himself "that this innocent amusement can scarce give offence to any person whatsoever, as every possible precaution will be used to prevent disorder and irregularity"[1]). But notwithstanding Mr. Bardin's appreciation of "the countenance already shewn him in this undertaking, a sufficient testimony of a general satisfact-tion"[2]) no reference to a continuation of these concerts appears during the following years and in March 1769 he announced, with a request to debtors and creditors alike to settle their bills, that his tavern was to be let[3]).

In the same year, in June, Mr. Samuel Francis announced that the "Vaux Hall Gardens" had been "newly fitted up" with "a very good Long Room, convenient for a ball or turtle entertainment . . . contiguous to the Garden"[4]) and that a concert of music vocal and instrumental would be offered to his guests twice a week. He also remarked that the gardens would have been opened earlier in the spring *but on account of the theatre!* The first concert was given on June 30th and if the instrumental "parts" were in keeping with the vocal "held" by Mr. Wools and Miss Hallam, it is to be regretted that Mr. Francis did not meet with sufficient encouragement to continue these concerts during the following years, if we allowed to infer this from the absence of advertisements. On the opening night[5]) were to be sung in

Act I.
By particular desire — 'Black Sloven', by Mr. Wools
'Ye Men of Gaza' (from Handel) by Miss Hallam.

Act II.
'Blest as the immortel gods is he', by Mr. Wools
'Fair Aurora' (Duet from Artaxerxes)[6]) by Mr. Wools and Miss Hallam.

---

1) N. Y. Post Boy, June 26, 1766.
2) N. V. Mercury, July 21, 1766.
3) N. Y. Journal, March 13, 1769.
4) N. Y. Journal, June 8, 1769.
5) N. Y. Journal, June 29, 1769.
6) Arne.

The introduction of subscription concerts, of course, immediately increased the number of benefit concerts, especially of those given for the benefit of musicians connected with the management of the subscription concerts. The first to thus expect a substantial appreciation of his labors was Mr. Leonard who announced a concert in June 1762[1]) and then a "concert of musick vocal and instrumental" at the Assembly Room for Feb. 15, 1763. It was to begin at 6 o'clock and to conclude "with an Ode on the Restauration of Peace, set to musick by Mr. Leadbetter; solo part to be sung by Mr. Jackson, with proper choruses"[2]). Mr. Leonard had further benefits on Jan. 10 and December 13, 1764[3]) and possibly also later. He disappears from the papers with a concert advertised for April 14, 1767[4]).

Benefit concerts were also given for Mr. Thomas Harrison on March 22, 1763 and April 12, 1764[5]), the latter at the New Assembly Room when there were to be introduced

"several new songs, and one cantata; and by particular desire, to conclude with the song and grand chorus *Rule Britannia*, etc., accompanied with drums and clarinets"!

As was the case with Mr. Leonard, Thomas Harrison disappears for a few years until he again announced benefit concerts for Nov. 16, 1769 and Dez. 11, 1770 with "a ball for the ladies".[6])

1) N. Y. Gazette, June 7, 1762.
2) N Y. Gazette, Feb. 7, 1763.
3) N. Y. Mercury, Jan. 2, 1764; N. Y. Gazette, Dec. 3, 1764.
4) N. Y. Mercury, April 6, 1767 (postponed from March 10th).
5) N. Y. Gazette, Feb. 28, 1763 and N. Y. Weekly Post Boy, April 12, 1764. If Mr. Krehbiel in his article on music in Trinity Church claims that Thomas Harrison had been brought over from England as organist as early as 1744 he evidently confused Thomas Harrison with John Rice. The probabilities are that Harrison became organist after Rice's removal to Boston in 1753. At any rate, he is positively mentioned as organist of Trinity Church in the N. Y. Gazette, February 1, 1762 in an advertisement where he also appears as dealer in all kinds of musical instruments. He seems to have been succeeded by James Leadbetter who was chosen organist for one year with the stipulation that he was to assist in tuning the new organ, on April 5, 1764. (Compare Dix). For this new organ already in 1761 500 pounds had been voted but it was not purchased (in England) until 1763 when (comp. N. Y. Gazette, Jan. 3, 1763) the old organ "consisting of 26 stops, 10 in the grand organ, 10 in the choir organ, and 6 in the swell, three sets of keys; with a frontispiece of gilt pipes and otherwise neatly adorned" was offered for sale. It was built 1739—1740 by Johann Gottlob Klemm (b. 1690 in Dresden, came to Philadelphia in 1736, moved to New York 1745, joined the United Brethren at Bethlehem, Pa. in 1757, died there 1762) and was the first organ installed in Trinity Church. That there was at least some talk of erecting an American built organ as early as 1703 appears from the vestry entry of "ye 4th of August, 1703" as printed in Baird's Early Records of Trinity Church', Hist. Mag. 3d series, 1872, p. 10:
"Order that ye Rever. Mr. Vesey, Rector, Coll. Wenham . . . confer with & discourse Mr. Henry Neering, Organ Maker about making & erecting an organ in Trinity Church in N. York and if they shall think meet to agree with him on as easy terms as possible".
Nothing however, appears to have been done in the matter, as Trinity Church was still in need of "a sett of organs" in 1709 and as the first organ mentioned in New York we might consider the one given by Governor Burnet, Dec. 28, 1727 to the Corporation of the Dutch Church. (Dix.)
6) N. Y. Mercury, Nov. 6, 1769 and Dec. 3, 1770.

Then we notice a "publick concert" on April 3, 1764[1]) for the benefit of Mr. A. Van Dienval, at the conclusion of which was to be sung "a grand chorus song, accompanied with drums, trumpets, *or* clariants", presumably *Rule Britannia*. Another musician, prominently connected with the Subscription Concert and long a resident of New York, appeared relatively late on the plan with benefit concerts. Mr. Hulett is meant, who gave his first on March 5, 1765[2]). The announcement of his second, on Oct. 5, 1765[3]) contained this meagre allusion to the program:

"The first violin to be performed by a gentleman lately arrived. A Solo on the Violin by the same Hand, the other instrumental parts by gentlemen of the town."

Nor is anything said of his concert on March 31, 1767[4]) except the date and the usual information as to tickets, etc. With reference to his "only concert this season at Mr. Burn's Room" on Dec. 3, 1767[5]) he at least ventured the information that it was to be "in two acts. The vocal parts by Mr. Wools and Miss Hallam". He also thought it worth his while to mention that at his concert on March 23, 1770[6]) a Mr. Stotherd was to perform by particular desire "several pieces on the French horn" and he became unusually communicative when he remarked in the announcement of his benefit concert at Hull's Assembly Room, April 27, 1773[7]) that

"the Concert [was] to be conducted and the first violin performed' by Mr. Zedtwitz (A capital performer from London). The other instrumental parts, by the gentlemen of the *Harmonic Society*.
In act the first, a duet, by Mr. Zedtwitz and Mr. Hulett. In act the second a solo by Mr. Zedtwitz."

Both gentlemen named by Mr. Hulett had their own benefit concerts, Mr. Stotherd on February 9, 1770[8]) and Mr. Zedtwitz on May 11, 1773[9]). In Mr. Stotherd's concert at Mr. Burn's Room the instrumental parts were performed by "several gentlemen who [were] pleased to patronize the concert and they must have been able amateurs to carry out this remarkable program:

ACT 1st.

1st Overture of Bach, Opera prima
3d Concerto of Avison, Opera quarta
A Hunting song — Black Sloven
A French Horn Concerto, by Mr. Stotherd
4th Concerto of Stanley

---

1) N. Y. Mercury, March 26, 1764.
2) N. Y. Gazette, Feb. 25, 1765.
3) N. Y. Mercury, Oct. 14, 1765.
4) N. Y. Journal, March 12, 1767.
5) N. Y. Post Boy, Dec. 3, 1767.
6) N. Y. Journal, March 15, 1770.
7) N. Y. Mercury, April 19, 1773.
8) N. Y. Journal, Feb. 1, 1770.
9) N. Y. Mercury, May 10, 1773.

Duet on the French Horn
8th Periodical Overture[1])

Act 2d.

Overture of Saul[2])
Select pieces for four French Horns
2d Concerto of Humphries
A Hunting Song
A French Horn Concerto, by Mr. Stotherd
3d Concerto of Corelli
Overture of Atalanta[2])
After the Concert, there will be a ball ...

If the announcement of the Subscription Concert on April 28, 1774, with exception of a program presented on May 17th by a Mr. Caze, contains the last reference to the Harmonic Society I was able to find, that of Mr. Zedtwitz in the New York Mercury, May 10, 1773 contained the first. The concert, at Mr. Hull's Assembly Room, was to be conducted and the first violin perform'd by himself, the other instrumental parts by the gentlemen of said Harmonic Society. Only a few numbers of the program were mentioned: in act the first, a Solo by Mr. Zedtwitz, by particular desire 'Vain is beauty's gaudy flower' and 'The Soldier tir'd' by Miss Hallam; in act the second, singing by Miss Storer, and a duet with Mr. Hulett's son, "ten years old", who thus probably holds the distinction of having been the first prodigy to appear on American soil.

But who was this musician of a name so suggestive of Prussian aristocracy? May be it would be more charitable to leave the question unanswered but the opportunity is too tempting to briefly trace the checkered career of this gentleman to whom nobody will allow this title after hearing of his ignominious end.

Hermann Zedtwitz expressed his intention to settle in New York in April 1773 and proposed "to teach a certain number of gentlemen the violin, in the present taste, having been a pupil of several of the most eminent masters now in London and Germany". This intention he carried out and his name also repeatedly appeared in connection with concerts, but apparently the musical profession was not lucrative enough and with the year 1775 he appears in the newspapers[3]) as the proprietor of "the Chimney office" first in Little Queen Street and then in Nassau and Fairstreet", extending his business into a primitive sort of *Trust*. Then came the war and therewith ended the career of Mr. Zedtwitz. The facts are briefly these[4]).

----

1) So called from the collection of 'Periodical Overtures' in 8 parts by the most fashionable composers of the day, issued monthly by Rob. Bremner.

2) Haendel.

3) N. Y. Journal, March 16, 1775 etc.

4) Compare N. Y. State Archives; Pennsylvania Archives; Force's American Archives; Pennsylvania Staatsbote, 1776; Washington's Writings, etc. In a letter

When the rupture between the Colonies and the Motherland became inevitable, (von) Zedtwitz who claimed to have seen military service under Frederick the Great, was appointed major and commissioned as lieutenant-colonel in the First New York regiment on March 8, 1776. He took part in General Montgomery's famous attack on Quebec as "a brave officer" but "was so disabled by a rupture occasioned by a fall from a precipice" that he became unfit for active duty. It was then suggested to put him in command of the forts on the North River near New York. Fortunately enough for the Americans the appointment had not yet become effective when a letter of Zedtwitz, written to Governor Tryon (British) was intercepted smacking of the worst kind of treason. He admitted having written the letter but, as he asserted, merely to fool Tryon and to recover certain sums due him for services rendered the British Crown in Germany. Naïve as this explanation was, the court was divided in its opinion as to Zedtwitz' guilt and maybe the valuable service rendered by him in influencing the Hessians to desert their colors had something to do with their clemency. He was cashiered, however, removed to Philadelphia and confined to the State prison. Somehow he managed in May 1779 to make his escape from Reading and was on his way to New York when he was taken up near Morristown, N. J. "dressed in Woman's clothes"[1]). It is pretty safe to say that this escapade ended most unpleasantly for our Hermann von Zedtwitz, music teacher, chimney sweep, lieutnant-colonel and traitor.

Mr. von Zedtwitz' career has carried us a few years beyond the period under discussion. In retracing our steps it might be well to first dispose of such entertainments as were only in part concerts. For instance, on July 15, 1767[2]) Mr. Douglas, actor and theatrical manager, delivered George Alexander Stevens' once so popular 'Lecture on Heads' in three parts. By particular desire, Mr. Wools who lived to be the Nestor of the American stage, was to sing at the end of the first part 'Thou like the Glorious sun' after the second 'Water parted from the sea', both airs from Arne's opera Artaxerxes and after the lecture the cantata 'Cymon and Iphigenia'. Similar entertainments were repeatedly given either like this at Burn's Assembly Room or "by permission" of the authorities at the theatre in John

preserved in copy at the N. Y. Public Library and dated August 20, 1778 the Hessian lieutenant Henckelmann has this to say about "von Settwitz. Er war vor der Rebellion Schornsteinfeger in New York, verliess seinen Posten, ging nach Philadelphia, recommandierte sich bei dem Hr. Penn durch Clavierspielen und Singen, dass dieser ihn zum Mitglied im Congress vorschlug, worin er aufgenommen wurde und noch eine Rolle spielt". As a matter of fact, of course, Zedtwitz never was a member of the Continental Congress but the letter may serve as an illustration of the absurd form gossip and rumors will take and how sceptical one should be in using letters for historical argument.

1) Virginia Gazette, Williamsburg, June 5, 1779.
2) N. Y. Gazette, July 6, 1767.

Street. In 1769 these lectures on heads, hearts, etc. were presented to the public under the more pretentions than appropriate heading of 'Attic Evening Entertainment' with "extracts from various authors read, and some of the most celebrated songs" sung. For instance the latter comprised on July 21[1]):

'A way to the fields' (a hunting song) by Mr. Hudgson.
A Song set by *Dr.* Henry Purcell, by Mr. Warwell
'The Linnets', by Mr. Hudgson.
A Martial Song, in character, by Mr. Warwell
A Two part song, by Mr. Warwell and Mr. Hudgson.

In the meantime the official antipathy against theatrical performances had abated and thereafter the actors only rarely found time or opportunity to deliver such lectures outside of the theatre. The idea was revived a few years later by a Mr. Hoar who, end of August and in Sept. 1772, delivered a "Syllabus in three parts with a concert of vocal and instrumental musick"[2]) and in 1773 utilized his "copy of Mr. George Alexander Stevens's new Lectures (with characteristic heads and dresses) as they are now delivered in London by that celebrated genius". Mr. Hoar was assisted between the acts by a "young lady" who sang a number of songs "with proper accompaniments"[3]).

It remains to trace a few concerts proper not hitherto mentioned. In 1767, on April 23[4]), "the Royal American Band of Musick", presumably a regimental band stationed at New York, gave for its own benefit a concert of vocal and instrumental music, of which nothing else is said. On June 13, 1769[5]) the actress and singer Mrs. Harman, assisted by her colleagues Miss Hallam, Miss M. Storer, Mr. Wools and Miss Wainwright had a benefit concert. This probably was one of a series of benefit concerts of which "a vocal entertainment at Mr. Burn's Long Room" on July 14, 1769 "by permission of His Excellency the Governor" was "the last night". From the fact that it was announced for nobody's special benefit, it may be surmised that it was a joint-benefit for the singers, who all belonged to Douglas' American Company, as mentioned on the program:

ACT 1st.

A Pastoral, by Mr. Warwell
'Come rouse brother Sportsman' (a hunting song) by Mr. Hudgson
'Bright author of my present flame', by Mr. Warwell.

ACT 2d.

'May Eve; or Kate of Aberdeen', by Mr. Hudgson
A Song in the Anacreontic taste, by Mr. Warwell
The Jest, set by Mr. Michael Arme, by Mr. Hudgson.

---

1) N. Y. Journal, July 20, 1769.
2) N. Y. Journal, Aug. 27; Sept. 3, 1772.
3) N. Y. Journal, Feb. 4, 1773.
4) N. Y. Gazette, April 13, 1767.
5) N. Y. Post Boy, June 5, 1769.

[Act 3d.

A Cantata, by Mr. Warwell
A Song, by Mr. Hudgson
A Duett, by Mr. Warwell and Mr. Hudgson.

Then came a concert on January 24, 1771[1]) at Mr. Bolton's Tavern for the benefit of John Mc Lane, "five major of the 29th regiment"[2]) and subsequently, as we have seen, instructor of the German flute at Philadelphia. As special attractions Mr. Mc Lane mentioned "a solo on the German flute" and after the concert "several pieces of music performed by the fifers and drummers of the said regiment".

Possibly it was also Mr. Mc Lane who took the second flute in a "duet on 2 flutes" which the flutist George Webster announced as the principal feature of his concert, scheduled for March 13th at Mr. Bolton's tavern, postponed from March 5, 1771[3].) The concert, adorned by other select pieces, was to conclude with the march in Haendel's Judas Maccabaeus "accompanied with a side drum". Shortly afterwards, on April 17th[3]) "by particular desire of several ladies of distinction" a concert of vocal and instrumental music was held for the benefit of a "respectable but distressed family of orphans" and said ladies expressed their hope "that so charitable a design [would] meet the countenance of every person of sensibility and benevolence".

So far, New Yorkers had not yet caught a glimpse of French and Italian virtuosos with exception of Signiora Mazzanti. A splendid opportunity came in May 1774 though it must be confessed that the programs smacked somewhat of the sensational. Certainly the announcement of Mr. Caze's concert with "orchestry's" pieces etc. leaves nothing to be desired in quaintness[4]):

MUSIC. On Tuesday Evening the 17th instant will be performed at Mr. Hull's Tavern, for the use of Mr. Caze, an extraordinary instrumental and vocal *Concert* in two acts, consisting of different solos, upon various instruments, unknown in this country, to be executed by the gentlemen of the Harmonic Society, who have been pleased to promise their assistance.

---

1) N. Y. Mercury, Jan. 7, 1771.
2) N. Y. Mercury, Jan. 14, 1771.
3) N. Y. Journal Feb. 14, N. Y. Mercury, March 4, 1771. George Webster is still to be traced at New York in 1785 as teacher of the flute. During the war, though he still gave music lessons, he drifted mainly into the liquor, grocery and shoe business at the sign of the Three Cannisters. For instance, in the Royal Gazette, Nov. 4, 1778 he announced *inter alia* that he would supply "Sergeants, of the army with any quantity of strong military shoes, likewise hard and soft shoe-brushes for the use of their men" and "gentlemen and ladies who are fond of preserved fruits in brandy ... with peaches, pears, plumbs and green gages". It is extremely doubtful whether Washington's army was equally provided with all the delicacies "in and out of season" nor could many of our soldiers boast of "strong military shoes".
4) N. Y. Mercury, May 9, 1774.

1st Act.

A grand Orchestry's Symphony
A French Ariette will be sung accompanied with the guitar and violin.
Mr. Caze will play his own composed music, on the violin with Mr. Zedtwitz.
A Concert on the Flute
A Sonada on the Spanish Guitar
The first Act to end with a March.

IId Act.

A Grand Orchestry's Symphonie
A French Ariette accompany'd with the Mandolin and Violin
A Solo on the Violin
A Duo on Mandoline and Violin
A Sonada of the Salterio; and d'Exaudet's Minuet with echos.
The Concert to finish with a March of the grand Orchestry.
After the Concert there will be a ball . . .

Not less quaint is the announcement[1]) of the joint benefit concert of the two *maestri* Nicholas Biferi and Pietro Sodi, the latter, it will be remembered from the chapter on Charleston, claiming to have had for many years the sole conduct of the dances at the Italian opera in London[2]):

At Mr. Hull's Assembly Room, will be performed a great *Concert* extraordinary, the 26th of this month, for the benefit of Mr. Biferi and Mr. Sodi, the said concert will be divided into two acts, each act composed of four pieces.

Mr. Biferi, master of music from Naples, will perform on the harpsichord a piece of music of his composition with the orchestra; ditto in the second act will perform a solo accompanied with the violin.

There will follow a ball, in which Mr. Sodi will dance the louvre, and the minuet with Miss Sodi, a young lady nine years of age; and Miss Sodi will dance a rigadoon with young Mr. Hulett.

Mr. Biferi again endeavoured to interest the public on March 23, 1775[3]) when he had a "concert and ball under the patronage of the Hon. Stephen Payne Galway, Esq. "at Mr. Hull's Tavern. This was followed by the last concert before the war" a publick concert for the benefit of a Band of Musick" at Mr. Hull's Assembly Room on April 27th[4]).

---

1) N. Y. Mercury, May 16, 1774.
2) Mr. Biferi and Mr. Sodi were two of the "three gentlemen lately [in April] arrived from London" who proposed in the N. Y. Gazetteer, May 5, 1774 to open "A new Academy for teaching musick, dancing and the Italian and French languages". The third was Joseph Corani, to whose lot it would have fallen to teach the languages, had the proposals met with success. Evidently they did not, for we met Sodi at Charleston in the following year and Nicholas Biferi subsequently advertised his paedagogic talents independently of the beautiful cooperative scheme. He taught "vocal music, the harpsichord, to play pieces of music and an easy method to learn the composition which he printed for the public at Paris; he composes all sorts of music, vocal and instrumental". Was this *Nicolas* Biferi from Naples possibly identical with the *Biferi* (Bifferi), *Francesco, fils*, who was born about 1739 at Naples, who lived at Paris about 1767 and who published there in 1770 his 'Traité de la musique dans lequel on traite du chant, de l'accompagnement, de la composition et de la fuge'? (Compare Eitner.)
3) N. Y. Mercury, Feb. 27, 1775.
4) N. Y. Mercury, April 17, 1775.

For certain reasons the name of one musician, and probably the best New York could boast in those days, has not yet been referred to in the record of concerts after 1760: William Tuckey. He had threatened to leave the city unless he met with better encouragement but either because his threat had the desired effect or because he did not see his way clear to more appreciative climes, Tuckey remained in New York and labored faithfully in the interest of the Charity School connected with Trinity Church. This part of his activity does not interest us here whereas his efforts to establish what we perhaps would call to-day, an Oratorio Society, or at any rate, his efforts to systematically bring church music before the general public deserves not only attention but lasting credit.

To ascertain the full extent of this pioneer-propaganda is no longer possible but Tuckey's rather minute announcements on several occasions afford a fairly good view of what he tried to accomplish and in part did accomplish. The announcements are so interesting and instructive in themselves that it will be better to use, as far as possible, Tuckey's own words than to paraphrase them and rob them of their delightful quaintness.

It will be remembered that already in 1754 he urged an "improvement" and "amendment" of "the singing in public congregations" in New York and it goes without saying that his energies remained bent in this direction. Then, in 1762, his appeal took a more concrete form in this advertisement in the New York Weekly Post Boy, September 4, 1762:

TO ALL LOVERS OF DIVINE HARMONY.

Whereas it is a custom in Protestant congregations in Europe, on times of rejoicing, as well on annual as particular days of thanksgiving, to sing the Te Deum therefore by particular desire a subscription is open'd for the encouragement of so laudable a practice in this city. Proposals as follows: Every lady, gentleman etc., to subscribe whatever they please, for which subscription money *William Tuckey*, has obligated himself to teach a sufficient number of persons, to perform the Te Deum, either with or without organ, or other instruments; and that it shall be as good a piece of music as any of the common Te Deums sung in any cathedral church in England. Performers to pay nothing for instruction (unless it be their pleasure) but it is expected that they will (as they are to be inhabitants of the city) be kind enough to join the choir on any particular occasion; especially at the opening of the new organ, which is expected soon.

Public subscriptions are taken in by Mr. Gaine, Mr. Weymann, and the printer of this paper, which moneys are to be left in the persons hands who receive it, 'till there is a rehearsal of the piece before the subscribers, of which rehearsal they shall have notice.

Mr. Tuckey desires all persons from lads of ten years old etc., as well as other persons of good repute, that has good voices and are willing to join the company, to be speedy in their application, and give in their names to Mr. Hildreth, Clerk of Trinity Church, or Mr. Silby, Clerk of St. George's Chappel; as he will begin immediately to instruct the performers and receive all qualify'd till there are 50 voices in the chorus.

Some response certainly must have been made to this call, but I found
no further allusion to the enterprise until 1766 when the New York Mercury on October 6, 1766 printed the following *news* which prove Mr. Tuckey
to have launched in the meantime at least one "Rehearsal of Church Musick",
alias concert. The announcement reads:

We are inform'd that Mr. Tuckey's Rehearsal of *Church Musick*, (which has given
such general satisfaction to the people of all ranks in this city, at the performance)
will very shortly by particular desire of a number of ladies and gentlemen (who are his
friends) be again rehearsed for his *benefit*, with a considerable addition: whereof notice
will be given in the weekly papers —

This *Concert* will consist of nothing but church musick; in which will be introduced,
a new Te Deum, Jubilate, Cantata Domini; and Deni [!] Misereatur, accompany'd with
a sufficient number of proper instruments. Mr. Tuckey would take it as a great favour
of any gentleman, who sing or play any instrument, to lend him their kind assistance
in the performance, and give him timely notice, that there may be a sufficient number
of parts wrote out."

The date was fixed for October 28th[1]) and the price of tickets at four shillings each to be had at Tuckey's home. It is also interesting to note that
the concert was not held in a church but at Mr. Burn's New Room. To
the pieces mentioned in the preliminary announcement was added

an Anthem (in which there is an obligato part for a harp, as there is also in the
Cantate Domino) with several other pieces of Church Musick, intermixed with other
instrumental performances in order to ease the voices: the whole to conclude with a
Martial Psalm, viz. the 46th, Tate and Brady's version, accompanied with all the instruments, and a pair of drums.

N. B. There will be more than forty voices and instruments in the chorus.

Whether the adjective "new" applied only to the Te Deum or to all the
pieces does not appear but it is highly probable that at least the Te Deum
was Tuckey's own composition[2]).

---

1) N. Y. Gazette, Oct. 20, 1766.
2) Students of American psalmody will have met with Tuckey's compositions
as contained in psalm-tune collections. Probably the first composition of his published
in America was 'An Anthem taken out of the 97th Psalm', embodied anonymously
in James Lyon's 'Urania', 1761 and subsequently popular as 'Liverpool'. We also
know from the Boston Evening Post, Dec. 15, 1760 that a Thanksgiving Anthem of
his was performed in December, 1760 in Trinity Church, New York. Consequently
his compositions became fairly well known, notwithstanding the fact that he failed
in his efforts to publish certain of his works by subscription. For want of better opportunity and in order to be of service to the historians of American church music,
I quote the respective advertisements here. On March 11, 1771 appeared in the N. Y.
Mercury the following.
Proposals for publishing (by subscription) Two select pieces of Church music.
1st. An Hymn (by way of an anthem) consisting of Solos, Duets, one Trio and
Chorus; together with a Psalm Tune, adapted for any charitable church collection,
and first design'd for the benefit of the Free School belonging to Trinity Church in
New York, to be perform'd in the churches at the annual collection; the school being
chiefly supported by charity; the words of the hymn by a gentleman of Kings' College.

It may be taken for granted that when on Oct. 30, 1766 the "new Episcopal Chapel, called St. Paul's and esteemed one of the most elegant edifices on the Continent was opened" it was William Tuckey who with "a suitable band of music vocal and instrumental" introduced "several pieces of church music" the "judicious execution" of which "contributed much to heighten the solemnity" as the New York Mercury expressed• it on November 3d. It appears that the introduction of a band, whatever its constitution might have been, was due to the expressed desire of Sir Henry Moore, a desire granted

---

2d. A performance adapted for a *funeral*, consisting of three Dirges, (or chorus) the words part of the burial service; together with an Anthem and a Psalm Tune suitable on the solemnity of a funeral or interment of any person of note, etc. The whole never yet perform'd being very lately set to music by *William Tuckey*, for some years a professor of the theory and practice of vocal music, Vicar Choral of the Cathedral Church of Bristol and Clerk of the Parish of St. Mary Port in said city, now resident in New York.

The subscribers to pay two shillings at the time of subscribing and two shillings more on the delivery of the work (New York currency) which is to be neatly engrav'd on copper plates, and work'd off on the best paper: and when ready to be deliver'd; notice will be inserted in the New York, Philadelphia and Boston papers: the subscribers to be at the expence of sending their subscriptions and for their books to New York either to Hugh Gaine or the proprietor, William Tuckey.

N. B. No more will be work'd off than what are subscribed for, so that none will be sold by any bookseller, but those who subscribe who will be entitled to the usual discount.

Though the following proposals were anonymous the fact that a number of the pieces were identical with those performed at Tuckey's concert of October 28, 1766 renders it certain that he was the composer, a supposition further strengthened by the tenor of the advertisement in the N. Y. Journal, July 1, 1773:

Church Music. Ready for engraving, and to be published by subscription, the following select pieces, consisting of a complete set of church service, viz. A *Te Deum laudamus*; *Jubilate Deo; Benedicite opera Domini; Cantate Domino* and *Deus misereatur;* a burial service and an anthem for any grand funeral; a complete and well adapted anthem to be sung at the time of any charitable contribution; a grand chorus, 'Hosanna to the Son of David, Blessed is he that cometh in the name of the Lord', etc. proper to be sung at any meeting; or convention of the clergy, of any denomination; as also an Anthem 133d Psalm, for a grand meeting of Free and Accepted Masons'; the whole to be published in score, which will contain to the best calculation sixty folio pages, to be engraved and worked off in the neatest manner and on the best paper, the work will receive the greatest dispatch as soon as a sufficient number of subscribers offer who are requested to be as speedy as possible to deliver in their names and places of abode. The piece to subscribers will be one dollar and a half; one half to be paid at the time of subscribing and the other half of the delivery of the book.

Subscriptions are taken in by Messrs. Gaine, Rivington and Holt, printers in New York . . . [and others from Rhode Island down to Charleston, S. C.!] All the subscription money is to be sent and deposited in the hands of Messrs. Rivington, Holt and Gaine, or either of these gentlemen in New York, who will take care that no money shall be paid to the compiler, till they have inspected the manuscript and seen it dispatched to the engraver; and in case a sufficient number of subscribers should not offer they will return the subscription money they have received.

N. B. There never was any complete set of church service made public, nor can any be procured but by friendship and a great expence; neither is any burial service of the kind to be purchased, unless it be that in Dr. Croft's anthems, which is sold for two guineas.

"on the condition that the band should only join in such part of the service as was usual and customary in like cases, and that no other pieces of music should be allowed but such only as were adapted to the service of the church on such solemn occasions".[1])

Suitable band of music! This recalls to our minds the plan Joh. Seb. Bach submitted to the city fathers of Leipzig (Spitta, II, p. 74). He therein demanded as *minimum* 2—3 first, 2—3 second violins, 2first, 2 second violas, 2 violoncelli, 1 double bass, 2—3 oboes, 1—2 bassoons, 3 trumpets, 1 kettle-drum, that is to say, in addition to organ and harpsichord not more than 22 instrumentalists as against a chorus of 12 to 16 (trained!) singers. These specifications are instructive. That they really were considered about normal we know from Mattheson who says in his 'Vollkommener Kapell-meister' that for choir and orchestra together "bevor ab in grossen[!]Stadt-kirchen" 30 persons are approximately needed. Finally, Joh. Samuel Petri, in his 'Anleitung zur praktischen Musik', 1767 recommends:

". . . . Man möchte nach der Menge der Instrumentalisten die Stimmen etwa so besetzen wenn eine *espece* von Concert herauskommen sollte: Ein sehr schwacher Chor. . . [7—8 instrumentalists] . . . Ein etwas stärkerer . . . [10—12] Ein vollständigerer . . . [21 to 24]"

specifying 2 flutes *or* oboes, 2 horns *or* clarinets and kettledrums. Consequently William Tuckey did not have much difficulty in finding at New York in 1766 a really suitable band, at least for "a somewhat fuller chorus"!

Confining himself thus to church music, William Tuckey appears to have laboured until 1769 when he again ventured to give a benefit concert on April 21st[2]). Of the program nothing is said except that the vocal parts were held by Miss Wainwright, Miss Hallam, Miss Maria Storer and Mr. Wools, with a ball after the concert. Choirmaster, actors and dancing, surely a curious combination but one which speaks well for the tolerance of by-gone days!

One other feature of the program was announced in the papers that should not pass unnoticed. If, as Mr. Cummings claims in his monograph on 'God save the king' the first recorded public performance of the British national hymn took place at London on Sept. 30, 1745 in Carey's arrange-ment as a trio with chorus refrain, there is every reason to believe that the hymn made its first appearance on an American program on the evening of Tuckey's benefit, April 21, 1769 for "by particular desire the concert [was] to end with God save the king". This concert was followed not quite a year later by one which deservedly aroused the interest of our historians. Said F. L. Ritter[3]): .

---

1) Krehbiel, quoting *loc. cit.* the records of the parish.
2) N. Y. Mercury, April 12 and N. Y. Journal, April 20, 1769.
3) Music in America, New ed. 1895, p. 135.

"on the 9th of January, 1770, Handel's 'Messiah' was performed in Trinity Church, repeated on the 3d of October the following year and again in April 1772".

Mr. Ritter did not mention his authorities and therefore other writers who copied this statement, so important for the history of oratorio in America, were justified in hesitating to accept it. The more so, as the statement happens to be incorrect and misleading. Though the first performance was originally announced for Jan. 9, 1770[1]), it was subsequently postponed to Jan. 16th[2]). In the second place, the concert was given, not in Trinity Church, but at Mr. Burn's Room. Furthermore, the statement reads as if the entire oratorio was performed whereas only the overture and sixteen numbers were given. Finally, I have not come across the announcement of performances in 1771 and 1772. This, however, may have been my fault, and until the dates given are removed as impossible, Ritter's reference will have to stand.

Before submitting the full announcement, one other observation. Haendel's 'Messiah', first performed at Dublin in 1742 and at London in 1743, soon conquered Great Britain but was slow to force its way into popularity on the continent. Indeed, Sittard in his book on concerts in Hamburg claimed that the first performance of the 'Messiah' in Germany was given at Hamburg under Michael Arne[3]) on April 15, 1772. The inference is plain enough: William Tuckey introduced the 'Messiah' to the citizens of New York one year before its first performance in Germany! To be sure, Tuckey gave only seventeen of the fifty-seven numbers, but is it absolutely certain that Haendel performed his masterwork in its *entirety* at Dublin? And did it not soon become customary to perform only more or less comprehensive extracts from the gigantic score as the limits of human endurance required merciless cuts? At any rate, Sittard's statement that *beyond doubt* the *whole* oratorio was performed at Hamburg and not only a selection is rather bold in view of the fact that the announcement contains nothing to uphold this contention and on the other hand mentions that the famous oratorio was to be followed by the Coronation Anthem! Be this as it may, the honor of having introduced the 'Messiah' to the American public belongs to William Tuckey and this alone would entitle him to lasting fame in the history of our musical life.

Unfortunately all we know of this pioneer-performance is contained in the following characteristic though meagre announcement in the New York Journal, January 4, 1770:

---

1) N. Y. Mercury, Dec. 25, 1769.
2) N. Y. Journal, Jan. 11, 1770 and N. Y. Journal, Jan. 4, 1770.
3) Sittard says Thomas Augustine Arne, but it was Michael.

CONCERT OF CHURCH MUSIC.

Will be performed at Mr. Burns's Room, on Tuesday the 9th of January, 1770 for the benefit of Mr. Tuckey.

 First Part. Some select instrumental pieces, chosen by the gentlemen who are performers: Particularly a *Concerto* on the French Horn by a gentleman juxt arrived from Dublin[1]).

 Second Part. A *Sacred Oratorio* on the prophecies concerning Christ and his coming; being an extract from the late Mr. Handel's grand oratorio, called the *Messiah*, consisting of the overture, and sixteen other pieces, viz. air, recitatives, and choruses. Never performed in America.

The words of the oratorio will be delivered gratis (to the ladies and gentlemen) who are pleased to patronize and encourage this *Concert*, or may be purchased of Mr. Tuckey, or by others for six Pence.

As it is impossible that a performance of this sort can be carried on without the kind assistance of gentlemen, who are lovers of music and performers on instruments; Mr. Tuckey will always gratefully acknowledge the favour of the gentlemen who assist him.

Tickets to be had of Mr. Tuckey at eight shillings each. To begin precisely at 6 o'clock.

To this may be added from his advertisement of postponement to January 16th that he had succeeded in engaging "a considerable number of ladies and gentlemen". How considerable this number was is a matter of conjecture but it is reasonably certain that it cannot have fallen much below the twenty-three singers and thirty-three instrumentalists as employed in the performance of the Messiah (the last at which Haendel was present) for the benefit of the Foundling Hospital, London, May 3, 1759.

As was said above, I have been unable to verify Ritter's dates for the two repetitions of the concert. Possibly he had October 3, 1770 instead of 1771 in mind when a sermon was preached in Trinity Church by the Rev. Dr. Auchmuty for the benefit of the 'Corporation for the Relief of the widows and children of clergymen in the Communion of the Church of England in America' and when incidentally were performed "several pieces of Church music by the most eminent composers; among others, part of the celebrated Mr. Handel's oratorio of the Messiah"[2]). However, as also Mr. Dix in his history of Trinity Church asserts that the Messiah was repeated there on October 3, 1771 "when no less than 28 clergymen were present" I leave it to others to wrestle with the apparent contradiction between contemporary announcement and historical statement.

William Tuckey's subsequent career is singularly elusive. He advertised no concerts and no further mention of his name is made in the papers. Possibly he remained at New York until the beginning of the war. Where he resided afterwards, is equally a mystery and only one fact stands forth: his death at Philadelphia in 1781.

---

1) Probably Mr. Stotherd.
2) N. Y. Mercury, Sept. 24, 1770.

During the war the musical life of New York did not come to a standstill as in other cities. The reasons are not far to seek. Lord Howe captured the city in Sept. 1776 and it remained in the hands of the British until the evacuation in November 1783. New York speedily assumed the appearance of a garrison city not overly troubled by the opposing army and naturally the officers and society-folk belonging to the tory party felt a desire to feel as comfortable as possible. This desire was not checked by the great fire of 1776 which broke out in a down-town brothel and laid 500 houses, — including Trinity Church, — about one Third of New York then a place of some odd twenty thousand inhabitants — in ashes. The absence of many of the gaiety-loving Whig families who had fled, was hardly felt as the tory ladies and such as "followed the drum" to use Dunlap's veiled but plain words vied with each other to let the English and Hessian officers and other gentlemen, loyal to the king, forget the *ennui* of their daily and by no means arduous routine.

Under the circumstances, and as there always' has been a good deal of amateur talent in the British army, it is not at all surprising that the gentlemen of the army and navy, assisted by their tory-friends, formed themselves into a theatrical company, of which at least the repertory was as good as that of their professional predecessors. The performances continued until shortly before the evacuation and the presence of regimental bands materially aided towards a satisfactory rendition of the current English operas and musical farces. Indeed, Dunlap asserts that the orchestra, formed of the bands, was better than that attached to Douglas' company. Dunlap mentions as further places of amusement the ball-room of the City Tavern and "the *Mall*, the walk in front of the ruins of Trinity Church, the resort of beaux and belles during the summer evenings, promenading in thoughtless gaiety or with measured steps to the music of the military bands placed by the officers amid the graves of the church yard".

Strange to say, he does not mention concerts, though such seem to have occupied the minds of the gentlemen as much as theatrical performances.

At first these concerts were merely tentative as for instance a concert on January 24, 1778[1]) but towards the end of the same year[2])

"some gentlemen being desirous of having Musical Parties this winter, have entered into a subscription of two guineas each for to have a *Concert* twice a week and to commence as soon as there are twelve subscribers that are performers.

As soon as the subscription is filled, Mr. Rivington [the printer] will call a meeting of the subscribers to settle in what manner the monies arising from said subscription shall be appropriated."

Though I found no further reference to these Musical Parties, little doubt

1) Royal Gazette, Jan. 24, 1778.
2) Royal Gazette, Nov. 25, 1778.

can be entertained that the gentlemen succeeded in finding the twelve per-
former-subscribers. At any rate, these subscription-concerts, though now
weekly, flourished from 1781 to 1783. Not only was the public informed
in April 1781[1]) that "there [would] be neither play nor concert during this
week" but we have a still better clue in the New York Mercury of April 16,
1781:

> *Public Concert.* The subscribers to the Concert at Roubalet's are desired to take
> notice that it will recommence to-morrow evening — and in future be continued every
> Tuesday."

In 1782 the first 'Subscription-Concert' began on January 19th "precisely at seven and finished at ten o'clock" and was to be continued on
every Wednesday[2]). The season closed with the *eighteenth* concert on
(Thursday) May 16th[3]). As curious details of management may be mentioned the request that the subscribers should write the names of the street
and number of their house on the back of their tickets, as otherwise it would
be impossible to return them with propriety[4]) and the announcement that
gentlemen, who were non-subscribers and not residents in town, would be
furnished with extra-tickets for admission at the door of the concert room
at a dollar each. The subscription was to be continued during the following
year under these conditions[5]):

> 1. The subscribers to consist of officers of the navy and army and the gentlemen
> of the city.
> 2. Each subscriber to pay one guinea on the delivery of one ticket for the season
> on which he will please to insert his name, street, and number of the house.
> 3. Each subscriber to have the privilege of introducing two ladies and one gentle-
> man, provided such gentleman is not resident in the city.
> The first concert will be at Roubalet's on Saturday the 30th instant, to commence
> precisely at 7 o'clock, and will be continued weekly of the same day.
> Officers of the Navy and Army who may not have been applied to by the mana-
> gers, will receive tickets at Roubalet's at one guinea each, and will please to leave
> their names etc. at the bar."

That the concerts actually took place may be proven by several advertisements in the Royal Gazette in January and February, 1783. If these
concerts were not ideal in rendition, they were at least abreast of the times
in spirit. If proof be required, we need but turn to the program of a concert,
given by the gentlemen of the army and navy, as were all these public entertainments, to alleviate the misfortunes of persons, affiliated in one form or
the other with the British cause. The interesting announcement, in the
Royal Gazette, April 27, 1782, reads:

---

1) N. Y. Mercury, April 9, 1781.
2) Royal Gazette, Jan. 16, 1782.
3) Royal Gazette, May 8, 1782.
4) Royal Gazette, Jan. 23, 1782.
5) Royal Gazette, Nov. 27, 1782, signed Nov. 22d.

THEATRE.

(By Permission)

This evening will be performed, a *Concert* of Vocal and Instrumental *Musick*, for the benefit of two distressed Refugee Families;

It is hoped the humanity of the respectable public will, on this laudable occasion, be particularly shewn, as they may depend upon every pains being taken to render the evening's amusement agreeable.

Act I

Sinfonie of	Toeschi
Quartetto of Davaux for violins	
Song by Mrs. Hyde 'Soldiers tir'd of Wars alarms'.	
Violino Solo Concerto of	Borchny
Quintetto of C. Bach for Flauto.	
Sinfonie of Stamitz.	

Act II

Sinfonie of Haydn	
Quartetto of Kammell, for violino	
Song by Mrs. Hyde, 'The lark's shrill notes'	
Hoboy Solo Concerto of C. Fisher	
Quartetto of Vanhall, for Flauto	
Sinfonie of	Haydn

Act III

Sinfonie of	Bach
Quartetto of Davaux, for violino	
Song by Mrs. Hyde 'If 'tis joy to wound a lover'	
Clarinetto Solo Concerto of	Mahoy
Quartetto of Toeschi, for Flauto	
Sinfonie of Mardino [Martini?]	

Tickets to be had of the different printers, at Mr. Strachan's Coffee House, and Mr. James M'Ewer's No. 242 Queenstreet. Boxes 8 *s.* Pit 8 *s.* Gallery 4 *s.*

The subscription concerts evidently fully satisfied the desire of the sons of Mars to have Musical Parties as independent benefit and other concerts were but seldom announced. Among them one deserves attention given on Sept. 10, 1780[1]) at John Mackenzie's 'White Conduit House', apparently an open air entertainment and more particularly the "Concerto Spirituale of three acts" given at the theatre on March 25, 1780 in evident (miniature) imitation of the Concert Spirituel of Paris. We are told that

each act will consist of an Overture. Song. Solo. Song. Trio. Song. Symphony. The whole to conclude with the Grand Chorus of the Messiah. The orchestra to be on the stage, which will be properly decorated on this occasion."

Finally Signior Franceschini, whose ability on the violin Charlestonians had an opportunity to enjoy from 1774 to 1782 had "by permission" a benefit on June 9, 1783[2]) and he was succeeded by William Brown, subsequently so prominent at Philadelphia, at whose benefit on August 8, 1783[3]) "Signior Franceschini was to play the first violin". Unless Brown was "honoured

---

1) Royal Gazette, Sept. 9, 1780.
2) Royal Gazette, May 31, 1783.
3) Royal Gazette, Aug. 6, 1783.

with a sufficient audience" at his proposed "second" concert at Roubalet's on August 15th[1]) his concert at August 8, 1783 may be said to have been the last given at New York under the British *régime*.

William Brown was also the first to appear before the concert-going public of New York after the war. He must have been not only a troublesome character, to judge from his quarrels with Bentley and Capron at Philadelphia, but also of a rather restless disposition. Hardly had he given his concerts of 1783 at New York when he went to Philadelphia, a journey then by no means very comfortable. Thence he proceeded to Baltimore where he is to be traced early in 1784. We further know from the chapter on concerts in Philadelphia that he ventured in the same year as far South as Charleston and back again to Philadelphia where he seems to have remained until fall of 1785 when he reappears at New York as the founder of the New York Subscription Concert. End of October[2]), the number of subscribers being "compleated", he requested the gentlemen to meet at Cape's Tavern to "fix on some regulations" relative to the enterprise. Beyond this and the announcement[3]) that the managers of the 'Gentlemen's Concert' found it agreeable that the "company should have tea and coffee served up to them in the tea rooms, in the interval betwixt the conclusion of the concert and the commencement of the dancing" we hear nothing concerning the entertainments except — and this is really the most important item — that, as Mr. Brown was permitted to note in the announcement, New York Daily Advertiser, March 14, 1786 of a benefit concert

"the managers of the Gentlemen's Concert [were] perfectly satisfied with the attention and assiduity of Mr. Brown in the conducting of the musical department during the season."

This testimonial, however, did not induce Mr. Brown to remain at New York and as there seems to have been no other musician of sufficient energy to take his place, the enterprise collapsed. Indeed, New York just then appears to have been, may be for political reasons, a rather uninviting place for musicians. Even an unquestionably able artist like Alexander Reinagle, "member of the Society of Musicians in London", found it to his advantage to leave New York after a brief sojourn.

He, like William Brown, found the Quaker City more hospitable and his return to New York in Sept. 1788 was due primarily to his connection with the Old American Company of comedians. With the return of this company things musical, too, received a fresh impetus at New York. The first fruit of Reinagle's energetic and experienced leadership was the revival of the

1) Royal Gazette, Aug. 6, 1783.
2) N. Y. Packet, Oct. 24, 1785.
3) N. Y. Daily Advertiser, Jan. 10, 1786.

'New York Subscription Concert' under his direction "the vocal parts by Mrs. Henry and Mr. Capron. The instrumental by Messrs. Reinagle, Capron, Bradford etc." The enterprise was planned on a modest scale as only three concerts were held at the City Tavern, on Sept. 15, Sept. 29 and October 13, 1788[1]) with the following "plans".

FIRST CONCERT
Act I

Overture	Stamitz
Song	Mrs. Henry
Concerto Violoncello	Mr. Bradford

Act II

Sonata Piano Forte	Mr. Reinagle
Song	Mrs. Henry
Overture of	Abel

Act III

Solo Violin	Mr. Reinagle
Song	Mrs. Henry
Overture of	Stamitz

SECOND CONCERT.
Act I

Grand Overture	Haydn
Song	Mrs. Henry
Concerto Violoncello	Capron

Act II

Sonata and Trio of Haydn and Schroter	Mr. Reinagle
Song	Mr. Capron
Quartetto, Flute, of	Bach

Act III

Trio of Boccherini	Messrs. Reinagle, Bradford and Capron
Song	[Mrs.] Henry
Overture of	Reinagle

THIRD CONCERT
Act I

Overture of	Gossec
Song	Mrs. Henry
Solo Violoncello	Mr. Capron

Act II

Concerto Pianoforte of Schroter	Mr. Reinagle
Song	Mrs. Henry
Quartetto, Flute	Vanhall

Act III

Miscellaneous Quartett	
Song	Mrs. Henry
Overture of	Stamitz

---

1) Daily Advertiser, Sept. 13, Sept. 27, Oct. 11, 1788.

In the following year, 1789, again only three concerts were offered "under the direction of Messrs. Reinagle and Capron" on Sept. 22, postponed from Sept. 15, Oct. 6 and Oct. 30th under the heading of "New York Subscription Concert of Vocal and Instrumental Music"[1]). The programs read:

FIRST CONCERT
Act 1st.

Overture of	Giordani
Song by	Mrs. Sewell
Concerto Violoncello	Mr. Capron
Overture of	Guglielmi

Act 2d.

Overture of	Stamitz
Song by	Mrs. Sewell
Sonata Piano Forte	Mr. Reinagle
Overture of	Gossec

After the first act will be performed a *Chorus*, to the words that were sung, as Gen. Washington passed the bridge at Trenton — the Music *now* composed by Mr. Reinagle.[2])

SECOND CONCERT.
Act 1st.

Overture of	J. Stamitz
Song .. ·	Mrs. Sewell
Concerto Clarinet	Mr. Wolfe
Solo Violoncello	Mr. Capron

---

1) Daily Advertiser, Sept. 15, Oct. 2, Oct. 20, 1789.

2) This chorus, to the words "Welcome, mighty chief! once more" was published in December 1789 unter the title of

Chorus sung before Gen. Washington as he passed under the triumphal arch raised on the bridge at Trenton April 21st 1789. Set to music and dedicated by permission to Mrs. Washington by A. Reinagle .. Philadelphia. Printed for the author ..."

In my Bibliography of Early Secular American Music, p. 25 I contend that Reinagles' piece was *not* sung on April 21st on the bridge at Trenton. The main reasons for this startling contention are these: 1) The concert announcement distinctly says "The music *now* composed by Mr. Reinagle". 2) The Sonata, as the original chorus was referred to in all the contemporaneous newspaper accounts was sung "by a number of young girls" unaccompanied whereas Reinagle's (rather indifferent) piece is engraved for "2 voice, 1 voice, 3 voice" with pianoforte accompanied apparently reduced from an orchestral score. Now, Reinagle's chorus is *not* identical with the President's March which in 1798 furnished the musical basis for Joseph Hopkinson's 'Hail Columbia'. Consequently, if Reinagle's chorus was not sung on April 21, 1789 on the bridge at Trenton, some other musician must have furnished the music for the patriotic musical address of welcome, which so impressed George Washington. According to certain traditions, this musician was Philip Phile and it is also claimed, (without knowledge of Reinagle's chorus etc.!) that the words were sung to the tune of the President's March of which either Phile or Philip Roth is said to have been the composer. In fact, Phile's authorship of the President's March hangs on a satisfactory solution of the problem whether the President's March was sung on the bridge or not. Those interested in this puzzle are referred to my 'Critical Notes on the origin of Hail Columbia' (Sammelbände d. IMG. 1901—2) where I mention *musical* reason for my opinion that the President's March was *not* sung on said occasion.

Act 2d.

Chorus[1])

Overture of	Vanhall
Song	Mrs. Sewell
Duett, Piano Forte and Violin of	Mozart
Overture	Ditters

THIRD CONCERT.

Act 1st.

Overture	Carlo Stamitz
Song	Mrs. Sewell
Solo Violoncello	Mr. Capron
Quartett Clarinet	Mr. Wolfe
Song	Mrs. Sewell

Act 2d.

The 6th Periodical Overture of	J. Stamitz
Song	Mrs. Sewell
Sonata Piano Forte	Mr. Reinagle
Symphonia	Gossec

The same number of concerts, at Corre's Hotel, was adhered to during the next three years. In the meantime, Reinagle had again moved to Philadelphia and it fell to Capron's lot to "open" the subscriptions. In this he was assisted during the winter of 1790—1791 by a Mr. Kullin. The first concert was to be on Jan. 3, 1791 and the others were to follow in fortnightly intervals[2]), but on Jan. 3d Capron found himself obliged by the "combination of many circumstances" to change the dates to Jan. 10th, Jan. 24th and Feb. 7th. Beyond this and the notice on Dec. 31st, 1790 that a "Mr. Luby will also perform on the Spanish guitar and sing" I have found no reference to the concerts in the Daily Advertiser except the usual details of management, f. i. that strangers could be admitted for ten shillings for each concert if introduced by a subscriber.

The series of 1792 also began rather late, on February 28th and was continued on March 13th and 20th[3]). Henri Capron divided the responsibilities and the profits between himself, Mr. Van Hagen, sen., who needs no further introduction to the reader, and George Edward Saliment, "professor of music lately arrived", teacher of singing in English and French, of the guitar and German flute on which he styled himself a master[4]). These three gentlemen submitted on Feb. 7th in the Daily Advertiser the following conditions of subscription:

I. A subscriber paying five dollars will receive a ticket which will admit to the three concerts, a gentleman, a lady, and two misses or masters, under fourteen years of age.

---

1) Apparently the same as sung at the first concert.
2) Daily Advertiser, Dec. 21, 1790.
3) Daily Advertiser, Feb. 25, March 13 and March 20, 1792.
4) Daily Advertiser, Aug. 18, 1791. Saliment remained true to New York but disappears from the directories after 1800.

II. A single subscriber paying three dollars, will receive a ticket which will admit a gentleman or lady to the three concerts.

III. A ticket to admit a gentleman or lady, to a single concert, ten shillings.

IV. A ticket to admit a gentleman and lady to a single concert two dollars.

V. The subscription money to be paid on delivery of the tickets.

After each Concert a Ball.

The conditions being satisfactory to the public, the concerts were held on the dates mentioned with these offerings:

FIRST CONCERT.
Act I
Symphony of	Pleyel
Piano Forte Concerto	Mr. Van Hagen
Song	Mrs. Hay
Violin Concerto	P. A. Van Hagen, jun.
Violoncello Concerto	Mr. Capron

Act II.
Symphony of	Pleyel
Flute Concerto	Mr. Saliment
Song	Mrs. Hay
Violin Concerto	Mr. Van Hagen
Symphony of	Pleyel

SECOND CONCERT.
Act I
Overture of Henry IV by	Martini
Piano Forte Concerto	Mr. Van Hagen
Song	Mrs. Hay
Violin Concerto	P. A. Van Hagen, jun.
Flute Concerto	Mr. Saliment

Act 2d.
Interlude of Henry IV by	Martini
Solo Violoncello	Mr. Capron
Song	Mrs. Hay
Violin Concerto	Mr. Van Hagen

THIRD CONCERT.
Act I
Overture	
Song	Mr. Capron
Forte Piano Sonata, by Pleyel	Mr. Van Hagen
Tenor Concerto	P. A. Van Hagen, jun.

Act II
Overture of the Deserter	[Dibdin or Monsigny]
Flute Concert	Mr. Saliment
Song	Mr. Capron
Violin Concerto	Mr. Van Hagen
Overture of Rose and Colas	[Monsigny]

Shortly afterwards Henry Capron took up his residence at Philadelphia and the Subscription-Concerts were continued at Corre's Hotel under the management of G. E. Saliment, who soon seems to have dropped out, and Mr. and Mrs. Van Hagen, lately from Amsterdam who was to perform "concertos, sonatas and accompanyments on the pianoforte" as we are informed in the proposals on Sept. 27, 1792 in the Daily Advertiser. The managers had also succeeded in engaging the "vocal powers" of the famous Mrs. Mechtler, "lately from England". As far as the solo numbers of the programs are concerned, they resulted more or less in an exhibition of the abilities of the Van Hagen family with a plentiful display of Pleyel's music. Here are the three programs of the three concerts on Oct. 15, Oct. 29 and Nov. 12, 1792[1]):

FIRST CONCERT.
Act I.

Grand Overture of	Pleyel
Song	Mrs. Mechtler
Forte Piano Concerto	Mrs. Van Hagen
Violin Concerto	P. A. Van Hagen, jun.
Flute Concerto	Mr. Saliment

Act II.

Violin Concerto	Mr. Van Hagen
Song	Mrs. Mechtler
Forte Piano Concerto	Mrs. Van Hagen
Sinfonia Finale of	Pleyel

Several gentlemen, amateurs, of the St. Cecilia Society in this city, have obligingly consented to honor the performance with their assistance.

SECOND CONCERT.
Act I.

Overture of	Pichel
Forte Piano Concerto	Mrs. Van Hagen
Song	Mrs. Mechtler
Flute Concerto	Mr. Saliment
Simphonie Concertante, of..	C. Stamitz

Act II.

Violin Concerto	Mr. Van Hagen
Song	Mrs. Mechtler
Forte Piano Concerto	Mrs. Van Hagen
Simphonie Finale of	Pleyel

THIRD CONCERT.
First Part.

Grand Overture of	Lackwith [!]
Violin Concerto	P. A. Van Hagen, jun.
Song	Mrs. Mechtler
Forte Piano Concerto	Mrs. Van Hagen

Second Part.

Flute Concert	Mr. Saliment
Song	Mrs. Mechtler
Violin Concerto	Mr. Van Hagen
Rondo of	Pleyel

1) Daily Advertiser, Oct. 10, Oct. 23, Nov. 3, 1792.

If the Van Hagens, contrary to tradition, gave their Subscription-Concerts in the fall of 1792 instead of in the winter, their reasons must have been weighty. Presumably they had heard that Messrs. James Hewitt, Jean Gehot, B. Bergmann and William Young contemplated an encroachment upon their monopoly and they hastened to reap a harvest before these formidable competitors became active who called themselves in the papers "professors of music from the opera house Hanoversquare and Professional Concerts under the direction of Haydn, Pleyel, etc. London" and who promised to make their enterprise "entertaining and instructive by introducing every novel performance that Europe has produced"[1]). In this the Van Hagens succeeded. Though the four gentlemen advertised the first of a series of concerts "by subscription for *twelve* nights" for Oct. 4, 1792[2]) they found themselves on the very day of performance compelled to postpone the entertainment which certainly would have been entertaining and instructive with this program[3]):

ACT I.

Overture	Rossetti
Quartetto	Wraniski [!]
Concerto Flute, Mr. Young	C. G. Gloesch
Concertante for violin, flute, tenor, and violoncello	Pleyel
Concerto Violoncello, Mr. Phillips	Phillips

ACT II.

Sinfonia	Ditters
Concerto Violin, Mr. Hewitt	C. Stamitz
Quartetto Flute	Schmittbauer
Grand Overture	Pleyel

More than likely the ambitious gentlemen had not studied their ground carefully enough. Twelve concerts were decidedly too many for New York, at least under the conditions proposed, namely that the subscriptions were to be

"for ladies, one guinea and a half each — for gentlemen, two guineas each — for a lady and gentleman, three guineas each — Non subscribers, one dollar each."

The enterprising quartet, or rather trio as William Young[4]) dropped out, soon saw the discrepancy between their proposals and the willingless

---

1) The best known of the four was Jean Gehot. According to Fétis he was born about 1756 in Belgium, travelled in Germany and France after 1780 and lived in London in 1784, but he must have been there as early as 1781 as Pohl ('Mozart u. Haydn in London', p. 370) traced him in London in that year as violin virtuoso. Eitner mentions numerous compositions by Gehot, 36 quartets, trios etc. and several theoretical works. The identity of this Gehot with the "American" Gehot appears from John R. Parker's Musical Reminiscences in the 'Euterpiad', 1822. Parker also states that Gehot died in obscurity and indigent circumstances. Of his compositions, composed in America, only very few, and they insignificant, are to be traced.
2) Daily Advertiser, Sept. 25, 1792.
3) Daily Advertiser, Oct. 4, 1792.
4) According to Dunlap he was sentenced to death in 1797 for having killed in a desperate mood the constable who came to arrest him for contracted debts.

of the New Yorkers, accustomed to a more meagre musical diet, to subscribe so much money for so many concerts.   To be sure, they stated on
November 3d that their reason for postponing their subscription concerts was
to obtain the celebrated singers, Mrs. Pownall (late Mrs. Wrighten) and Mrs. Hodgkinson, both recently from England, and as they were determined to engage the first singers
in America have spared no expence nor trouble (by separate journeys to Philadelphia,
etc. etc.) to gratify the amateurs of music.

However, the fact that they further announced that the first concert
would be held "as soon as the subscription [was] adequate to the expence"
and that, when this finally happened, they limited themselves to six concerts
instead of twelve clearly indicates other reasons besides the one published.
Nor did they, as will be seen, adhere to the original plan of introducing
"catches and glees by many other eminent singers from London", meaning,
of course, the singing members of the Old American Company.

Not before the middle of January, 1793 did Messrs. Hewitt, Bergman,
and Phillips — he too from London — meet with sufficient encouragement
to launch their enterprise.   The first concert took place at Corre's Hotel on
January 23, 1793, the second on February 21st, and so forth on March 2d,
March 16th, March 25th and April 6th[1]).   A peculiar detail of management
was this that subscriptions were kept open until the end of the series with
gradually decreasing prices.   But more important is the fact that works by
Wanhal and Haydn were played from manuscript and that the latter's
'Passion of our Saviour' perhaps had its first performance in America on
March 25, 1793.   This 'Passion' was none other than the 'Seven Words'
composed in 1785 for the cathedral of Cadiz, and shortly afterwards performed
at London under the title of 'Passione Instrumentale':

FIRST CONCERT.
Act I.

Overture	Haydn
Song	Mrs. Pownall
Quartetto	Girowetz
Song	Mrs. Hodgkinson
Concerto Violoncello	Mr. Phillips

Act II.

Concerto Violin	Mr. Hewitt
Song	Mrs. Hodgkinson
Song	Mrs. Pownall
Finale[2])	

SECOND CONCERT.
Act I.

Overture	Haydn
Song	Mrs. Pownall

---

1) Daily Advertiser, Jan. 19, Feb. 16, March 13, March 23, March 28, 1793.   To
avoid confusion it might be well to state that several postponements and changes of
program were made. *Only the final* the dates and programs have been entered here.
2) The balls following the concerts were conducted by Mr. Phillips.

Trio .. .. Schmidt
Song .. .. Mrs. Hodgkinson
Concerto Violoncello .. .. Mr. Phillips

Act II.

Concerto Violin .. .. Mr. Hewitt
Song .. .. Mrs. Hodgkinson
Duetto, Violin and Viola .. .. Messrs. Hewitt and [?]
Song .. .. Mrs. Pownall
Overture .. .. Ditters
By particular desire
Song, 'The Primrose Girl' .. .. Mrs. Pownall

THIRD CONCERT.

Act I.

Sinfonia .. .. Vanhall, M. S.
Song .. .. Mrs. Hodgkinson
Quartetto .. .. Pleyel
Song .. .. Mrs. Pownall
Concerto, Violoncello .. .. Mr. Phillips

Act II.

Concerto Violin .. .. Mr. Hewitt
Song .. .. Mrs. Pownall
Overture .. .. Stamitz
Song .. .. Mrs. Hodgkinson
Finale .. .. Haydn

FOURTH CONCERT.

Act I.

New Overture .. .. Haydn, M. S.
Song .. .. Mrs. Pownall
Quartetto .. .. Pleyel
Song .. .. Mrs. Hodgkinson
Concerto Violoncello .. .. Mr. Phillips

Act II.

Celebrated concertante, Violin, viola, clarinetto,
and violoncello .. .. Pleyel
Song .. .. Mrs. Pownall
Sinfonia .. .. Rosetti
Song .. .. Mrs. Hodgkinson
Finale, Battle Overture .. .. Hewitt[1])

FIFTH CONCERT.

Act I.

Overture, La Chasse .. .. Haydn
Song .. .. Mrs. Hodgkinson
Quartetto .. .. Pleyel
Song .. .. :. .. .. :. .. .. .. Mrs. Pownall
Concerto Violoncello .. .. Mr. Phillips.

---

1) This naïvely programmatic piece was first played on Sept. 26, 1792. The 'program' will be given under benefit-concerts.

Act II.

The Passion of our Saviour, expressed in instrumental parts, composed by Haydn.

    Part 1. Introduction
        2. Father [for]give them, they know not what they do.
        3. To day thou shalt be with me in Paradise
        4. Woman — behold thy son
        5. My God, my God, why hast thou forsaken me
        6. I thirst
        7. It is finished
        8. Into thy hands I command my spirit.
To conclude with the representation of an Earthquake.

Song	Mrs. Hodgkinson
Sinfonia	Stamitz
Song	Mrs. Pownal
Finale	Haydn

SIXTH CONCERT.
Act I.

Overture	Van Hall
Song	Mrs. Hodgkinson
Quartetto	Stamitz
Song	Mrs. Pownall
Concerto Violoncello	Mr. Phillips

Act 2 d.

Concertante	Pleyel
Song	Mrs. Hodgkinson
Overture	Stamitz
Song	Mrs. Pownall
Full piece	Haydn[1])

In the following year the rival organisations again appeared on the plan with a slight interchange of forces. Under the direction of Messrs. Capron, Hewitt and Saliment with Hulett as conductor of the balls, a series of three 'City Concerts' was given at the City Tavern on Dec. 27, 1793, Jan. 9 and

---

1) For reasons not mentioned this concert was "removed" from Corre's Hotel to the City Tavern. The date was originally fixed for April 6, with this program, devoted entirely to Corelli and Haendel, and certainly more interesting than the one performed

Act I.

Overture, Sampson	Haendel
Song 'Come ever smiling liberty' from the Oratorium of Judas Maccabaeus	Mr. Pownall
1st Concerto	Corelli
Duetto 'O lovely peace with plenty crown'd'	Mrs. Hodgkinson and Mrs. Pownall
Overture, Ariadne	Haendel

Act II.

Overture, Jephta	Haendel
Song 'I know that my Redeemer liveth', from the 'Messiah'	Mrs. Pownall
2d Concerto	Corelli
Recit. and song 'Comfort ye my people', from the Messiah	Mrs. Hodgkinson
Overture, Occasional	Haendel

Jan. 23, 1794[1]). Mr. and Mrs. Van Hagen and Mr. Phillips, in charge of the Terpsichorean features, in turn and evidently jealous of their antecedents, opened both in French and English a subscription for three '*Old City Concerts*', held at Corre's Hotel on Jan. 7, Jan. 21 and Feb. 4, 1794[2]). The City Concerts were predominantly instrumental in character, the only singer engaged being Mrs. Pownall, assisted occasionally in French duets by Mr. Capron. On the other hand, in the Old City Concerts vocal and instrumental music were more evenly distributed. Against Mrs. Pownall were pitched Mr. and Mrs. Hodgkinson and Mr. Prigmore, also the precocious talents of Master Van Hagen being *featured*. A slight difference appears further in the arrangement of the programs. In the Old City Concerts the virtuoso element clearly reigned supreme and no definite place seems to have governed the selection of the orchestral numbers, whereas the pillar, as Theodore Thomas would have said, in the programs offered by Capron clearly was formed by Haydn, whose name appears not once on the programs of the Old City Concerts. Otherwise the concerts had much in common and the similarity between the conditions of subscription was probably more an outcome of business considerations than of a competition for public favor. The terms at the City Concerts, for instance, were these. Each subscriber paid 5 dollars which entitled him to a ticket to admit himself and two ladies. A "single" subscriber paid 3 dollars and a non-subscriber 10 shillings for each concert. The price of admission for a young lady or gentleman under 14 years of age was 5 shillings, a condition somewhat recalling to our mind the — to Americans, at least, — odd custom prevailing in German where "Kinder und Militär zahlen die Hälfte". The programs read:

CITY CONCERTS.

FIRST CONCERT.

ACT I.
Overture .. .. Haydn
Concerto Piano Forte .. .. Mr. Rausch
Song .. .. Mrs. Pownall
Concerto Flute .. .. Mr. Saliment

ACT II.
Concerto Violoncello .. .. Capron
Song .. .. Mrs. Pownall
Solo, French Horn .. .. Mr. Pelissier
French Duet for 2 voices .. .. .. Mrs. Pownall and Mr. Capron
Finale .. .. Pleyel

1) Daily Advertiser, Dec. 26, 1793; Jan. 7, and 20, 1794.
2) Daily Advertiser, Jan. 3, 15 and 30, 1794.

13*

SECOND CONCERT.

Act I.

Sinfonie	Vanhall, M. S.
Song	Mrs. Pownall
Quartetto, Pleyel	Messrs. Hewitt, Bergman. Du Champ and Capron
Duett for 2 voices 'How sweet is the breath of morn'	Mrs. Pownall and Mr. Capron
Sonata Piano forte	Madame de Seze.

Act II.

Concerto Flute	Mr. Saliment
Song, accompanied on the PianoForte	Madame De Seze
Duett, Violin and Violoncello	Messrs. Hewitt and Capron
Song	Mrs. Pownall
Finale	Haydn

THIRD CONCERT.

Act I.

Overture, La Reine	Haydn
Song, accompanied on the Piano Forte	Madame de Seze.
Quartetto	Messrs. Saliment, Hewitt, Du Camp and Capron
Song	Mrs. Pownall
Concerto Violin	Mr. Hewitt

Act II.

Concerto Piano Forte	Mr. Rausch
Song, accompanied on the Pedal Harp	Madame De Seze
Concerto Violoncello	Mr. Capron
Song	Mrs. Pownall
Finale, La Chasse	Haydn

OLD CITY CONCERTS.

FIRST CONCERT.

Act I.

Overture	Pleyel
Song 'Mansion of peace'	Mr. Hodgkinson
Concerto Tenor	Master Van Hagen
Song 'Answer to the Mansion of peace'	Mrs. Hodgkinson
Concerto, grand Piano Forte	Mrs. Van Hagen
Duett 'How sweet in the woodlands'	Messrs. Hodgkinson and Prigmore

Act II.

Concerto Clarinett	Mr. Wolf
Song 'Blue ey'd Patty'	Mr. Prigmore
Solo, French horn	Mr. Pellesier
Bravoura, 'Cease gay seducers'	Mrs. Hodgkinson
Sonata on the Forte Piano for four hands	Mr. and Mrs. Hodgkinson
Duett 'Could you to battle march away'	Mr. and Mrs. Hodgkinson
Concerto Violin	Mr. Van Hagen

SECOND CONCERT.
Act I.
Overture	Stamitz
Hunting Song	Mr. Prigmore
Concerto Tenor	Master Van Hagen
Bravura 'The bleak wind whistles' ..	Mrs. Hodgkinson
Sonata, Piano Forte	Mrs. Van Hagen

Act II.
Overture, Henry 4th	Martini
Song 'Poor Richard'	Mr. Hodgkinson
Concerto Violin	Mr. Van Hagen
Song, accompanied by the clarinet, 'Sympathetic echo'	Mrs. Hodgkinson
Concerto Pianoforte	Mrs. Van Hagen
Comic Duett	Mr. & Mrs. Hodgkinson
Finale	De Zaides.[1])

THIRD CONCERT.
Act I.
Overture by	Plyel
Trio 'Incitement to virtue'	Mr. & Mrs. Hodgkinson & Mr. Prigmore
Concerto Violin	Master Van Hagen
Song 'Humanity'	Mr. Hodgkinson
Sonata on the Piano Forte	Mrs. Van Hagen

Act II.
Entre Acte of Henry the Fourth Song 'Generous wine'	Mr. Hodgkinson
Concerto Violin	Mr. Van Hagen
Song 'Remembrance'	Mrs. Hodgkinson
Concerto on the Piano Forte	Mrs. Van Hagen
(By desire) Confic Duett 'The jealous man, etc.'	Mr. & Mrs. Hodgkinson
Finale, the Deserter	Grétry [!]

During the same year, the rival managers must have come to an understanding and a junction of their forces was effected, for when the concert-season opened, the Daily Advertiser on Dec. 12, and 18, 1794, possibly much to the surprise of its readers, announced that Mr. and Mrs. Van Hagen, Messrs. Hewitt and Saliment — Capron had again left for Philadelphia — would co-operate in a series of three concerts at the New Assembly Room in William Street "upon a much larger scale than heretofore", the vocal parts to be held by Mrs. Hodgkinson, Mrs. Pownall and Mr. Benjamin Carr. Wherein this larger scale consisted is difficult to see but perhaps some plausible explanation was deemed necessary in view of the fact that the subscription-price was raised from 5 to 6 dollars for two ladies and a gentleman, from 3 to $4^1/_2$ dollars for one lady and a gentleman, etc. Of course, this advance in the price of subscription was due primarily to the fact that

---

1) Dezède, 1740—92.

otherwise a co-operation would have been to the disadvantage of the managers rather than to their advantage. Finally, it is noteworthy that the series was not entitled Old City Concerts, but City Concerts. They were held on Feb. 21, March 5 and March 19, 1795 with these programs[1]):

FIRST CONCERT
Act I.

Sinfonie	Pleyel
Ballad	Mrs. Pownall
Concerto Flute	Mr. Saliment
Song	Mr. Carr
A Concerto Piano Forte	Mrs. Van Hagen

Act II.

Overture	Girovetz
Song	Mrs. Hodgkinson
Quartetto	Messrs. Hewitt, Bergman, Van Hagen, jun., Rosendall
Song .. .., ...	Mrs. Pownall
Full Piece	Haydn

SECOND CONCERT.
Act I.

Storm Overture	Mr. Hewitt
Song	Mr. Carr
Concerto Piano Forte	Mr. Van Hagen
Song	Mrs. Hodgkinson
Concerto Flute	Mr. Saliment

Act II.

Concerto Violin	Mr. Hewitt
Song	Mrs. Pownall
Duet, for violin and viola	Messrs. Hewitt and Van Hagen, jun.
Song	Mr. Carr
Finale	Pichl

THIRD CONCERT.
Act I.

Grand Symphony	Pichl
Song	Mrs. Hodgkinson
Quartetto	Messrs. Van Hagen jun , Van Hagen, sen., Bergman and Hewitt
Song	Mrs. Pownall
Concerto Pianoforte	Mrs. Van Hagen

Act II.

Concerto Flute	Mr. Saliment
Song	Mr. Carr
Concerto Violin	Mr. Van Hagen
Song	Mrs. Hodgkinson
Finale	Pleyel

---

1) Daily Advertiser, Feb. 18, March 2, March 17, 1795.

This co-operation appears not to have been to the taste of Hewitt and Saliment. They withdrew and left the field to Mr. and Mrs. Van Hagen who went into partnership with Frederick Rausch, music teacher and dealer in instruments, and John Christopher Moller, late of Philadelphia. At first, on Dec. 4, 1795 in the American Minerva, they announced under the suggestive heading of *Old* City Concert a series of four concerts but contented themselves a few weeks later, on Dec. 26th, with a subscription for three. The concerts were held at the New Assembly Room on Jan. 12, Jan. 21 and Feb. 2, 1796 with Miss Broadhurst as attraction in the "vocal parts"[1]).

FIRST CONCERT.
ACT I.
Sinfonia	Gyrovetz
Concerto Flute, by a gentleman lately from Europe	
Song 'Amidst the allusions'	Miss Broadhurst
Duetto Piano Forte	Mrs. Van Hagen and Mr. Rausch
Concertante	Mr. V. Hagen and Van Hagen, jun.

ACT II.
Sinfonia	Pichl
Concerto Piano Forte	Mrs. Van Hagen
Song 'How can I forget the fond hour' ..	Miss. Broadhurst
Concert	Mr. V. Hagen
Finale	Haydn

SECOND CONCERT.
ACT I.
Sinfonia	Pleval
Song, 'Court one not to scenes of pleasure ..	Miss Broadhurst
Fantasie with a rondo	Mr. Rausch
Song Bravoura	Miss Broadhurst
Concerto Violin	Mr. Van Hagen

ACT II.
Sinfonia .. .., ...	Pichl
Song 'Twas within a mile of Edinburg town'	Miss Broadhurst
Duetto Piano Forte and Tenor.	Messrs. Moller, Van Hagen
Finale	Haydn

THIRD CONCERT.
ACT I.
Grand Overture	Wranitzky
Song 'Kind Zephyr wast my passing sighs' ..	Miss Broadhurst
Sonata on the harp	Mr. Relain
Song 'Tho, by the tempest'	Miss Broadhurst
Concerto Piano Forte	Mr. Moller

ACT II.
Overture, Henry 4th	Martini
Song 'O Nancy wilt thou fly with me'	Miss Broadhurst
Concerto Violin	Mr. Vanhagen
Finale	Pleyel

---

1) American Minerva, Jan. 7, Jan. 18, Jan. 28, 1796.

So far it had been Philadelphia that robbed New York of some of her best musicians but now Boston was beginning to act as a magnet. Thus New York lost in 1796 the useful and energetic services of the Van Hagens. Logically the continuation of the Old City Concerts fell upon Mr. Moller's shoulders but unfortunately I am unable to submit data of consequence beyond the mere fact that he actually did continue the concerts. Presumably the programs and other data referring to the three Old City Concerts of 1797 for which Moller "by advice of his friends" opened a subscription in the Minerva on Dec. 27, 1796 are hidden in one or the other of the daily papers, but they escaped me. Or, possibly, he fared not better than did Messrs. Hewitt, Rausch and Saliment who intended to revive the City Concerts under the name of the City Subscription Concert in competition with Moller's series[1]) but not finding the subscription adequate to the expense saw their way clear for one concert only. Though this "annual" concert of Feb. 7, 1797[2]) properly belongs to the benefit-concerts, its program may be inserted here as it also represents the last sign of life of the City Concerts started by Hewitt and his associates in 1793.

Act I.

Overture	Haydn
Song	Mr. Tyler
Concerto Pianoforte	Mr. Rausch
Song	Mrs. Hodgkinson
Glee 'Come live with me and be my love'	
Battle of Prague, arranged for a full orchestra by	Hewitt

Act II.

Concerto Violin	Mr. Hewitt
Song	Mr. Tyler
Concerto Flute	Mr. Saliment
Song	Mrs. Hodgkinson
Glee 'Adieu to the village delights'	
Finale .:	Pichl

Nor did the Old City Concert last much longer. On Feb. 12, 1798 Mr. Moller advertised in the Daily Advertiser subscription-concerts in which would be introduced parts of the 'Messiah' but it does not appear that he was successful in continuing the concerts beyond the first. In fact, on the same day, while giving the *plan* of the first concert, he was not in a position to announce the exact date — it was to be advertised "in due time". As the same advertisement was still running as late as March 14th it may be inferred that the concert did not take place at all. At any rate, a series of concerts was not given. The program of the first and last concert reads:

1) Minerva, Dec. 24, 1796.
2) Daily Advertiser, Jan. 30, 1797.

PART I.

Overture	Pleyel
Song	Miss Moller
Concertante	Messrs. Nicolas and
	Averdile
Song	Miss Broadhurst
Duett, grand Piano Forte	Miss Moller and Mr. Geib
Full piece	Hayden

PART II.

New Overture	J. C. Moller
Song 'Comfort ye my people'	Miss Broadhurst
Concertante Flute	Mr. Saliment
Song 'I know that my Redeemer liveth'	Miss Moller

Chorus (and the Glory) [!] The principal parts by Messieurs
Piercon, Shiptons and Lee, and by MissBroadhurst and Miss
Moller.

After this no subscription-concerts are mentioned during the last years of the century. However, if undoubtedly the interest in such enterprises had been waning, it should not be surmised that New York was without concerts in addition to the usual benefit entertainments. As far as private enterprises of a sustained character are concerned, it will be seen that the center of the concert-season in New York, too, had merely shifted from the winter to the summer and besides this it must be taken into consideration that the activity of the several musical societies, though very little is known of them, naturally and as was also the case in smaller European cities, seriously interfered with subscription concerts as undertaken independently by individual musicians.

The Harmonic Society of pre-revolutionary times seems to have died a natural death when the war-clouds began to hover over New York. It was to my knowledge the only musical society founded in the city before the war but Mr. F. L. Ritter, while not mentioning the Harmonic Society, refers to an Apollo Society of which he says (on p. 135 of his History) that it seems to have been the foremost among those musical societies ... established in New York about the middle of the last century. A very interesting statement, but unfortunately Ritter forgot to mention his source and therefore we feel justified in treating his statement with scepticism! However, after the war, soon another attempt was made to unite the music lovers into a society and this attempt was followed by others with various fortunes.

On Nov. 9, 1786 the Daily Advertiser announced that "the Society for promoting vocal music [would] meet at 6 o'clock this evening at Mr. Hulett's[1])

---

1) This was John Hamilton Hulett, dancing master, son and successor to old Hulett who had died in 1785. John H. Hulett is still to be traced in the New York Directory of 1805, but he does not appear in that of 1810.

School Room in Little Queen Street, agreeable to adjournment". Consequently this meeting was not called to *found* the society. It therefore remains open to further investigation whether or not the society was founded prior to 1786 and it is also a matter of further research to ascertain what became of it.

One year later, the same paper on Dec. 27, 1787 addressed "all lovers of music" with proposals of "several musical amateurs, to establish a musical society, both vocal and instrumental" and a meeting at which "to consider and adopt some fundamental rules", was called at the Charity Schoolroom in John Street first for Dec. 29th and then for Jan. 5, 1788 — when "performers *only* [were] requested to attend". The meeting evidently led to something tangible for on Feb. 6th, in the Daily Advertiser, John Wood, Secretary by order of the moderator, called a special meeting of the members of the *"Musical Society* of the City of New York".

Concerning the first year of the society's activity the newspapers observe silence and not until June 1789 do we hear of the object of the society. Then, on June 12th in the Daily Gazette, a concert of sacred music was advertised for June 18th at the Lutheran Church "by a few lovers of music having formed themselves into a Society for the purpose of promoting that noble art", *i. e.* sacred music. The proceeds were to cover the payment of an organ already purchased by way of individual contributions and to otherwise forward the designs of the society. That these 'few lovers of music" constituted the members of the Musical Society becomes apparent from the advertisement in the Daily Gazette of June 13th when it was said that on June 18th the "Musical Society of the City of New York together with the assistance of a Band of instrumental musicians" would perform the following pieces:

1. Overture by .. .. Vanhall
2. Anthem, from Psalm 150 by .. Arnold
3. Jonah, an oratorio by .. .. .. Felsted[1])
4. Symphony by .. .. Kammell
5. Anthem, from Psalm 80, by .. Woodward
6. Violin Concerto by .. .. Phile
7. Anthem, from 1. Cor. 15, by .. Keefe
8. Simphony Finale.

This is the only program of the society I have been able to discover and the few remaining data on the Musical Society of the City of New York were gleaned from the New York directories. Thus it would appear that George Gilfert, musician and subsequently of some prominence as music dealer, was the "director", *scil.* president, in 1789, followed in 1791 by Isaac Van Vleek, notary public and from 1792 to 1794 by Henry Will, pewterer.

---

1) More about this rather obscure oratorio under Boston.

The society, which had its meeting place in John Street, is not mentioned in the directory of 1795 nor later and therefore apparently had ceased to exist.

In the meantime a society had been founded which, though not under its original name, lived far into the nineteenth century[1]). It was the *St. Cecilia Society*, "instituted", as we learn from the New York directory of 1795, "in 1791, with a view to cultivate the science of music, and a good taste in its education [execution?]. The concerts [were] held weekly, on Saturday evenings; the principal professors of music [in the city being] members and performers at these concerts". The officers originally in charge (see N. Y. Directory, 1792) were David Mitchelson as president, Lewis Ogden as treasurer, and Isaac Van Vleek as secretary. Mr. Mitchelson held his office for four years, when succeeded by Mr. Lewis Ogden. The last year of the society's independent existence, 1799, then saw Mr. Joseph Fitch at the helm, Frederick Rausch, the musician, being vice-president.

If this society clearly cultivated instrumental music, the very name of another points to an activity in the realms of church music. When the 'Uranian Society' was founded and when it went out of existence is doubtful. The first reference to it is found in the Daily Advertiser, March 7, 1793 when a special meeting was to be held on the same evening at the City Hall and the last may be gleaned from the directory of 1798 under the heading 'Uranian Musical Society', with Mr. Joseph Kimball as president and a surprisingly long list of well-to-do and prominent citizens as members. In the directory of 1797 it is expressly stated that "this society was instituted for improvement in sacred vocal music. Elect the first Wednesday in January, and meet every Wednesday".

---

1) Mr. Ritter had this to say (on p. 135):

"In 1791 a St. Cecilia Society was established but it lasted only a few years; the cultivation of instrumental music was its aim. Mr. S. Johnson tells me that, about 1838, a gentleman, Mr. Ming, who belonged to it, told him that the St. Cecilia Society failed because the public did not appreciate classical music. When a small band of seven or eight musicians one night attempted to play in the theatre a portion of a Haydn symphony, the "gods" in the gallery cried out "Stop that noise; give us 'Bonypart crossing the Rhine', 'Washington's March', or 'Yankee Doodle'." On the following night, when the musicians repeated the "offense" by again attempting to play Haydn, they were greeted with "cat calls", rotten eggs, and bouquets of a variety of vegetables".

This anecdote is amusing, but it is an anecdote and should not be taken seriously. It is very characteristic of Ritter's attitude towards early music in America that he mentions this occurrence in the same breath with the activity of the St. Cecilia Society though it did not happen at its concerts and without asking himself whether such things did not happen elsewhere besides in America and whether it really happened "because the public did not appreciate classical music". As a matter of fact, he might have gleaned from Dunlap that the public, responsible for said incident, consisted of two drunken ship-captains!

It may also be opportune to remark here that nothing goes to show that the 'Euterpean Society', still flourishing (?) when in 1842 the New York Philharmonic Society was founded and looking back on a career of several decades was founded *before* 1800. If, as Mr. Ritter says on p. 223, about 1840 "this society was considered as perhaps

Merely mentioning a 'Polyhymnian Society' which must have existed in 1799[1]) and possibly was founded in 1798 as in April 1799 at the "first quarterly meeting " "new" officers were to be elected, I submit the few data I found concerning the Columbian Anacreontic Society. The name implies an imitation, and as the model-society was dissolved in 1786, even a revival on American soil of the Anacreontic Society of London. The latter had been established by several noblemen and wealthy amateurs towards the close of the 18th century and its fortnightly concerts were held at the Crown and Anchor Tavern in the Strand. The concerts, in which the leading members of the musical profession took part as honorary members, were followed by a supper, after which the president or his deputy sang the constitutional song 'To Anacreon in Heaven' (which later on was to furnish us Americans the musical substratum of both 'Adams and Liberty' and 'The Star Spangled Banner'). This apostrophe was succeeded by songs in every style and especially by catches and glees sung by the most eminent vocalists of the day (Grove). That these songs — sung *after* supper in a society for men only — were unfit for the ears of the Duchess of Devonshire is not surprising. Still the indignation and disgust of this lady, then leader of the *haut-ton* who, as Parke in his anecdotic Memoirs narrates, was foolish enough to clandestinely attend one of the meetings, was so annoying to the members that the society soon afterwards, in 1786, declared itself dissolved.

In New York, to be sure, there were no noble men but there were wealthy amateurs enough of a convivial bend of mind, who had no objections against a broad joke, if they could swallow it with a bumper of Madeira, who liked music in general, and whom the spirit easily would move to sing out drinking

the oldest musical society in the United States" and "was regarded as the lineal descendant of the old Apollo", at least the last part of his statement should be encircled with question-marks. Had the compiler of the city directories for 1800 continued the practice of enumerating the musical societies, it would be easy enough to ascertain the year of foundation of the Euterpean Society, but unfortunately he did not.

Now, Mr. Thomas Goodwin, whose 'Sketches and impressions' from his 'after dinner-talk' R. Osgood Mason published in 1887 had this to say: "The Euterpean, an amateur orchestra, was already an old organisation half a century ago. It had been well managed, and owned a small library and several valuable instruments ... I have a program of its forty-eighth anniversary concert, given January 21, 1847, which would carry its organisation back to the last century". This means that the society was founded either on Jan. 21, 1799 or on Jan. 21, 1800. I am inclined to accept the latter possibility, for these reasons. While the fact that the Euterpean Society is not mentioned in the papers of 1799 and 1800, not even meetings being called through the medium of the press, as was customary, may not carry much weight, the other fact, that in the account of the procession in memory of George Washington on Dec. 31, 1799 both the Philharmonic and the Columbian Anacreontic Society are mentioned but not the Euterpean, makes me suspicious! The more so, as the Euterpean Society is not even enumerated among the musical societies in the directory of 1799, issued *after* January, 1799! For these reasons, I doubt very much that the Euterpean Society was founded before January 21, 1800.

1) Daily Advertiser, April 4, 1799.

songs like 'To Anacreon in Heaven' or catches and glees in Anglo-Saxon fashion. It needed but a "jolly, good fellow" with recollections of the happy days of the Anacreontic Society in dear, old London to mould his kindred into a society and him they found in John Hodgkinson, a disciple of Bacchus and irrisistible as actor and singer, whom Dunlap called "the soul of our musical societies". At any rate, it is not a violent supposition to consider Hodgkinson the moving spirit in the foundation of the Columbian Anacreontic Society in 1795 in view of the fact that he was the president during the first four years of the club's existence[1]) with this formidable array of convivial talent to assist him in the furtherment of Anacreontic ideals:

> John C. Shaw, first Vice-President
> Aquila Giles, second Vice-President
> John Bleecker, Secretary
> John Ferrers, Treasurer
> William Richardson, William H. Robinson, Henry
> Livingston, James Maitland, James Cuyler, John
> K. Beckman, *Harmonics.*
> George Pollock, B. Winthrop, Joseph Stansbury,
> Edward Moore, Richard Morris, A. Giles and James
> Hewitt, standing Committee.

That the society was founded in 1795, at any rate not later, becomes apparent from a concert program announced by Messrs. Hewitt and Saliment in the Daily Advertiser, June 6, 1795. As last number figures:

"Collin's Odes on the Passions, to be spoken by Mr. Hodgkinson. With music representative of each passion, as performed at the *Anacreontic Society,* composed by J. Hewitt,"

in all probability the earliest example of melodramatic music composed in America. Beyond this and personal data on the board of managers, very little information is to be gleaned from contemporary sources, but that the society flourished for a number, of years, is certain. Possibly some day the constitution, and by-laws, the original as well as the revised and amended laws and regulations "of March 1800[2]) will turn up and also a goodly collection of programs which would enable us to trace what music and when it was performed at the regular concerts, usually given at the Tontine Coffee House following the business meetings. In the absence of such documents the supposition may not be amiss that the Columbian Anacreontic Society gave quite a stimulus to the musical life of New York, particularly towards the cultivation of glees and kindred music. One feature, and in this the New York society seems to have differed from its model, clearly stands forth from the many business-advertisements of the society: the annual 'Ladies Concert' towards spring. Nor were the regular concerts

---

1) N. Y. Directories, 1797 and 1798.
2) Daily Advertiser, Nov. 4, 1800.

given behind closed doors, so to speak, for it appears to have been the privilege of the members to share the entertainments in company of the visitors. Thus managed, the society could not possibly arouse the suspicions of *Le Donne Curiose* and gentlemen of the stamp of the Duchess of Devonshire and at least during the first years of its existence the Columbian Anacreontic Society enjoyed an excellent reputation. Otherwise the gentlemen in charge of the procession in memory of George Washington on Dec. 31, 1799 would hardly have dared to accord the Columbian Anacreontic Society a prominent place in the procession together with the Philharmonic Society, the only other musical society then existing in New York. The event must have been regarded as a climax in the society's career for the members went about the selection and arrangement of the music to be performed in celebration of the obsequies of General Washington with much care[1]). It was unanimously resolved to meet at the Green Room of the theatre one hour previously to the moving of the general procession; the secretary was directed to shroud the badges of the society (an Irish harp) with black; the members were instructed to wear a knot of black love ribbon attached to the centre of the rose to which the line was pendant and finally the latter two resolutions remained in full force during the meeting of the society for the remainder of the season[2]). Thus attired the Columbian Anacreontic Society certainly did not cut a poor figure in the procession of which and of the subsequent sacred concert the Daily Advertiser printed in form of a broadside the following account on Jan. 3, 1800 as furnished by the committee on arrangements:

On the 31st of December 1799, the day appointed by the citizens of New York to pay the most solemn funeral honors to the Memory of their beloved Chief and Fellow Citizen General George Washington .... the Citizens in their military and civil habiliments, with the foreigners of various nations all eager to join in the testimonies of veneration for the *Great Deceased*, having assembled in their appointed order, the procession moved under the guidance of signals, to the mournful sounds of minute guns and muffled bells, in the following order:

Officer and eight dragoons.

Sixth Regiment, in platoon, by the left, with arms and colours reversed — drums and fifes in mourning ... [followed Cavalry, Major. Gen. Hamilton and suite, St. Stephen's Society and Tammany Society, Masonic lodges, commercial companies, college professors, consuls etc.]

Music.

Anacreontic and Philharmonic Societies in complete mourning — the grand officers bearing wands, decorated with crape — the members wearing their badges with crape and. bows of love ribbon.

---

1) Daily Advertiser, Dec. 27, 1799.
2) Daily Advertiser, Dec. 30, 1799. As an early illustration of the amusing pride we Americans take in club-badges may serve the following. On May 17, 1798 such members of the Columbian Anacreontic Society who "chuse" to attend the theatre on May 21st in "compliment to their president" John Hodgkinson who had his benefit, were informed in the N. Y. Gazette that seats would be reserved for them in the "Shakespeare Box" and that they "will wear their badges".

[Then came the clergy, the bier etc. etc. The procession moved to St. Paul's Church.]
The following are the words of sacred music performed on the 31st ult. at St. Paul's Church by the Anacreontic and Philharmonic Societies.

Solo.

Sons of Columbia, now lament
Your spear is broke, your bow's unbent
Your glory's fled
Amongst the dead
Your Hero lies
Ever, forever clos'd his eyes.

Chorus.

Columbians weep! weep still in louder moan
Your Hero, Patriot, Friend and Father's gone.

Dead March.

Then Recitative Solo
    Female voices
    General Chorus
    Conclusion

SECOND PART

Elegy

How sleep the brave, who sink to rest
By all their Country's wishes blest?
By Fairy hands, their knell is rung
By Forms unseen, their dirge is sung
    Recitativo Solo
    Song
    Grand Chorus
The Lord God omnipotent reigneth, etc . . . .

Still less is known of the artistic activity of the 'Harmonical Society', instituted as the directory of 1797 stated, "on March 17, 1796 for the purpose of cultivating the knowledge of vocal and instrumental music". From the directory of the preceding year it is to be learned that the society met on Tuesdays and that the management originally lay in the hands of John Richardson, President, John S. Hunn, Secretary and John B. Cozine, Treasurer, three gentlemen who with a slight exchange of office controlled the destinies of the society for the first three years. As in 1798 a second secretary became necessary, it may be surmised that the business of the Harmonical Society had grown considerably. The place of meeting seems to have varied, Little's Tavern, the City Hall, Gaultier's Assembly Room, De la Croix', Broadway and Vaux Hall, Broadway being mentioned. Unfortunately neither the number of concerts nor the programs are mentioned in the papers and we hear only that the "instrumental harmony" began usually at 7 o'clock. Finally, on Dec. 3, 1799, through the columns of the Daily Advertiser, a punctual attendance of the members of the Harmonical Society on Dec. 5th at their Concert Room in Broadway was requested on business of great importance. The result of this meeting was a junction of the St. Cecilia Society of 1791 and the Harmonical Society, thus announced in the Daily Advertiser Dec. 9, 1799:

Philharmonic Society

The Members of the St. Cecilia and Harmonical Societies, are informed that a junction of these two has been formed under the name of the Philharmonic Society.

The first annual concert of the Philharmonic Society was held at the Tontine Hotel in Broadway on Dec. 23, 1800 "with a variety of vocal and instrumental music by the most celebrated performers in the city"[1]); but the new society had made its first public appearance, as we know, on that memorable day of Dec. 31, 1799. How long the society lasted, I am not prepared to prove but it would not surprise me to learn that the several attempts at a Philharmonic Society during the first decades of the nineteenth century, of which we read in histories, all refer to the career of the same one Philharmonic Society founded in 1799 and growing out of the St. Cecilia of 1791 and the Harmonical Society of 1796.

It was intimated above that towards the close of the century the centre of the concert-season shifted from the winter to the summer, as far as concerts are concerned that were independent of musical societies. This peculiar but not unprecedented development was principally due to the establishment of Joseph Delacroix' Vaux Hall Gardens and Joseph Corre's Columbia Gardens and Mount Vernon Gardens. It will also be seen that the repertory there was by no means inferior to that of the subscription concerts the place of which these summer-concerts took chronologically and absolutely.

The probabilities are that New York possessed "rural felicities" before 1796 like Mrs. Armory's Vaux Hall in Great George Street where, with a Mr. Miller's tight rope dancing as main attraction, on June 25, 1793 a concert of

"the most favourite overtures and pieces from the compositions of Fisher and Handel" was given, "the orchestra being placed in the middle of a large tree" in order to render the prospect of the garden "beautifully illuminated in the Chinese stile with upwards of 500 glass lamps."[2])

However, to have made good orchestral and vocal music a regular feature belongs to the initiative of Joseph Delacroix, the caterer, unrivalled for his delicious ice-cream, then not so common as now.

As a fore-taste of what he contemplated doing he gave at his elegantly illuminated "Salloon", the Ice House Garden, no. 112 Broadway on the

1) Daily Advertiser, Dec. 23, 1800.
2) Daily Advertiser, June 24, 1793.

evening of Sept. 15, 1794 with James Hewitt as leader of the band a "grand concert of vocal & instrumental music" with this high-toned program[1]):

Act I.

Overture	Haydn
Song 'The Wish'	Miss Broadhurst
Concerto Piano Forte	Mr. Rausch
Song 'Bravoure'	Miss Broadhurst
Symphony	Pleyel

Act II.

Concerto Flute	Mr. Bingley
Song 'Keep your distance'	Miss Broadhurst
Quartetto Violin	Mr. Hewitt, etc.
Song 'When the mind is in tune'	Miss Broadhurst
Finale	Stamitz

Then, end of May 1797, he informed the public that he had elegantly decorated his gardens — from now on called Vaux Hall Gardens — in "a new taste" and provided accommodations for fifteen of the best musicians who with the beginning of June would give a vocal and instrumental concert three times a week, on Tuesday, Thursday and Saturday evenings. The price of admittance was four shillings with a deduction to holders of season tickets[2]). To the keen disappointment of his guests Delacroix saw himself obliged to take down the decorations of his garden on the night fixed for the opening, June 13th and to postpone the entertainment to June 15th, but thereafter things moved smoothly and in case of rain the concerts were performed in the "great room". Of course, July 4th was a *gala*-night and on such occasions everything was done to "call to mind the American heroes". It did not require much to attain this, for now as then a "transparent likeness" of George Washington would arouse the liveliest enthusiasm of the company and once 'Hail Columbia' had been given to our nation this song, of course, would achieve the same result. The first season was not without accidents. For instance, in July the band was obliged to leave New York in order to fill a theatrical engagement at Boston, but Mr. Delacroix was not to be discouraged. He postponed the concerts for a week in order to recruit another band and when he continued his entertainments he had added vocal performers to his forces and was bold enough to give concerts every evening[3]).

In the following year Joseph Delacroix rented for a term of several years "the house and garden of the late alderman Bayard, near Bunker's Hill"[4]). He again called the premises 'Vaux Hall Gardens' and continued his summer-concerts, first three, later on four a week shutting his place end of July for

---

1) Minerva, Sept. 13, 1796.
2) Daily Advertiser, May 22, 1797.
3) Daily Advertiser, July 12, 1797.
4) Daily Advertiser, May 5, 1798.

several weeks. During this year he lowered the price of admission to 2 shillings and generously entitled for this sum the bearer "to a glass of ice cream punch". In 1799 he added fire-works "made by the celebrated Mr. Ambrose" to the attractions which consisted, besides the usual refreshments, illuminations etc., of the band, first under Hewitt and then under Everdell, and of the vocal exhibitions of (mainly) Mrs. Oldmixon, Miss E. Westray and Mr. Jefferson[1]). It also affords a curious glimpse into by-gone times if Delacroix briefly announces "No lanthorn — no exhibition" or remarks "the large barn in front of Broadway will be open for the accommodation of carriages. The horses can be securely tied". But New Yorkers ever have been fickle in patronizing such enterprises and so it came to pass that on July 18th[2]) the "Vauxhall Garden [was] to let or for sale, for the term of six years". Whilst they lasted, the concerts at Delacroix' Vauxhall contributed decidedly to the musical life of New York and a few programs may follow to prove this.

JUNE, 10, 1797
Act I.

Overture	Haydn
Song 'I never loved any dear Mary but you' ..	Mr. Tyler
Sinfonie La Chasse	Stamitz
Song 'Three sweethearts I boast'..	Miss Moller, Messrs. Tyler and Lee
Full piece	Vanhall

Act II.

Concerto Flute	Mr. Saliment
Song 'Hunting cantata of Diana'	Mr. Tyler
Sinfonie	Pleyel
Song 'tho' by the tempest'	Miss Moller
Glee 'Adieu to the village delight'	Miss Moller, and Messrs. Tyler and Lee
Finale	Kozeluch

JUNE 17, 1797
Act I.

Overture	Haydn
Song 'Lucy, or Selima's companion'	Mr. Tyler
Sinfonia	Vanhall
Song 'No more I'll heave the tender fish' ..	Miss Moller
Catch 'How great is the pleasure'	Miss Moller, Messrs. Tyler and Lee
Concertant Pleyel	Messrs. Hewitt, Saliment, Moller and Sammo

Act II.

Overture	Pleyel
Song 'Diana and Hebe'	Mr. Tyler
Sinfonia	Kozeluch

---

1) Daily Advertiser, May 14 and July 17, 1799.
2) N. Y. Gazette.

Song 'No that will never do' .. ..   Miss Moller
Glee 'How merrily we live' .. ..   Miss Moller, Messrs. Tyler
                                            and Lee
Full piece .. ..   Stamitz
The concert to begin precisely at 8 o'clock and the whole season.

JUNE 23, 1797
Act I.

Overture .. ..   Poloniska
Song 'Sweet lass of Richmond hill' .. .. ..   Mr. Tyler
Sinfonie .. ..   Vanhall
Song 'The Female cryer' .. ..   Miss Moller
Concertante .. ..   Pleyel

Act II.

Overture .. ..   Wranisky
Song 'Old Towler' .. ..   Mr. Tyler
Quartetto, Pleyel .. ..   Messrs. Hewitt, etc.
Song 'How can I forget' .. ..   Miss Moller
Glee 'Hark the hollow hills resounding' .. ..   Miss Moller, Messrs. Tyler
                                            and Lee
Finale .. ..   Schmittbauer

JUNE 26, 1797
Act I

Overture .. ..   Toeschi
Song 'The sweet little girl that I love' .. ..   Mr. Tyler
Sinfonie .. ..   Kozeluch
Song 'The poor little gipsy' .. ..   Mrs. Seymour
Entre act .. ..   Martini
Song 'How can I forget' .. ..   Miss Moller
Full piece .. ..   Haydn

Act II

Overture .. ..   Dibble
Song 'Lovely Nan' .. ..   Mr. Tyler
Concerto Piano Forte .. ..   Mr. Moller
Favourite Hunting Song .. ˋ .. ..   Mrs. Seymour
Serenata .. ..   Davaux
Song 'How d'ye do' .. ..   Miss Moller
Finale .. ..   Kreutzer [R. Kreutzer]

JUNE 28, 1797
Act I

Overture .. ..   Haydn
Song 'Fa la la' .. ..   Mrs. Seymour
Quartetto .. ..   Pleyel
Song 'And hear her sigh adieu' .. ..   Mr. Tyler
Duett 'One short moment' .. ..   Miss Moller and M. Tyler
Allegro .. ..   Treller
Song 'Tis in vain' .. ..   Miss Moller
Finale .. ..   Vanhall

Act II

Sinfonie .. ..   Toeschi
Song 'As t'other day' .. ..   Mr. Tyler

14*

Overture	Pichl
Song 'The Tobacco box'	Mrs. Seymour
Presto	Leffler
Song 'No that will never do'	Miss Moller
Glee 'How merrily we live'	Miss Moller, Mr. Tyler etc.
Finale	Toeschi

JULY 4, 1797
ACT I

Grand Overture	Haydn
Song 'Little Sally'	Miss Moller
Quartetto for the French horn, violin, tenor and basso	Messrs. Dupuis, Hewitt, Gilfert and Deseze.
Song 'Three sweethearts I boast'..	Miss Moller
Glee 'Lightly tread this hollowground'	
Battle Overture, in commemoration of the 4th July	Hewitt

ACT II

Concerto Flute	Saliment
Song 'Tantivy, bark forward'	Miss Moller
Sonata Piano Forte	Mr. Moller
Glee 'Here in cold Grot'	
Finale	Pleyel

JULY 6, 1797
ACT I

Overture	Paderchi
Song 'The Wish'	Miss Moller
Quintetto, Hewitt, Saliment, etc.	Pleyel
Song 'How d'ye do'	Miss Moller
Sinfonie	Vanhall
Glee 'Hark the lark'	Miss Moller, etc.
Presto	Stamitz

ACT II

L'Allegro	Perdoni
Song 'Tho'by the tempest'	Miss Moller
Rondo 'A pretty little plow boy ', Piano Forte	Mr. Moller
Glee 'Hail social pleasure'	Miss Moller, etc.
Finale	Pleyel

JULY 8, 1797
ACT I

Overture	Wiska [?]
Song 'Ruby Aurora'	Miss Moller
Quintetto, French horn	Mr. Dupuis
Song 'Winsome Kate'	Miss Moller
Sinfonie	Bach

ACT II

Concertante, Violin	Hewitt
Song 'From the Eliza'	Miss Moller
Overture	Canabichi [!]
Song 'No that will never do'	Miss Moller
Finale	Mustcropo [!]

Somewhat different in character was the music offered at B. Isherwood's Ranelagh Garden, near the Battery and "known by the varigated lamps over the door"[1]). Though announced as nightly concerts of vocal *and* instrumental music, the very form of the announcement shows that the instrumental music was of minor importance. It was furnished by "Messrs. Everdell, Seymour, Nicoli etc."[2]). Nor was the vocal music of a high grade, but perhaps New York wanted just then a plentiful supply of *popular* songs. Mr. Isherwood certainly supplied this demand as long as Ranelagh Garden interested the city, that is to say, during the summers of 1798 and 1799. The following three programs may serve to illustrate the point and show to a degree what were then considered *catchy, sweet, popular* songs.

JUNE 28, 1798

Father, mother and Luke	Mr. Jefferson
Hoot awa ye loon	Mrs. Seymour
The Waving willow	Miss Broadhurst
Duet of Hey dance to the fiddle and tabor ..	Mrs. Seymour and Mr. Jefferson
The First of my amours	Williamson
The Kiss	Seymour
John Bull was a bumpkin born	Jefferson
The Female cryer	
Hymen's evening post	Williamson

July 4, 1798

Ye sons of dull sloth	Mrs. Seymour
Knowing Joe, or Plowman turned actor ..	Mr. Jefferson
How can I forget the fond hour	Miss Broadhurst
In honour of the day, the Boston Patriotic Song, Adams and Liberty	Mr. Williamson
Where is the harm of that	Mrs. Seymour
Dickey Gossip	Mr. Jefferson
Duett Hey dance to the fiddle and tabor ..	Mrs. Seymour and Mr. Jefferson
Bonny Charley	Miss Broadhurst
The New York Federal song 'Washington and the Constitution'	Mr. Williamson
The little farthing rush-light	Mr. Jefferson
And, 'Hail Columbia'	Mr. Williamson

JUNE 1, 1799.

Act 1st. Songs — 'Alone by the light of the moon', Mr. Perkins — 'Sweet Nan of Hampton Green', Mrs. M'Donald — 'The Highland laddie', Mrs. Oldmixon — 'Nong Tong Paw', Mr. Jefferson — 'On the lake of Killarney', Mrs. Seymour — 'From scenes of love', Mr. Perkins — 'The Wedding day', Mrs. M'Donald — 'The Soldier tir'd of war's alarms', Mrs. Oldmixon — 'The Waiter', Mr. Jefferson — The Sailor boy, Mrs. Seymour.

---

1) Daily Advertiser, July 3, 1798.
2) N. Y. Gazette, May 30, 1799.

Neither Mr. Delacroix nor Mr. Isherwood were destined to monopolize the interest taken by New Yorkers in summer-concerts. Absorbing the good points in the enterprises of both, Joseph Corre, proprietor of Corre's Hotel, "compleated" 'Columbia Garden', adjoining his house and facing the Battery in May 1798 and forthwith engaged a "grand" band which was to play three times a week[1]). Corre catered from the beginning, possibly warned by the experience of his rivals, to the better class of citizens and politely informed the public of his intention "to keep good order and strict rules" in the hope that "no person [would] attempt to be admitted that would not be agreeable and conduct themselves accordingly". He had gone to the expense of installing an organ in his place, played every evening by J. Chr. Moller[2]), and being a man of ideas he did not content himself with an orchestra. For weeks at a time "Mr. Henry and the band of wind instruments" would take its place[3]) and this was also the case on evenings devoted mainly to popular or patriotic songs as for instance on July 4, 1798. Who conducted the orchestra during 1798 and 1800 does not appear but in 1799 George Everdell seems to have been the conductor[4]). Furthermore, it will be seen that Joseph Corre freely placed his garden at the disposal of such artists engaged by him who wished to give benefit concerts and this certainly went far to increase his popularity both with them and their friends.

These concerts at Columbia Garden lasted at least until July 1800[5]). In the meantime, Joseph Corre had "created" the 'Mount Vernon Garden' in Leonardstreet, two blocks above the hospital. It was opened on a similar plan as his Columbia Garden on May 22, 1800 with James Hewitt as leader of the band and the programs certainly left nothing to be desired. But Corre was not satisfied with concerts only. Early in July[6]) he turned the Mount Vernon Garden into a summer-theatre and gave theatricals with several of the principal performers of the regular winter-company three times a week. These performances were discontinued early in August and when they were taken up again it was on "an improved plan". Not only was there presented "a select dramatic piece of two, and sometimes three acts, each night" as f. i. the Purse, The Romp, The Adopted Child, The Highland Reel, but also regularly a "grand concert" under James Hewitt. For both the theatrical and concert numbers Corre had engaged at a considerable expense Mr. and Mrs. Hodgkinson, Mr. and Mrs. Hogg, Mr. Fox,

1) N. Y. Gazette, May 14, 1798.
2) Daily Advertiser, June 13, 1798.
3) Daily Advertiser, July 9, 1799.
4) N. Y. Gazette, July 26, 1799.
5) Daily Advertiser, July 10, 1800.
6) Daily Advertiser, July 8, 1800.

Mr. Hallam jun., Mr. M'Donald, Mr. Lee, Mr. Jefferson, Miss Westray, Miss Brett, Miss Harding and others[1]), who, of course, in accordance with theatrical traditions, each came in for a benefit-night. In this manner the performances flourished until September 19th, "positively the last night". It really seems to have been the last night as already on August 29th[2]), Joseph Corre "intending to retire from public business" advertised his "Mount Vernon Theatrical Garden" as for sale. Corre must have considered the purchase of his property quite an investment, for, said he:

In the course of two or three years it will be the handsomest spot on the continent for the above purpose, the street when regulated will raise the Garden from 12 to 20 feet above the level of the street, all around which will form a proper Mount, with a fine circulation of air which will make the performance very agreeable to the audience. The main street is now paving to the very corner of the street which will render the walk much easier; there is a well of water as good as any in the city. To give any further information about the garden and building is needless as the public are well acquainted with the place by this time.

It is only fair to Mr. Corre to add here, as was done in the case of Mr. Delacroix, a number of programs to illustrate what debt of gratitude the music lovers of New York owed him:

COLUMBIA GARDEN.

JUNE 13, 1798
ACT I

Sinfonie	Kozeluch
Glee 'Adieu to the village delights'	Messrs.Tyler,Shapter and Lee
Duet, Violin and alto	Messrs. Berault and Hewitt
Song 'The Cottagers daughter'	Mr. Tyler
Allegro	Haydn
Song 'The Highland laddie'	Mrs. Oldmixon
Overture	Pleyel

ACT II

Concerto Organ .. .. ʊ	Moller
Glee 'Fare the well, thou native vale'	Mrs. Oldmixon, Tyler, Shapter and Lee
Song 'The Soldier tir'd'	Mrs. Oldmixon
Concerto Flute	Mr. Saliment
Song 'The Green Mountain farmer'	Mr. Tyler
Catch 'Give the sweet delight of love'	Messrs. Tyler, Shapter, Lee
Full piece	Wranitzky

JULY 3, 1798
PART I

Song	Mr. Tyler
Song 'The Silver moon'	Miss E. Westray
Song 'Life's a country dance'	Mr. Hodgkinson
Song 'Ere I fly to meet my love'	Miss Brett
Song 'Come Kiss me'	Mrs. Hodgkinson

---

1) Daily Advertiser, Aug. 11, 1800.
2) Daily Advertiser.

PART II

Song 'The Capture or Sea fight' .. .. Mrs. Hodgkinson
Song 'For chase' .. .. Miss Brett
Song 'Down the bourn,' etc. .. .. Mrs. Hodgkinson
Song .. .. Mr. Tyler
Song 'Young Sandy once a wooing came' .. Miss E. Westray

JULY 4, 1798

PART I

Song 'Adams and Liberty' .. .. Mr. Hodgkinson
Song 'As sure as a gun' .. .. Miss E. Westray
Song 'The Bird when summers charm no more' Mrs. Hodgkinson
Song .. .. Mr. Tyler
Song 'Jane of Aberdeen'' .. .. Miss Brett
Duo 'Time has not thinn'd my flowing hair' Mr. and Mrs. Hodgkinson

PART II

Song .. .. Mr. Tyler
Song 'The Silver moon' .. .. Miss E. Westray
Song 'Tantivy' .. .. Miss Brett
Song 'Je ne vois, entend pas, monsieur' .. .. Mr. Hodgkinson
Ladies' new patriotic song 'Washington's March' Mrs. Hodgkinson

JULY 6, 1798

PART I

Song 'Adams and Liberty', by desire .. .. Mr. Hodgkinson
Song 'In my pleasant native plains' .. .. .. Miss Brett
Song .. .. Miss E. Westray
Song .. .. Mr. Tyler
Song 'Come buy of poor Kate' .. .. Mrs. Hodgkinson
Song 'I die for no shepherd, not I' .. .. .. The Young lady[1])

PART II

Song .. .. Miss E. Westray
Song 'Je ne vois, entend pas, monsieur' by desire Mr. Hodgkinson
Song 'Fox chase' .. .. Miss Brett
Song 'O dearly I love somebody' .. .. .. The Young lady
Song .. .. Mr. Tyler
Song 'Prithee fool be quiet' .. .. Mrs. Hodgkinson

JULY 7, 1798

PART I

Song .. .. Mr. Tyler
Song 'Bonny of Aberdeen' .. .. Miss Brett
Song .. .. Miss Westray
Song 'The Heiress' .. .. Mrs. Hodgkinson
Song 'Jack Junck' .. .. Mr. Hodgkinson

---

1) The announcement to the day in the Daily Advertiser was headed: "For the benefit of the distrest widow and daughter of a late American officer, and a brother mason, on which occasion a young lady (the daughter alluded to above) will make her first and only appearance in public".

PART II

Song	Miss Westray
Song 'Brighton Sly'	Mr. Hodgkinson
Song 'I fly to meet my love'	Miss Brett
Song	Mr. Tyler
Song 'Drop a tear and bid adieu'	Mrs. Hodgkinson

JUNE 11, 1799

ACT I

Sinfonia	Kozeluch
Glee 'Fair Flora decks'	Messrs. Tyler, Chapter & Lee
Quartetto Violin	Mr. Hewitt
Song 'When the sails catch the breeze'	Mr. Tyler
Minuetto	Hayden
Song 'The tuneful lark'	Miss E. Westray
Glee 'How shall we mortals spend our hours'	Messrs. Tyler, Shapter and Lee
Song 'The Female cryer'	Mrs. Oldmixon
Full piece	Pleyel

ACT II

Concerto Organ	Mr. Moller
Song 'Let fame sound the trumpet'	Mr. Tyler
Quartett Fluto	Mr. Saliment
Song	Miss E. Westray
Catch, 'Poor Thomas Day'	Messrs. Tyler, Shapter & Lee
Song 'Ah! how hapless is the maid'	Mrs. Oldmixon
Finale	Ditters

JUNE 24, 1799

ACT I

Overture	Haydn
Catch	Messrs. Tyler, Shapter and Lee
Andante	Stamitz
Song 'Bright chantilleur'	Mr. Tyler
Trio, Flute	Mr. Saliment
Song 'Fair Rosaline'	Miss E. Westray
Glee	Messrs. Tyler, Shapter and Lee
Sinfonie	Pleyel

ACT II

Overture	Cambini
Song 'Sweet Myra of the Vale'	Mr. Tyler
Minuetto	Haydn
Song	Miss E. Westray
Catch 'Poor Thomas Day'	Messrs. Tyler, Shapter & Lee
Finale	Sterckel

JULY 1, 1799

ACT I

Overture	Kozeluch
Glee 'Adieu to the sailor's delights'	Messrs. Shapter, Tyler and Lee
Allegro	Cambini
Song 'Primroses deck'	Mr. Tyler
Concertante	Stamitz
Song 'The Primrose girl'	Mrs. Seymour
Sinfonie	Pleyel

Act II

Full piece	Hoffmeister
Song	Mr. Tyler
Andante	Wranitzky
Song 'Ower of Glandower'..	Mrs. Seymour
Catch 'Eie, nay John'	Messrs. Tyler, Shapter and Lee
Finale	Haydn

JULY 9, 1799

Act I

Song 'You tell me, dear girl'	Mr. Tyler

Song, Mrs. Seymour, 'The poor little gipsy'
Song, Mr. Bates 'John loves Jane, and Jane
loves John'

Act II

Song, Mr. Tyler, 'The Soldier's adieu'
Song, Mrs. Seymour 'What can a lassie do'
Song, Mr. Bates 'Jack at the windlass'
To conclude with 'Adams and Liberty'

N. B. The subscriber begs leave to inform the ladies and gentlemen that he has engaged Mr. Henry and the Band of wind instruments to play every evening.

JULY 16, 1799

Act I

Cottage on the Moor	Mr. Tyler
Cheering Rosary	Mrs. Seymour
The Pleasures of London	Mr. Bates

Act II

Diana	Mr. Tyler
Edinburgh town	Mrs. Seymour
A Tar for all weathers	Mr. Bates

JULY 25, 1729

Act I

Overture of the Frescatana[1]), executed by the wind instruments

Song 'the Negro boy'	Mr. Tyler

Minuet of Pleyel and Andante by Haydn

Song 'May I never be married'	Mrs. Seymour

Act II

Overture of Peter the Great[2])

Song 'Old Towler'	Mr. Tyler
Minuet	Haydn
Song 'Hope thou balmy comfort shed'	Mrs. Seymour
Duetto 'The Tobacco box'	Mr. Tyler and Mrs. Seymour

JULY 4, 1800

Act I

Overture	Hayden
Song 'Tally ho'	Miss Brett

1) Either Guglielmi, Paesiello or Cimarosa.
2) Probably Grétry.

Andante .. .. Kreutzer
Song 'Hail Columbia' .. .. Mr. Fox
Minuetto .. .. Stamitz
Song 'The Singing girl' .. .. Mrs. Hodgkinson
Allegro .. .. Kozeluch
Song 'To the memory of Washington' .. .. Mr. Hodgkinson
Full piece .. .. Pleyel

Act II

Sinfonie .. .. Sterckel
Song 'Adams and Liberty' .. .. Mr. Fox
Andante .. .. Hayden
Song 'Dearest youth' .. .. Miss Brett
Minuetto .. .. Van Hall
Song 'The moment Aurora' .. .. Mr. Hodgkinson
Allegro .. .. Cornell [!]
Song 'Prithee fool be quiet' .. .. Mrs. Hodgkinson
Full piece .. .. Hayden

MOUNT VERNONT GARDEN.

MAY 22, 1800

Act I

Overture .. .. Haydn
Song 'The Cottager's daughter' .. .. .. Mr. Tyler
Allegro .. .. Pleyel
Song 'The Caledonian laddie' .. .. Mrs. Seymour
Naval duett .. .. Messrs. Hodgkinson and Tyler
Andante .. .. Kozeluch
Song 'Come Kiss me, said he' .. .. Mrs. Hodgkinson
Sinfonie .. .. Dussek

Act II

Overture .. .. Stamitz
Song 'The Sailor boy' .. .. Mrs. Seymour
Duett 'How sweet is the breath of morn' .. Mr. and Mrs. Hodgkinson
Presto .. .. Wranitzky
Song 'the Beaux of the year 1800' .. .. Mrs. Hodgkinson
Sinfonie .. .. Abel
Song 'Away to the chase' .. .. Mr. Hodgkinson
Full piece .. .. Hayden

MAY 29, 1800

Act I

Overture .. .. Hayden
Song 'Diana', a hunting cantata .. .. .. Mr. Tyler
Andante .. .. Stamitz
Song 'The Father of Nancy' .. .. Mrs. Seymour
Allegro .. .. Kozeluch
Song 'Nong, tong, paw' .. .. Mr. Hodgkinson
Minuetto .. .. Sterckel
Song 'The Waving willow' .. .. Mrs. Hodgkinson
Sinfonie .. .. Gyrowetz

Act 2 d.

Overture	Wranitzky
Song 'The Bonny bold soldier, Young Willy for me'	Mrs. Seymour
Polonaise	Clementi
Song	Mr. Tyler
Andante	Hayden
Song 'Little thinks the soldiers wife'	Mrs. Hodgkinson
Allegro	Borghi
Song 'Life's a country dance'	Mrs. Hodgkinson
Full piece	Hayden

JUNE 3, 1800
Act I

Overture	Kreutzer
Song 'Fragrant chaplets'	Mrs. Seymour
Allegro	Kotzeluch
Song	Mrs. Hodgkinson
Andante	Stamitz
Song	Miss Brett
Sinfonie	Hayden

Act II

Overture	Haydn
Song 'Little Sally'	Mrs. Seymour
Minuetto	Sterckel
Song	Mrs. Hodgkinson
Andante	Pichl
Song	Miss Brett
Full piece	Pleyel

JUNE 5, 1800
Act I

Overture	Hayden
Song 'Tom Tackle'	Mr. Hodgkinson
Andante	Pichl
Song 'The Shepherds boy'	Miss Brett
Trio for Violin and Violoncello	Messrs. Hewitt, Saino and Miniere
Song 'Cheering Rosary'	Mrs. Hodgkinson
Minuette	Kozeluch
Song 'Death stole my lad away'	Mrs. Seymour
Allegro	Sterckel

Act II

Sinfonie	Pleyel
Hunting song	Miss Brett
Andante	Wranitzky
Song 'Group of lovers'	Mr. Hodgkinson
Minuetto	Kozeluch
Song 'The Little gipsy'	Mrs. Seymour
Allegro	Dusik [Dussek]
Song 'Sweet echo', accompanied on the flute by Mr. Hodgkinson	Mrs. Hodgkinson
Full piece	Hayden

JUNE 13, 1800

Act I

Overture	Hayden
Song 'The Pipe upon the mountain'	Miss Brett
Andante	Pleyel
Song 'Sailor's journal'	Mr. Hodgkinson
Minuette	Wranitzky
Song 'Crazy Jane'	Mrs. Hodgkinson
Allegro	Carlo Stamitz

Act II

Sinfonia	Clementi
Song 'The Fox chase'	Miss Brett
Andante	Dussick
Song 'Life's a country dance'	Mr. Hodgkinson
Presto	Hoffmeister
Song 'Prithee fool be quiet'	Mr. Hodgkinson
Full piece	Hayden

JUNE 16, 1800

Act I

Overture	Pleyel
Song 'When Ruddy Aurora'	Miss Brett
Andante	Pichl
Song 'The Man and his wife'	Mr. Hodgkinson
Minuetto	Stamitz
Song 'Down the Bourne'	Mrs. Hodgkinson
Finale	Haydn

Act II

Sinfonie	Sterckel
Song 'Ellen or the Primrose girl'	Mr. Hodgkinson
Andante	Monchausen [!]
Song 'William and Mary'	Miss Brett
Minuetto	Kreutzer
Duett 'To thee each joy possessing'	Mr. & Mrs. Hodgkinson
Full piece	Filtz

JUNE 19, 1800

Act I

Overture	Stamitz
Song 'Love for love'	Miss Brett
Andante	Bottelswiller
Song 'The Soldiers adieu'	Mr. Hodgkinson
Minuetto	Sterckel
Song 'The Lake of Killarney'	Mrs. Hodgkinson
Allegro	Pleyel

Act II

Sinfonie	Haydn
Song 'n vain I deck the lonely grave'	Miss Brett
Andante	Von Duelman
Song 'The London Buck'	Mr. Hodgkinson
Minuetto	Clementi
Song 'I attempt from love's sickness to fly ..	Mr. Hodgkinson
Finale	Dussick

JUNE 21, 1800

ACT I

Overture	Haydn
Song 'The Little waist'	Miss Brett
Andante	Stamitz
Song 'The Wounded hussar'	Mr. Hodgkinson
Minuetto	Porrelli [Corrclli]
Song 'The Merry maids a Maying go'	Mrs. Hodgkinson
Allegro	Kozeluch

ACT II

Sinfonie	Pleyel
Song 'Tally ho'	Miss Brett
Andante	Stamitz
Song 'The Groupe of lovers'	Mr. Hodgkinson
Minuetto	Bach
Song 'My love's on shore'	Mrs. Hodgkinson
Full piece	Haydn

JUNE 27, 1800

ACT I

Overture	Hayden
Song 'When the men a courting came'	Miss Bett
Andante	Wranisky
Song 'The Wounded hussar'	Mr. Hodgkinson
Minuetto	Minschini
Song 'He's aye a kissing me'	Mrs. Hodgkinson
Allegro	Stamitz
Song	Mr. Fox
Overture	Kozeluch

ACT II

Sinfonie	Pleyel
Song 'Tuneful lark'	Miss Brett
Andante	Van Hall
Song 'The Group of lovers'	Mr. Hodgkinson
Allegro	Puzzlestopper [!]
Song 'The Masquerade'	Mrs. Hodgkinson
Minuetto	Eickner
Song	Mr. Fox
Full piece	Pleyel

JULY 7, 1800

ACT I

Overture	Kozeluch
Song	Miss Brett
Andante	Stamitz
Song 'What is a woman like'	Mr. Hodgkinson
Allegro	Clementi
Song 'The Joy of the chase'	Mrs. Hodgkinson
Finale	Pleyel

ACT II

Sinfonie	Haydn
Song 'How charming the camp'	Miss Brett
Andante	Wranizki
Song, The celebrated 'Laughing Song', by desire	Mr. Hodgkinson
Minuetto	Cambini
Song 'The Wedding day'	Mrs. Hodgkinson
Full piece	Haydn

AUG. 11, 1800

The musical piece in 2 acts, of the *Purse*, or the American Tars' Return . . .

Grand Concert interspersed with recitations

1. An Adress on the impossibility of pleasing everybody, exemplified in the fable of the Old Man, the Boy and the Ass by Jefferson
2. Echo song 'How d'ye do' .. .. Mrs. Hodgkinson, echoed by Miss Brett
3. Address to the memory of Columbus .. Miss Harding
4. Song 'The Last shilling' .. .. Mr. Hodgkinson
5. Address 'Belles have at ye all' .. .. .. Miss Westray
6. Song 'The Twins of Latona' .. .. Mr. Fox
7. Rondeau by the orchestra .. .. Plyell
8. Song 'A Sailor loved a lass' .. .. Miss Brett
9. Song 'The London sportsman' .. .. .. Mr. Jefferson

AUG. 13, 1800

1. Sinfonie .. .. Haydn
2. Song 'The tuneful lark' .. .. Miss Brett
3. Allegro .. .. Pleyel
4. Song .. .. Mr. Fox
5. Recitation — Pindar's Razor grinder .. Mr. Jefferson
6. Song 'Bonny Jem of Aberdeen' .. .. .. Mrs. Hodgkinson
7. Song 'Henry's Cottage maid' .. .. .. Miss Harding
8. Address 'On False pride' with a few lines to the memory of Howard .. .. Mrs. Hogg
9. Song 'Father and mother and Sukey' .. .. Mr. Hodgkinson

[This program was preceded by a comedy]

AUG. 15, 1800

1. Periodical Overture .. .. Haydn
2. Song 'Sanely's [?] tale of love' .. .. .. Miss Brett
3. Recitation On false pride .. .. Mrs. Hoog
4. Song 'Ellen arise' .. .. Mr. Hodgkinson
5. Recitation Belles have at ye all .. .. .. Miss Westray
6. Song 'The Learned pig' .. .. Mr. Jefferson
7. Minuetto .. .. : .. .. .. Pleyel
8. Ballad 'My poor dog Tray' .. .. Mr. Fox
9. Duett 'Sweet is the breath of morn' .. .. Mr. and Mrs. Hodgkinson

[This program was followed by Dibdin's 'The Romp']

With their revenues from teaching, selling, copying music, with several societies and theatrical companies to engage them for their orchestras and with the salaries accruing from a participation in subscription-concerts, the half hundred musicians, to be traced towards 1800 at New York, were able to eke out a living, and very few only were skillful or enterprising enough to risk benefit-concerts. That these few reaped anything like a harvest may also be doubted for concerts have always and everywhere been a precarious matter and presumably, if such statistics were available, the money lost by musicians with the pardonable ambition to appear for their benefit before the public would more than equal the money made. On the whole, it may be said that concerts are nowadays managed on a sounder business-basis, though often not on a sound ethical basis, whereas in the eighteenth century the benefit concerts savored of charity. By dint of having given his services cheaply or gratis to the musical societies, a musician would speculate on the good-will and gratitude of their members but we need not go as far as Vienna and her Tonkünstler Sozietät to know that such societies frequently would not feel under the slightest obligation to the generous virtuoso. In New York probably the attitude of the music lovers became somewhat similar once the idea of musical societies had gained ground but this did not deter the "celebrated performers" and with their benefit-concerts they added perceptibly to the musical life of the city.

Possibly the first benefit concert after the war was given by William Brown on March 16, 1786 at the Assembly Room "consisting of one act, in which [were] performed sundry select pieces of musick and a harmonical piece taken from Ladies' favourite tunes with variations"[1]. That Brown had engaged an orchestra for the occasion becomes evident from the fact that after the concert

"the orchestra [was to] be removed in order that the ladies and gentlemen may not be incommodated in their dancing".

As the ball was under the direction of the managers of the "Gentleman's Concert", presumably they also furnished their orchestra. Indeed Brown, clever business man as he was, practically gave the concert under their protectorate and seeing their perfect satisfaction with his attention and assiduity as conductor of the subscription concerts, gained their permission to further the sale of tickets by adding to his announcement a "recommendatory testimonial of their approbation".

Somewhere in his history, F. L. Ritter reflecting upon summer entertainments remarks that in those days the summers at New York cannot have been as hot as nowadays and if I am not mistaken this remark, evidently written with a sigh, is meteorilogically correct. Still, those musicians and concert-goers who assembled on July 20, 1786 to perform in and listen to Alexander Reinagle's "Grand concert" at the Assembly Room in Broad-

---

1) Daily Advertiser, March 14, 1786.

way, certainly not an airy place, must have possessed a wonderful endurance if they survived this program, so peculiarly printed in the New York Packet, July 13:

ACT FIRST

Overture	Haydn
Song	Miss Storer
Sonata, Piano Forte	Mr. Reinagle
Song	Ditto
Concerto Violin	Mr. Phile
Song	Miss Storer

ACT SECUOND

Overture	Haydn
Song	Miss Storer
Duetto, Violin and Violoncello	Messrs. Phile and Reinagle
Duetto	Miss Storer and Mr. Reinagle
Miscellaneous Quartet	
Laughing Song	Mr. Reinagle
Overture	Haydn

ACT FIRST

Song — from the oratorio of the Messiah
   Recit. — 'Comfort ye my people, saith your God . . . .
   Aria — 'Every valley shall be exalted . . . .
Song — From the oratorio of Samson
   'Return O God of Hosts, behold thy servant in distress' . . .
Song — From the Oratorio of the Messiah
   'I know that my Redeemer liveth' . . .

ACT SECOND

Song — From the opera of La Bona Figliuola (Piccini)
   'Furia di Donna irata in mio soccorso invoco' . . .
Duetto — 'O lovely peace, with plenty crown'd' . . .
Song — 'Now the time for mirth and glee
         Laugh, and love, and sing with me;
         Cupid is my theme of story.
         'Tis his god-ships' fame and glory;
         All must yield unto his law:
            Ha! ha! ha! ha! ha! ha! ha!'

The first part was confessedly, though with a rather wide stretch of imagination, in imitation of "Handel's Sacred Music, as performed in Westminster Abbey". Reinagle further took pains to acquaint the public that Miss Maria Storer had sung the principal parts in Haendel's oratorios at the musical festivals in Bath, Salisbury etc.

During the year 1787, to my knowledge, no benefit-concerts were given. Then, on June 6, 1788, the Daily Advertiser informed the public that on June 11th would be performed at the German Church in Nassau Street for the relief of the German Reformed Church in the city of Albany the following "Divine Music":

1. Grand Overture by Martini
2. Anthem from the 34th Psalm
3. Jonah, an oratorio, composed by S. Felsted
4. Sinfonia
5. Anthem from Sundry scriptures
6. Sinfonia finale.

To prevent disorder, care was taken by the managers headed by the Rev. Dr. Kunze that only such a number of tickets were sold as to accommodate the auditory with seats and printed bills, containing "particulars" *i. e.* programs, were given with the tickets, a common-sense custom to which we Americans fortunately still adhere.

The only other benefit concert of the year was ventured upon by Henry Capron who just then expressed his desire to settle in New York as teacher of singing, pianoforte, violin and guitar[1]). The admission to his concert, announced for Oct. 23d[2]), was strictly limited to advance-subscribers, a clause very seldom attached to announcements of benefit concerts. Capron presented this "plan" at the City Tavern:

ACT I
Grand Overture   .. .. ..   Stamitz
Song
Concerto Violoncello   .. ..   Mr. Capron
ACT II
Sonata, Piano Forte   .. ..   Mr. Reinagle
Song
Quartet, Flute
ACT III
Solo, Violin   .. ..   Reinagle
Song
Overture   .. ..   Haydn

In the following year, so memorable in our country's history, a Mrs. Sewell solicited the kind patronage of the public for a concert to be held on Oct. 31st[3]) but no further details were mentioned. Her methods evidently differed widely from those of Mr. P. A. Van Hagen who not only inserted the full program of his benefit at the City Assembly, Dec. 1, 1789[4]) but also remarked that he sold all sorts of instruments and that he would teach at "6 dollars a month (or 12 lessons) and one pound entrance" any of the following instruments: violin, harpsichord, tenor, violoncello, German flute, hautboy, clarinet, bassoon — and singing. A versatility which would have made a German Stadtpfeifer blush with envy! And to all these accomplishments Mr. Van Hagen seems to have added on said occasion an exhibition of the latent musicability of iron nails!

---

1) Daily Advertiser, Nov. 5, 1788.
2) Daily Advertiser, Oct. 23, 1788.
3) Daily Advertiser, Oct. 28, 1789.
4) Daily Advertiser, Nov. 20, 1789.

ACT I

Symphony of	Pleyel
Concerto on the Violin	Mr. Van Hagen
Song	Mr. Van Hagen, junior
	(eight years of age)
Quartetto of	Pleyel
Concerto on the Tenor	Mr. Van Hagen
Concerto on the Piano Forte	Mr. Van Hagen, jun.

ACT II

Concerto on the Violin	Mr. Van Hagen
Trio. Piano Forte	
Song Duet	Messrs. Frobel and Van Hagen
Solo upon iron nails, called Violin Harmonika (never performed)	
Symphony De Chasse, Finale	C. Stamitz

In the following year 1790, a troupe of Frenchmen, presumably political refugees, invaded New York and gave the city a first taste of French operas in French, the tender root out of which, with all due respect for the arguments occasionally advanced in favor of the system, the polyglot understanding powers of the New Yorkers in opera gradually grew within a century into a monstrous cactus. The troupe was headed by Mr. St. Aivre, singer and dancing master, we may argue, more from necessity than inclination. The operatic performances were preceded on Sept. 10th[1]) by a concert at the City Tavern for which the assistance of the Van Hagens, Henri Capron and John Christopher Moller had been gained. This rather miscellaneous program was presented:

ACT I

1. The Overture from the Deserter[2])
2. Song — 'Alas! I sigh' by Mr. St. Aivre
3. Solo Violoncello, by Mr. Capron
4. Song 'To the sounds of the drums' by Mr. Cammas
5. Trio 'Sweet hope', by Madame and M. St. Aivre and M. Cammas
6. Symphony
7. Quartetto, by M. Van Hagen and son
8. Cantus from 'The Fair Arsenia'[3]) by Madame and M. St. Aivre and M. Cammas.

ACT II

1. The Overture, from the Fair Arsenia
2. Song 'I dare to meet the strokes of fate', by M. Cammas
3. Sonata on the Harpsichord, by Mr. Moller
4. Duetto 'In the bosom of a father', by M. and Madame St. Aivre
5. Concerto Violoncello, by M. Van Hagen, sen.
6. Trio from 'Felix'[4]), by M. and Madame St. Aivre and M. Cammas
7. Duett 'Yes! I must go to-morrow morn' by M. St. Aivre and M. Cammas
8. The Overture of Henry IV or the Battle of Ivry[5])
After the Concert will be a grand Ball.

---

1) Daily Advertiser, Sept. 4, 1790.
2) Monsigny.
3) Monsigny.
4) Monsigny.
5) Martini.

On the program for Dec. 1, 1789 young Van Hagen's age had been given as eight years. This his father either had forgotten or, as it sometimes happens to fathers of prodigies, he really did not remember the exact age of his precocious son when he announced in a style, not unworthy of Leopold Mozart, to subscribers and non-subscribers a benefit concert for "P. A. Van Hagen, jun. only nine years of age" for Feb. 21, 1791 with the following somewhat vague "order of the music":

Act I

Symphony, just received from Europe per the *Eliza*, Capt. Armour [!]
Concert on the Harpsichord, of Giordani, by Mr. Van Hagen, jun.
Song of Felix[2]); by Mr. Cammas
Concert on the Violin, by Mr. Van Hagen, jun.
Symphonie Concertante, of Davau, by Mr. Van Hagen and Son
Song Duet of Gretry, by M. and Mrs. St. Aivre
Concert on the Harpsichord, by Mr. Van Hagen
Concert on the Violin, by do.

Act II

A new Symphony, never before performed
Song of Felix, by Mr. St. Aivre
Concerto on the Tenor, by Mr. Van Hagen, jun.
Song, in the English language, by Mr. St. Aivre
Air on the Violin, by Mr. Van Hagen
Favorite Overture de Blaise et Babet[3])

A few days preceding this concert, on Feb. 12th, Mr. Kullin, pianist, acquainted the public of his intention to give a benefit concert with the asisstance of Mr. Capron and Mrs. Haye, "lately from Paris . . . whose voice he had every reason to hope [would] be considered as a great acquisition to his concert". And as his subscription had already been honored with a number of the most respectable names he had further reason to flatter himself — he said — with such success as would enable him to procure a first rate violin performer from Philadelphia or elsewhere[4]). In this he was disappointed for when he finally fixed the date of the concert for March 7th[5]) the name of no violin performer from Philadelphia or elsewhere appeared on the program. As a kind of substitute, however, Mr. Kullin hastened to remark that he would "perform on a Grand Concert Pianoforte, entirely of a new invention and just finished by Messrs. Dodds and Claus, of this city', certainly one of the very first instances of the custom to advertise the *piano used:*

---

1) Daily Advertiser, Feb. 15, 1791.
2) Monsigny.
3) Dezède.
4) Daily Advertiser, Feb. 25, 1791.
5) Daily Advertiser, March 4, 1791.

ACT I

Symphony .. .. Pleyel
Song, by Mrs. Haye
Sonata for the Forte Piano, with accompaniments for
    the violin, by Messrs. Kullin and Van Hagen .. Sacchini
Quartetto .. .. Plyel
A Four hand piece on the Piano Forte, by Messrs.
    Kullin and Van Hagen
Solo for the Violoncello, by Mr. Capron
Symphony

ACT II

Symphony
Duo for the Tenor and violin, by Mr. Van Hagen
    and Son
Air with variations for the Pianoforte and violoncello
A Song by Mrs. Haye
Concerto for the Violin, by Mr. Van Hagen
Concerto for the Pianoforte, by Mr. Kullin

Finally, on June 27, 1791[1]) Mr. and Mrs. Solomon, "vocal performers
from the Southward, having performed the *Summer's Evening Brush* in
South Carolina, Georgia, Virginia and Boston" gave a similar entertainment
at the City Assembly Room

"consisting of recent and fashionable songs and duetts, interspersed with the
recitation of several pieces, prosaic and in verse, from the most celebrated authors
and the songs connected with them."

By March 30, 1792 P. A. Van Hagen, jun. had become "ten years of
age" and he respectfully informed the public through the Daily Advertiser
that he had opened the subscription for his benefit this season on April 17th
and on the day of performance he added to the program "with the assistance
of Mr. Capron and Mr. Saliment". The "order of the concert" — another
of those circumscriptive terms instead of which the simple word program
had not yet made its appearance whereas the term "act" for part has now
been relegated to vaudeville — reads:

ACT I

Overture by Pichl, performed at the crowning of the
    Emperor Leopold IId.
Concert on the Harpsichord
Concert on the violin, by P. A. Van Hagen, jun.
Song, by do.
Rondo .. .. Pleyel

ACT II

Concerto on the Tenor, by P. A. Van Hagen, jun.
Song, ditto.
Concerto on the Violin, by Mr. P. A. Van Hagen

Overture of the Two Savoyards[2])

---

1) Daily Advertiser, June 27, 1791.
2) Dalayrac.

A few months later, as will be remembered, New York's musical life received a stimulus by the arrival of "Messrs. Hewitt, Gehot, Bergman, Young and Phillips, professors of music from the Opera house, Hanover-square and Professional Concerts under the direction of Haydn, Pleyel, etc. London"[1]). We can well imagine how the curiosity of the concert-goers was aroused by the program of their first concert on American soil, a program which seems to have thrown the first dangerous bomb of program music into our musical life. Possibly James Hewitt never witnessed a battle — ample excuse for putting one into an overture — but Jean Gehot had just ended his voyage from England to America — ample reason for recording it in a sort of musical diary — and if he possessed at all the trick for writing suggestive, imitative, programmatic, symbolical music, his overture in twelve movements must have been an entertaining bit of autobiography. That it met with public approval is certain. Not so much because such self-evident music generally pleases but because it otherwise would not have been repeated at the subscription concerts. Another innovation was this that the Messrs. Hewitt, etc. faithfully inserted in their program the "composer's names". They "humbly hoped to experience the kind patronage of the ladies and gentlemen, and public in general" on Sept. 21, 1792 at Corre's Hotel with this really interesting program[2]):

Act I

	Composers' names
Overture	Haydn
Quartetto .. .. ~..	Pleyel
Symphony	C. Stamitz
Concerto Violoncello, Mr. Philips	Philips
Overture in 9 movements, expressive of a battle, etc. ..	Hewitt

No. 1. Introduction.
2. Grand march; the army in motion
3. The Charge for the attack
4. A National Air
5. The Attack commences in which the confusion of an engagement is heard
6. The Enemy surrender
7. The Grief of those who are made prisoners
8. The Conqueror's quickmarch
9. The Finale.

Act II

Concerto Violin, Mr. Hewitt	Hewitt
Flute Quartetto, Mr. Young	C. Stamitz
Overture, in 12 movements, expressive of a voyage from England to America	Gehot.

No. 1. Introduction

---

1) Daily Advertiser, Sept. 20, 1792.
2) Daily Advertiser, Sept. 20, 1792.

2. Meeting of the adventurers, consultation and their determination on departure
3. March from London to Gravesend
4. Affectionate separation from their friends
5. Going on board, and pleasure at recollecting the encouragement they hope to meet with in a land where merit is sure to gain reward
6. Preparation for sailing, carpenter's hammering, crowing of the cock, weighing anchor etc.
7. A Storm
8. A Calm
9. Dance on deck by the passengers
10. Universal joy on seeing land
11. Thanksgiving for safe arrival
12. Finale

The Concert to begin at half past seven. After which will be a Ball, conducted by Mr. Philips, who for several seasons conducted the Pantheon and City Balls, and will, on that evening, introduce some new English dances, which, if the ladies and gentlemen request, will be performed by the concert band.

Almost entirely a Van Hagen family affair was the last benefit concert, of 1792, on Dec. 2d[1]) as the *pièces de résistance* lay in the hands and throats of Mr. Van Hagen, Master Van Hagen, Miss Van Hagen *"about* 13 years old" and Mrs. Van Hagen:

FIRST PART

Overture of	Pleyel
Violin Concerto	P. A. van Hagen, jun.
Song Duetto by	Miss and Master Van Hagen
Flute Concerto	Mr. Saliment
Forte Piano Sonata	Mrs. Van Hagen

SECOND PART

Tenor Concerto	Mr. Van Hagen
Song Trio by	Mrs., Miss and Master Van Hagen
Forte Piano Concerto	Mrs. Van Hagen
Finale of	Pleyel

Of the Van Hagen family, Mrs. Van Hagen in a way was the most interesting member and it is perhaps worth while to quote here what she had to say in her behalf in the Daily Advertiser, Nov. 8, 1792:

Mrs. Van Hagen, lately from Amsterdam respectfully informs the ladies of this city that she intends to teach the theory and practice of music on the harpsichord and Piano Forte with thoroughbass, if desired; also, the principles of vocal music and singing according to the most approved method and the present taste in Europe.

As she has been for several years organist in the churches at Namur, Middleburg, Vlissingen and Bergen op den zoom, she also teaches on that instrument, as well church music, as lessons, sonatas, concertos, etc.

Mrs. Van Hagen hopes from her theoretic knowledge and successful experience in the science of music, to be as fortunate in the progress of her pupils in this city, as she has been in some of the first families in Holland.

---

1) Daily Advertiser, Nov. 3, 1792.
2) Daily Advertiser, Jan. 13, 1793.

As motives of delicacy may induce parents to commit the tuition of young ladies in this branch of education to one of their own sex, and the female voice from its being in unison, is better adapted to teach them singing than that of the other sex, which is an octave below, she flatters herself that she shall be indulged with their approbation and the protection of a respectable public.

The following year, 1793, brought a Mrs. Armory the distinction of having introduced in our country on Jan. 23 "between the hours of 6 and 8 o'clock", "in the Fields" the *"Harmonia Celesta,* this excellent and admired instrument blended in sound between the grandeur of the organ and the ravishing softness of the heart thrilling lute". Though not strictly a concert, the presentation of *Select Extracts* from the most eminent authors recited by particular request by Mrs. Melmoth "from the Theatres Royal of London and Dublin" on April 9th at the City Assembly Room[1]) call for attention here as Mrs. Melmoth in order to enhance the entertainment procured a band of music under James Hewitt for the opening and closing members of each part of the program. This program undoubtedly would be attractive even to-day if her part was taken by an actress of her calibre and though Hewitt's band probably lacked the finish of our modern orchestras it was still in touch with the true tradition of rendering eighteenth century music, nowadays lost to all except very few conductors:

PART THE FIRST

Overture .. .. Haydn

Exordium
Antony's Soliloquy over the body of Caesar .. .. Shakespeare
Celadon and Amelia .. .. Thomson
Scene from the tragedy of Macbeth .. .. Shakespeare
Quartetto .. .. Girovets

PART THE SECOND

Sinfonie .. .. Stamitz
Satan's Soliloquy to the Sun .. .. Milton
Eve's dream .. .. ibid.
The Story of Maria .. .. Sterne
Concerto Violin .. .. Mr. Hewitt

PART THE THIRD

Sinfonie .. .. Vanhall
Scene from Julius Caesar, in which
    Cassius excites Brutus to oppose .. .. Shakespeare
    Caesar's power .. .. Mr. Barbauld
Pity, an allegory
Collin's Ode to the Passions

The other benefit concerts of the year, as far as I found them, were all crowded into the month of June. On the eleventh[2]), Mrs. Pownall appeared

1) Daily Advertiser, March 26, 1773.
2) Daily Advertiser, June 8, 1793.

at the City Theatre both as singer and composer with this miscellaneous program:

ACT 1st

New Overture	Vanhall
Song 'Sweet Echo' accompanied on the flute by Mr. Saliment	Mrs. Pownall
Quartetto Flute, Messrs. Saliment, Hewitt, etc.	Hoffmeister
Song 'Whither my love'	Mrs. Hodgkinson
Concerto Violin	Mr. Hewitt
Glee 'Hark the lark at Heaven's gate sings'	Mrs. Pownall
Mr. West, Mr. Prigmore, Mr. Robins, and Mrs. Hodgkinson.	

Catch 'They say there is Echo here', as performed with great applause in Vauxhall Gardens, London, Mrs. Hodgkinson, Mrs. West, Mr. Prigmore, Mr. Robins, and echoed by Mrs. Pownall

ACT 2 d.

Sinfonie	Pleyel
Song (by desire) 'Tally ho'	Mrs. Pownall
Concerto Flute	Mr. Saliment
Song 'Soldier tir'd'	Mrs. Hodgkinson
New Overture	Haydn
Glee 'Adieu to the village delights'	Mrs. Pownall
	Mr. Prigmore, Mr. West and Mr. Robins
To conclude with the comic dialogue of Jamie and Susan	Mrs. Pownall and Mr. Prigmore.

To reciprocate, Mrs. Pownall assisted with readings and songs at the benefit concert of Hewitt and Saliment on June 18th at the City Tavern. The announcement in the Daily Advertiser of June 14th was headed "last concert this season" but, of course, it did not properly belong to Hewitt and Saliment's series of subscription concerts. The second act of the concert was opened with Hewitt's Battle Overture and the entertainment began at half past seven, an hour gradually gaining in favor over seven o'clock:

ACT I

Sinfonie	Pleyel
Song	Mrs. Hodgkinson
Quartetto Flute	Mezger
New Song	Mrs. Pownall
Concerto Violin	Mr. Hewitt
The act will conclude with a recitation from the tragedy of Zara, by	Mrs. Pownall

ACT 2.

Battle Overture, in which will be introduced the Duke of Yorks' celebrated march	Hewitt
Song, Mrs. Hodgkinson, last time this season	
Concerto Flute	Mr. Saliment
Hunting song, last time this season	Mrs. Pownall
Finale	Haydn

After which Mrs. Pownall will read the story of Old Edwards taken from the Man of Feelings in which will be introduced a song taken from the poem of Lavinia, and composed by her.

Finally, Mrs. Hodgkinson was to give an entertainment on June 17th at the City Tavern which consisted mainly of select readings and songs. The only instrumental numbers announced were a violin concerto played by Mr. Van Hagen and a concerto played on the "grand Piano Forte" by a Mr. Smith. However, Mrs. Hodgkinson's personal attendance was rendered impossible by her safe delivery of a daughter on June 16th and therefore Mr. Hodgkinson saw himself under the necessity of substituting for the two songs advertised to be sung by his wife his own new song of "Bow Wow" and a favorite one by Dibdin, "never sung here" called 'None so pretty' which he hoped the emergency of the occasion would render acceptable. In this he certainly was not disappointed and it would be interesting to know how much of the applause usually showered on him on this occasion went to John Hodgkinson, *Papa* instead of to John Hodgkinson, the vocalist.

The year 1794 was ushered in by two benefits for Madame De Seze on Jan. 14th and Jan. 28th[1]). As might be expected the programs are decidedly French in character and the second is rendered especially interesting because it gave to New Yorkers an occasion to form an acquaintance with the style of Méhul.

Unless previous operatic ventures or other private affairs had plunged Mr. and Mrs. De Seze into debt, if may be surmised that the concerts were financially disastrous as Mr. Hauterive, the French consul, saw himself obliged to sell at auction on Feb. 11th their trunks and instruments[2]). This step poor De Seze considered unwarranted and he hoped that "no good feeling man" would bid on his things. The programs of the two concerts read:

JAN. 14, 1794

ACT I

Symphony	Hayden
Song	Madame De Seze
Sonata Piano Forte, accompanied by Messrs.	
Hewitt and De Seze [!]	
Song	Mrs. Pownall
Pleyel's celebrated Concertante for violins,	
tenor, clarinett and violoncello, by Messrs.	Hewitt, Du Camp, Woolfe and Capron

ACT II

Sonata Harp	Mad. De Seze
Song accompanied on the harp	Mad. De Seze
Trio for the flute	Mr. Saliment
Song, accompanied on the Piano Forte	Mad. Deseze

---

1) Daily Advertiser, Jan. 13 and Jan. 28, 1794.
2) American Minerva, Feb. 10, 1794.

Quartetto Cambini	Messrs. Hewitt, Bergman, Du Camp and Capron
Favorite Airs on the harp	Mad. De Seze
Finale	Rossetti

JAN. 28, 1794

ACT I

Simphony	Haydn
Song, on the Piano Forte, 'Dieu! .. .. Ce n'est pas pour moi, etc.'	Mad. De Seze
Concerto on the Piano Forte	Mad. de Seze
Song	Mrs. Pownall
Concertante	Hewitt, Saliment, Capron, etc.

ACT II

Sonata on the Harp	Mad. De Seze
Song of the opera of Atys[1]), on the harp ..	Mad. De Seze
Quartett of Pleyel, by	Messrs. Hewitt, Bergman, Du Camp and Capron
The most celebrated song in the beautiful French opera of Euphrosine[2]), beginning with these words 'Quand le guerrier vole au combat' on the Piano Forte by	Mad. de Seze
The pretty French potpourri, on the harp, with many favorite airs	Mad. De Seze
Finale	Haydn

These two concerts were followed in rapid succession by several others. First by Mrs. Pownall's benefit at the City Tavern on Feb. 6th[3]) with this program:

ACT 1 st.

Duett, 'Fair Aurora' from the opera of Artaxerxes[4])	Mrs. Pownall and Mr. Bergman
Quartetto, Messrs. Hewitt, Bergmann, Ducamp and Capron	Pleyel
Song 'On the rapid whirl wind's wing'	Mrs. Pownall
Concerto Horn	Mr. Pelipier [Pelissier]
Song, accompanied on the harp	Madame Desone [Deseze?]
Concerto on the grand Piano Forte	Mr. Rausche
Song the Lovely lad of the lowlands	Mrs. Pownall
Sinfonie	Pleyel

ACT II

Concerto, Violin	Mr. Hewitt
Song 'Love thou teazing pleasing pain'	Mrs. Pownall
Quartetto, Flute	Messrs. Saliment, Hewitt, Ducamp and Capron
Song 'Tally Ho'	Mrs. Pownall
Duett	Messrs. Hewitt and Capron
'Ma Chère amie', harmonized for three voices	Mrs. Pownall, Mr. Capron and Bergmann

Full piece

---

1) Piccinni.
2) Euphrosine et Corradin by Méhul.
3) Daily Advertiser, Jan. 31, 1794.
4) Arne.

Then Henri Capron presented this program on Feb. 26th[1]).

ACT 1 st.

Grand Overture 'La Reine' by	Mr. Haydn
Song by	Mrs. Pownall
Concerto Violoncello	Mr. Capron
Song, accompanied with the Piano Forte ..	Mad. De Seze
Concerto on the Flute	Mr. Saliment

ACT II

Concerto on the Piano Forte	Mrs. De Seze
A Hunting song by	Mrs. Pownall
Concerto Violin	Mr. Hewitt
Song on the harp	Mad. De Seze
A Duet sung by Mad. De Seze and Mr. Capron	Gretri
Finale	Mr. Haydn.

This concert had been preceded on Feb. 20th by Mrs. Hodgkinson's "concert and ball"[2]) with the "kind" assistance of Mrs. Melmoth, an adjective then probably more than now implying a *bona fide* act of unselfish professional courtesy:

ACT 1st.

Grand Overture by	Stamitz
Song (by desire) 'Sweet Echo'	Mrs. Hodgkinson
Concerto Violin	Master Van Hagen
Song 'The Hardy sailor'	Mrs. Melmoth
Quintetto, ...	Mr. and Master Van Hagen, Mr. Du Camp, etc.
Duett 'Adieu Poor Jack'	Mr. and Mrs. Hodgkinson
Sonata, Piano Forte	Mrs. Van Hagen

ACT 2 d.

Song 'Sweet lillies of the valley'	Mrs. Hodgkinson
Concerto Violin	Mr. Van Hagen
Song 'Disdainful you fly me'	Mrs. Melmoth
Concerto Piano Forte	Mrs. Van Hagen
Song 'Amid a thousand sighing swains'	Mrs. Hodgkinson
Duett 'Time has not thinn'd my flowing hair'	Mr. and Mrs. Hodgkinson
Finale	De Zaides [Dezède]

Hewitt's Battle Overture was again in prominence at the benefit concert of his partner in the Subscription Concerts venture, Mr. Saliment, on March 11th at the City Tavern[3]):

ACT 1st.

Battle Overture, Composed by	Mr. Hewitt
Song	Mrs. Pownall
Sonata Piano Forte	Madame De Seze
Solo Violin	Mr. Hewitt

---

1) Daily Advertiser, Feb. 15, 1794.
2) Daily Advertiser, Feb. 13, 1794. As a rule "and ball" was not longer added in the announcements but the instances were exceedingly few in those days when concerts were not followed by balls, usually conducted in New York by Mr. Hulett.
3) Daily Advertiser, March 3, 1794.

ACT II

Concerto Flute	Mr. Saliment
Duett for 2 voices (by particular desire)	
'Time has not thinned my flowing hair'	Mrs. Pownall and Mr. Bergmann
Solo Violoncello	Mr. Capron
Song, accompanied on the harp	Mad. De Seze
Finale	Haydn

The announcements of all these concerts were simple in style but when P. A. Van Hagen, junior again was to appear on the concert stage at Corre's Hotel on March 25th before subscribers only including "a Miss or Master under 14 years" at 5 shillings, he or rather his father indulged in this amusing advance notice in the Daily Advertiser, March 4th:

To render this entertainment as pleasing as possible, a selection will be made of new music and such as has received the repeated applause of the present refined taste in Europe, in addition to Mr. Mrs. and Master Van Hagen's best exertions to please, the brilliant vocal powers of Mrs. Hodgkinson are promised; Mrs. Melmoth has also obligingly consented to give two favourite songs, her mellifluous voice, correct style and pleasing taste in singing, which at a late public concert surprised the audience with delight, want no commendation to those who were present.

His program — it must be admitted that our prodigy modestly kept in the background — reads[1]):

ACT I

Overture Henry 4th and Entre Act ..	Martini
Song of Nina	Mrs. Melmoth
Concerto on the Violin	Master Van Hagen
Song 'Sweet lillies of the valley'	Mrs. Hodgkinson
Sonata Grand Piano Forte	Mrs. Van Hagen

ACT II

Overture of	Pleyel
Song 'The Highland laddie'	Mrs. Melmoth
Concerto on the Violin	Mr. Van Hagen
Song 'Sympathetic Echo', accompanied	
by the Clarinet	Mr. Hodgkinson
Concerto Grand Piano Forte	Mrs. Van Hagen
Duett 'Cher object', ...	Miss and Master Van Hagen
Concerto (by particular desire) on the	
Carillion, or Musical Glasses. Com-	
posed by	Mr. Van Hagen
Finale by	Ditto

If James Hewitt's program of Sept., 1792 furnished ample proof of his sympathies with programmatic music, the concert he gave on April 1, 1794[2]) — a rather ominous day — strengthens this impression. In his 'Voyage from England to America' he had paid but slight attention to the disagreeable qualities of *Oceanos*. This gap he now filled in with his 'New Overture, to conclude with the representation of a storm at sea'. The other

1) Daily Advertiser, March 21, 1794.
2) Daily Advertiser, March 21, 1794.

programmatic pillar of the program was the finale, Haydn's "celebrated Earthquake", from the "Seven Words':

ACT I

New Overture, to conclude with the representation of a storm at sea, composed by	Mr. J. Hewitt
Song, (by particular desire) 'Poll of Plymouth'	Mrs. Pownall
Quartetto, for 2 violins, tenor and base[!] by	Messrs. Hewitt, Bergman, Pellier and Capron
Song, accompanied on the harp, ...	Madame De Seze
Concerto Flute	Mr. Saliment
A Glee and a catch, by Mrs. Pownall, Messrs. Bergmann, King and Robins.	

ACT II

Concerto Clarinet	Mr. Wolfe
Song	Mrs. Pownall
Sonata Piano Forte	Madame De Seze
A Glee and catch, by	Mrs. Pownall, Messrs. Bergman, King and Robins
Finale, the celebrated Earthquarke	Haydn

In the meantime Mr. De Seze had opened a French school for young ladies from ten to sixteen years of age and correspondingly a French school for young gentlemen. Also Madame De Seze appears to have renounced temporarily the laurels of the concert stage for she gave a "last" concert on April 8th[1]) at the City Tavern with this program:

ACT I

Symphony	Haydn
Song on the harp	Mad. De Seze
Concerto on the Piano Forte..	Mad. De Seze
Song	Mrs. Pownall
Quartetto on the flute	Mr. Saliment, Hewitt, Capron etc.

ACT II

Sonata on the harp, accompanied by	Messrs. Hewitt and De Seze
An English song on the harp 'A Lovely rose', composed by	Mr. Capron and Mad. De Seze
The celebrated song 'Comme un', of the French opera, called 'Eclair, la fausse magie'[2]) on the Piano Forte	Mad. De Seze
Concerto on the violin	Mr. Hewitt
French Duet for two voices 'Dans le sein d'un pere'	Mad. De Seze and Mr. Capron
After wich Mad. De Seze will sing an English song, to thank the public of their kindness, this song is on the tune, 'Ah! no, no, no' accompanied on the Piano Forte.	
Finale	Haydn

1) Daily Advertiser, April 2, 1794.
2) Grétry.

With Mrs. Pownall's selection of the Belvedere House for her benefit concert on Sept. 4th, previous to her departure to Philadelphia, we possibly have the first instance of benefit concerts given in the open, for though the entertainment was to be held in the ball room in case of inclement weather, the plan was to permit, if possible, the company to hear the music on the bowling green where an "occasional orchestra" had been erected "on the balcony, in the manner of Vauxhall gardens"[1]. Also the program was clearly modelled after those heard at Vauxhall in London with its happy blending of popular and *heavy classic* music:

ACT I

Overture by	Haydn
Irish song 'Pat of Killarney' by	Mrs. Pownall
Sinfonia	Pleyel
Song 'Advice to the ladies of America' composed and to be sung by	Mrs. Pownall
Sinfonie	Hoffmeister
Rondeau 'My bonny Joe is gone to sea', by	Mrs. Pownall
Quatuor, Pleyel	Messrs. Hewitt and De Pellier

ACT II

Concerto Flute	Mr. Saliment
'A Soldier for me' by	Mrs. Pownall
Concerto Horn	Mons. Pelissier
A Cantata called 'The Happy rencontre, or, Second thoughts are best' by	Mrs. Pownall
Sinfonie	Abel
'Tally ho' by	Mrs. Pownall
Full piece.	

Mrs. Pownall's *al fresco* benefit was not to remain the last of its kind. Indeed, as soon as about 1798 the center of gravity had shifted from the winter to the summer, it was only logical that the prominent musicians would frequently prefer the summer to the winter for their benefits, the more so as this was the dead season in the activity of the musical societies which latter may reasonably be held responsible for the decreasing — certainly not in creasing — number of benefit concerts given in those years during the winter. On the whole it might be said that in this direction the concert life of New York came to a standstill instead of progressing lustily. For instance, the year 1795 cannot have seen many more than the three benefit concerts I traced in the Daily Advertiser. The first was given by Mrs. Van Hagen at the New Assembly Room on April 16th[1]) at which Benjamin Carr, so much better known as composer, organist, publisher, appeared as vocalist:

---

1) Daily Advertiser, Sept. 3, 1794.

Act I

Grand Symphony	Pleyel
Song	Mr. Carr
Sonata Piano Forte	Mrs. Van Hagen
Song	Mrs. Hodgkinson
Concerto on the Tenor	Mr. Van Hagen

Act II

Concerto Piano Forte	Mrs. Van Hagen
Song	Mr. Carr
Concerto Violin	Mr. Van Hagen, jun.
Song	Mrs. Hodgkinson
Overture, Blaise et Babette	Dezaldes [Dezède]

The two other concerts were given by the Dioscures Hewitt and Saliment and it is the program of the first, on June 11th, which furnished the clue to the year of foundation of the Columbian Anacreontic Society and also gave occasion to suspect James Hewitt guilty of the first piece of melo-dramatic music written in America, (now called 'Song recitations'), with his setting to Collin's Ode on the passions. The other concert, their "annual concert and ball", on December 29th, presented but the usual juxtaposition of orchestral and chamber-music, then, however, from the entirely different number of instruments employed in considerably smaller localities for more *intime* music, vastly less objectionable than it would be or is to-day. Here are the programs:

JUNE 11, 1795

Act I

Overture . . . The Battle of Prague, adap- ted for a full band, by	J. C. Schecky [Schetky]
Song	Mr. Carr
Concerto Flute	Mr. Saliment
Song	Mr. Hodgkinson
Glee 'Hark the lark' .. .. ∴	Mr. Cook
Concerto Piano Forte	Mrs. Van Hagen

Act II

Double Concerto for Flute and Violin	Messrs. Saliment and Hewitt
Song	Mrs. Melmoth, who has kindly offered for that night to sing the song from the opera Artaxerxes [Arne] 'Disdainful you fly me'.
Concerto Violin	Mr. Hewitt
Song	Mr. Carr
Glee 'Hope'	Mr. Hewitt

Collin's Ode on the Passions, to be spoken by Mr. Hodgkinson. With music representative of each passion, as performed at the Ana-creontic Society, composed by J. Hewitt.

DEC. 29, 1795

ACT I

Symphony	Pleyel
Song	Mr. Carr
Quartetto Flute	Messrs. Saliment, Hewitt, etc.
French Ariette, accompanied on the Piano Forte, by a lady who has kindly offered her assistance for that night only	
Overture	Van Hall

ACT II

Concertante for Violin and flute	Messrs. Hewitt and Saliment
Song	Mrs. Melmoth
Sonata Piano Forte	Mr. Carr
French Ariette, accompanied on the harp, by a lady.	
Finale	Haydn

For the year 1796 I have traced only two benefit concerts and for 1797 none. I trust that local historians will be more fortunate in completing the record though I doubt that the historical aspect will be changed very much. The program of the benefit for the very popular operatic star Miss Broadhurst on Nov. 15th[1]) at the Assembly Room was this, leaving it open to conjecture whether the Battle Overture performed was that by James Hewitt:

ACT I

Sinfonie	Pleyel
Song 'The Waving willow'	Miss Broadhurst
Concerto Piano Forte	Mr. Moller
Song 'The Cottage of the grove'	Mr. Tyler
Concertante for flute and violin	Messrs. Saliment and Hewitt
Bravoura Song	Miss Broadhurst

ACT II.

Battle Overture	
Song 'O come, sweet Mary, come to me',	Mr. Tyler, Miss Broadhurst[!]
Concerto Flute	Mr. Saliment
Song 'The Cheering rosary'	Miss Broadhurst
Glee	Miss Broadhurst, Messrs. Tyler, Johnson and Lee
Finale	Haydn

On Dec. 6th[2]) Mr. Moller, the manager of the Old City Concert, offered at the same place for his benefit in

ACT I

Overture	Pleyel
Song	Miss Broadhurst
Concerto Violin	Mr. Nicolai
Song	Miss Broadhurst
Duetto Grand Piano Forte	Mr. and Mrs. Moller

---

1) Minerva, Nov. 11, 1796.
2) Minerva, Nov. 30 and Dec. 2, 1796. It was first announced for Dec. 8th but the date was changed to Dec. 6th "on account of the City Assembly".

ACT II

Concerto Piano Forte	Miss Moller
Duett	Miss Broadhurst and Mr. Tyler
Concerto Clarinet	Mr. Henry
Bravoura Song	Miss Broadhurst
Finale	Pleyel

The first benefit concert of 1798 — those of 1797 must have escaped me — was given by Filippo Trisobio on Jan. 12th. The announcement was characteristic of this gentleman who died, as we know, in the same year at Philadelphia. Said he in the Daily Advertiser, January 8th:

A GRAND CONCERT.

Signor Trisobio, from Italy, professor of vocal music, established in Philadelphia, being a passenger in this city for a few days, has the honor to announce to the public, a *Concert* for Friday Evening the 12th inst. Also, that he has engaged Miss Broadhurst, with whom he will sing some Italian duettos of the first composition. He will sing in English, French and Italian. The band will be directed by Mr. Collet at the Tontine City Tavern . . . .

Signor Trisobio hopes to experience the same generous indulgence as he has received in several cities of this continent.

§§§ A numerous collection of Italian songs of the best composers may be had of Signor Trisobio, price three dollars.

The concert given on July 24, 1798 at the New City Tavern, Broadway by Mr. Lee[1]) with Messrs. Tyler, Jefferson, Miss Broadhurst, Mrs. Seymour, etc. as principal vocalists, "accompanyments by Messrs. Hewitt, Everdell, etc." was to conclude with "Hail Columbia, by Mr. Tyler and full chorus". This is also the only item worth recording of Mr. Lee's benefit concert at Columbia Garden on July 28th[2]). What a hold Joseph Hopkinson's hastily written lines, set to the 'President's March' — the memory of his father's 'Temple of Minerva' and other patriotic songs haunting his mind — was speedily gaining on the public may be inferred from the fact that also Mr. Adde's "grand" benefit at Columbia Garden on Sept. 4th[3]) concluded with this our first really national hymn:

ACT 1st.

Sinfonia	Hyden
Song	Mrs. Seymour
Concerto on the Horn	Mr. Libeschisky
Song	Mrs. Seymour
Sinfonia	Gerowetz

ACT 2d.

Concerto on the Violin	Mr. Nicholas
Song	Mrs. Seymour
Sinfonia	Hayden

1) Daily Advertiser, July 23, 1798.
2) Daily Advertiser, July 28, 1798.
3) New York Gazette, Aug. 31, 1798.

Concerto on the Clarinet .. .. Mr. Henry
The whole to be concluded with *Hail Columbia*, by Mrs. Seymour
*** Tickets at 4 s, to be had of Mr. Gilfert, Broadway, will
entitle the bearer to a glass of Ice cream or punch.

In the meantime, owing to Joseph Corre's half diplomatic, half generous willingness to supply his garden, not less than five benefit concerts had been given at Columbia Garden and to these must be added one for the benefit of Mr. Jefferson at Ranelagh Garden on Aug. 6th[1]). Certainly a corroboration of the theory advanced above with reference to the open-air benefit concerts!

First Miss Broadhurst and Mr. Tyler, who seems to have been a special favorite with the public as singer of patriotic songs, gave their joint benefit on Aug. 1st. Their program contained songs only, at least, songs only were announced in the Daily Advertiser, July 31st. but it goes without saying that the band and the virtuosos brought some variety into the entertainment:

PART 1st.

Song 'The Negro boy' .. .. Mr. Tyler
Song 'Where's the harm of that' .. .. .. Mrs. Seymour
A favorite Comic Song .. .. Mr. Jefferson
Song 'Sweet echo' .. .. Miss Broadhurst
The mock Italian trio 'Ting, tang, ta' .. .. Mr. Tyler, Mrs.
Seymour and Miss Broadhurst

PART II

Song 'Comely Ned, that child at sea' .. .. Mr. Tyler
Song 'The Cherry girl' .. .. Mrs. Seymour
A favourite Comic Song .. .. Mr. Jefferson
Song 'Jemmy of the glen' .. .. Miss Broadhurst
Song 'Adams and Liberty' .. .. Mr. Tyler

Then came on August 7th and again on Aug. 28th the band-master and clarinetist Henry and the horn virtuoso Libeschesky with joint benefits, mainly of instrumental music[2]) as the "arrangement of the music" shows:

PART I

Overture Henry 4th .. .. Martini
Song 'Too happy when Edward was kind' .. Miss Broadhurst
Solo, French horn .. .. Mr. Libeschesky
Song 'Tom Truelove's kneel' .. .. Mr. Tyler
Concerto Clarinet .. .. Mr. Henry
Allegro .. .. Pleyel

PART II.

Overture Demophon .. .. Vogel
Song 'Comely Ned that died at sea' .. .. Mr. Tyler
Concerto French Horn .. .. Mr. Libeschesky
Song 'Jemmy on the glen' .. .. Miss Broadhurst
Finale .. .. Haydn

---

1) Daily Advertiser, Aug. 4, 1798.
2) Daily Advertiser, Aug. 6 and Aug. 27, 1798.

16*

AUGUST 28, 1798
PART I

Grand Sinfonia	Paul Wraswsky [Wranitzky]
Song	Mrs. Seymour
Duet, Clarinet and French horn	Messrs. Henry and Libeschesky
Song	Mr. Tyler
Concerto Clarinet	Mr. Henry

PART II

Sinfonia	Gerowet [Girowetz]
Song	Mr. Tyler
Concerto French Horn, first time	Mr. Libischisky
Song	Mrs. Seymour
Finale	Pleyel

The same two gentlemen were engaged by desire of several ladies and gentlemen by a Mr. De La Mausse for his benefit concert with full orchestra, August 14, 1798[1]) and finally Messrs. Pelissier and Hoffmann announced that they would have their concert on Sept. 1st[2]). Particulars were to be expressed in the bills of the day but, unless they meant by bills programs distributed at the concert, one would look in vain for these particulars in the Daily Advertiser of Sept. 1st. Of Victor Pelissier, by the way, Dunlap drew this pen picture in his History of the American Theatre (p. 207):

He was a short old gentleman, and so near-sighted as to be nearly blind. Always cheerful, and his thoughts as fully occupied by notes as any banker or broker in Wall Street.

Though not strictly a benefit concert, unless we choose to be facetious, a "grand" concert may be mentioned here which was given on Nov. 26th at the "Pantheon, formerly New-Circus ... in commemoration of the evacuation of New York by the English"[3]). Strange to say no patriotic songs appear on the program, only such ditties as 'The Country club' being mentioned. With its songs, a quartet, three symphonies and two overtures besides the one to Arne's Artaxerxes and a "grand overture, double orchestra" by the London Bach the program is one of the longest on record:

ACT I

Grand Overture, double orchestra	Back
Song 'The Sailor Boy'	Mrs. Seymour
Song 'The Country Club'	Mr. Jefferson
Sinfonie	March
Song 'Let same sound the trumpet'	Mr. Tyler
Song 'Hope the balmy comfort send'	Mrs. Seymour
Overture	
Glee	Mrs. Seymour, Messrs.. Tyler and Lee
Grand Sinfonie with kettle drums	

1) Daily Advertiser, Aug. 13, 1798.
2) Daily Advertiser, August 28, 1798.
3) Daily Advertiser, Nov. 26, 1798.

ACT II

Overture
Song 'The Kiss' .. .. Mrs. Seymour
Song 'Mong, tong, paw' .. .. Mr. Jefferson
Quartetto .. .. Mr. Everdell, Samo,
                                           Nichola, Abel
Song .. .. Mr. Tyler
Sinfonie
Glee .. .. Mrs. Seymour, Messrs.
                                           Tyler and Lee

[Overture to] Artaxerxes with kettle drums.
Afterwards a Ball, to be continued till two o'clock in the morning.

Merely mentioning Mr. Mitchell's "Music-Balls" at the Assembly Room
in 1799[1]), Miss White's benefit concert on June 27, 1799[2]), that of a Mr.
Perkins at Ranelagh Garden on July 9, 1799[3]) and Mr. Myler's cruelty —
not to animals — but to his own flesh and blood in presenting "to the lovers
of harmony" on Nov. 15, 1799 at Lovett's Hotel his musical children, these
"phenomena of musical abilities" being "a boy not seven years old" and
"his sister, an infant just turned of four years" I submit a program which
possibly has more interest for the historian of fire-works in our country
than of music.

Joseph Delacroix informed the public through the New York Gazette
of July 26, 1799 that on the same evening would be executed at Vaux Hall
Garden:

AN ELEGANT & BRILLIANT FIRE WORK.

Never displayed before on this Continent — with *A Grand-Concert* Vocal and
Instrumental. The music conducted by Mr. Everdell and the singing by Mr. Barett
and Mr. Jefferson.

ACT I

Overture .. .. Haydn
Song 'Meg of Wapping' .. .. Mr. Jefferson
Song 'Independent we will be' .. .. Mr. Barett
Song 'The Village Recruit' .. .. Mr. Jefferson

ACT II

1. The Arms of the United States in coloured fire-works, with a
   horizontal sun
2. A Royal balloon with stars
3. A Brilliant wheel
4. Two Roman candles
5. A Horizontal wheel, with stars and report
6. A fixed Roman pyramid with an illuminated pedestal
7. A large Vestual wheel, forming a full body of coloured fire
8. Two Roman candles
9. Two Cohorn balloons with report
10. A large Chinese fire wheel

---

1) N. Y. Gazette, April 25, 1799.
2) Daily Advertiser, June 24, 1799.
3) Daily Advertiser, July 9, 1799.

Act III

1. Song 'To arms Columbia' .. .. Mr. Barrett
2. Song 'The Country club' .. .. Mr. Jefferson
3. Song 'Adams and Liberty' .. .. Mr. Barrett

Act IV

[Fireworks]

The programs of the few benefit concerts given in 1800 may also follow here. On Feb. 27th at Lovett's Hotel[1]) Messrs. Hewitt, Saliment, Henry and C. H. Gilfert offered this really good program:

Act I

Overture, Lodoiska, composed by .. .. .. Kreutzer
Song .. .. Mr. Hodgkinson
Concerto, Pianoforte .. .. Mr. C. H. Gilfert
                                       lately from Europe
Song .. .. Mrs. Hodgkinson
Duet, Flute and Tenor .. .. Messrs. Saliment,
                  and Hewitt, composed by J. Hewitt
Overture, Demophon, composed by .. .. .. Vogel

Act II

Concerto Clarinet .. .. Mr. Henry
Song .. .. Mrs. Hodgkinson
Concerto Flute .. .. Mr. Saliment
Song .. .. Mr. Hodgkinson
Overture d'Ephigene [sic] composed by .. .. Gluck

This was followed on March 11th[2]) by Mr. Weldon's concert and ball at the Tontine City Hotel with the following "order of the music":

Act I

Sinfonie
Song, Mrs. Grattan 'Soldier tir'd'
Grand Duet for two performers on one Piano
      Forte, Messrs. Moller and Weldon
Violin Quartet, Messrs. Berault, Noel, Abel and Minere
Song, Mrs. Grattan, Italian bravura
Rondeau, Pleyel

Act 2d.

Concerto Piano Forte, Mr. Weldon
Song, Mrs. Hodgkinson
Concerto Clarinet, Mr. Berno
Song, Mrs. Hodgkinson
Overture, Lodoiska, Kreutzer.

Then came, the program not being mentioned, a benefit for Mrs. Grattan, the lady manager of Philadelphia fame, on April 22d[3]) and on August 27th[4]) a concert given by a Miss White at Vaux Hall Garden with these selections:

1) Daily Advertiser, Feb. 21, 1800.
2) Daily Advertiser, March. 8, 1800.
3) Daily Advertiser, April 21, 1800.
4) Daily Advertiser, Aug. 26, 1800.

ACT I

Overture	Pleyel
Song 'No, not yet'	Miss White
Andante	Arogart [Mozart?]
Song 'The Unfortunate sailor'	Mr. Fox
Minuetto	Kotzeluch
Song 'Come kiss me, said she'	Mrs. Hodgkinson
Allegro	Sterckel
Song 'Henry lov'd his Emma well'	Miss Brett
Finale	Stamitz

ACT II

Sinfonie	Haydn
Song 'The Black cockade'	Miss White
Allegro	Pleyel
Song 'The Wounded hussar'	Mr. Fox
Overture	Cambini
Song 'Gray Jane', (by particular desire)	Mrs. Hodgkinson
Minuetto	Wraniski
Song 'When Sandy told his tale of love'	Miss Brett
Full piece	Stamitz

Finally, after several years of seclusion in her boarding school, Madame De Seze again ventured before the public in a concert at J. Adams junr.'s Hotel on Dec. 9th[1]) with the following rather indifferent program, monopolized by Pleyel:

ACT I

Symphony	Pleyel
Song	Madame Deseze
Concerto on the Piano Forte	do.
Quintet	Messrs. Henry, Deseze, etc.
Song	Madame Deseze
Rondo	Pleyel

ACT II

Concerto on the Violin, by an amateur	
Song, accompanied on the harp, ...	Madame Deseze
Concertante on the Harp and flute	do. etc. [!]
The much admired Song 'C'est pour toi que je les arrange', accompanied by the harp ..	do.
Finale	Pleyel

The chapter on concerts at New York, taking New York as a musical center, could be closed here as the vicinity of New York was practically a musical wilderness. True, in Princeton there had been a musical awakening about 1760 owing to James Lyon's activity while at college, and to the North, West, East and South of New York singing-schools, psalmodists, organs and organists and what Printz would have called *Bierfidler* were not missing. Also a few music teachers would venture outside of New York; theatricals including ballad-operas were given on a very modest scale, and

---

1) Daily Advertiser, Dec. 5, 1800.

now and then some local publisher would issue a psalm-tune collection, but all this is hardly worth mentioning here. As to concerts, they were so few that it is mere luck if one stumbles across them in the papers. However, in order to be of service to local historians, a few references may follow here to such concerts I accidentally found in my wearisome wanderings through New Jersey papers and those published at Albany, the *Athens* of the Dutch, and Poughkeepsie.

Shortly before New Jersey was to resound from the military bands of the Hessians — the most famous in Germany — Mr. Hoar, whom we met in New York, strolled to Princeton. He was to have a concert at Mr. Whitehead's Long Room on August 22, 1774[1]) and hoped for the patronage of the ladies and gentlemen of the neighborhood as he had not only engaged the best local performers but was to have from New York the assistance of two gentlemen and a young lady. The concert was to be divided in three parts, with four songs in each and the whole was to conclude with a ball "conducted on the same plan, as at Bath, Turnbridge, Scarborough and all the polite assemblies in London or any other part of Great Britain". Among the vocal music, consisting of a select and "well chosen number of songs, cantatas, and duets" were the following:

> The Highborn Queen
> Say little foolish fluttering thing
> Were I a shepherd's maid
> Cleone, a cantata
> The British fair
> May Day, a Cantata
> The Gaudy Tulip
> The Lass with one eye
> Sweet Willy O —
> The English Padlock
> The Sheep in her clusters
> A new favourite Hunting song.

By permission of the magistrate, Mrs. M'Donald announced a "grand" concert for July 31, 1799 at the Court House, Newark, N. J. in the Centinel of Freedom, July 23. Also by permission, the half-blind Mr. Salter, on his drift to Charleston, S. C., gave a musical entertainment at the City Hotel in Trenton, N. J. on Dec. 18, 1798 (State Gazette, same day) to which admittance could be gained for the ridiculously low sum of 25 cents — „children *half* price" — and the same unfortunate musician announced in the Guardian, or, New Brunswick Advertiser, Dec. 11, 1798 that "they" would give a concert of vocal and instrumental music with "speaking and elegant dancing" between the parts on the same evening at Mr. Sutton's.

---

1) **New York Journal, August 11, 1774 under date of Princetown, N. Y. 6th August, 1774.**

In Albany[1]), J. H. Schmidt, "esteemed of the best performers" on the piano-forte, appeared before a public, proverbially close-fisted, at Mr. Angus' Assembly Room on April 18, 1797 (Albany Gazette, April 17) with the following program which leaves it open to doubt whether he was surrounded by a *miniature* orchestra or whether Mr. Schmidt — and this would be historically interesting — played piano-forte arrangements of the orchestral pieces mentioned as becomes at least plausible from the words in the advertisement: "several musical pieces on the pianoforte":

Act I

Overture .. .. Vanhal
Grand Concerto on the
    Pianoforte, with accompaniments, by .. Mr. Schmidt
Trio for two violins and bass
'Be never jealous' — a favorite duet for two voices
The celebrated Sonata of Dr. Haydn, for two
    performers on one piano-forte, by Messrs. Schmidt and Weisbecher

Act II

Symphonia .. .. Stamitz
The 'Heaving of the lead' — a favorite song
    by Mr. Schmidt
A Duett concertante, for two violins
The Battle of Prague, on the Forte-piano, by
    Mr. Schmidt
Overture .. .. Haydn

---

1) Population: 1790—3498; 1800—5289 inhabitants.

BOSTON AND NEW ENGLAND.

THOUGH heretofore the early musical life of Boston has aroused the interest of historians to the neglect of other musical centers, this partiality has led to some substantial results, clearing as it did the historical undergrowth. Still, it will be seen that the works of Hood, Ritter, Brooks, Perkins and Dwight and more recently Mr. Elson's sympathetic History of American Music have by no means fully covered the ground as far as the concert-life of Boston and New England in general is concerned. Now, with a greater mass of data at our disposal, we shall no longer hesitate to call Boston a musical city even in the eighteenth century. Had she not been, Boston, with a population[1] much smaller than that of New York would hardly have succeeded in suddenly gaining within a few decades a position in the musical life of our country similar to that of Munich *versus* Berlin in Germany. —

The musical advertisements in the early Boston papers[2] bear substantial evidence to the fact that during the first decades of the eighteenth century sacred music predominated in Massachusetts, but, it must be insisted upon, not to such an extent as most historians would make us believe. One of the strongest points against the prevalent theory is this that public concerts were given at Boston at quite an early date.

The first concert recorded in our Colonial papers was advertised in the Boston Weekly News Letter, Dec. 16—23, 1731 but this does not necessarily imply that it was the first given! Also a bare possibility remains that concerts might have been advertised in such earlier numbers of this weekly,

---

1) Population: 1722—10567; 1765—15520; 1790—18038; 1800—24937 inhabitants.
2) The first real newspaper, the 'Boston News Letter' was founded as early as 1704!

founded in 1704, as seem to be lost forever. However, undoubtedly Boston's concert-life dates back to at least 1731 and everything considered this is quite early. The announcement in the Weekly News Letter reads thus:

On Thursday the 30th of this instant December, there will be performed a *Concert of Music* on sundry Instruments at Mr. Pelham's great Room, being the House of the late Doctor Noyes near the Sun Tavern.

Tickets to be delivered at the place of performance at *Five shillings* each. The Concert to begin exactly at Six o'clock, and no Tickets will be delivered after Five the day of performance.

N. B. There will be no admittance after Six.

This first concert was followed on Nov. 23 and Dec. 28, 1732 by two "Consorts of Musick performed of sundry instruments"[1]. Both were held "at the Concert Room in Wing's Lane near the Town Dock", from which announcement we may infer that Boston possessed some kind of a concert hall as early as 1732. Shortly afterwards, on Jan. 29, 1733, the same paper informed the public of a further concert to be given on Feb. 1, 1733. The advertisement is interesting as it contains the earliest reference to the duration of the entertainment. It was "to begin at Six o'clock and end at Nine". This concert, however, was postponed to February 15th. The next I came across was advertised in the Boston News Letter for March 11, 1736 and from the fact that the concert was to begin "at half an Hour after Six and end at Nine", it might be inferred that then as now two hours and a half had come to be considered the limit of human endurance.

Besides leaving us in the dark concerning the music played, the newspapers never allude to the musician or musicians who thus introduced concerts at Boston. The only clue is the notice that the first concert was to take place "at Mr. Pelham's great Room". Now, this Pelham was identical with Peter Pelham, the engraver, dancing master, manager of the subscription assembly (in Puritan Boston!), boarding-school-keeper, instructor in "writing, arithmetic, reading, painting upon glass", and dealer in the "best Virginia Tobacco"[2]. A man of such versatility may also have been proficient enough as a musician to give concerts. This hypothesis is strengthened by the fact that he appreciated the difficulties of the musical art sufficiently to put his son for nine long years "under the Tuition of an Accomplish'd Professor of the Art of Musick". Then, after his return to Boston in 1743, "Mr. Peter Pelham, jun." advertised his readiness to give

1) New England Weekly Journal, Nov. 13 and Dec. 15, 1732.
2) News Letter, Feb. 22, 1728; Boston Gazette, Jan. 1, Jan. 16, May 8, 1733; Boston Evening Post, Jan. 16, Sept. 1744; Sept. 12, 1748.

lessons on the harpsichord and in the "Rudiments of Psalmody, Hymns, Anthems, etc."[1]).

That young Pelham's training easily made him the foremost musician of Boston is more than likely, but, strange to say, I have not found his name mentioned again in the Boston papers. Perhaps he moved soon afterwards to Virginia, where he is to be traced later on. He certainly does not appear in connection with a concert given more than a year after his return and erroneousy claimed to have been Boston's first concert. It was thus advertised in the Boston Gazette on Nov. 27, 1744:

> This is to inform the Public, that by the Permission of the Select Men, a *Concert of Musick* for the Benefit of the Poor of the Town, is to be perform'd at Faneuil Hall[2]) on Thursday the Sixth of December, which will begin at half an Hour after Five in the Evening. Tickets may be had at the House of Mr. Stephen D(e) Blois in Queen-street at Ten Shillings each. As the Money raised will be put into the Hands of the Select Men, those who are so charitably disposed as to give any thing extraordinary may depend upon its being apply'd to the laudable Purpose aforesaid.
>
> N. B. No person will be admitted without a ticket.

In the meantime music had definitely entered into the *public* life of the Bostonians and the fact that concerts were now beginning to be considered a proper tribute of respect to the king, proves pretty conclusively, in my opinion, that the New England Puritans were human, after all, on six days of the week and not so frightfully bigoted, ascetic and narrow-minded as they usually are pictured and that they did not consider music, to use Hullah's words, a stolen pleasure, a popular legend so brillantly scouted by Davey in his History of English music.

It naturally suggested itself to pay some attention to the Boston Select-men minutes as reprinted in the Boston Town Records and the result was quite gratifying. For instance, it is recorded of the meeting of Oct. 10, 1744 that:

> "Mr. William Sheaf with a number of Gentlemen desire the Liberty of Faneuil Hall to-morrow in the Afternoon being the King's Coronation Day in Order to Cele-brate the Day with a Concert of Musick.
>
> Voted that the Liberty be granted they making good all Damages & that it be no President for the future."

However, the *President* had been established and the select men very soon were called upon to wrestle with it. Accordingly they granted in their meeting of Oct. 24, 1744

---

1) Boston Evening Post, May 30, 1743. According to William H. Whitmore in 'The Early Printers and Engravers of New England' (Mass. Hist. Soc. Proc. 1866—67) he was baptised at St. Paul's Covent Garden, London, Dec. 17, 1721.

2) This venerable landmark of Boston, a combination of market and assembly building, was built in 1742 by Peter Faneuil as a gift to the city.

"Liberty . . . to Mr. William Sheafe & a Number of Gentlemen for a Concert of Musick in Faneuil Hall on Tuesday next, it being the Majesty's Birth Day, the Gentlemen proposing the Benefit arising by the Tickets at Ten Shillings Old Tenor to be for the Benefit of the Poor of the Town to be disposed of at Discretion of the Select Men."

For some reason or the other the proposed concert did not take place for we read in the minutes of the meeting on Nov. 21, 1744

"Mr. William Sheafe & a Number of Gentlemen desire the Use of Faneuil Hall for a Concert of Musick in the room of that which was to have been performed on His Majesty's Birth Day, & as the Days are very short, that they might have it in the Evening to break up at nine o'Clock, the Benefit arising by the Tickets to be for the Use of the Poor of the Town as the Select men shall direct."
Liberty is granted to them accordingly."

The poor of the town had every reason to congratulate themselves on the musical enthusiasm of Mr. William Sheafe and a number of gentlemen for it was reported in the meeting of Dec. 12, 1744 that

"the Selectmen received of Mr. Stephen Deblois two hundred & five pounds five shillings old Tenor being collected by a Concert of Musick in Faneuil Hall for the Use of the Poor of the Town."

Presumably the selectmen gave their consent to similar requests during the next years but no reference to such appears in the printed minutes until May 4, 1747 when

Mr. Thomas Hancock applied to the Selectmen in the name of his Excellency Governor Knowles (with his Complements [!] to them to be there) Desiring he might have the use of Faneuil Hall, one Evening this week for a Concert of Musick which was unanimously consented to by the Select Men[1]).

Several years elapsed before a public concert was advertised in the papers. It was to take place on Jan. 9, 1755[2]) at the Concert Hall in Queen-

---

1) It is necessary to call attention here to the fact that Mr. A. B. Brown in his book on Faneuil Hall (p. 89) in referring to this request quotes that Mr. Thomas Hancock applied for the use of the hall "one evening in *each* week, for a concert of music". On the basis of this quotation I claimed in my article on 'Early Concerts in America' (New Music Review, June, 1906) that Boston possessed weekly amateur concerts as early as 1747. Later on I ran across the official version and as the contradiction between the two versions was apparent Mr. Edward Burlingame Hill of Boston kindly consented to consult the original minutes. Mr. Brown's version unfortunately is incorrect.

2) Weekly News Letter, Jan. 2, 1755. See also Elson, who, by the way, states that Concert Hall was built in 1756, obviously a slip of the pen. When Concert Hall was built, is unknown. It existed already in 1754, though not called by that name in a deed of Sept. 1754 by which Gilbert and Lewis Deblois, brasiers, conveyed it to Stephen Deblois for 2000 pounds. In 1769 the latter sold it to William Turner for 1000 pounds. The hall later on passed into the hands of the Amory family and stood until 1869 when it was torn down to make way for the widening of Hanover Street. (See Drake's History and antiquities of Boston, 1856 and his Old Landmarks of Boston.) The Amory family cannot have purchased the hall from Turner before Sept. 1787 when the Mass. Centinel, advertised it for sale. Turner, however, kept a dancing school at Concert Hall for years afterwards.

street. We are not told for whose benefit the entertainment was held, but it might have been John Rice who came to Boston from New York as music teacher and organist of Trinity Church during fall of 1753[1]). At any rate his name is positively connected with a concert advertised in the Evening Post, March 31, 1755 for April 10th, as it was to be given "for the benefit of John Rice".

If this advertisement was the first to clearly identify a particular musician with these early concerts, one that appeared in the Evening Post, Jan. 31, 1757 for the first time dimly alludes to the program:

> For the benefit of Mr. *Dipper*, at Concert Hall, on Thursday next, the third of February, will be perform'd, a *Concert* of Vocal and Instrumental Musick to consist of Select Pieces by the best Masters.
> Tickets to be had at the Crown and Comb the corner of Queenstreet, and at the Golden Eagle in Dock Square, at half a Dollar each. To begin at Six o'clock.

Again it was Mr. Thomas Dipper who gave concerts on March 30, 1758 (deferred from March 14th); Jan. 4, 1759, Jan. 10, 1760, February 3, 1761 (postponed from Jan. 20th)[2]) but beyond the usual information as to the price of tickets etc. we are not acquainted with further details, except that these concerts, too, consisted of "Select pieces by the best masters", a form of advertisement which remained traditional in Boston for many years. The only additional hint is contained in the announcement of the concert on Feb. 3, 1761 when "many" of the pieces were to be "accompany'd by two French horns" and the whole program was divided "into three acts".

This was the last concert announced under Thomas Dipper's name but not the last in which he took part as may be inferred from the fact that tickets for concerts on Nov. 6 and Nov. 12, 1761 were to be had of the printers *and* of Mr. Dipper, at half a dollar each[3]). Possibly Thomas Dipper, who had been imported from London as organist of King's Chapel in 1756, still held this position part of 1762 but that no concerts or other musical events at Boston can be linked with his name after 1762 becomes apparent from a notice in the Evening Post, June 6, 1763:

> "We hear from Jamaica, that Mr. Thomas Dipper, late organist of King's Chapel in this town, died there a few months ago."

Possibly the concert of Feb. 3, 1761 was the first of a series as the original announcement for Jan. 20th was headed "Mr. Dipper's Public Concert will *begin* on Tuesday the 20th instant." This possibility leads to some rather puzzling problems. In the first place, the term "public" concert is so un-

---

1) Boston Evening Post, Nov. 19, 1753.
2) Evening Post, March 13 and 27, 1758; Jan. 1, 1759; News Letter, Jan. 10, 1760; Evening Post, Jan. 12, and Feb. 2, 1761.
3) Boston Evening Post, Oct. 26 and Nov. 22, 1761. Possibly the concert on Nov. 12th was merely postponed from Nov. 6th.

usual in Colonial Times as to invite the suspicion that in contradistinction to this and other serial public concerts announced for no particular musician's benefit, there also existed at Boston *private* concerts, as a rule not accessible to non-subscribers. Now the latter species does not necessarily imply that an organized society of "gentlemen-performers" existed at Boston, but, if they met at more or less regular intervals, of necessity some kind of organisation must have bound them together. Furthermore, should it appear that one or the other of the prominent musicians not only gave benefit concerts but managed serial subscription concerts, the query naturally would arise whether the latter ran parallel to the *collegium musicum*, if we may call it so, or were identical with it. Before attempting an answer, if an answer is possible, perhaps it will be best to gather in chronological order the few data that throw light on the puzzle.

Said the News Letter on April 29, 1762:

"The members of the Concert, usually performed [!] at Concert Hall, are hereby notified that the same is deferred to the end of the Summer months. And it is desired that in the meantime each member would settle his respective arreage with Stephen Deblois, with whom the several accounts are lodged for that purpose."

Usually performed at Concert Hall! This certainly does not read as if the anonymous organisation of which Mr. Stephan Deblois seems to have been the treasurer, was founded recently and who knows but that these musical gatherings had their spiritual father in William Sheafe and his friends or at least sprang into life simultaneously or soon after the erection of Concert Hall? Or, maybe Thomas Dipper had a hand in the organisation and if the concerts were accessible to non-subscribers, then he possibly alluded to the concerts at Concert Hall and not to an independent undertaking when announcing in Feb. 1761 "Mr. Dipper's public concert".

Next we read in the Massachusetts Gazette, Oct. 2, 1766 that a Concert of Musick was to begin on Oct. 7th and "to be continued every Tuesday evening for eight months" at Concert Hall. Gentlemen inclining to become members were directed to Mr. Stephen Deblois for further information. Then, on Jan. 12, 1769, the same paper speaks of 'the private concert' which was to begin on Wednesday evening the 25th. However, from the Boston Evening Post of Feb. 2d we know that the opening night was postponed to Feb. 10th and that the concerts thereafter continued every other Wednesday until May 31st.[1]) Hence the name of "Wednesday Night Concert". That it was not strictly private appears from the same announcement as non-subscribers were admitted on paying half a dollar each. During 1770 Tuesday again seems to have been the night of meeting, at least the

---

1) Boston Evening Post, May 29, 1769.

last concert for the season was announced for Tuesday, July 17, 1770[1]).
It was to begin at the unusually late hour of eight o'clock.

During the winter of 1770—1771 at least two series of subscription
concerts were given, one under the direction of William Turner and the
other under Thomas Hartley. Mr. Turner seems to have been not less
prominent as musician than as dancing and fencing master. In fact,
he first appeared on the plan in the latter capacity by becoming in 1765
successor to his father Ephraim who had taught dancing and fencing at
Boston for many years and who died after a lingering illness in October
1765[2]). William Turner presumably was also active on the concert stage
during those years but I failed to find his name mentioned in connection
with concerts until December 7, 1770 when *his* concert was to open by subscription[3]). That this was not merely a benefit concert but really constituted the first in a series appears between the lines of the account of his
troubles with Mr. Morgan, the violinist, published in the Boston Gazette,
April 26, 1773. How long William Turner continued the enterprise is not
certain. Mr. Seilhamer when speaking of Burgoyne's Thespians in Boston
(1775—1776) mentions a concert given by Turner. This may or may not
have been a benefit concert but it is also to be gleaned from his exposure
of Mr. Morgan that this gentlemen threatened in April 1773, if not employed
by Turner, to "lead Mr. Propert's concert" against him. Consequently
William Turner was still busy with subscription concerts early in 1773. He
then seems to have gone to London from where he returned during the
summer of 1774 continuing to teach, "the polite arts of dancing and fencing
in the newest and most approved method, at Concert Hall"[4]) and with
these accomplishments more than with music he appears to have made
his living in after-years.

Simultaneously with Turner, Thomas Hartley seems to have been connected with subscription concerts during the winter of 1770—1771 as he,
in the Boston Evening Post of March 11, 1771, begged leave to

"acquaint *his* subscribers, that to avoid the Assembly and Passion Week, his two
remaining concerts will be held on Wednesday the 20th instant, and on Wednesday
the 10th of April."

Evidently John Rowe referred to one of these subscriptions concerts
with this entry in his diary on Jan. 3, 1771

"Spent the evening at Concert Hall, where there was a concert performed by
Hartly, Morgan and others; after the concert a dance. The Commodore and all the

---

1) Boston Evening Post, July 16, 1770.
2) Massachusetts Gazette, June 13, 1765 and Boston Evening Post, Oct. 21,
1765.
3) Boston Evening Post, Dec. 3, 1770.
4) Boston Evening Post, June 6, 1774.

captains of the navy here was there and Colo. Dalrymple and fifty or sixty gentlemen and the same number of ladies present."

The next reference, or rather references to serial concerts appear in the papers for 1773. On January 7th, Mr. David Propert, organist of Trinity Church, acquainted the gentlemen subscribers and the rest of his friends through the Massachusetts Gazette that "he is in expectation soon of a Capital performer;.and then he will open the concert for the winter season". This preliminary notice was supplemented in the Boston Evening Post by the following quaint announcement:

Mr. Propert acquaints the Gentlemen Subscribers that he intends to open the *Concert* at the British Coffee House in Kingstreet on Wednesday the 3d day of February. Wishes he could have had a larger room, which by the next season he hopes to accomplish, this being the best he can accommodate them at present. The performer he expected is come, and he is also favour'd with the band of the 64th: the little boys under his care will in a short time be able to sing out of Mr. Handel's oratorios, as they have a very distinguishing ear and power of voice: He returns thanks to those gentlemen who are lovers of the art and have favor'd him with their support, and assures them (as difficult as it may be) he will persevere to exert his abilities to give them all the satisfaction in his power. —

Every night will be performed select pieces upon the harpsichord with accompaniment compos'd by the most celebrated masters of Italy and London; to begin at half after six.

N. B. As the season is so far advanced the subscription is a guinea for three months.

From John Rowe's diary it appears that at least three concerts of the series took place on March 3, 17, 31, 1773 with "good music" before "a very genteel company".

We already know that Mr. Propert had a rival in William Turner and consequently musical Boston again enjoyed at least two series of subscription concerts during part of the year 1773. This interesting fact is corroborated by a glance into the Boston Evening Post of April 19th and in fairness to William Turner his announcement also follows in full:

Mr. Turner respectfully begs leave to acquaint his subscribers that his last concert for this season will be on Tuesday evening the 27th current, at which time will be performed a variety of music received from London by Capt. Scott, which never has been performed in this place—compos'd by the most eminent masters in Europe.

Mr. Turner also takes this public opportunity of returning his most grateful thanks to his friends and subscribers for their support of his Concert during the past season, and begs leave at the same time to acquaint them that he expects in June next an elegant organ, made by the celebrated Mr. John Snitzler, and as he is determined to spare no pains or expence to give satisfaction he hopes to merit a continuation of their favors for next season, tho' many attempts have been made to injure him.

He also thinks it an act of justice to inform the public and his friends that he is not interested in Mr. Propert's Concert, advertised for Thursday 22d, as has been reported.

The rivalry between the two musicians ended with a victory for David Propert as the latter on Nov. 4, 1773 in the Massachusetts Gazette acquainted the gentlemen subscribers to his Concert that it would be opened at Concert Hall on Wednesday Nov. 10th and continue on that day once a fortnight. However, Turner soon was to have his revenge and we may imagine his satisfaction when he read in the Boston Evening Post of Oct. 3, 1774 the following melancholical lines:

Mr. Propert begs leave to acquaint the gentlemen subscribers to the Concert that he could not succeed in a number sufficient to defray the expences and finds the town in general not composed enough to enjoy or encourage any diversions at this unhappy time of publick calamity and distress, therefore he has dropt all thought of a concert for the present.

And yet a few more subscription concerts must have taken place before the war turned the interests of the gentlemen subscribers into less peaceful channels than the enjoyment of overtures, concertos and symphonies! Foreshadowing the end, "the managers of the concert" gave public notice in the Massachusetts Gazette Jan. 26, 1775 that the next meeting of the gentlemen subscribers was adjourned to the first Thursday in March

"in order to settle with the performers for the time past — and to raise an additional subscription to the stock in hand, to enable them to carry it on for two months longer.

That these concerts were conducted not by David Propert but by W. S. Morgan is also pretty certain as otherwise it would not have rested with the managers to appoint Feb. 2d for a "grand" concert of vocal and instrumental music for Mr. Morgan's benefit[1]). On the other hand it is not quite clear whether the managers raised enough additional stock to carry on the concerts during March and April and if Morgan, regardless of the signs of approaching war, on April 3d announced "his first evening's entertainment" in the Boston Evening Post the form of his announcement almost leads us to infer that the contemplated series was an enterprise of his own:

Mr. Morgan requests leave to acquaint his subscribers and the public in general that his first evening's entertainment will be on Tuesday the 11th instant; when will be performed a Concert of Vocal and Instrumental Music; between the parts of which will be delivered (gratis) several comic Lectures an various subjects.

Tickets at three shillings sterling each to be had at the British Coffee House, and of Mr. Morgan at his chamber near the Mill bridge, where such gentlemen as chuse to subscribe may be inform'd of the proposals.

These are the scattered data on the basis of which an answer may be ventured to the queries suggested above. Personally I am inclined to believe that at the very least from 1761 on, without any or with temporary interruptions only, a sort of musical society existed at Boston until 1775 and that independently a few prominent musicians managed subscription concerts. At any rate, semi-public subscription-concerts flourished and it is a pity that we know so very little of the repertory, studied and played by the gentlemen-performers with the assistance and under the

---

1) Boston Evening Post, Jan. 30, 1775.

guidance of the best available professional musicians, such as Dipper, Hartley, Turner, Propert and Morgan.

Having ventured one conjecture with reference to these subscription-concerts another may follow here before *terra firma* is again touched with the benefit concerts given by the musicians just mentioned and Messrs. Flagg, Juhan, Selby, Asby, Mc Lean, Stieglitz and Stamper.

It is this. Beginning with 1763 a number of "public" concerts may be traced apparently belonging to no series nor announced for the benefit of any particular musician. But somebody must have been responsible for them, and the question arises, who gave them? As they generally were held at Concert Hall, the idea would not seem far-fetched that Concert-Hall was erected by the Deblois as a business-proposition just for that purpose. In other words, those concerts might have been given by the proprietor or lessee of Concert Hall for the benefit of Concert Hall. Another explanation is equally plausible. How, if they were public appearances of the gentlemen-performers who thus found it convenient and easier to defray the current expenses of their "private" concert? Whatever explanation is accepted the fact remains that public concerts were given which belonged neither to any series nor were announced for the benefit of any particular musician. The announcements were generally clad in the formula "consisting of the most agreeable compositions from the best authors" but otherwise they throw little light on these somewhat mysterious entertainments. The dates, together with such bits of information as might prove interesting, were these: May 31, 1763 postponed from May 26th; Nov. 9, 1764; Oct. 24, 1765; Dec. 5, 1768; Jan. 13, 1769; June 20, 1770; Dec. 24, 1773[1]). The concert of 1763 "opened" the latest acquisition of Concert Hall, "a delicate and melodious new organ, made by the first hand and lately imported from London in Capt Burges", and declared to have been "perhaps the finest instrument in America". An item of interest connected with the concert on Nov. 9, 1764 is this, that tickets were also to be had at Mr. Billings's shop near the Post-office, and possibly we have in this the earliest musical reference in the papers to William Billings, tanner, psalmodist and composer whose music was to exercise such a strange fascination over our people for thirty long years. The announcements of the other concerts are indifferent, that of June 20, 1770 excepted. It shows that the Concert really was an opera performance in disguise as the advertisement reads:

"A vocal entertainment of three acts. The songs (which are numerous) are taken from a new celebrated opera, call'd, *Lionel and Clarissa*".

Following this clue, it is then easily ascertained that in 1770 several

---

1) Boston Evening Post, May 16 and 30, 1763, Nov. 5, 1764, Oct. 7, 1765, June 18, 1770, Dec. 20, 1773; Boston Chronicle, Nov. 21-28, 1768, Jan. 2-9, 1769.

others besides this opera by Dibdin were given in concert-form. Perhaps
Mr. Joan, of whom more later on, was responsible for these entertainments.
At any rate, John Rowe, not sufficiently weighed down by his wide business
interests to neglect his entertaining diary recently published, entered under
March 23, 1770:

"In the evening I went to the Concert Hall to hear Mr. Joan read the Beggar's
Opera & sing the songs. He read but indifferently, but sung in taste. There were
upwards one hundred people there."

Turning to benefit concerts, given either at the virtuoso's own risk or
with the assistance and under the auspices of the gentlemen performers on
the principle of *do ut des*, (which is not always clear) it would seem that
Thomas Hartley's benefit concert of Jan. 15, 1767[1]) at Concert Hall was
the first given at Boston after Thomas Dipper's departure to Jamaica. Of
course, the program consisted "of select pieces by the most eminent masters"
which leaves a rather wide margin to our reconstructive imagination. When
announcing his "grand" concert on April 28, 1769[2]) Mr. Hartley even re-
frained from giving this meagre formula but he remarked that "the vocal
parts" would be held by a "gentleman from London" whose identity, however, is not disclosed. Finally, of his last benefit concert to be traced in the
papers, f. i. in the Boston Evening Post, Jan. 1, 1770, we know nothing except the date. It was to be held on Jan. 5, 1770 postponed from Dec. 29,
1769. In 1771 we found him connected with subscription concerts but
after that he cannot have resided much longer at Boston since we found
him playing first violin at a concert in Charleston, S. C. in January 1773.
His subsequent career is unknown to me.

In the meantime the doors of Concert Hall had been opened to the public
on March 16, 1769 for the benefit "of the fife-major of the 29th regiment"
The concert certainly took place, for John Rowe, the Boston captain of
industry, entered in his diary under March 16, 1769

". . . . Spent the evening at the Fife-Major's concert at Concert-Hall — there was
a genteel Company & the best Musick I have heard performed there."

Tickets at the then usual price of half a dollar were to be purchased
at the London Bookstore, by the printers of the Boston Chronicle which
announced the concert on March 9—13th — and at Mr. M'Lean's, watchmaker in Kingstreet. It will be remembered that a fife-major by the name
of John M'Lean gave a concert at New York in 1771. In case the 29th
regiment was a militia regiment, it is possible that the anonymous fife-
major of the 29th regiment, Mr. M'Lean the watchmaker and the fife-
major M'Lean were identical. If this correlation should prove to be

---

1) Boston Evening Post, Jan. 12, 1767.
2) Boston Chronicle, April 3 and April 27, 1769.

impossible, then this particular concert might be linked with the name of a musician who in the Boston Evening Post, Oct. 11, 1713 claimed to have been "the first founder and having at great expense of time, trouble, etc. instructed a band of music to perform before the regiment of militia in this town". This energetic musician was Josiah Flagg, born possibly about Nov. 5, 1738[1]) and best known as Boston's authority in psalmody before William Billings appeared on the plan.

In 1764 Josiah Flagg had published his 'Collection of the best Psalm tunes ... approv'd of by the best masters in Boston. New England'. The book was engraved, on paper made in the Colonies, by Paul Revere. This coincidence is deeply regretted by those who collect early American psalm tune collections for their value from the standpoint of musical history and not from that of the history of engraving. Admitting that Paul Revere did his work well, though he might have given credit to Henry Dawkins whose title page to Lyon's 'Urania' he — to put it mildly and as was his habit — deftly borrowed, Flagg's collection would not bring to-day the exorbitant price of 52 dollars, had it not in after-years fallen to Paul Revere's lot to become famous, under circumstances not wholly clear, as the man of the 'Mid-night ride'. Be this as it may, Josiah Flagg compiled a useful collection and met with sufficient encouragement to publish in 1766 'A collection of all Tansur's and a number of other anthems'[2]). But psalmody did not satisfy ambitious Josiah Flagg and he soon ventured into the spheres of secular music of which tendency traces may even be found in his collection of 1764. To found and drill at great expense and trouble a militia band, is still considered a creditable undertaking, but Flagg did more than this. He gave quite acceptable concerts and merits the particular sympathy and admiration of the historian because he occasionally condescended to mention his programs. This, however, was not the case with the first concert actually announced for his benefit which took place after a postponement of date on June 29, 1769 at Concert Hall[3]). Still, Josiah Flagg merits some applause for having at least remarked that the "vocal part [was] to be performed by four voices, and to conclude with the *British Grenadiers*". As this public concert was the "last" this season, logically it must have been preceded by others and it would be interesting to know whether it belonged to a series of subscription concerts or whether Josiah Flagg had friends and admirers enough to risk more than one benefit concert during that year. His next benefit concert, on June 7, 1770[4]) was adorned by "a duet to

---

1) In the Records of the Church in Brattle Square, Boston, 1902 appears on p. 161 in the "List of Persons baptized" "Josiah Flag. November 5, 1738"
2) See my book on Francis Hopkinson and James Lyon, 1905.
3) Boston Chronicle, June 26/29, 1769.
4) Massachusetts Gazette, June 7, 1770.

be sung by a gentleman who lately read and sung in Concert Hall[1]) and Mr. Flagg".

All this reads harmless enough so far, but that Josiah Flagg really was conversant with the best music of the time and possessed ambitions and taste far beyond that of the average psalmodist — if he really was an exception — is strikingly illustrated by the following programs. For May 17, 1771[2]) he solicited the patronage of the public with this really remarkable selection of "vocal and instrumental musick accompanied by French horns, hautboys, etc. by the band of the 64th Regiment".

ACT I.	Overture Ptolomy	Handel
	Song 'From the East breaks the morn'	
	Concerto 1st	Stanley
	Symphony 3d	Bach
ACT II.	Overture 1st	Schwindl
	Duet to 'Turn fair Clora'	
	Organ concerto	
	Periodical Symphony	Stamitz
ACT III.	Overture 1st	Abel
	Duetto 'When Phoebus the tops of the hills'	
	Solo Violin	
	A new Hunting Song, set to music by	Mr. Morgan
	Periodical Symphony	Pasquale Ricci

Nor did he lower his standard when less than half a year later, on Oct. 4th, he gave another benefit concert at Concert Hall. That it was not customary to appeal to the public twice within half a year, or rather that it was customary to defer benefit concerts to the end of the season would appear from a *N. B.* in the announcement in the Massachusetts Gazette, Oct. 3d where Flagg emphatically denied that "his being thus early with his concert is not with intention to interfere with any other person". As a side-light on advertising methods of the time it may also be observed that the announcements in the papers differed. Whereas he gave to the Massachusetts Gazette the news that his concert would be

"conducted (and a solo on the violin) by Mr. Morgan, organist of Newport"

and that in the concert would be

"introduced several of the airs, dueto's and chorus's in Acis and Galathea, composed by Mr. Handel. — And in act the 2d a Concerto on the organ, by a gentleman lately arrived from London"

the Massachusetts Spy, Oct. 3, 1771 was intrusted with the publication of the full program:

---

1) Either Joan or Douglas, who both gave operatic readings in 1770.
2) Boston Evening Post, May 13, 1771.

ACT I. Overture and the first chorus in Acis and Galathea, (by
        ten voices) 'O the pleasure of the plains, etc.
        Sixth Concerto of Stanley
        Solo on the violin by Mr. Morgan
        Song 'Love sounds the alarms, etc.'
        Fourth Periodical Symphony

ACT II. Overture in Pastor Fido
        Duetto 'He comes, etc.'
        Organ Concerto by Mr. Selby
        First Concerto by Mr. Humphrys
        Duetto and Chorus in Acis and Galatea
        'Happy we etc.'
        Overture by Ld. Kelly

His admiration for Haendel found further expression in a concert at
which Josiah Flagg possibly made his final bow to the public of Boston.
It was then that he reminded them of their obligations to him for having
founded and drilled the first regular militia band of Boston. He made his
appeal to the public purse still stronger by notifying his friends that he was
"about to leave the Province soon" and hoped that they would "enable
him to do it in an independant manner"[1]). Thus the "Grand Concert of
vocal and instrumental music to be led by Mr. Morgan" and for which he
had obtained leave "of the gentlemen selectmen" for the use of Faneuil
Hall on Oct. 28, 1773 partook of the character of a testimonial concert for
Josiah Flagg with this program:

THE FIRST PART.

An Overture
Song
An Overture in the Shepherd's Lottery[2])
Song
Harpsichord Concerto
A Chorus in the Messiah

THE SECOND PART

Coronation Anthem
Solo Violin, 'The Hero comes'
Overture
Liberty Song[3])
There will be upwards of 50 performers.

Whether or not Josiah Flagg left Boston, I do not know but the probabilities are that he did, for otherwise an ambitious and energetic man
like Flagg would have been heard from subsequently. Any further data on
his career would be welcomed as Boston was not too generously favored
with pioneers like Josiah Flagg in those days. That his services were kept
in good remembrance long after his death would appear from the accounts

1) Boston Evening Post, Oct. 18, 1773.
2) W. Boyce.
3) Words by John Dickinson to 'Heart of oak'.

of a concert given on Jan. 31, 1795 by the flutist Mr. Stone for the relief of the widow Flagg. This concert netted the handsome sum of one hundred and two dollars. That this was Josiah Flagg's widow I infer from the fact that she was the mother of the dentist and "vile miscreant son" Josiah Flagg, junr. But of this concert more will be said later on.

It is peculiar how suddenly and mysteriously many of our early musicians appear on the horizon and disappear again leaving either no clue whatever to their antecedents or allowing the inquisitive biographer only momentary glimpses into the different periods of their life or again leaving no traces behind them, once they have proved fairly interesting subjects of investigation. In the majority of cases this fragmentary condition of their biographies will cause no heart burning but when we have to deal with men like Josiah Flagg, William Tuckey and others we certainly sigh for more data. Though by no means as important a figure as these two musicians, James Juhan furnishes a further typical example of such a meteoric career. Indeed in his case, conjecture has to furnish more or less broken links in the biographical chain, fragmentary at its best.

On Oct. 20, 1768 the Boston Weekly News Letter contained an advertisement to the effect that a James Joan taught the French language, instrumental music, dancing and the minuet privately to ladies and gentlemen in the commodious and large building opposite "Dr. Coopers Meeting". So far this advertisement reads like so many others but Joan added that he also made and sold neat violin bows, thereby becoming entitled to a possible serious consideration in a history of violin making in America. The suspicion is correct, for we read in the Boston Chronicle, July 31, 1769 that he indead made and sold "below the Sterling price violins, screw-bows, and cases, equal in goodness to the best imported". It is the same old cry of protest against the fictitious and yet not fictitious supremacy of the Cremonese instruments! However, what truth Joan's assertion might have contained, he conceived — and probably it was the first experiment of the kind in our country — the idea of allowing the unbiased public to decide upon the superiority, inferiority or equal value of his instruments. On March 1, 1770[1]) our ambitious Frenchman gave a benefit concert at Concert Hall, where he had taken up his abode in the meantime as teacher of the violin, German flute and bass-viol. At this concert *"all the violins that [were to] be used [had] been manufactured here by the said Juan"*[2]). To the historian this bit of information is of decidedly more interest than the notice that the program contained "two grand choruses for four voices, the words

---

1) Boston Evening Post, Feb. 19, 1770.
2) To save others the trouble of fruitless reference, I remark that no violin maker by the name of Joan, Juan or Juhan appears in v. Lüttgendorff.

will adapted to the times [and] two other excellent songs". But we are glad to hear this and also that *James* Joan in September of said year[1]) still carried on "the manufacture of violins, bass-viols etc. in the greatest perfection from two to ten guineas price". Possibly Mr. Joan repeated his experiment when he gave a "grand" concert, Mr. David Propert performing some select pieces on the fortepiano and guitar between the acts at Concert Hall on March 21, 1771[2]), but this is not recorded.

It will have been noticed that the name of our would be Stradivari is given in two different forms: James Joan and Juan. Now no musician of either name appears again in the Boston papers but we read under date of Sept. 12, 1771 in the South Carolina Gazette of Charleston:

James *Juhan*, lately arrived in this province ... proposes teaching violin, German flute and guittar, he likewise proposes tuning harpsichords, spinets etc. by the year, quarter or otherwise, and repairs .. all sorts of musical instruments ... has to sell a *few excellent violins*

and in a like capacity we still find James Juhan at Charleston in April 1772[3]). Therefore the conjecture might not be considered unreasonable that James Joan or Juan who displayed his violins in a concert at Boston and the James Juhan of Charleston, S. C. are identical. What became of this James Juhan until he reappears in 1783 at Philadelphia, "lately arrived ... with his family" as music teacher and manufacturer of the "Great North American Fortepiano"[4]) is again a puzzle. Possibly he died at Philadelphia but certainly he left his mark on the city's musical life through his son, for we do not hesitate in believing that James was the father of Alexander Juhan, *junior* who from 1783 on played such a prominent part in the musical affairs of the Quaker City.

Merely mentioning a concert of vocal and instrumental music at Concert Hall on April 20, 1770[5]) for the benefit of a Mr. Asby who at the end of the entertainment was to appear "in the character of a clown" in the cantata 'Cymon and Siphigenia', our attention turns for a while to the "capital performer" whom David Propert had been so anxiously awaiting. W. S. Morgan, shortly after his arrival in Boston on Nov. 1770 hastened to notify the public that he was a "pupil of Signior Giardini", that he purposed "instructing ladies and gentlemen on the harpsichord, violin etc. on the easiest terms and by the most approv'd methods" and that he was to be spoke with at his Academy Room from the hours of nine in the morning to one o'clock.

---

1) Massachusetts Gazette, Sept. 6, 1770.
2) Massachusetts Gazette, March 7, 1771.
3) South Carolina Gazette, April 16, 1772.
4) Pennsylvania Gazette, June 25, 1783. Spillane, Ford, Brooks and others by some strange error give the name as Julian.
5) Mass. Gaz. March 29 and April 19, 1770.
6) Massachusetts Gaz. Nov. 8 and Nov. 22, 1770.

But Mr. Morgan's path in the Colonies was not to be strewn with roses and for this he had nobody to blame but himself. Mr. W. S. Morgan seems to have been somewhat of an adventurer, spendthrift, drunkard and all-around rascal. In a letter addressed to the "impartial" public in self defense to certain actions of his, in the Boston Gazette, April 26, 1773, William Turner not only draws a vivid picture of Morgan's character but incidentally becomes his biographer. Said he:

As my conduct towards Mr. Morgan has been much censur'd, I beg leave to offer a number of real facts, which I am thoroughly convinc'd will alter the opinion of every prejudic'd person and point out them that I'm the only injur'd man. —

On Mr. Morgan's first arrival here, Mr. W. F. W. a gentleman belonging to the navy apply'd to me and ask'd me to employ said Morgan, on which I told him, if he was capable to play either first or second fiddle in the Concert I would do it. Accordingly, Mr. W. F. W. desir'd him to call on me and convince me of his capacity, which was done. After which I inform'd Mr. W. F. W. he'd answer my purpose and that he should be employ'd as soon as the Concert open'd and should receive a benefit concert for Assistance."

Soon after, says Turner, he received a note from Morgan that he was in the hands of the sheriff not having paid his board bill. Turner paid the sum in order to keep Morgan out of prison. Not only this, he takes him to his home, introduces him to his friends and supports him "with board and money" "upwards of six months", in consequence of which Morgan promised utmost friendship.

". . . . he then having an opportunity of doing something for himself, by going to Newport, desir'd a letter of recommendation . . . which was readily granted, the contents of which got him into business that brought him in at the rate of £ 150 Sterling per annum, but he being imprudent lost his business and friends and was obliged to quit Newport . . .

A week later Turner received a letter from Rochester asking him to help him (Morgan) out of troubles, which he did. By this time it had become impossible to interest his friends in Morgan. Finally they sent him to Portsmouth and

"he again got into good business and might have continued so till this day, if he had behav'd like a gentleman but being oblig'd to quit that place, he once more return'd here, and call'd at my house in the evening and told me, if I did not employ him he should lead Mr. Propert's Concert against me; I having company, and finding him not in a capacity to talk with, desir'd he would let me know where he lodg'd, and I'd call and talk with him in the morning. This he declined and went off leaving me in the dark. This happen'd on Friday Evening and I never heard anything of him 'till I read Monday's paper and found he'd come to assist Mr. Propert against me although he had repeatedly declar'd he never wou'd perform against me on account of my great friendship towards him.

But to come to the point, this said Morgan being indebted to me ever since the year 1770 and I finding him to be ungrateful, requested my just due, and desir'd he would settle with me and pay the balance or at least give security for it."

Of course, Morgan makes all sorts of promises but Turner does not receive a penny, whereupon he sends an officer with a writ.

"Now I appeal to all unprejudiced persons if this was impolite behaviour to a man that has acted so ungrateful a part. Further, so far from my being desirous of hindering the company that attented at Mr. Propert's concert on the 22d instant of Mr. Morgan's performance, I desir'd the officer M. Otis, if he cou'd not get bail, to discharge him, and I'd pay cost, as I despis'd an ill natur'd action . . ."

In every other walk of life Mr. Morgan would have been ostracized after this exposure, so easily to be verified by inquiries at Newport and the other scenes of his escapades, but he was an artist and in an artist usually such conduct is gladly condoned as long as he pleases as a capital performer. This W. S. Morgan undoubtedly was in the eyes of the public and musicians of Boston during the few years of his intermittent residence there. After having proved his abilities as violinist in Turner's first subscription concert of 1770—1771, Morgan saw his way clear to give on Feb. 8, 1771 his first benefit concert[1]) at Concert Hall with a band. This was followed by a second benefit assisted by the band of the 64th Regiment on May 10th[2]). After his disastrous expedition to Newport, Rochester and Portsmouth he returned to Boston early in April 1773 and immediately announced a "grand" concert, he himself to play the violin and D. Propert the harpsichord, for April 22d. The first act was to conclude "with the celebrated Highland Laddie concerto never performed here. And by particular desire [was to] be sung, the favorite song of Mongo, out of the Padlock", by Dibdin[3]). The entertainment was postponed to April 26th as on April 22d, owing to what Messrs. Morgan and Propert probably considered an "ill natur'd action" on Turner's part, Mr. Morgan had made the forced acquaintance of Mr. Otis, officer of the law. He again appeared before the public in a benefit concert on March 10, 1774[4]) and then went into a kind of partnership with a Mr. Stieglitz, a "capital performer on the German flute" who had arrived from London in December 1773 and had introduced himself to the Bostonians with a "grand" benefit concert on Dec. 28th[5]). Having received assurance of the patronage and assistance of the Musical Gentlemen Messrs. Morgan and Stieglitz combined their fortunes with the assistance of the band of the 64th Regiment on April 20, 1774 at Concert Hall[6]). At the end of the concert Morgan appeared in a new capacity, as orchestral composer and unless his Military Symphony suffered in the neighborhood of Stamitz and Arne, it cannot have been half so worthless as its author. But Mr. Morgan's sins shall be forgiven, as he was generous enough to insert the full program:

1) Mass. Gaz. Feb. 8, 1771. The concert was postponed from Jan. 25th by particular desire.
2) Mass. Gaz. May 9, 1771.
3) Mass. Gaz. April 8, 16, 26, 1773.
4) Mass. Gaz. Feb. 10, March 10, 1774.
5) Boston Evening Post, Dec. 27, 1773.
6) Boston Evening Post, April 4, 1774.

ACT I

Overture .. .. Stamitz, 1st
Concerto — German flute
Song — 'My dear Mistress'
Harpsichord Concerto by Mr. Selby
Symphony — Artaxerxes[1])

ACT 2d.

Overture .. .. Stamitz 4th
Hunting Song ..
Solo, German Flute
Song — 'Oh! my Delia'
Solo Violin

To conclude with a grand Military Simphony accompanied by kettle drums, etc. compos'd by Mr. Morgan.

Tickets at half a dollar each ...

N. B. Copies of the songs to be delivered out (gratis) with the tickets. — To begin at seven o'clock precisely.

Emboldened by their success and at the particular request of a number of gentlemen Messrs. Morgan and Stieglitz — of course, again with the assistance of the band of the 64th Regiment — gave a second joint-benefit at Concert Hall on May 18th[2]) with a different but not less interesting program:

ACT I

Overture .. .. Guglielmi 1st
Concerto .. .. Brabant
Song 'All in the downs'
Harpsichord Concerto, Mr. Selby
Simphony — G. Flute, accompanied with kettledrums [!]

ACT 2d.

Overture .. .. Gossec 33d
Song
Solo— G. Flute
Song 'Soldier tir'd of war's alarms', from the opera of Artaxerxes, accompanied with the kettledrums, etc.
Solo Violin

To conclude with a grand Simphony by Lord Kelly, accompanied by kettledrums, etc.

Then the two ambitious gentlemen separated their fortunes again though continuing to exchange professional courtesies. Thus Mr. Stieglitz with the promised assistance of the Gentlemen Performers gave a benefit concert on Feb. 21, 1775[3]) and Mr. Morgan one on Sept. 8, 1774[4]). Though the program is not mentioned the meagre announcement is of great historical

1) Arne.
2) Boston Evening Post, May 9, 1774.
3) Massachusetts Gazette, Feb. 9, 1775.
4) Boston Evening Post, Sept. 5, 1774. Postponed from Sept. 5th.

importance as it proves that the *full orchestra of the period, including clarinets* was employed and from the tenor of the advertisement it must be
inferred that on this occasion the orchestra was of unusual size. The announcement reads in part:

First violin, Mr. *Morgan.* German flute, Mr. *Stieglitz.* Harpsichord, Mr. *Selby.*
Accompanied with clarinets, hautboys, bassoons, French horns, trumpets, kettledrums, etc. etc.

N. B. The Gentlemen Performers of the Army, Navy and of the Town, have pro-
mis'd Mr. Morgan their assistance in [this] Concert; likewise some of the best performers
from the several bands of music of the line.

With exception of the benefit concert tendered him by the managers of
the Gentlemen-performers' concert on Feb. 2, 1775[1]) and of his attempted
revival of the subscription concerts in April of 1774, this concert on Feb. 2,
1775 was the last in which W. S. Morgan seems to have appeared before
the public of Boston and I do not know what became of him after 1775.

During the last years of his career at Boston, W. S. Morgan sided, as
was seen, with David Propert against Mr. Turner. This musician "professor of musick" moved from New York where he taught music and "gave
out plans for organs, from 35 l. to 500 l." to Boston late in 1770[2]). He divided his energy between teaching half a dozen instruments and selling
"a variety of [imported] new musick and musical instruments", but devoted
himself in after-years almost exclusively to dealing in instruments. In 1771
David Propert became organist of Trinity Church and in that capacity he
announced benefit concerts at Concert Hall for Oct. 15, 1771 when he had
"a good company upwards of 200" (J. Rowe) and Oct. 13, 1772[3]) before he
assumed charge of the subscription concerts mentioned.

We further know that on Sept. 22, 1773 in celebration of the King's
Coronation a "grand concert of musick" was given at Concert Hall[4]), and
that on Oct 24, 1774 on the anniversary of the King's birth there was a
"grand" concert at Faneuil Hall" in honor of royalty"[5]). Finally, from the
Massachusetts Gazette, Dec. 29, 1774 it would appear that a concert, previously announced for Dec. 12th for the benefit of a Mrs. Stamper who was
in distressed circumstances, was postponed to that day. It was to be "compos'd of the greatest variety of instruments . . . in town".

While William Turner and David Propert who occasionally played at
John Rowe's home and whom the genial merchant called a "fine hand"
were fighting for supremacy in matters musical, a musician was gradually

---

1) Boston Evening Post, Jan. 30, 1775.
2) N. Y. Mercury, Sept. 17, 1770; Mass. Gaz. Dec. 27, 1770. Propert reappeared
again at Boston in 1789.
3) Mass. Gaz. Sept. 26, 1771 and Boston Evening Post, Sept. 28, 1772.
4) See Brooks, p. 157.
5) See Abram English Brown's 'Faneuil Hall', 1900, p. 89.

forging to the front to whom more than to Gottlieb Graupner or any other musician the glory is due of having indirectly laid the foundation for the Handel and Haydn Society, indeed the glory of having prepared the musical future of Boston more than any other musician before or after him. This musician was William Selby and if in the 'History of the Handel and Haydn Society not even' his name is mentioned, I can only repeat what I have said in my Bibliography of Early Secular American Music:

The rapid progress of music at Boston was largely prepared by him and it is unfair not to mention William Selby among the musical pioneers of Boston.

As the name implies, William Selby was an Englishman and we probably have to recognize in him the organist of St. Sepulchre's in London who at the anniversary of the Charity School in 1767 accompanied on the organ the anthem composed by Kiley and sung by the Charity Children. Had Selby remained for any length of time in London, certainly his name would appear in other sources (accessible to me) besides in Pohl's 'Mozart and Haydn in London', v. II, p. 212. This, as far as I can see, is not the case. However, one fact stands forth: in Josiah Flagg's concert of Oct. 4, 1771 a concerto on the organ was performed by a "gentleman lately arrived from London" and this gentleman undoubtedly was William Selby, whose talents as harpsichord player and organist were soon recognized by those who gave concerts at Boston.

It would be interesting to know if William Selby left London because he had received a call as organist by the vestry of King's Chapel, (after the war temporarily called Stone Chapel) a position which he must have held in 1772 as a benefit concert was given in Oct. 1772 by "Mr. Selby, organist at the King's Chapel". Either late in 1773 or early in January 1774 he became organist of Trinity Church at Newport, R. I. as appears from an advertisement in the Mercury, Jan. 24, 1774 where he also announced his intention of opening a dancing school! Whether this combination of occupations displeased Newport or whether Newport displeased Selby, he cannot have remained organist of Trinity Church far into September, as Sept. 16, 1774 a benefit concert was announced by "Mr. Knoetschel, organist of Trinity Church". But Selby still held the position in August as he then announced a concert for his own benefit[1]). He subsequently returned to Boston and again became organist of King's Chapel as the church records remark under date of Easter Monday, 1777:

A public collection for his benefit was ordered. It amounted to £ 2. 13 only but £ 20 additional were voted out of the church stock[2]). He fared

---

1) See Brooks, Olden Time Music, p. 63.
2) Foote's Annals of King's Chapel, II, p. 309.

much better in the following year, for John Rowe entered in his diary under Nov. 8, 1778:

"Mr. Selby had a collection this afternoon it amounted L 97. *very handsome.*"

Still, Selby at one time during the war evidently saw himself obliged to look for other revenues besides those accruing to him as organist and music teacher, as in 1780 he is mentioned as selling at his shop near Broomfield's Lane "Port, Teneriffe, Malaga Wines, Tea, Brown and Loaf sugar, logwood, English soap, etc."[1]). However, with the year 1782 he stepped out of the liquor and grocery business and lived again the musical life. Possibly from 1779 to 1782 owing to the condition of the church, Selby was not organist at the Stone Chapel but in Oct. 1782 he is again mentioned as such in the papers. He held the position until succeeded by P. A. Van Hagen in 1799. He died early in December 1798 for we read under the death news in the Columbian Centinel Dec. 12, 1798: "In this town, Mr. William Selby, Aet. 59". Consequently he was born in 1738[2]).

In addition to his activity as harpsichordist, organist, music teacher and above all as manager of concerts, William Selby strived for the laurels of a composer and compiler and in this respect, too, he should not be under-estimated. Possibly one or the other of the concertos which he played at concerts were the fruit of his activity as composer and that he really did compose an organ concerto will appear a few lines below. But not until 1782 do we possess tangible proof of his ambitions as composer. It was in this year that he proposed to "the friends of music and the fine arts" to publish by subscription, in monthly installments his 'New Minstrel' which was in fact to be a collection of "original" compositions. I have given in my Bibliography the full text of these proposals, remarkable not only for

---

1) Continental Journal, Jan. 13, 1780.

2) These statements contradict Foote's Annals of King's Chapel where we read (v. II, p. 403) that William Selby was organist from 1782 to 1804 at a salary of L. 66. 13 s. 4 d. being succeeded by Mrs. Elizabeth Van Hagen, 1804—18 10. It is also stated that his immediate succeesors were not able to efface the memories of his superior abilities. This I was willing to believe but the year 1804 aroused my suspicions. Indeed it could not be correct. In the first place, P. A. Van Hagen, junr. is positively mentioned as "organist of the Stone Chapel" when advertising in the Columbian Centinel, Jan. 4, 1800 the publication of his 'Funeral Dirge on the death of George Washington! Further-more "*Selby*, William, musician Tremontstreet" figures in the Boston Directory of 1796, as "organist, Tremontstreet" in that of 1798, but no longer in that of 1800 nor 1803. In the one for 1800, however, we find "Selby, Sarah, Tremontstreet" and the supposition will not be considered violent that she was his widow. (The only item con-flicting is this that in the Boston marriage records of 1792 his bride's name is given as Susannah (Parker) but the address, in my mind, carries more circumstantial evidence than the difference in the Christian name). Finally Mrs. Van Hagen is not mentioned as organist in the directories before 1805 whereas we find "Von Hagen, P. A. jun. or-ganist" in that of 1803. If therefore his mother became organist in 1804 he seems to have held the position from 1799 to 1803. As my request Mr. Edward Burlingame Hill of Boston took the matter up and he succeeded in finding Selby's death notice in the Columbian Centinel as quoted.

the boldness of the plan, but also for the proud spirit and strong love of his art and for the confidence Selby had in the musical future of his adopted country. I also stated there that his appeals do not seem to have fallen on willing ears. Still, Bostonians must have held him in some esteem as a composer. Otherwise the Massachusetts Magazine would hardly have offered to its subscribers in 1789 and 1790 such songs of his as 'The Lovely lass', 'The Ode for the New Year', 1789, the 'Ode on Musick', 'The Rural retreat', partly reprinted in after-years in the American Musical Miscellany, 1798.

In the meantime, as will be seen, his 'Ode in honour of General Washington', his anthems 'O be joyful in the Lord', 'Jubilate Deo', 'Now unto the King eternal' were performed in public as also 'An Ode to Independence' at the Stone Chapel in celebration of the 11th anniversary of American Independence on July 7, 1787[1]). We also know that two anthems by William Selby

"one taken from the 100th Psalm for four voices (that was performed at the Stone Chapel on the 30th of April [1782], the other taken from the 17th Psalm, for three voices, composed in an easy and familiar style, and adapted for the use of Singing Societies"

were published in Aug. 1782[2]). By glancing over the psalm tune collections etc. of the last two decades of the eighteenth century, it will further be observed that the compilers occasionally embodied some of Selby's works, which goes far enough to prove that he had become favorably known as composer. However, Selby himself thought well enough of his efforts to again approach the music lovers in 1790 and 1791 with proposals for publishing, if not all, at least a considerable number of his compositions on a similar plan as the 'New Minstrel', of 1782. This time he selected the fetching title 'Apollo, and the Muse's musical compositions'.

The work was to comprise:

"Anthems in four parts, with symphonies for the organ — Voluntaries or fuges for the organ or harpsichord. Sonatas or lessons for the harpsichord or pianoforte — Songs set for the voice and harpsichord or pianoforte, also, transposed for the German flute and guitar — A piece with variations for the harpsichord or pianoforte, in concert with the violin and guittar — A concerto for the organ or harpsichord with instrumental parts — A Sonata for two violins and violoncellos."

A veritable catalogue of William Selby's works up to 1790, but again it is not clear whether 'Apollo' left the press. Parts perhaps, for I am now inclined to believe that an engraved torso of pieces buried in a volume

---

1) Massachusetts Centinel, Boston, July 7, 1787. The ode beginning 'All Hail! Sublime she moves along' was said to have been "inimitably" performed. The solo parts by Mr. Deverell, a watchmaker by trade, and the chorus by a select company of singers at the end of the service.

2) Boston Gazette, Aug. 26, 1782.

of tracts at the Massachusetts Historical Society and in which appear (first) a 'Lesson', a song called 'Silvia', an 'Ode as performed at the Stone Chapel, Boston [1789] before the President of the United States of America', 'In Acis and Galatea', and a 'Fuge or voluntary' made part of this edition of William Selby's collected works.

That a man of such ambitions would leave his mark on the musical situation at Boston, was natural, but, as was stated above, William Selby, at least as far as the concert-life is concerned, did not become the leading musical personality of Boston until after the war. Of course, he came in for a share of the benefit concerts during the last years preceding the war and his programs were by no means inferior to those already mentioned. For instance, that of his concert postponed to Oct. 26, 1772[1]), the anniversary of George III accession to the throne, in order not to "do anything to the injury of Mr. Propert", who had likewise announced a benefit, will be read with interest by those who perhaps desire to contribute to the so-called Renaissance-movement with a typical eighteenth century program. Mr. Selby "organist at the King's Chapel" presented the following selection at Concert Hall:

ACT FIRST

1st. Periodical sinphonia   ..   Bach
Song
2d. Correlli's Concerto's [!]
Song
4th. Periodical Sinphonia   ..   Filtz

2d Act.

1st. Abel's 7th opera
Song
Harpsichord
20th Periodical Sinphonia   ..   Piccini
Handel's Grand Coronation Anthem in
     22 parts.

. . . N. B. The above concert will be assisted by the band of his Majesty's 64 th Regiment and the concerto designed for the harpsichord will be performed on an organ.

If this program was mainly instrumental, Selby's benefit concert on Sept. 22, 1773[2]), the anniversary of the Kings coronation, partook more of the character of a choral concert in honor of Haendel. With the same band under W. S. Morgan as leader and violin soloist, Selby, presumably with the choir of King's Chapel, rendered this program at Concert Hall:

---

1) Boston Evening Post, Oct. 5 and Oct. 12, 1772.
2) Boston Evening Post, Sept. 19, 1773.

FIRST ACT.

Overture .. .. Mr. Handel
Song, Duet and Chorus
Organ Concerto
Song
Hallelujah, Grand chorus in Mr. Handel's
  oratorio of the Messiah

SECOND ACT

Sinphonia
Glee in three parts, composed in the
  year 1600
Solo Violin .. .. Mr. Morgan
Handel's Grand Coronation Anthem
  in 22 parts.

*** Tickets at half a dollar each . . .
To begin at 7 o'clock precisely, and no money will be taken at the door.
Mr. Selby having been at great pains and expence to have his concert performed elegantly, humbly hopes to be patronized by his friends and the public.

Not until 1782 does Selby's name again positively appear in connection with concerts and thereafter he seems to have bent his energies less on good orchestral than on choral concerts. Therein lies his claim to be called an indirect founder of the Handel and Haydn Society. With this statement it is not intended to underestimate the pioneer work done since about 1720 by the 'singing schools', and the several choirs of Boston which undoubtedly profited by the efforts of the singing schools to prepare young and old for a better understanding and a better rendition of the hymns, psalms and anthems used in the churches. That also in both the singing schools and church choirs excerpts from Haendel's works were studied with enthusiasm may be taken for granted but neither Billings nor his rival psalmodists seem to have possessed the necessary energy to bend opportunities towards a more systematic and artistic study of sacred cantatas not only but of oratorios. In this respect William Selby was destined to fulfill a mission and to give the musical life of Boston a stimulus in the right direction.

The concert alluded to, a veritable musical landmark of Boston, was to be conducted by William Selby for the benefit of the poor of Boston in the afternoon of April 23, 1782 at the Stone Chapel, but was postponed on account of the weather to the last day in April[1]). Tickets were to cost four shillings, the doors were to be opened at three and the performance to begin at 4 o'clock and "books of the performance" were printed and sold at the Chapel. Not having been fortunate enough to discover one of these printed books, of necessity, I must restrict myself to a quotation of the program as announced in the press of this

---

1) Boston Gazette, April 15, 1782; Boston Evening Post, April 27, 1782.

Musica Spiritualis, or Sacred Music being a Collection of Airs. Duetts and Choruses, selected from the oritories [!] of Mr. Stanly, Mr. Smith and the late celebrated Mr. Handel; together with a favourite Dirge, set to music by Thomas Augustus Arne, Doctor in Music. Also, a Concert on the organ, by Mr. Selby.

But Mr. Selby's ambitions ran still higher. We may trust that though he had become an American, the news of the gigantic Handel Commemoration at Westminster Abbey in 1784 filled his soul with pride and that it awakened a desire in him, if possible and as far as possible, to unite the musical forces of Boston in a concert which would assume the proportions of a festival and would show his fellow-citizen what could be done even in a small city like Boston. This opportunity was soon to come. The revolting conditions of our prisons in those days is a matter of history. But be it said in honor of the more humane part of the young nation, the number of those who not only deprecated the conditions but sought to relieve the misery of the poor, unfortunate prisoners was steadily increasing. After very careful preparations the Musical Society of Boston, presumably founded in 1785 and of which William Selby undoubtedly was the musical guide, resolved to contribute its share in the movement. Then on Jan. 2, 1786 the Massachusetts Gazette printed the following long but historically very important announcement[1]).

We hear that the *Musical Society* in this town agreed, on the 20th of last month, to perform a Concert of *sacred* Musick, vocal and instrumental, at the *Chapel Church*, on Tuesday, the 10th day of this present month of January, for the benefit and relief of the poor prisoners confined in the jail in this town, and that the *Musick*, and Morning Service of the Church, are then to be performed as follows, viz.

As soon as the Church doors are shut, precisely at 11 o'clock in the forenoon of that day.

I. That the Overture in the sacred Oratorio, called the *Occasional Oratorio*, composed by the late celebrated Mr. Handel, be performed by all the musical, instrumental band.

II. That the first, famous and justly celebrated Recitative, in the Oratorio of the *Messiah*, composed by the inspired Handel, be sung, accompanied by the first and second violin, the tenor and bass instruments. — The words, 'Comfort ye, comfort ye my people' . . .

III. That the first Song in the same most sacred Oratorio, to be sung, accompanied by the proper instruments. The words, 'Every valley shall be exalted' . . .

IV. The Morning Service of the Church is then to begin; and after the *Lord's Prayer*, and the four versicles following, then the Doxology, or Glory to God, — 'Now unto the King eternal, immortal, invisible', etc. as set to musick by Mr. *Selby*, is to be performed by all the voices, accompanied by the organ only.

V. That the Anthem from the 95th Psalm, in the usual Morning Service of the Church, 'O come let us sing unto the Lord', etc. be sung or said.

VI. That the 41st, 112th, and 146th be read as the proper Psalms for the day; after each of which, the same Doxology, as set to musick by Mr. *Selby*, be performed by all the voices, accompanied by the organ and all the instruments.

VII. That the 4th Concerto of *Amizon*, musica de capella, opa. 7 be performed by the organ and all the instruments, as and for the Voluntary.

---

1) Copied from Brooks, Olden Time Music, p. 90—94.

VIII. That the first lesson for the day, taken from the 4th chapter of *Tobit*, from the 3d to the end of the 11th verse, with the 16th verse of the same chapter, be read.

IX. Then that the Te Deum ... be chanted.

X. Than that the second lesson for the day, taken from the 25th chapter of Matthew, from the 31st to the end of verse the 40th, be read.

XI. Then the *Jubilate Deo*, or, 'O be joyful in the Lord, all ye lands', is to be sung, as and for an Anthem, by the voices, accompanied by all the instruments.

XII. That the Apostles' Creed be read.

XIII. Immediately after that Creed, the song from the oratorio of the Messiah 'The trumpet shall sound' ... is to be sung, accompanied by the trumpet etc.

XIV. Then the Versicles after the Creed, with the first Collect for the day are to be read. And after the same.

XV. The song from the Oratorio of Sampson is to be sung ... the words ... 'Let the bright Cherubims' ...

XVI. Then the second and third Collects, the Prayer for Congress, and the Prayer for all sorts and conditions of men, be read.

XVII. Then the second Organ Concerto of Mr. Handel is to be performed.

XVIII. Then the general Thanksgiving and the concluding prayers are to be read.

XIX. Mr. *Selby* will then play a Solo, Piano, on the organ; during which the sentences in the Offertory will be read, the boxes at the same time being carried about to receive the contributions and donations of the charitable and humane.

XX. Then 'the Prayer for the whole state of Christ's Church militant here on earth' is to be read, and the Morning Service of the church is to end with the usual concluding prayers and blessing.

XXI. Lastly, the musical band will perform a favourite overture by Mr. Bach.

N. B. Tickets for this Charity, at three shillings each, as we are informed, will be offered for sale in every part of the town.

We are further informed that all the ministers of all the several religious societies and persuasions in this form, with Joseph Henderson, Esq. the High-Sheriff of the County, Samuel Breck, Esq. and Thomas Dawes, Esq. Members of the town, Joseph Barrell, Esq. Doctor Charles Jarvis and Samuel Henshaw, Esq. are chosen, by the *Musical Society*, to be a committee, for the purpose of appropriating all monies, to be raised by the sale of the tickets, and which may accrue from the donations and contributions of the charitable and humane towards the support of this charity.

The first appropriation of the money, for the affording necessary cloathing, firing and provisions to the most necessitious prisoners for debt.

We hope none will be backward in bestowing, according to their ability, for this truly benevolent purpose.

It is almost commonplace to remark that such a liturgical-musical festival like this cannot very well have been carried out in primitive musical surroundings and to further insist, after all that has been said in this book, that the musical life in our principal cities was far beyond the primitive stage would be an insult to the reader. Still, this particular 'Musica spiritualis' far surpassed what Americans were used to and this impression soon found its echo outside of Boston. Referring to the dates of receipt of several communications from correspondents, the Pennsylvania Herald printed on January 28, 1786 what we may call a fairly appropriate criticism of the Boston festival and perhaps other reports had a very stimulating effect, as we remember, on the Selby of Philadelphia: Andrew Adgate. The Penn-

sylvania Heralds published its correspondence, headed "Boston, January 12"
as follows:

(19) On Tuesday last was performed at the chapel in this town, a concert of vocal
and instrumental music, for the benefit of the unfortunate and distressed prisoners
now lying in the jail of this county. — The church prayers which were read by the
rev. Mr. Freeman, were agreeably and judiciously intermix'd with the music, in such a
manner as to give relief alternately to the reader and performers, and prevent the ear
of the auditor from being fatigued. The whole was conducted with the greatest order
and decorum, saving a theatrical clap at the conclusion, which can only be imputed
to the pitch of enthusiasm to which the excellent overture of Mr. Bach wound up the
enraptured auditors. —

The vocal and instrumental parts were executed in a manner that reflects the highest
honour on the musical abilities of the gentlemen who composed the band. The church
was thronged with all classes of people, and we were particularly happy in seeing so
many of the softer sex present on the occasion; whom we cannot suppose otherwise
influenced than by the mild affections of humanity. —

To soften the calamities of our fellow creatures, and pour gladness in the heart
of the wretched; to clothe the naked, and set the prisoner free, are duties; which our
feeling as men, and our religion as Christians, require us to fulfil . . .

(20) A correspondent remarks that the doxology composed by Mr. Selby, gave
great satisfaction on Tuesday last at the Chapel church, and was only excelled by
his anthem, in which he has not disgraced the inspired, royal author of the 100 psalm.

(21) Mr. Selby's execution on the organ appeared masterly throughout the whole
performance, but more particularly so in the second organ concerto of Handel.

(22) The first recitative and the first song in the Messiah were sung as to have
done no discredit to any capital singer at the theatre in Covent Garden; but the song
of 'Let the bright cherubims in burning row, etc.' in the opinion of several who had
heard the oratorio of Sampson at Covent Gardenhouse, was sung, as least as well, in
the Chapel Church, on Tuesday by our townsman, as they had ever before heard."

If proof be needed that William Selby really was the moving spirit of
the Musical Society and therefore of this concert, it is furnished in the *NB*
of the announcement of his benefit concert on April 27, 1786[1]) at Concert
Hall when

"among other select pieces and songs [were to be] performed, An *Ode in honour
of General Washington*, composed by Mr. William Selby — likewise, the favourite catch
of 'Hark the bonny Christ bell' . . .

N. B. The above mentioned concert is to be performed in consequence of a resolve
of the Musical Society, and the money arising from the sale of the tickets to be present:d
to Mr. Selby, for his singular services rendered the society.

Just as Andrew Adgate and the Uranian Academy were encouraged by
the success of their first to give a second "grand" concert, so were William
Selby and the Musical Society. Hardly a year had elapsed since the benefit
for those, unfortunate enough to be entombed in a New England county
jail, when the managers announced — evidently the fame of the Concert
Spirituel had travelled far — for Jan. 16, 1787 with the assistance of a
"band hired by them"[2]) a '*Spiritual Concert* for the benefit of those who

1) Boston Gazette, April 17, 1786.
2) Massachusetts Centinel, Jan. 10, 1787.

have known better days'. The full program was thus published in the
Boston Gazette, Jan. 15th:

Charitable Concert. The following we are assured, will be the order of the several
musical performances, and of the service of the Chapel Church at the performance
of the Concert of Sacred Musick, to-morrow.

1. The 20th periodical overture, *la Buona Figliuola*, composed by Piccini, (the
last presto to be omited, instead of which will be introduced a celebrated march adapted
to the occasion.

2. Then the first, famous and justly celebrated Recitative in the oratorio of *the
Messiah* composed by the inspired Handel, to be sung by Mr. Ray, accompanied by
the first and second violin, the tenor and bass instruments. — The words 'Comfort
ye, comfort ye my people' . . .

3. Then the first song, in the same most sacred oratorio, is to be sung, accompanied by the proper instruments. The words: 'Every valley shall be exalted' . . .

4. The Morning Service of the church is then to begin — and after the Lord's
Prayer, and the four versicles following, then the Doxology, or Glory to God — 'Now
unto the King eternal, immortal, invisible', etc. as set to musick by Mr. Selby, is to
be performed by all the voices, accompanied by the organ only.

5. The Psalms adopted for the occasion, are then to be read; after each of which
the same doxology, as set to musick by Mr. Selby, is to performed by all the voices,
accompanied by the organ and all the instruments.

6. A violin Concerto is then to be performed as and for the voluntary.

7. Then the first lesson for the day is to be read.

8. Then the Te Deum, or, 'We praise thee, o Lord' — is to be chanted.

9. Then the 2d lesson for the day will be read.

10. Then the Jubilate Deo, or 'O be joyful in the Lord' . . . as set to musick by
Mr. Selby is to be sung as and for an anthem, by the voices, accompanied by all the
instruments.

11. Then the Apostle's Creed will be read.

12. Then a Solo from the Sacred oratorio of *Jonah*[1]), will be sung by Mr. Deverell,
accompanied by the organ, and all the instruments, etc. — The words 'Out of the deep,
O God, I cry' . . . [two stanzas]

13. Then the versicles after the Creed with the first Collect of the Day, are to
be read. And after the same.

14. Then from the Oratorio of *Sampson* is to be sung these words — 'Let the bright
cherubims in burning row' . . .

15. Immediately after which will be performed the Chorus* from Handel's Messiah
'Hallelujah, the Lord God omnipotent reigneth' . . .

16. Then the second and third collects, and the prayer for all sort and condition
of men will be read.

17. Then an Organ Concert to be performed by Mr. Selby.

18. Then the general thanksgiving and the concluding prayers are to be read.

19. Lastly, the musical band will perform a favourite Overture, composed by
Carlo *Ditter*.

* At the performance of this Divine Chorus, called by way of eminence the *Thunder
Chorus*, it is usual for the whole audience to rise from their seats, and be upon their
feet the whole time of the Chorus, in testimony of the humble adoration of the Supreme
Governor of the Universe, our great and universal Parent, and in honor of our blessed
Redeemer.

This time we need not look to Philadelphia papers for a full description
and contemporary report of the impression made by these festivals on the

---

1) S. Felsted.

public. All historical curiosity is satisfied by the report as printed in the Boston Gazette of Jan. 22d[1]) and it is exceedingly interesting to contrast the *succès d'estime* of Selby as composer and the somewhat reserved opinion of the merits of Dittersdorf's favourite overture with the enraptured exstasies of the critic over "Handel! Handel! Handel!" and especially his "Thunder Chorus":

Boston, January 22.

Last Tuesday was performed, at the Chapel Church in this town, the *Spiritual Concert* for the benefit of those among us who have known better days. The Musick began at half an hour after 11 o'clock, with the Overture in the opera of La *Buona Figliuola* ... in the march adopted on the occasion instead of the presto movements of Piccini, the drums had a very pleasing effect. The overpowering pathos of *Handel* in the first recitative of his *Messiah*, was excellently sung, and forcibly felt by every musical ear present, Mr. Selby's Doxology ... filled every ear with pleasure. —

The prayers of the church were most agreeably intermixed with the musical performances, and alternately relieved the gentlemen of the Musical Society and the auditory. Mr. *Arnold's* Te Deum was inimitably sung, and Mr. Rea's distinct, sweet over-powering countertenor voice, was eminently distinguishing in this part of the performance, as in all others in which he bore a share: this Te Deum, we are assured, is infinitely more musical and effecting than the common, sing song, half-squalling, half-reading Te Deum usually performed in the cathedrals of England. —

The Jubilate Deo, or C. Psalm, set to musick by Mr. Selby, gave universal satisfaction, the choruses in which are worth of admiration. — The Song from the oratorio of Jonah, sung by Mr. Deverell, was beautifully affecting but *Handel! Handel! Handel!* The song from his oratorio of Sampson 'Let the bright Cherubim, etc.' sung by our townsman, Mr. Rea, could not be excelled by anything but the Hallelujah Chorus in the Messiah, in which there appears perfect illumination — the surprise and astonishment of the audience, at the performance of this divine Chorus, cannot well be described, especially at those parts where the *drums* so unexpectedly thundered in and joined in the glorious Hallelujahs to the 'King of Kings and Lord of Lords, etc.' Great delicacy was shewn in directing this vast effort of genius, to follow the inimitable song in Sampson 'Let the bright Cherubim etc.' and this we are told we owe to Mr. Selby. In the organ concerto this gentleman shewed great delicacy and execution. — The last overture, composed by Ditter, was forcibly and well executed. The horns produced in this an excellent effect.

We have only to lament that the very short notice of this well executed and benevolent entertainment and the present distressed situation of the town, with *some* other concurring circumstances, prevented the church from being *crouded*, as was the case last year.

As it may be of interest to compare our modern ways of managing *monstre*-affairs — and such this charitable concert was for the Boston of those days — with the methods of yore, the instructions "to the public" as printed in the Boston Gazette, also on Jan. 15th, may follow here:

The *Public* are hereby notified that the Concert of Sacred Musick to be performed on the morrow at the Chapel Church, will begin precisely at half an hour after eleven o'clock in the forenoon, — that one half of the South door will be opened at ten o'clock (when the first bell will ring) for the reception of the audience; that no one will, or can, be admitted without a ticket, that no change will be given to those who may delay

---

1) Literally the same appeared in the Massachusetts Centinel, Jan. 17, 1787.

purchasing tickets until they come to the church; that precisely at half an hour after eleven o'clock the doors will be shut and fastened, when the bell will cease tolling; that the pews no 1 and 2 at the upper end of the middle aisle, opposite to the reading desk and pulpit, are reserved for the reverend the ministers of the town of all denominations, and into which it is earnestly requested no other persons will attempt to sit.

Tickets for the charity, at 3 s. each, are sold at the Post Office; by Mr. Burke, at Concert-Hall; at Messieurs Green and Cleverley's Newbury Street and by Mr. Deverell watchmaker, next door south of the Treasury, Marlboro-Street.

N. B. As the order of the musick and of the service of the church on this laudable occasion is published in this paper, we advise our customers to take the papers with them to the church, as a proper assistant.

On January 29th the Musical Society notified the public through the Boston Gazette that it had appointed a committee consisting of gentlemen of the clergy to distribute the monies collected by the sale of tickets, amounting to $ 162 after deduction of all expenses. As this sum must have seemed surprisingly small to all concerned, they also enumerated the concurring circumstances which had prevented the church from being crowded as in 1786:

The shortness of the notice given of the performance. — The scarcity of money — The military expedition and the call on the inhabitants for raising and equipping their men with General Sheppard against ca. 2000 insurgents under Capt. Shays in the vicinity of Springfield . . .

Of course, such concerts represented only the extraordinary events in the career of both the Musical Society and William Selby. Their normal activity restricted itself to the usual musical meetings and subscription concerts. It would appear from a request addressed in Sept. 1787[1]) to "those gentlemen who are desirous that the concert should be carried on through the ensuing season upon the same terms it was last winter" that the Musical Society first instituted such regular entertainments in 1786. Unless proof is furnished to the contrary it may be taken for granted that William Selby was the conductor of the society during this and the season of 1787/1788. In that case it is plausible enough that the members of the Musical Society turned out in full force to show their appreciation on the night of Selby's benefit concert at Concert Hall, Sept. 10, 1787[2]). Had he not been the regularly appointed conductor the subscribers to the Musical Society would hardly have been desired to take notice in the Massachusetts Centinel, January 16, 1788 that their next concert was postponed to Feb. 7th, as the hall on Thursday, January 24th was to be appropriated to the benefit of Mr. Selby, when there would be a "public" concert with this program:

1) Massachusetts Gazette, Sept. 15, 1787.
2) Mass. Centenel, Sept. 8, 1787.

FIRST ACT.

Overture
A Double piece on the harpsichord
Song
Full piece

SECOND ACT.

The Country Courtship, a musical entertainment. The characters, Dorus, Alexis and Pastora.

The season lasted at least into March as the concert scheduled for March 6th was postponed to March 13th, many of the performers being out of town[1]). For the season of 1788—1789 the Musical Society agreed on six public performances at Concert-Hall for a limited number of subscribers[2]). Those of the preceding year who desired to subscribe for these six concerts were requested to send in their names so that the gentlemen who stood proposed as new members could be admitted, should there be any vacancies. Strangers could be admitted if introduced by a subscriber. Then, on Nov. 22d, the public was notified that the first concert of the series would be held on Nov. 28th[3]). A continuance of these concerts under the auspices of the Musical Society is doubtful, not only because such were not advertised in 1790 but also because it is at least possible that the Musical Society had ceased to exist. Something to this effect may be inferred between the lines of an advertisement in Massachusetts Gazette, March 14, 1789 when the subscribers were notified that the amount of their subscriptions was absolutely necessary to the defraying the expense of another concert!

On the other hand, there is evidence that in 1787 the Musical Society no longer monopolized opportunities for lending their voices for charity as on Sept. 22, 1787 the Massachusetts Centinel notified the public that the proceeds from a Concert of Sacred Musick on October 4th would be appropriated to assist rebuilding the Meeting House in Hollis Street, destroyed by fire

"agreeably to the generous intentions of the Musical *Societies* in this town who have projected this concert".

The program is remarkable in so far as William Billings' name appeared twice, whereas previously his music hardly ever was performed in public concerts. The program reads:

ACT I

10th Periodical Overture .. .. Filtz
Anthem — 'Except the Lord build the House' .. Billings
Anthem — 'O be joyful in the Lord' .. .. Selby
Organ Concerto

---

1) Mass. Centinel, March 4, 1788.
2) Mass. Centinel, Oct. 22, 1788.
3) Massachusetts Centinel, Nov. 22, 1788.

Act II

Anthem — 'O Lord God of Israel' .. .. Williams
Song from the oratorio of Sampson
Anthem — 'And I saw a mightly angel' .. .. .. Billings
Handel's grand Hallelujah Chorus from the sacred
oratorio, Messiah, accompanied with kettledrums.

William Selby not being mentioned as conductor of this co-operative effort of the several musical societies of Boston, the contention that he was in charge of the performance is, of course, a conjecture by way of elimination. However, he certainly conducted a Concert of "Sacred Musick Vocal and Instrumental" which the proprietors of Christ Church gave there on May 21, 1788[1]) in the afternoon as it is distinctly said "under the direction of Mr. William Selby" and with the generous assistance of the Musical Society.

By order of the vestry, Amos Windship and John Stoddard informed the public that the proceeds would be appropriated to lessen the expenses that had arisen from the repairs of the church and particularly of the organ and to secure also "the tower, which, if not very soon done, will be insufficient to support the bells it contains". The program reads:

First Part

Symphony
Song ... 'In Paradise lost', sung by Mr. Brewer
Piece for Clarinetts and horn
Anthem, composed by Doctor Green, sung by Mr. Deverell
Full piece

Second Part

Organ concerto, performed by Mr. Selby
Song in the Messiah, sung by Mr. Rea
Violin Concerto
Song in Sampson, sung by Mr. Deverell
Symphony.

Whether any of the musical societies assisted, is not mentioned. Presumably not, as the only choral number on the program could very well be rendered by a church choir, such as Christ Church possessed.

It was different when, end of 1789, George Washington came to Boston during his famous inaugural tour through the States. Everybody vied with everybody to show the illustrious general in what unbounded love he was universally held and all party-strife and party-bickerings were dropped to receive him and to entertain him with outbursts of gratitude and admiration. A triumphal arch had been erected. Through this he was escorted in a magnificent procession, in which a band was not missing, to the Senate Chamber. Thence the President passed through the Representatives' Chamber to a *Colonnade*, erected for the occasion in the West-end of the

---

1) Massachusetts Gazette, May 20, 1788.

State House and composed of six large columns, fifteen feet high, and a ballustrade hung in front with Persian carpets on which were wrought thirteen roles, symbolising the thirteen States. As soon as the President entered the Colonnade, he was saluted by three huzzas from the citizens and by an *Ode*[1]) sung by a select choir of singers, with Mr. Rea at their head, in the Triumphal Arch, adjacent to the Colonnade. After the ode was sung, the procession passed the President and proceeded into Courtstreet, where the whole were dismissed.

But these were merely the preliminaries to the festivities and though perhaps originally no special musical entertainment adorned the plans in honor of George Washington, it so happened that a few days later an opportunity arose to show him what Bostonians could do in the way of music. On Oct. 14th the Massachusetts printed the following:

FOR PUBLICK ORNAMENT.
An *Oratorio*, or, Concert of Sacred Musick.

On Wednesday next, will be performed at the Stone Chapel in this town, an Oratorio, or, Concert of Sacred Musick, to assist in finishing the Colonnade or Portico of said chapel, agreeably to the original design.

PART THE FIRST
1. Full anthem — composed by Mr. Selby
2. The favourite air in the Messiah, (composed by the celebrated Handel) 'Comfort ye my people' — by Mr. Rea
3. Organ Concerto — by Mr. Selby
4. The favourite air in the oratorio of Samson (composed by the celebrated Handel) 'Let the bright Seraphim' — by Mr. Rea
5. Full anthem, composed by Mr. Selby

PART THE SECOND
The oratorio of *Jonah*, complete, the solos by Messrs. Rea, Ray, Brewer and Dr. Rogerson. The chorusses by the *Independent Musical Society;* the instrumental parts by a Society of Gentlemen with the band of his Most Christian Majesty's Fleet.

As the above oratorio has been highly applauded by the best judges, and has never been performed in America[2]); and as the first performers of this country will be joined by the excellent band of this Most Christian Majesty's squadron, the Publick will have every reason to expect a more finished and delightful Performance than ever was exhibited in the United States.

---

1) Under 'Castalian Fount', the Massachusetts Centinel in which this account appeared, Oct. 28, 1789, printed on the same day the words of this 'Ode to Columbia's Favourite Son'. The first stanza runs:
> Great Washington the Hero's come
> Each heart exulting hears the sound
> Thousands to their Deliverer throng,
> And shout him welcome around.
> Now in full chorus join the song,
> And shout aloud great Washington!

The President had to submit to seven stanzas of this awful stuff!

2) This was not correct, as "Jonah, an oratorio, composed by S. Felsted" was performed at New York on June 11, 1788.

The musick to begin at half past 2 o'clock. Tickets at half a dollar each, may be had at Dr. Winship's, Union Street — at B. Guild's Book Store, and at the Post Office in Cornhill, and at J. Templeman's, W. Burley's and R. Russel's Offices in State Street.

This somewhat boastful announcement may be pardoned in view of the fact that it probably was the first time in Boston's musical history that a musical society ventured on the rendition of a complete oratorio, even if it was only 'Jonah, an oratorio, disposed for voices and harps', by the obscure Samuel Felsted[1]) who seems to have been better known in America than in England. Probably we are near the truth in surmising that again William Selby was the moving spirit and conductor of the concert. However, on Oct. 21st, the day of performance the public was notified that the concert was postponed for a few days and the supposition is plausible enough that the managers postponed the affair in order to turn the benefit for the portico of Stone Chapel into a "publick ornament" in honor of George Washington, just then in their midst. This is, indeed certain, for on Oct. 27th one of the papers announced that the oratorio would be performed in presence of the President of the United States and that the concert would begin with a congratulatory *Ode*[2]) to the President instead of Selby's full anthem. The words of this ode, written by a Mr. Brown of Boston, were printed in the Massachusetts Gazette on Oct. 31st[3]). George Washington was indeed to be congratulated if the composer, possibly Selby, did not inflict such wounds on him as did Mr. Brown with this fearful patriotic poetry:

RECITATIVE

Behold the man! whom virtues raise
The highest of the patriot throng!
To him the Muse her hommage pays,
And tunes the gratulary song.

AIR.

Illustrious Visitant! Design'd
By the Heavn's invincible decree
T'enoble and exalt the mind
And teach the nation to be free!
[Follow five more stanzas]

Now it is well known how heartily George Washington disliked such apostrophes and a sigh of relief must have escaped him if this "gratulary song" was not launched on his ears, for the indispositon of several of the first

---

1) Printed under this title in 1775 at London. A copy is in the British Museum. (Eitner.) Of Felsted's life very little seems to be known and how obscure a musician he was or at least has become, is evident from the fact that his name is not even mentioned by Brown and Stratton.

2) See Brooks, p. 97.

3) Words and music were subsequently published together. A copy of the ode is at the Mass. Hist. Soc. (See my Bibliography.)

performers interfered with the well-meaning plans of the managers and again the concert had to be postponed. However, as the President "honoured the Stone Chapel with his presence to hear the concert of sacred musick" on Oct. 27th several pieces were performed which merited and received applause[1]). At last, after the Massachusetts Centinel had contributed to the mishaps by announcing a wrong date, the Oratorio was given on December 2d with the original program, an original poem delivered by Mr. Whitwell and a brilliant illumination of the chapel[2]). It would be interesting to know the public opinion on said occasion as recorded by some gentleman-critic, but though the papers printed the full text of Felsted's Jonah, they did not, to my knowledge, adorn their columns with an elaborate and uplifting *resumé* of the public impressions.

After this concert, no musical society is mentioned by name in connection with further concerts, choral or instrumental, for about ten years, though occasionally references to several musical societies may be found in the papers[3]). Therefore undoubtedly such existed in Boston during the last decade of the eighteenth century but it seems that they, for some reason or the other, no longer played a prominent part in public. Certainly the subscription concerts to be traced in 1790 and later were independent enterprises as not once a connection appears between them and those mysterious concerts. Nor is it clear who was responsible for these concerts themselves, about which exceedingly little is to be gleaned from the papers. For instance, all the information I am able to submit for the season of 1790—1791 consists in this that "the subscribers to the concerts" were notified on March 12th in the Massachusetts Centinel that the sixth and last concert would be on March 17th. Then on Oct. 19, 1791 the "members of the subscription concerts" were requested to meet at Concert Hall on October 21st upon particular business and by tracing such notices we find that again six concerts were given during the winter of 1791—1792, the last on April 12th. The supposition that William Selby must have been connected with these concerts in some capacity is logical enough and the conjecture that he was the manager

---

1) Massachusetts Continel, Oct. 28, 1789.
2) Massachusetts Centinel, Dec. 2, 1789.
3) In Perkins and Dwight's History of the Boston Handel and Haydn Society it is claimed (on p. 29) that the Independent Musical Society was founded in 1786 and that it took part in commemorating the death of Washington (Dec. 14, 1799) on his first succeeding birthday. The sources of both dates are not mentioned and really nothing goes to show their accuracy. The date of foundation might be correct if the Musical Society and the Independent Musical Society were identical, which is obviously improbable. That the Independent Musical Society — I believe it had long ceased to exist — took part during the 'Sepulchral Service' on Feb. 22, 1800 with Oliver Holden's music is also very improbable as the minute report of Feb. 26th in the Columbian Centinel mentions the "ablest choir of vocal masters we ever recollect to have heard", but no Independent or any other musical society.

and conductor is corroborated by a notice to the subscribers in the Massachusetts Centinel, March 17th headed: *Mr. Selby's Concert* and under the same heading a continuance of these concerts was announced in the Columbian Centinel, Sept. 29, 1792. The first was to be on Oct. 18th[1] "the musick to begin precisely at 6 and end at 8 o'clock — when the room [would] be cleared for country dances". Presumably the series contained less than six concerts for otherwise the subscribers would hardly have been informed on January 30, 1793[2] that a subscription paper was open at Mr. Vila's for four additional concerts upon the same plan as hitherto conducted and that if one hundred subscribers appeared the first concert would be on February 7th. The entertainments of this series were to begin at 7 o'clock, the country dances at nine and to end at 1 o'clock! These data are meagre enough, not once an allusion being made to the programs, a fact proving convincingly the private character of the concerts, but at least they leave no doubt as to the existence of subscription concerts during these years whereas for the remaining years of the century subscription concerts may be considered hypothetical in absence of even such meagre data in the papers.

Quite in keeping with these doubts, based, of course, only on the files I had occasion to examine, is the fact that from 1793 on, William Selby's name gradually disappears from the papers. Now and then he would assist in benefits given by other musicians but these occasions became fewer and fewer and to my knowledge the last benefit concert given for Selby himself in conjunction with Jacobus Pick took place at Concert Hall on June 20, 1793 with the following program[3]:

The Overture of Henry IVth[4]
A French Song by Mr. Mallet
A Clarinet Concerto by M. Foucard
A French Song by Madame Douvillier
A Violin Concerto, by Mr. Boullay
An Italian Duetto, by Messrs. Pick and Mallet
A Flute Concerto, by Mr. Stone
La Chasse, composed by Hoffmeister
A Piano Forte Sonata, by Mr. Selby
A French Trio, by Madame Douvillier, Messrs. Pick and Mallet
A Duetto on the Harmonica, by Messrs. Pick and Petit
A Symphony, composed by Pichell

William Selby's career has carried us far beyond the Revolutionary War, but in the case of Boston it would have been historically unwarranted, though convenient, to break off the narrative before the battle of Lexington and

1) Columbian Centinel, Oct. 13, 1792.
2) *ibidem.*
3) Columbian Centinel, June 15, 1793.
4) Martini.

to resume it after Lord Cornwallis' surrender at Yorktown because, of all our principal cities, Boston, a few months excepted, remained undisturbed by the movements and counter-movements of the opposing armies. That the war interfered at first with the development of Boston's musical life, goes without saying but already in 1779 we notice signs of a revival of the interest in music other than in Billings' forceful battle hymn 'Chester' and that the moving spirit of this revival, at the very least from 1782 until 1793, was William Selby I believe to have made an historical fact. Indeed, though — and also because — his name is not mentioned with reference to the several concerts from 1779 to 1782 there remains at least the possibility of his con- nection even with these entertainments. Consequently, as William Selby was prominent for years before the war, Boston's musical history during the last thirty years of the eighteenth century may be said to have centered in the personality of this interesting and ambitious musician.

The first concert given during the war, was characteristic of the peaceful conditions prevailing at Boston. It was announced for July 5, 1779[1]) in celebration of the *Independence of America* with an 'Ode, suitable to the occasion', as principal number. It affords a curious glimpse into by-gone times if we hear that the attendance of gentlemen performers at the rehearsal of July 3d would be esteemed a favor. However, "the severity of the season made it necessary to make large additions in the (Concert) Hall for the ac- commodation of so large a company" as was expected and hence the managers, with apologies to the public, saw themselves obliged to postpone the patriotic concert to July 9th. Presumably other concerts were given between 1779 and 1782 but not until the latter year did I run across advertisements to that effect. Then not less than four were given, one on February 21st[2]), another on March 7th[3]) "by particular desire", the third on March 21st[4]) with "Three English songs in the first act", (these three at Concert Hall) and the fourth in Trinity Church on October 3d[5]) for the benefit of the poor in the Boston Alms-House. The overseers apologized for appealing to the "well known humanity" of their fellow citizens and flattered them- selves that a repetition of the offence would in future be removed by a more punctual and competent supply to the treasury. But the most important item is contained in the rather awkward announcement of the program, proving, as it does, that Boston then possessed a musical society deriving its name from that medieval genius and terrible inventor of the Guidonian hand: Aretinian Society. The concert was plainly one of

1) Continental Journal, July 1, 1779.
2) Boston Evening Post, Feb. 16, 1782.
3) ditto, March 2, 1782.
4) Boston Gazette, March 18, 1782.
5) Boston Gazette, Sept. 23, 1782.

Sacred Music being a collection from Williams, Stephenson, Billings and others — Also an interlude on the organ between each vocal piece, by Mr. Bellsted.
The Vocal music will be performed by the Aretinian Society.

The concerts advertised between 1782 and 1790, all being connected with William Selby's career, have already been recorded except one, with which he probably had nothing to do. It was given on Oct. 9, 1788[1]) at the request of a number of respectable characters for the benefit of Mrs. Smith who together with her husband, "both lately from the Southward" had entertained during the month of September fashionable Boston with dramatic and lyric recitations interspersed with songs, so-called 'Moral Lectures'. As Mr. and Mrs. Smith's connections called them to Europe, they hoped for the patronage of a generous public when presenting the following "vocal parts":

1. An Ode on his Excellency Gen. Washington
2. The song, 'Dauphin of France'.
3. The air, 'Lads of the Village'
4. Advice to the Fair
5. Bright Phoebus, an admired Hunting song
6. A New Sea song
7. The admired song of 'The Gipsies'
8. Major André's Farewell
9. The admired song of 'Tallio' [!]
10. The Ballad dialogue
11. Lark's shrill notes.

On Sept. 16, 1790[2]) a benefit concert was given at Concert Hall for Mr. Oliver Barron, "one of the unhappy men who were cast away on Grand Manan, by which accident he had the misfortune to freeze to such a degree as to be under the necessity of having them cut off which has rendered him unable to support himself". Neither of this nor of a concert given on Dec. 21, 1790[3]) at Stone Chapel is any reference made to the program but the latter was intended for the benefit of no less a man than William Billings. He was just then at the zenith of his career. His 'New England Psalm Singer' of 1770 and his 'Singing Master's Assistant' of 1778 and later collections of his hymns and psalm-tunes had attracted — not for their musical grammar, which was conspicuously absent, but for the undeniable spark of something

---

1) Massachusetts Centinel, Oct. 8, 1788. The following *"criticism"* of one of Mr. and Mrs. Smith's Moral Lectures will surely prove amusing reading. On Sept. 12th the Mass. Gaz. had this to say:
"At Concert Hall last Wednesday evening, was performed by Mr. and Mrs. Smith, lately from the Southward, before a large collection of gentlemen, and a few ladies, some of them of the first fashion, and in gorgeous attire, a variety of scenes, selected from the most celebrated plays, both tragick and comick, intermixed with well chosen prologues and epilogues; the whole enriched by a variety of airs, duets, etc. ... The audience were highly entertained, and the hall shook with their plaudits. The songs were sung in a stile which discovered, as well as an harmonious voice, a delicacy of taste, which Apollo himself might envy ..."
2) Columbian Centinel, Sept. 8, 1790.
3) Columbian Centinel, Dec. 15, 1790.

kin to originality and individuality — attention to his name wherever psalms were sung in the Northern and Middle States and hardly a single psalm-tune collection by other American psalmodists of that period is to be found in which Billings' Muse does not preminently figure. In short, his name and fame resounded in the remotest church choir and so-called singing schools and without doubt he was the most popular composer in his days. Yet Billings, and this will cause surprise, was in rather reduced circumstances, for a correspondent in the Columbian Centinel Dec. 8, 1790 expressed his satisfaction

"in hearing that a number of benevolent characters are determined to bring forward a Concert of Sacred Musick for the benefit of Mr. William Billings of this town — whose distress is real, and whose merit in that science, is generally acknowledged"

and the announcement of the concert closed with these significant remarks:

"The pieces to be performed will consist of a great and, it is expected, a pleasant variety, and whilst the charitable will rejoice in this opportunity to exercise their benevolence, the amateurs of musick, will no doubt be abundantly gratified.

> The heart that feels for other's woes,
> Shall find each selfish sorrow less,
> That breast which happiness bestows
> Reflected happiness shall bless.

For the honor of Boston we hope that a sufficient number of tickets at 2 shillings each were sold to be of substantial benefit to Gov. Samuel Adams' proud but poor friend. Still, if we remember that Billings, born at Boston Oct. 7, 1744 had still to live almost ten years until he died on Sept. 29, 1800, we cannot but regret that the last years of this remarkable man should have been spent in poverty. Remarkable not only for his musical *naïveté*, enthusiasm, latent talent and amateurish utterances, but also in appearance. If Billings, "somewhat deformed, blind of one eye, one leg shorter than the other, one arm somewhat withered; and . . . given to the habit of continually taking snuff"[1]) attended the testimonial concert, we may feel sure that Bostonians looked with pity and sympathy on this tanner-musician.

To dwell on the "concerts of vocal musick of the most fashionable songs and duets" as given repeatedly by Mr. and Mrs. Solomon, "vocal performers from the Southward", at Concert Hall in the summer of 1791 is unnecessary as they belonged to the category of Moral Lectures, Spectaculum Vitae, etc. The fashionable songs and duets and the name of concert were merely vehicles to force drama and opera on the public in a form against which the blue-laws of 1750 were powerless. To the same category belonged the

---

1) See Ritter, Music in America, 1895, p. 60. In spite of his sneers at Billings', amateurish utterances, Ritter's description of Billings and his ambitions will give every impartial raeder the impression that this Yankee was a very forceful character.

"grand concert" under the direction of Alexander Reinagle on Oct. 9, 1792[1]) after which was to be given "a musical entertainment called the *Poor Soldier* delivered" by such well-known actors as Harper, Morris and Mrs. Solomon. Finally the antediluvian law against theatres was repealed and at last Bostonians were at liberty to enjoy drama and opera. This change had its effects also on the concert-life of Boston and it requires only a very superficial knowledge of the history of drama at Boston to notice these effects in many of the programs, submitted in the following pages, as from now on until the end of the century the vocalists and members of the orchestras of the several theatrical companies that invaded Boston, came in for a large, if not the largest, share of the concerts given.

Faint signs of the new era already appear in the program as offered by Mons. Jacobus Pick for his benefit at Concert Hall on Nov. 27, 1792[2]):

A Grand Symphony, composed by Haydn
Song, by a lady
A Sonata on the Piano Forte, by a young lady
A Flute Concerto, by a Gentleman amateur
A Song, by Mons. Pick
A Grand Symphony, composed by Pleyel
The Song of Bellisarius, by Mr. Powell
A Grand Overture
A Grand Symphony, by Fils
Song, by a lady
A Hautboy Concerto, by Mr. Stone
A Quintetto, composed by Pleyel, and performed by the Gentlemen amateurs of Boston
Several pieces on the Harmonica, by Mons. Pick,
A Grand Overture.

The Subscription to be one dollar — each subscriber to be entitled to one lady's ticket.

Theatrical influences are still more unmistakable in the program as announced for the benefit of Messrs. Petit, Boullay, Mallet, Foucard and Madame Douvillier at Concert Hall on May 15, 1793[3])

FIRST PART.

A Grand Overture of Henry Fourth[4])
An Italian Song by Mr. Mallet
Clarinette concerto .. .. Mr. Foucard
An English Song .. .. Mr. Powell

1) Columbian Centinel, Oct. 6, 1792.
2) Columbian Centinel, Nov. 21, 1792. From the same paper, Feb. 23, 1793 when Mons. Pick expressed his desire to teach "the principles of vocal music by note" and nearly all orchestral instruments, we learn that he had "made the science of music his study at the Academy of Bruxelles".
3) Columbian Centinel, May 11, 1793. This concert had originally been announced for March 27th but was postponed.
4) Martini.

Violin Concerto, with four known tunes .. .. Mr. Boullay
A French Song .. .. Mad. Douvillier
A Grand Symphony
An Italian Duet .. .. Messrs. Pick and Mallet

SECOND PART.

Grand Overture, Music of Mr. Gretry
Song, by .. .. Mr. Pick
Quartetto, by Messrs. Petit, Boullay, Foucard and Mallet[1])
An English Song .. .. Mr. Harper
Violin Concerto .. .. Mr. Petit

With one, more curious than notable, exception all the other concerts of 1793 were given by the same gentlemen in form of benefits. Monsieur Petit had his on May 30th[2]), Monsieur Louis Boullay his on June 13th[3]) and again on November 14th (postponed from Oct. 31st)[4]), Monsieur Mallet on Nov. 29th[5]), Monsieur Jacobus Pick again on Dec. 12th[6]) and likewise Louis Boullay on Dec. 26th[7]). As this was announced as the last, the concerts formed practically a series of benefit concerts at Concert-Hall by subscription with programs strikingly differing from those of former years in combination, taste and tendency. Clearly a wedge was being driven into the standards of Colonial Times and the era of cosmopolitanism was fast dawning even in Boston. The "Distribution" was this:

MAY 30, 1793

FIRST PART.

Grand Overture, musick of Haydn
An Italian Song .. .. Mr. Mallet
Clarinet Concerto .. .. Mr. Foucard
An Italian Song .. .. Mr. Pick
Quartetto (by Pleyel) .. .. Messrs. Petit, Boullay,
                                             Foucard and Le Roy

---

1) Óf Francis Mallet, who was destined to play a prominent part in Boston's musical life General Oliver says in his 'First Centenary of the North Church Salem' (see Brooks, p. 167):

"Monsieur Mallet was a French gentleman of much respectability who came to this country with Lafayette and served in the army of the Revolution to the end of the war. He then settled in Boston as a teacher of music, declining to receive any pension. He was among the earliest publishers of music in Boston, the friend and business partner of the celebrated Dr. G. K. Jackson and predecessor of Graupner, the famous double bass player, whose music store was in Franklin Street."

To this may be added that Mallet in 1798 is mentioned as organist to the "Rev. Mr. Kirkland's congregation". It is also clear that the biographical note in my Bibliography is a trifle incorrect as Mallet settled in Boston at least as early as 1793. Still I doubt that he came to Boston immediately after the war. It is more probable that he came to the United States as a refugee from Hispaniola.

2) Columbian Centinel, May 25, 1793.
3) Col. Cent. June 12, 1793.
4) ibidem, Oct. 30, Nov. 13, 1793.
5) ibidem, Nov. 20th.
6) ibidem, Dec. 7, 1793.
7) ibidem, Dec. 25, 1793.

A French Song	Mad. Douvillier
Violin Concerto	Mr. Boullay
An English Song	Mr. Powell
A Sonate and a Song with accompaniment of guitar	Mr. Le Roy
An Overture	Musick of Gretry

SECOND PART

A Concertant Symphony for two violins and a tenor	Messrs. Petit,
	Boullay and Le Roy
An English Song	Mad. Placide
La Bataille de Prague[1]), upon the pianoforte and	
and English Romance	Mr. Mallet
An English Song	Mr. Harper
A Violin Concerto	Mr. Petit
A French Trio .. ·	Madame Douvillier
	Messrs. Pick and Mallet

End of the Concert, the Overture of Henry the IVth[2])
Mr. Petit will neglect nothing for the execution of the music.

JUNE 13, 1793

FIRST PART

Grand Overture, D'Iphigenia	M. Gluck
An Italian Song	Mr. Mallet
Clarinette Quartetto with variations	M. Foucard
French Song	Mad. Douvillier
Sonata [on the] Pianoforte	Mr. Mallet
English Song	Mr. Powell
Violin Concerto	Mr. Boullay
An English Song	Mrs. Mechtler

SECOND PART

Grand Simphonia	
An Italian Song	M. Pick
Concertant Simphonia	Messrs. Petit, Boullay, and
	Le Roy (Amateur)
An English Song	Mad. Placide
Violin Concerto	M. Petit
An English Song	Mr. Harper
A Grand Overture	

NOV. 14, 1793

1st ACT

Grand Overture
French Song
A Quartett, by Messrs. Boullay, Pick, Mallet and an amateur
Song. by Mr. Pick
Violin Concerto by Mr. Boullay
A Grand Symphony

---

1) Kotzwara.
2) Martini.

2d Act

Grand Overture
Flute concerto, by Mr. Stone
Duet on the Fiddle and bass, by Mr. Boullay
Fortepiano sonata, by Messrs. Selby and Boullay
Several airs with variations, Mr. Boullay
A Duet Song, by Messrs. Pick and Mallet
A Finale

NOV. 29, 1793
1st Act.

Grand Symphony, composed by the celebrated Haydn
Italian Song, by M. Mallet
Quartette of Airs, with variations, by an amateur, Messrs. Boullay,
    Pick & Mallet
A Duet on clarinets
French Song, by Mr. Pick
Quartette on the Fortepiano,
    composed by Pleyel, by M. Mallet & amateurs
Overture of Henry IVth.[1])

2d Act.

Grand Symphony, of Pleyel
Flute Quartette
Violin Concerto, by M. Boullay
Overture of Iphigenia[2]) on the Forte-Piano and an English Air, by M. Mallet
Quartette of Pleyel, Concertante by three amateurs and M. Mallet
Italian Duet, sung by Messrs. Pick and Mallet
Finale, of Hoffmeister, with a hunting Air on the horn, by M. Pick

DEC. 12, 1793
1st Part

A grand Symphony composed by Pichel
A French Song, by Mr. Mallet
Hautboy Concerto, by Mr. Stone
An Italian Song, by Mr. Pick (with an Hautboy accompaniment)

2d Part

A grand Overture
A French Song with the accompaniment of the Spanish guitar and violin,
    by two amateurs
A Violin Concerto, by Mr. Boullay
A Clarinet Concerto, by Mr. Granger, Boullay, Mallet and Pick
The Overture of Henry IVth[3])
A French Duetto, by Mr. Pick and Mallet
A Sonata on the Harmonica with several known airs, by Mr. Pick
A Grand Symphony, composed by Pleyel

DEC. 26, 1793
1st Act

Grand Symphony
An Italian Song, by M. Pick
Quartett, by M. Boullay and amateurs

---

1) Martini.
2) Gluck.
3) Martini.

Song, by M. Mallet
Flute Duetto, by an amateur and a professor
Violin Concerto, by Mr. Boullay
A grand Overture of Iphigenia, composed by Gluck

2d Aст.

Grand Overture, composed by Aiden [Haydn!]
French Song, by M. Mallet
Varied airs, by M. Boullay
French Song, accompanied with a guitar, by an amateur
A Violin Concerto, by M. Boullay

To these concerts must be added the joint benefit of Messrs. Boullay, Pick and Mallet on Oct. 22d[1]) and a concert of sacred music, held at the Universal Meeting House, for the benefit of Master Peter Dolliver, organist of that church, on July 4, 1793[2]). The date speaks for itself and the manner in which Master Dolliver's *impresario* announced this patriotic concert will afford a few moments of amusing reading:

THE DECLARATION OF INDEPENDENCE.

At the Universal Meeting House, to-morrow, July 4, precisely at 6 o'clock in the morning. A wish, not to intrude on the various services of this justly celebrated Day, prompted to the above early hour, when those persons who please to attend, may have an opportunity of being gratified, without immediately interfering with the serious business, or the innocent pleasure of the day.

A celebrated band of singers, eminently distinguished for their accurate knowledge in the science of vocal harmony, having generously offered their assistance, on the present occasion, a much admired *Ode to Independence* [by William Selby] will open the performance. A momentary pause at the 120th line of the poem, will be succeeded by an *Ode to Freedom*, generally supposed to have been composed by Della Crusca, and allowed to be unrivalled in the compass of language. A second momentary rest will be made at the 234th line, and afford room for the introduction of 'Columbia, Columbia, to glory arise' written by the animated and animating Dr. Dwight. At the conclusion of the 360th line, an original Anthem, of the high Hallelujah metre, and never before published, will be sung, accompanied by instruments.

Concluding *Anthem*, composed for Thursday Morning, July 4, 1793
Hail! The first the greatest blessing
God hath giv'n to Man below
. . . .

Surprisingly few concerts were given during the year 1794. We cannot be far from the truth if we see in this the direct or indirect influence of Boston's first regular theatrical season at the new Federal Street Theatre under the management of Charles Stuart Powell after the repeal of the anti-drama law and this influence on the concert-life is only too noticeable during the remaining years of the century. The company played from Feb. 3 to July 4 and during these five months not a single concert has come to my notice. Nor were such given during the latter part of the year, the company

---

1) Columbian Centinel, Oct. 19, 1793.
2) Col. Cent. July 3, 1793. The concert was postponed from June 25th.

resuming its unsuccessful career in Boston middle of September. Only during the summer-months, concerts seem to have been given. Probably more would have been announced had not Boston just then been visited by a conflagration which naturally enough temporarily stifled the slumbering enthusiasm of the afflicted city for concerts and other public entertainments.

For July 10, 1794[1]) a Mr. Nelson, member of Powell's company, advertised a concert plainly in imitation of Vauxhall entertainments though it took place at Concert-Hall. He and Messrs. Bartlett and Collins sang such popular songs as 'Sweet Poll of Plymouth', 'When Phoebus the tops of the hills does adorn', 'The Heaving of the lead', 'Poor Jack', 'Alone by the light of the moon' and the trio of 'Poor Thomas Day'. Of a different character was the program offered by Mrs. Pownall on July 22[2]) for her benefit at the theatre, which the trustees, not with out being subjected to narrow-minded censure, had generously put at her disposal. The program, in which Mrs. Pownall, as on other occasions elsewhere, appeared as composer, reads:

Act I

Overture	Haydn
Song 'Advice to the ladies of Boston, composed and to be sung, by	Mrs. Pownall
Roxelane	Haydn
Song 'A Soldier for me'	Mrs. Pownall
Sonata, on the Piano Forte	Mr. Selby

Act II

Concerto on the Violin	M. Boullay
A Cantata called 'The Happy rencontre, or Second thoughts are best', composed and sung by Mrs.	Pownall
Symphony	Pleyel
Song 'Sweet echo', by	Mrs. Pownall
Accompanied on the flute, Mr. Stone	

Act III

Concerto on the Flute	Mr. Stone
Air with Variations	Mr. Boullay
Song 'Tally Ho', in the character of Diana, huntress of the woods	Mrs. Pownall
Grand Symphony	Hoffmeister

Mrs. Pownall had headed her announcement "for one night only" but she met with such a liberal patronage that she resolved to engage the theatre, by particular desire of many ladies and gentlemen who attended the first, for a "second and last" concert on August 1st[3]). She had selected this pleasing program:

---

1) Columbian Centinel, July 9, 1794.
2) Columbian Centinel, July 19, 1794.
3) Columbian Centinel, July 30, 1794.

Act 1st.

Overture
An Irish ballad 'Killarney is a charming place' .. Mrs. Pownall
Symphony
Washington, a song written by Mrs. Pownall
Full piece
'Pauvre Jacques', French rondeau, Mrs. Pownall

Act 2d.

'The Lark's shrill notes', composed by Carter .. .. Mrs. Pownall
Piece [Full piece?] .. .. Stamitz
'Jemmy of the Glen', written and composed by .. Mrs. Pownall
Concerto .. .. Boullay
'A Soldier for me' (by desire) .. .. Mrs. Pownall

Act 3d.

'Sweeth Poll of Plymouth' .. .. Mrs. Pownall
Concerto .. .. Stone
'The Primroses' .. .. Mrs. Pownall
Symphony
'The Nabob', a cantata .. .. Mrs. Pownall
Full piece
An Occasional Address, written by Mrs. Pownall[1])

In the meantime, on July 31st, the city was visited by the conflagration mentioned and Mrs. Pownall's concert could not take place. The date was changed to August 3[2]) and whatever opinions the more puritanical Bostonians held of the morals of plays and players, they cannot have failed to read with a blush and perhaps with doubts as to these very opinions, Mrs. Pownall's announcement:

To afford some alleviation to these accumulated distresses, Mrs. Pownall has postponed her intention of a concert for her own emolument, as advertised in Wednesday's Centinel, and will appropriate the receipts of the evening to the relief and accommodation of those whom the merciless ravages of the most destructive of elements have reduced to the necessity of throwing themselves for redress into the arms of their fellow citizens.

With regret Mrs. Pownall commented after the concert on the "thinness" of the house netting only 200 dollars "and attributed this disappointing result of her generosity "to the heat of the weather and the recent calamity"[3]). It was a fair indication of what she might expect from her own benefit concert, but an opportunity for this did not arise, fortunately enough for her. Mrs. Pownall inserted on the same day, on which she made the financial results of her charity public, this amiable and polite *card:*

Mrs. Pownall presents her best respects to the citizens of Boston, and regrets an engagement that deprives her of the happiness of a longer visit; — but while she laments the necessity of relinquishing the concert she had postponed, she flatters herself with the pleasing anticipation of a second tour to this delightful part of America.

1) This address made part of the first act after the postponement.
2) Columbian Centinel, Aug. 2, 1794.
3) Columbian Centinel, August 9, 1794.

If only 200 dollars were netted for the victims of the conflagration, it may well be doubted if Mrs. Jacobus Pick covered expenses when she, regardless of the depression caused by the fire, announced a benefit concert at Concert Hall for August 28[1]) at one dollar a ticket with the following pieces and possibly she even found herself obliged to desist from giving it:

1st Part.

A grand Symphony by	Pepichell [Pichl]
Song by	Mrs. Pick
Flute quartetto by	An amateur etc.
Song by	Mr. Pick
Overture to the Deserter[2])	
Song by	Mrs. Pick
Chace [La Chasse] by Stamitz, the horn part by	Mr. Pick

2d Part.

Overture of Blase Babet[3])	
Italian Duetto, by	Messrs. Pick and Mallet
A Violin Concerto by	Mr. Boullay
Song by	Mrs. Pick
Overture	
Duetto by	Mr. and Mrs. Pick
Several airs on the Harmonica by	Mr. Pick
The Battle of Ivri[4])	

The first concert of the year 1795 brought into prominence "a deserving youth" who

"Tho 'he mourns a prison'd sense
Has music in his soul"[5])

This youth was none other than the blind Dr. John L. Berkenhead who in 1796 became organist of Trinity Church, Newport R. I. and continued in that position for eight years[6]). For his benefit was performed at the Universal Meeting House a concert of sacred music on January 6, 1795. The program was thus announced:

To commence with a *Symphony* on the organ, accompanied with other instruments.

---

1) Columbian Centinel, Aug. 23, 1794.
2) Dibdin or Monsigny.
3) Dezède.
4) Martini.
5) Columbian Centinel, Jan. 3, 1795.
6) Brooks, p. 56 where an amusing anecdote is told of Berkenhead. On his way to church he would indulge at his friend John Frazer, the schoolmaster's house, in a drop of old Scotch rye. After one of these visits, he managed to play a wrong tune. The clerk called out from the desk "Mr. Birkenhead you are playing a wrong tune", where upon blind John L. pulled the curtain apart and called the clerk a liar. The vestry, greatly shocked by this reply, in their further employment of the doctor, who knew a good thing even if he could not see it, put in a proviso "during good behaviour and punctual attendance"

Dedicatory anthem will follow
    Next a prayer

Then select pieces, collected from approved authors, with an *Ode*, composed for the occasion, and an Exordium corresponding therewith, concluding with Handel's celebrated *Hallelujah* chorus.

Bills of the pieces will be put into the pews. Floor tickets, 25 s. Gallery tickets, 1 *s* 6 . . . .

This was followed by the concert mentioned previously in connection with Josiah Flagg's career. It seems that his widow was in very distressed circumstances, owing in part to some serious misunderstanding with her son, the surgeon-dentist Dr. Josiah Flagg, *junr*. Hearing of this, the flutist Stone conceived the idea of enlisting public sympathy in her behalf by means of a concert on January 31 at Concert Hall. In this he met with the approval of a gentleman who signed himself *C. P.*, evidently Charles Powell, the theatrical manager, and who assisted in making the appeal urgent by requesting the editor of the Columbian Centinel to insert a long poem, dated, Boston, January 29, 1795 in which the hero, or rather the villain, was Mrs. Flagg's "miscreant son". The editor, of course, hastened to comply with the request and the poem was printed on January 31. The poet, leaving to an "abler pen" the task to "expose his crimes"

> . . . . To drag forth his Gothic deeds to open day —
> Shew how to every sense of feeling lost
> He could the misery of his parents boast"

appealed to his fellow-citizens to

> Stretch forth, ye wealthy souls, the liberal hand,
> And join to stimulate the Ingenious Band
> The glorious theme propos'd by Stone espouse,
> And ling'ring want to cheery hopes arouse."

We certainly do not feel grateful to Mr. C. P. for his wretched poetry but we are under obligations to him for naming in a footnote the "ingenious band". It was 'The Society of the Sons of Apollo', evidently a musical society, of which, however, nothing further is known to me. This ingenious band, together with members of Powell's theatrical company, and John L. Berkenhead performed the following lengthy and rather miscellaneous program[1]):

PART 1st.

Symphony	Haydn
Flute Concerto	Mr. Stone
Song 'Blow, blow, thou winter's wind'	Mr. Bartlett
Quartetto on the Clarinet	
Glee 'Here's a health to all good lasses'	Messrs. Jones, Collins and Hipworth
The Demolition of the Bastile on the harpsichord or Piano Forte, by	Mr. Berkenhead

---

1) Columbian Centinel, Jan. 28, 1795.

PART 2d.

Grand Overture	
Song 'Adieu, adieu, my only life'	Mr. Jones
Violin Concerto	Mr. Mallet
Song 'Washington's Counsel'	Mr. Clifford
Glee 'Three flutes'	
Duet 'The Stag thro' the forest'	Messrs. Bartlett and Collins

PART 3d.

Full piece	
Duet on the Clarinet	Messrs. Stone and Granger
Song 'Dear Nancy I've sailed the world all around'	Mr. Clifford
Grand Lesson by Hook	Mr. Berkenhead
Song 'Come thou Goddess fair and free'	Mr. Bartlett
Grand Finale.	

The proceeds amounted to one hundred and two dollars which — the Columbian Centinel on February 4 said —

"considered the disadvantages unavoidably attending the business, must be considered as handsome. The thanks of the friends of humanity are due to Mr. Stone, and the gentlemen who assisted in the Concert, for their effort to relieve a suffering and deserving family. The assembly was brilliant and the performance highly satisfactory."

The widow Elizabeth Flagg and daughters, however, waited until middle of April with the expression of their gratitude, at the same time informing the public and their friends that they "carried on the business of riveting and mending China and glass, and needle work of all kinds".

On the same day, April 15th, Mr. Berkenhead announced a second benefit concert to be held at the assembly room of the New Theatre on April 23 and subsequently the Columbian Centinel printed the program in which again his 'Demolition of the Bastile' appeared:

PART I

Grand Symphony	Haydn
Song 'Ploughman turned Sailor," Mr. Bartlett, accompanied by the grand Piano Forte by	Dr. Berkenhead
Flute Concerto	Mr. Stone
Glee 'Here's a health to all good lasses'	Messrs. Jones, Collins and Hipworth
Sonata on the grand Piano Forte, composed by Dr. Arnold, and performed by Miss Doliver, a young lady of 9 years of age.	
Song 'Old Tom Day'	
Carelia Song	Dr. Berkenhead
Song 'From night until morn'	Messrs. Collins and Hipworth

PART II

Demolition of the Bastile, on the Grand Piano Forte	Dr. Berkenhead
Song 'Cottage Maid'	Miss Doliver

Overture of Henri IVth[1])
Song 'Learned pig' .. ..   Mr. Jones
Lesson on the Piano Forte .. ..   Dr. Berkenhead
Violin Concerto .. ..   Mr. Mallet
Song 'For England when with sorrowing gale'   Mr. Bartlett
Overture by Vanhall .. ..   Dr. Berkenhaed
Song 'Wedding day' .. ..   Mrs. Hellyer

PART III.

Grand Symphony
Song 'Flowing can' .. ..   Mr. Jones
Clarinet Concerto .. ..   Mr. Granger
Song 'Hush every breeze' .. ..   Mrs. Hellyer
Grand Lesson on the Piano Forte .. .. ..   Dr. Berkenhead
Song 'Maria' .. ..   Mrs. Hellyer
Grand Lesson .. ..   Dr. Berkenhead
Song "Bonny Will" .. ..   Mrs. Hellyer
Finale.

This concert was followed on June 18[2]) by a joint benefit for Messrs. Mallett and Jones at Concert Hall but though they had both repeatedly stepped forward in charitable entertainments and notwithstanding their exertions during the season they were considerable losers on the occasion, as a correspondent to the Columbian Centinel indignantly remarked on June 24. The few lovers of music, however, who attended were highly pleased with the performance of the program, again adorned by the 'Demolition of the Bastille':

PART I

Grand Overture by the celebrated Gretry
Favourite Air, by Mr. Bartlett
Duetto on the German flute .. ..   Mr. Stone and amateur
Song 'Bachelor's Hall with accompaniments'..   Mr. Hipworth
Hautboy Concerto .. ..   Mr. Stone
Song 'Hush every breeze' .. ..   Mrs. Hellyer
Demolition of the Bastille .. ..   Mr. Berkenhead
Catch 'How great in the pleasure' .. .. ..   Messrs. Hipworth, Jones and Collins

PART II

Full Piece
Song .. ..   Mr. Collins
Violin Concerto .. ..   Amateur
Song 'The Ploughboy's escape' .. ..   Mr. Jones
Duetto on the Clarinet .. ..   Messrs. Stone and Granger
A few select Airs, by .. ..   Amateur of this town
Grand Concerto on the Piano Forte .. ..   Mr. Berkenhead
Song .. ..   Mrs. Hellyer
Glee in the Mountaineers[3]), etc. .. .. ..   Messrs. Collins, Bartlett and Mallet.

---

1) Martini.
2) Columbian Centinel, June 17, 1795.
3) Arnold.

In the meantime Powell's company had failed and Colonel Royal Tyler, the author of 'The Contrast', who had been master of ceremonies, assumed the management of the theatre. He re-engaged part of Powell's company and succeeded in securing part of Hallam and Henry's Old American Company and with this strong combination he re-opened the theatre on November 2. Thus it happened that Mrs. Pownall's "pleasing anticipation of a second tour to this delightful part of America" came true. Well knowing that her duties at the theatre would be too arduous for a division of energy between opera and concert, she hastened to hold a benefit before the theatre opened. It was given on October 7. at the theatre and evidently was very successful for Mrs. Pownall felt sufficiently encouraged to add two other benefit concerts in surprisingly rapid succession as her "third and last night" was announced already for October 13[1]). In the first, Bostonians received a glimpse of a prodigy much younger than Miss Dolliver, it being Felix Pownall's first attempt in public, which we may well believe as this young gentleman was only four years of age. The "selections" contained as further *pillar* an americanised version of Kotzwara's 'Battle of Prague' which, we are told, still raged on both sides of the Atlantic as late as 1850:

ACT I

Song (by desire) 'Soldier for me'	Mrs. Pownall
Concerto Violin	Mr. Bergmann
Duett 'The Way worn travellers' from the Mountaineers, by the Misses Wrightens[2])	
Solo Flute	Mr. Stone
Song 'Little Felix is your name', by Felix Pownall, a child only four years of age, being his first attempt in public.	

ACT II

'Sweet echo', by Mrs. Pownall, accompanied on the flute by Mr. Stone	
Battle of Prague (on the pianoforte, with accompanyments) consisting of a Slow march. 2. Words of command, first signal Cannon. 3. Bugle horn for the cavalry and second signal cannon. 4. The trumpet call. 5. The General attack. 6. The Attack with swords. 7. The Light dragons advancing. 8. Trumpets of recall. 9. Cries of the wounded. 10. Trumpet of victory. 11. President's march. 12. Turkish music. 13. Finale	Miss M. A. Wrighten
Song 'My Henry swore at his parting'. Words by a gentleman of New York and music by	Mrs. Pownall

1) Columbian Centinel, Oct. 3, 7, 13, 1795.
2) Arnold. Daughters of Mrs. Pownall.

Quartette	Mr. Bergman, St. Amand, Pick and Mallet
Trio 'Magic lantern'	Misses Wrightens and Mrs. Pownall
Bravoura Song 'On the rapid whirlwind' by	Mrs. Pownall

Decidedly better than the concerts of this year were the few of 1796. Dr. Berkenhead presented this program at Bowen's Hall, head of the Mall, on February 25[1]) and it will be noticed that he figured not less than three times as composer, his 'Demolition' in the mean while having become the 'Abolition':

Act I

Grand Symphony	Haydn
Lesson on the Grand Piano Forte	Mr. Dolliver
Song by the celebrated Mrs. Arnold	
Lesson (composed by Clementi) on the Grand Piano Forte by Dr. Berkenhead	
Song (composed by Dr. Berkenhead)	Miss Maxwell
Lesson	Miss Dolliver
Song	Miss Dolliver
Solo on the flute	Mr. Stone
Billet doux, by Miss Maxwell and Miss Dolliver, accompanied on the grand Piano Forte, by Dr. Berkenhead.	

Act II

Grand Overture	
Song	Miss Maxwell
The Abolition of the Bastile, on the Grand Piano Forte	Dr. Berkenhead
Song	Miss Dolliver
Pleyel's Concertante	Miss Maxwell
Song	Mrs. Arnold
Song, composed by Dr. Berkenhead	Miss Maxwell
Lesson	Dr. Berkenhead
Grand Overture	

Historically more interesting than this was the program offered on March 24[2]) at Bowen's Columbian Museum by Mr. Nugent who, being a dancing master, waited until after the concert to show his talents in hornpipes and *pas seuls:*

1. A Grand Overture by the whole orchestra
2. A Clarinet Duet, by Messrs. Anderson and Granger
3. The Overture Chimine[3]) by wind instruments
4. A Quartette, by Messrs. Leaumont, Schaffer, Pick and Feckner
5. A Grand Chasse, composed by Stamitz.

The Concert will be followed by a ball, to be conducted by Mr. Nugent, in the course of which several hornpipes by Mr. Nugents' scholars and a *pas seul* by Mr. Nugent.

---

1) Columbian Centinel, Feb. 20, 1796.
2) Columbian Centinel, March 16, 1796.
3) Sacchini.

Different in character and mainly made up of sacred music by American composers was the concert given for the benefit of Peter Dolliver, junr. at the Universal Meeting House, where he was organist, on March 31[1]):

Voluntary by .. .. Dr. Berkenhead (
Holden's Dedicatory Anthem, accompanied by
   the organ and other instruments
Occasional Ode by Ladies
Billings's Easter Anthem
Ode, by Miss Amelia Dolliver
Cooper's Anthem
Solo by Miss Dolliver
"Ye Sons of Men" by .. .. Reeves
Solo, by a lady
Voluntary, by Mr. Dolliver
A Hymn-Music by Dr. Berkenhead
The whole to conclude with the celebrated
   Hallelujah Chorus by .. .. Handel

Not for his own benefit but for a benevolent purpose Mr. Stone announced a concert for May 23[2]) at Bowen's Museum. His program showed a return to more legitimate symphony-concert programs than Bostonians had been accustomed to for some time past. It contained in

ACT I
Grand Overture to Henry the 4th, with the
   entracts[3]).
Song 'Fair Rosalie' .. .. Mrs. Arnold
Flute Concerto .. .. Mr. Stone
Solo on the grand Piano Forte, composed by .. Dr. Berkenhead
Violin Quartetto by .. .. Pleyel
Song 'By moor light on the green' .. .. .. Mrs. Arnold
A favorite Symphony by .. .. Hayden

ACT II
A Grand Chasse, composed by .. .. C. Stamitz
A Clarinet Duetto by .. .. Michel
A new Hunting Song .. .. Mrs. Arnold
Hautboy Concerto .. .. Mr. Stone
Symphony on the grand Piano Forte, by Cle-
   menti .. .. Dr. Berkenhead
Violin Quartetto by .. .. Franzill [!]
The whole to conclude with a particular Full Piece.

The announcement of Mrs. Arnold's concert at Theatre Hall, June 1st[4]) is important as this lady, a popular actress and singer, did not forget to mention the names of the most eminent instrumentalists in the theatre orchestra who had offered her their assistance. Thus we are enabled to prove contrary to contemporary reminiscences that the orchestras of those

---

1) Columbian Centinel, March 26, 1796.
2) Columbian Centinel, May 21, 1796.
3) Martini.
4) Columbian Centinel, June 1, 1796.

days contained more than "half a dozen musicians". On this particular occasion the orchestra contained at least fourteen principal performers, the *etc. etc.* standing, of course, for the less prominent members, whereby the exact size is left to our more or less friendly imagination:

> Vocal performers, Mrs. & Miss Arnold
> Instrumental performers, Messrs. Shaffer, Mallet, Stone, La Barre, Granger, Anderson, Bonnemort, Sweeny, Vakner [Feckner?], Austin, Muck, L'Epouse, Calligan, etc. etc.
> Leader of the band, Mr. Leaumont
> Grand Piano Forte, D. Berkenhead

ACT 1st.

Grand Overture	
Song, by particular desire, 'Ellen, or the Richmond Primrose Girl', accompanied on the flute, by Mr. Stone	Mrs. Arnold
Solo on the grand Piano Forte	Dr. Berkenhead
Song 'The Market Lass'	Miss Arnold
Solo on a new instrument, called Spiccato, invented and played by	Mr. Shaffer
Manuscript Song 'The Cottage Gate', words by R. B. Sheridan, Esq. and music by the celebrated Haydn, accompanied on the grand Piano Forte by Dr. Berkenhead ..	Mrs. Arnold
Solo on Flute	Mr. Stone
Manuscript Hunting Song, with full band ..	Mrs. Arnold

ACT 2d.

Grand Symphony	Haydn
Manuscript Song 'Collin and Nancy'	Mrs. Arnold
Quartetto, in which the favorite Air of the Plough Boy' with variations will be introduced by	Mr. Leaumont
Song 'Henry's Cottage Maid'	Mrs. Arnold
Duet, Clarinet	Messrs. Anderson and Granger
New Song, sung last year at Vauxhall Garden, London, with great applause, 'Listen, listen to the voice of love'	Mrs. Arnold
Lovely Nymph assuage my anguish, on the spiccato, by	Mr. Shaffer
By desire, the popular song of the 'Heaving of the lead', with all the original parts, as performed at the Convent Garden Theatre by Shield	Mrs. Arnold
To conclude with La Grand Chasse[1])	

Compared with this, a program like that of Mrs. Sully and Mr. Collet at Concert Hall on September 13, the last concert in 1796, shrinks into insignificance[2]):

---

1) K. Stamitz.
2) Columbian Centinel, Sept. 10. 1796.

ACT I.

Symphony of Haydn
Sonata of Pleyel, on the Forte Piano by ..   Mrs. Sully
Ariet .. ..   Mrs. Pick
Concerto of Jarnowick on the violin .. ..   Mr. Collet
Rondo of Pleyel

ACT II.

Grand Overture
Ariet by .. ..   Mrs. Pick
Concerto of Herman on the Piano Forte
The celebrated Trio of Felix, song, by .. ..   Mr. Mallet, Mr. Pick
  and Mrs. Sully
Concerto on the Clarinet by .. ..   Mr. Dubois
Finale.

It was said towards the end of the chapter on New York that the Van Hagens moved to Boston late in 1796. Remembering how actively they were engaged in concert-work at New York, it will seem strange that both P. A. Van Hagen sen. and junr. taught music at their Musical Academy, played in the theatre orchestra, became organists of the best churches, opened a flourishing music store under the name of 'Musical Magazine' and otherwise became prominent in the musical affairs of Boston but, to my knowledge, did *not announce a single benefit concert between* 1797 *and* 1800. This alone would go far to prove that in Boston, as in New York and Philadelphia, for reasons not wholly on the surface, concert-life was at a very low ebb during the last years of the eighteenth century. And if further proof is needed, we need but examine the newspapers. For instance, I found but one concert advertised in 1797. It took place on September 14[1]) at the Columbian Museum with this indifferent program:

ACT FIRST

1. An Overture
2. A Quartette on the French horn. By Messrs. Rozier, etc.
3. A French Song, accompanied with the grand Piano Forte. By Mr. Mallet
4. A Quartette on the German flute. By Messrs. Stone, etc.
5. A Grand Symphony

ACT SECOND

1. An Overture
2. A Symphony on the Grand Piano Forte. By Messrs. Mallet, etc.
3. A Quartette on the Violin. By Messrs. Leaumont, etc.
4. An English Song, accompanied with the Grand Piano Forte. By Mr. Mallet
5. To conclude with a grand Symphony, full orchestra.

Mr. Brown respectfully informs ... that the Museum will appear to great advantage on that evening.

Slightly less meagre was the output of the year 1798 and if the proposals of Messrs. J. B. Baker and S. Powell to erect a 'Columbian Vauxhall', at the estimated cost of 10 000 dollars, "a species of Summer entertainment",

---

1) Columbian Centinel, Sept. 13, 1797.

combining "salubrity. with amusement and novelty with taste"[1]) if these
proposals met with sufficient encouragement then Bostonians had at least an
opportunity to enjoy open-air concerts as did Americans in other cities. But
before the Columbian Vauxhall could have been opened, almost all the concerts, to my knowledge given in 1798, had taken place. First in order and
importance was that announced by Mrs. Graupner for March 14[1]) at Bowen's
Columbian Museum. The program escaped me, but it is safe to say that
Gottlieb Graupner, her husband, assisted. It was not to be his last appearance before the public of Boston, for, just as William Selby had been the
musical center of the city during the years 1782—1792 so Gottlieb Graupner
became the musical oracle of Boston from now on until the foundation of
the Handel and Haydn society in 1815, of which he, too, was an original
member[2]). The concert of Mrs. Graupner was followed on April 2[3]) at
Mr. Vila's Concert Hall by a joint benefit for Messrs. Pick and Rosier, when
F. Schaffer, the clarinetist, was to play a concerto of his own:

Act I

A Grand Symphony of	Pleyel
The celebrated Song 'O Richard by my love'	Mrs. Pick
A French Duet	Mr. and Mrs. Rosier
Concerto on the Clarinet, composed and per-	
formed by	Mr. Shaffer
A Duet in the Siege of Belgrade[4])	Mr. and Mrs. Pick
A French Song	Mr. Rosier
A Concert and Symphony	Messrs. Von Hagen, sen. and jun.

Act II

A Concert on the French horn	Mr. Rosier
A French Song	Mr. Pick
A Concerto on the flute	Mr. Stone
The favorite Song 'Whither my love'	Mrs. Pick
Trio for two horns and a clarinet	Mr. and Mrs. Rosier and Shaffer
Concerto on the Violin	Mr. Von Hagen, sen.
Quartette on the French Horn	Messrs. Rosier,
	Von Hagen, sen. and jun.
A Song 'The Black bird's a sweet whistle' ..	Mrs. Pick
Finale	

---

1) Columbian Centinel. March 7, 1798.

2) Not in 1798, as has been generally accepted, but early in 1797 did Gottlieb
Graupner settle in Boston. He came there as oboist in the Federal Street Theatre
orchestra and advertised in March his services as teacher of the oboe, German flute,
violin etc. According to the several accounts of his life in Perkins and Dwight, Jones,
and other books, Graupner was born about 1740, became oboist in a Hanoverian regiment
and went to London in 1788 where he played under Haydn. From London he went
to Prince Edwards Island whence he arrived at Charleston, S. C. in 1795 where he
married. With some friends he later on, in 1810 or 1811 founded in Boston a 'Philharmonic Society' which existed until 1824. About 1800 Graupner opened a music
store. He also engraved and published music. The year of his death seems to be unknown. Mrs. Catherine Graupner, before her marriage known as Mrs. Hellyer, was a
prominent vocalist on the American stage. She is said (by Jones) to have died in 1821.

3) Columbian Centinel, March 21, 1798.

4) Storace.

Then came R. Leaumont, leader of the theatre orchestra and subsequently to be traced at Charleston, S. C. in the same capacity, with a benefit on April 20[1]) and F. Schaffer on May 2[2]) when he was to introduce a new instrument invented by him, possibly his spiccato, though the name is not given. On May 15[3]) the Columbian Museum was "opened" (tickets half a doilar, children 25 cents) for the benefit of Peter Dolliver who was to perform several pieces on the grand pianoforte assisted by Miss Amelia Dolliver who by particular request of her brother "accompanied for that evening the pianoforte with her voice". Then followed the last and only really important concert of the year on May 31[4]), a 'Spiritual Concert', also called an 'Oratorio', at the New South Meeting House in Summer Street. It was to be for the benefit of Francis Mallet, the organist of Rev. Kirkland's congregation, who had procured the first vocal and instrumental performers of Boston and who respectfully solicited the patronage of those ladies and gentlemen who united to a love of the liberal art of music, the disposition of alleviating real misfortune. The performance was to begin at 4 o'clock in the afternoon and the price of tickets was "first seat 75 cts.; second, 50 cts.; and third 25 cts."; perhaps the first instance in Boston's musical history of a graduation of prices beyond two. The pillar of the program was Haendel by whom Mr. Trille La Barre's 'Latin Oratorio' probably was placed in an embarrassing position:

ACT 1st.

Overture of Esther, composed by Handel
A Chorus 'Before Jehovah's awful throne'
A Song 'Bright Seraphim' (by Handel) .. .. Mrs. Graupner
A Quintetto, (a French horn and hautboys,
    principals) .. .. M. M. Rosier and Graupner
A Duet 'Lovely Peace' (by Handel) .. .. .. Mr. Pick & Mallet
A Latin Oratorio (by desire) composed by Trille La Barre

ACT 2d.

A grand Symphony, composed by Pleyel
A chorus 'When all thy mercies', adapted by Mallet
A Song 'Comfort ye my people' (by Handel) Mr. Ray
A Sonata on the organ .. .. Mr. Mallet
A Chorus 'Hallelujah' (by Handel)
Finale, Handel's Coronation

The concerts of 1799 were still fewer. First we notice a benefit for Peter Dolliver at the Columbian Museum on Jan. 24[5]). Again, "by the request

---

1) Columbian Centinel, April 14, 1798.
2) Col. Cent. April 25, 1798.
3) See Brooks, p. 102 where the date of "Tuesday evening next 1st of May" is obviously an error, the more so as Mr. Brooks copied the announcement from the "Columbian Centinel, [Wednesday] May 9, 1798".
4) Columbian Centinel, May 9, 26, 1798.
5) Columbian Centinel, January 23, 1799.

of her brother", Miss Amelia assisted. She sang a song, accompanied by Peter on the clarinet, and played a voluntary on the organ. Indeed, as Peter Dolliver and Mr. Linley, who had kindly offered his co-operation, also performed several pieces on the organ, this concert may be classed as one of the first organ recitals given at Boston. The organ, together with some musical clocks, formed one of the main attractions of Mr. Bowen's Museum and, when on Feb. 8 the public was invited to admire among a variety of new additions "a large cat of the mountain", together with "the likenesses of President Adams and General Washington", the organ was again brought into prominence by a performance of "that much admired solemn march, which was played by the band of music in France, when Louis 16th suffered under the guillotine"[1]). But Mr. Bowen was still more progressive and, though he was not an organist but merely a clever business man, those among our organists who delight in turning their vaunted king of instrument, as I have said elsewhere, into a kind of *orchestrion* for which anything will do from a fugue to an operatic pot-pourris, may see in Mr. Bowen a pioneer.

In the summer of 1799[2]) Mr. Bowen notified the public that beginning with July 30 there would be performances of his Concert Organ every Tuesday, Thursday and Friday evenings and as a specimen program he inserted that for the opening night:

The music will commence precisely at 8 o'clock with the Battle of Prague; Within a mile of Edinburgh; Dead of the night; Fal la la; The topsail shivers in the wind; Heaving the lead; Sailor's journal; Tom Bowling; You gentlemen of England and Little Sally; On Board the Arethusa; Lullaby; Old Towler; Bachelor's hall; Pleasures of the chase; How sweet in the woodland; Listen to the voice of love; Sweet little girl that I love; Lilly's of the valley; and the Woodman,

Dutch fishmonger; British grenadier; Freemason's song; Meg of Wapping; Dolly Thimble; Delights of the chase; Faint and wearily; Drink to me only; Kate of Aberdeen; Freemason's march.

In the meantime Gottlieb Graupner had announced under the heading of 'Subscription Assembly' that, encouraged by the very flattering marks of approbation on Mrs. Graupner's concert of 1798, he intended giving a benefit concert for himself which, he promised, would be one of the most brilliant performances ever produced in Boston — as soon as the subscription was adequate to the expense. This announcement appeared as early as April 17 in the Columbian Centinel but the subscriptions were so slow coming in that the concert did not take place until May 20[3]). A condition, highly significant for the state of concert affairs in Boston at the end of the century! Whatever the program was — presumably it was worthy of a

1) Col. Cent. Feb. 6, 1799.
2) Columbian Centinel, July 27, 1799.
3) Columbian Centinel, May 18, 1799. The program is not mentioned.

man who had played under Haydn — it cannot but have differed from that
offered by William Kendall by permission of the Universal Society in Mr.
Murray's Meeting House on December 12 for his "exclusive benefit"[1]):

1. Ode, Descend ye Nine
2. *do.* Introductory
3. Voluntary on organ
4. Solo, Italy
5. Ode, 'Tis thine sweet power
6. Chorus, Vital spark of heavenly flame
7. Voluntary on organ
8. Solo, Hail sacred art
9. Chorus, Drundon
10. Duet, Anesbury
11. Voluntary
12. Duet, Beneficence
13. Chorus, Angels toll the rock away
14. Solo, Let the bright Seraphim

Merely mentioning Mr. Bates' "Medley entertainment in three parts,
called 'Fashionable variety'; or, Characters drawn from life, consisting of
various descriptions, moral reflections, comic songs", the latter sung by
Mrs. Graupner, on March 20, 1800[2]) and on June 26, 1800 the appearance
of those phenomena of musical abilities, a boy of seven and an infant of
four years, whose acquaintance was already formed at New York[2]), I close
this chapter with an advertisement which proves that, however insignificant
the musical life of Boston had become in public, in private circles the love
of music had not died out.   We read in the Columbian Centinel, April 6,
1799:

Philharmonic Society

A general and punctual attendance of the members is requested this evening, as
business of importance will be laid before the society.   By order

W. H. M'Neill, Secretary.

Of this Philharmonic Society nothing further is known.   It is not even
mentioned by other historians but certainly the supposition will not be
considered violent that Gottlieb Graupner was one of the founders.   Is it
possible, after all, that the Philharmonic Society which Perkins and Dwight
claim to have been founded by Graupner and his friends in 1810 or 1811
and which gave its last concert on November 24, 1824, was identical with
that existing in 1799?

*   *   *

On Dec. 15, 1790 the Essex Journal of Newburyport informed its readers
that according to a late enumeration in the county of Essex with a total of
57908 the town of Newburyport contained 4837, Salem 7921, Marblehead

---

1) Columbian Centinel, Dec. 11, 1799.
2) The father closed the announcement with this *NB* "If the children do not
perform what is in the bills [marches, airs, hornpipes, duets, etc.] those who come
shall have their money back"!

5660, Glocester 5317, Ipswich 4562, Beverly 3290 and so on down to Methuen
with 1293 inhabitants. This curious bit of statistics strikingly illustrates
one important point: the difference between the States commonly comprised
under the collective name of New England and for instance the States of
New York and Pennsylvania. When thinking of cities or towns as they
thrived in the Middle States about 1790 our memory begins to fail after
having mentioned New York, Albany, Philadelphia, Bethlehem, Lancaster.
It is entirely different with New England. While most of the towns mentioned above were insignificant enough yet it would reveal a very limited
knowledge of general history if besides Boston, at least, Salem, Newport,
Worcester, Newburyport, Providence, New Haven, Hartford were not taken
into consideration. Undoubtedly Boston had by this become the center
of gravitation in these relatively thickly settled States but she had not yet
hopelessly out-distanced other towns, once her rivals, and (*mutatis mutandis*)
this struggle against her supremacy has continued ever since. Especially
in intellectual matters! We need but think of the many learned societies
and institutions, of the net of well-equipped and well-managed libraries
spread over New England and the neighboring States to recognize the
truth of this observation and to understand how the mighty and general
intellectual development of New England resulted from the absence of absolute centralisation of intellectual forces. The same observation holds
true if applied to the history of music in New England and more particularly
during the formative period. But the early musical history of New England
is peculiar. Undeniably the interest taken in music by the Yankees was
keen, earnest and sincere but outside of Boston it moved predominantly
in the narrow channel of what we call psalmody, cultivated by the innumerable singing schools and singing societies. For instance, where we find
in the newspapers one advertisement of a dancing master or a musician
anxious to teach the German flute, harpsichord, violin etc. we run across
a dozen advertisements of singing schools, or of the publication of the psalm-
tune collections (now so scarce) compiled by Stickney, Billings, Jocelyn,
Read, Holyoke, Law, Holden and others. It would be a thankful task for
a historian interested more in the history of our early sacred than secular
music to rigidly apply the projective method — more difficult, may be,
but also more correct and fruitful than the mere critical or esthetic method —
to this phase of our country's musical development. It would be seen how,
even in the field of psalmody, England was taken as the model with a full
knowledge and an enthusiastic imitation of the standards of psalmody prevailing in the mother country and how the New Englanders added to this
literature in a fashion peculiar to their own needs and requirements. One
important lesson would be learned and it is this that, if psalmody in America

was crude and amateurish, it was not very much more so than in England as represented by Tansur, Williams etc., that Billings was a character, a personality more than a pioneer, that his and the tendencies of his rivals and imitators were working with tremendous force for the good of the future of choral music, — in short that it is easier to ridicule the technical short-comings of these "singing teachers" than to give them credit for their actual musical abilities and to ascertain their real historical importance.

To what extent sacred music dominated the interests of music lovers outside of Boston may further be illustrated without difficulty. There existed at Cambridge in 1789 a 'Singing Club of the University' and though undoubtedly the Harvard boys knew strains very much more secular and even profane than those contained in the 'Harmonia Americana' compiled by their fellow-student Samuel Holyoke, the manner in which the members of the club publicly endorsed this collection proves that the 'Singing Club' was devoted mainly if not exclusively to the study of psalmody, "this im-portant part of divine worship"[1]). There also existed a musical club about 1786 at New Haven[2]) called 'The Musical Society of Yale College' and the same inference as to its tendencies may be drawn from the elaborate ad-vertisement in which Amos Doolittle and Daniel Read solicited subscriptions for their 'American Musical Magazine' in which no piece not previously examined and approved by said society was to be published[3]). However, sacred music did not predominate in the *provincial* cities of New England to the exclusion of secular music. Such a pre-conceived theory without actual proofs deducted from available data would be an absurdity, for, where toasts are drunk to the king, to the United States, to the Presidents to popular tunes of the day, where the lads woe the lasses, where mothers rock their babies to sleep, where the courtly minuet alternated with the sprightly jig, where the "martial band" sets the soldiers marching, where the harp-sichord, the violin, the guitar, the German flute are advertised for sale, and where patriotic songs are sung to the strains of Anacreontic airs, there, of necessity, must have existed an inherited and replenished store of secular music and consequently a vivid interest in secular music, at least during six days of the week. Moreover, with all the ethical arguments and legal restrictions against theatrical entertainments, the *Beggar's Opera* and other ballad operas invaded New England at an early date and when finally in the last decade of the eighteenth century the barriers against theatrical entertainments collapsed, the people of Providence, Salem, Hartford, New-port and elsewhere enjoyed, and what means more, were prepared to enjoy

1) Massachusetts Spy, Worcester, June 25, 1789.
2) Population in 1800 — only 4049 inhabitants!
3) Connecticut Journal, New Haven, March 29, 1786.

English opera just as much as the Bostonians or New Yorker. But in the realm of concerts — and this is peculiar — New England, Boston excepted, does not furnish much of interest to the historian. It would he more accurate to say outside of Boston and her immediate vicinity, for such towns like Salem, Charlestown, Cambridge naturally partook of everything offered at Boston in the form of public entertainments, and *vice versa.*

Thus, for instance, Bostonians were duly notified through the columns of the Massachusetts Gazette of a concert to be given by a Mr. Coleman in the Court House at Cambridge on Commencement day, July 15, 1772 and those who cared to attend the "grand" concert of vocal and instrumental music with Mrs. Spencer, Mrs. Berkenhead, Mr. T. Spencer and Dr. Berkenhead as principal performers at Warren's Tavern on January 15, 1798 or Peter Dolliver, the organist's concert of sacred music at the Meeting House in Charlestown on June 13, 1799 found the announcements in the Columbian Centinel. Since it was no longer necessary as of yore to use a rude ferryboat plying between the North End of Boston and Charlestown, as Cox had gained an international reputation by spanning Charlesriver in 1786 by a bridge, the short trip to Charlestown possessed the incidental features of a pleasant outing. It took somewhat longer to drive or ride to Salem, but, as the Salem Gazette printed advertisements of concerts to be given at Boston and the Boston papers such of concerts to be given at Salem, it is clear that the musical intercourse between the two cities must have been feasible and frequent. For many years Salem depended almost entirely on the offerings of Boston but it is interesting to note that towards the close of the century Salem possessed a concert-life independent of Boston.

As private singing societies were established at Salem as early as 1772, (according to Brooks), it is possible that more or less public concerts with programs made up of hymns and anthems were given there before the war, but the first real public concert held at Salem seems to have been the one at Concert Hall [!] on January 17, 1783. The interesting announcement in the Salem Gazette, January 16, reads:

The *Massachusetts Band of Musick* being at home a few days on furlough, propose, with permission, to perform at Concert Hall, in Salem, to-morrow evening. This band belongs to Col. Crane's Artillery, is complete, and will have the assistance of two or three capital performers.

The Musick will consist of *Overtures, Symphonies, Harmony and Military Musick,* Solos, duets on the horns, and some favourite songs by the band. To begin at six o'clock and end at half past nine.

Tickets at six shillings each, to be had at the Printing Office to-morrow.

The Massachusetts Band "performed to so great acceptance" that a few days later, on January 24, it was engaged to assist in a Concert for the Poor at Concert Hall[1]).

---

1) Salem Gazette, January 23, 1783.

Next we notice a Concert of Sacred Musick, Vocal and Instrumental planned for November 25, 1790 in St. Peter's Church for the purpose of repairing the organ of the church[1]). This time it was "the Band from Boston" which did the musical honors and William Selby was to play on the organ. Tickets for the ground floor were to cost 1 s. 6 and for the gallery 9d. For July 10, 1792[2]) was announced a concert but as between its parts was to be delivered "the tragic and moral lecture, called *Douglas* with various songs", the hybrid entertainment does not call for much attention here. It is different with the concert advertised for September 9, 1794[3]) at the Assembly Room for the benefit of Mr. and Mrs. Jacobus Pick, Messrs. Louis Boullay, Francis Mallet and Frederick Granger, as the program was as substantial as any offered at Boston during those years:

FIRST PART.
1. Blaise and Babet Overture[4]) — full orchestra
2. Song of Jordany [!], sung by Mrs. Pick
3. Quartetto on the flute, by a amateur, Messrs. Boullay, Pick and Mallet
4. French Song, by Mr. Pick
5. Overture in the 'Two Misers'[5]) — full orchestra
6. A favorite new Song, by Mrs. Pick
7. The Chasse of Stamitz, the horn part by Mr. Pick
8. A favorite Italian duet, sung by Messrs. Mallet and Pick

SECOND PART.
1. Grand Overture in Rosière de Salenci, composed by Gretry
2. A Comic Italian Song, by Mr. Mallet
3. Violin Concerto, by Mr. Boullay
4. A favorite new Song, by Mrs. Pick
5. Quartetto on the Clarinet, by Messrs. Granger, Boullay, Pick and Mallet
6. English Duett, sung by Mr. and Mrs. Pick
7. Grand Symphony of Pleyel.

Then we notice an organ recital given by William Blodgett at St. Peters' on December 7, 1796[6]), Mrs. Tubbs' song recital at Washington Hall in March 1797[7]) and on April 13, 1797[8]) a curious miscellaneous entertainment called

"Just in Time or Such things have been — Such things may be — Such things are. Mirth, Song and Sentiment by Chalmers and Williams from the Theatres, Boston,

---

1) Salem Gazette, Nov. 23, 1790. This must have been the organ made by Thomas Johnston of Boston for St. Peter's in 1754 but which was not erected there until 1770 when the church made an exchange with Johnston, giving him their old organ, purchased in 1743 by subscription from Mr. John Clark. For further information consult Brooks, p. 65.
2) Salem Gazette, July 10, 1792.
3) Salem Gazette, Sept. 2, 9, 1794.
4) Dezède.
5) Dibdin.
6) Salem Gazette, Dec. 6, 1796.
7) Salem Gazette, March 10, 1797.
8) Salem Gazette, April 11, 1797.

consisting of pieces, serious, comic, moral and entertaining in readings, recitations and songs. Performed at Dibdin's Vauxhall and the theatres in Europe."

In the following year, sometime in February, Washington Hall was the scene of a triumph for Mr. Spencer, the vocalist, and in connection with this concert was used, to my knowledge, for the first time in our musical history, the term *encore*. Said a correspondent in the Columbian Centinel, Boston, February 21, 1798:

Dr. Berkenhead and Co. entertained the inhabitants of Salem with a "Concert" on Thursday evening. — Washington Hall was well filled. Mrs. Berkenhead, though indisposed, sang with feeling and taste; Mrs. Spencer with emphasis and correctness; and Mr. Spencer was loudly applauded and repeatedly *encored*, by the gallery boys! The Bastile, by the Doctor, was admirably played on an elegant harpsichord, belonging to a respectable family in that town.

About this time, Salem came into possession of a 'New Concert Hall', in Marketstreet and it was here that Gottlieb Graupner with the assistance of "the best musicians from Boston" gave what he promised to be "more pleasing than any performance of the kind hitherto offered to the inhabitants of Salem"[1]). The memorable event took place on May 15, 1798 with a program in which chamber music figured pre-eminently:

PART 1st.

Grand Symphony by	Pleyl
Song 'On by the spur of valour goaded', Mr. Collins ..	Shield
Clarinet Quartetto, Messrs. Granger, Laumont, Von Hagen and Graupner	Vogel
Song 'He pipes so sweet', Mrs. Graupner	Hook
Concerto on the French horn, Mr. Rosier	Ponton [Punto?]
A favourite new Song 'Little Sally's wooden ware', Miss Solomon	Arnold
Full piece	Hayden

PART 2d.

Quartetto 'Who shall deserve the glowing praise', Mrs. Graupner, Mr. Granger, Mr. Collins, and Mr. Mallet	Linly
Concerto on the Clarinet, composed and performed by Mr. Shaffer	
A new favourite Echo song 'How do you do', Mrs. Graupner, accompanied on the hautboy by Mr. Graupner	Hook
Concerto on the violin, Laumont	Foder [Fodor]
A comic Irish Song 'Boston news', Mrs. Collins	
Concerto on the Hautboy, the composition of the celebrated Fisher, Mr. Graupner.	
Duet, 'Hey dance to the fiddle and tabor', from the much admired opera of Lock and Key[2]), Mrs. Graupner and	Mr. Collins
Finale	Pleyl

Number of performers 12 — Doors to be opened at 6 o'clock and the performance to begin precisely at half after seven. In consequence of the advice of some friends, Mr. Graupner has reduced the price of tickets to half a dollar each . . .

---

1) Salem Gazette, May 11, 15, 1798.
2) Shield.

This concert should have been followed on May 29[1]) by Mr. and Mrs. Rosier's benefit, but first Mr. Rosier's "public duties on Election Day" obliged him to postpone it to June 5 and then "his engagements to the Boston Cavalry" once more to June 7. Of course the Rosiers were very profuse in their apologies for those alterations.

The statement was made in the preceding pages that the Van Hagens do not seem to have risked a possible loss by giving benefit concerts at Boston. For this reason it is all the more interesting that young Peter A. Van Hagen — since they moved to Boston the Van became a Von — resolved to give a concert at Salem, his temporary residence, in the summer of 1798. That really the thrifty Van Hagens cared less for the glory of public appearance at Boston than for an actual benefit may be inferred from the fact that the Salem concert was only "to commence as soon as the subscription [was] found adequate to the expences" which he hoped to cover by his "terms — A subscriber for a ticket to admit a lady and gentleman, 1 dollar 50 cents; *do.* for one person 88 cents[!]; a non-subscriber, 1 dollar"[2]). It does not appear whether or not the inhabitants of Salem agreed to these odd 88 cents. It would almost seem that young Van Hagen postponed his concert by fully half a year as he again announced a concert for his benefit under almost literally the same terms on January 25, 1799, the only difference being that "a subscriber for a ticket for one person" received a rebate of 25 cents instead of 12. This change must have pleased the Salemites for the concert actually took place on February 5, 1799 with the assistance of his parents, Mr. and Mrs. Graupner, and "several of the best performers in Boston"[3]). Unfortunately the program was not mentioned, but probably it was arranged on very much the same lines as that presented on June 25, 1799 by Mrs. Graupner at the Concert Hall, Market Street for her benefit with Mr. Van Hagen, [sen.] as leader of the band "from Boston"[4]).

PART 1st.

Overture, composed by	Pleyel
Song by Mr. Munto	Dr. Arnold
A Sonata on the Grand Forte Piano	Kozeluch
for 4 hands, by Mrs. Von Hagen and Mr. Von Hagen, jun.	
'By my tender passion', a favourite song in the Haunted	
Tower, by Mrs. Graupner	Storace
Solo on the Clarinet, by Mr. Granger	Vogel
Lullaby, a favourite Glee for four voices, Mrs. Graupner,	
Mr. Granger, Mr. Mallet and Mr. Munto	Harrison
Concerto on the Violin by Mr. Von Hagen	Jearnowick

1) Salem Gazette, May 18, May 22, June 5, 1798.
2) Salem Gazette, Aug. 14, 1798.
3) Salem Gazette, January 25 and Feb. 5, 1799.
4) Salem Gazette, June 25, 1799.

PART 2d.

Concerto on the Piano Forte, by Mrs. Von Hagen .. ..   Haydn
Columbia's Bold Eagle, a patriotic song, words by a gentle-
    man of Salem. Music by Mr. Graupner and sung by
    Mrs. Graupner
Concerto on the Hautboy, by Mr. Graupner .. ..   Le Brun
The Play'd in Air, a much admired Glee in the Castle
    Spectre[1]), by Mrs. Graupner, Mr. Granger, Mr. Mallet
    and Mr. Munto
Quartetto by Messrs. von Hagen, sen. and jun., Mr. Lau-
    mont, and Mrs. Graupner.
'To Arms, to arms', a new patriotic song, written by Thomas
    Paine, A. M. sung by Mrs. Graupner and music by
    Mr. von Hagen, jun.
Finale .. ..   Haydn

For this concert 'A Citizen' addressed to Mr. Cushing, the owner of the
Salem Gazette, on June 25 a curious advance-criticism, highly flattering
to the participants. Said the citizen:

Mr. Cushing,

    I observe that a *Concert of Music* is advertised in your last paper, to be performed
on this evening for the benefit of Mrs. Graupner. It is to be hoped that, as the company expressed a great satisfaction for the last excellent Concert which was given
by Mr. Graupner, they will receive no less pleasure from this. To render the entertainment more complete, we are informed, that there will be added to the other instruments an excellent piano forte. The beauties of this instrument will be displayed in
the brilliant execution of Mrs. Von Hagen whose taste and talents procured her, when
in Holland, the admiration of the Court at the Hague, as they have since in America
commanded the applause of all who have heard her perform.
    To the claim which Mr. Graupner's abilities give him to the public patronage,
his misfortune in being burnt out of his house by the late fire at Boston will, it is hoped,
be duly considered by every human mind. Those that attend this concert, will have
added to the enjoyment of music, the satisfaction resulting from aiding those who
have suffered from a calamity which they themselves, as inhabitants of a wooden
town, are peculiarly exposed to.

A Citizen.

Finally "the excellent organ made by the celebrated Avery" for Rev.
Dr. Prince's Meeting House was to be "opened with several voluntaries by
an eminent master" during an afternoon-concert of sacred vocal and instrumental music on Sept. 19, 1800, for which, as usual, the best performers
in Boston had been engaged, but on account of the indisposition of one of
them the concert was unavoidably postponed and does not seem to have
taken place[2]). —

    "The Want of instruments, together with the Niggardliness of the People of this
Place, and their not having a Taste of Musick, render it impossible for any one of my
Profession to get a competent Maintenance here; and their Feuds and Animosities
are so great concerning their Government, that a Man can take but little Satisfaction
in being among them: so that, it is no better than burying one's self alive . . ."

---

1) Michael Kelly.
2) Salem Gazette, Sept. 16, 19, 1800.

Certainly this was anything but a compliment which John Owen Jacobi, the organist of Trinity Church, paid to the inhabitants of Newport, R. J. in a letter to Peter Evans of Philadelphia in March 1739[1]). Nor can it be maintained that the interest taken in music at Newport in after-years was very lively. Still, a few concerts are on record. Possibly the first given at Newport was the "grand" concert announced by a "number of the first performers from Boston, etc." for May 5, 1772 at the Court House[2]). In the following year, as will be remembered, William Selby became the organist of Trinity Church and he announced a benefit concert for August 3, 1774[3]). A few days later he resigned his position and a Mr. Knoetchel became his successor[4]). This gentleman then gave an afternoon-concert in the Colony House on September 18, 1774, the price of tickets being *three pounds* each, but, as Mr. Brooks who unearthed the announcement remarks, this fabulous sum was in depreciated currency and the price of the ticket would now be about fifty cents in silver. No other concert, it seems, was advertised until long after the war, when the announcement in the Newport Mercury, March 25, 1793 undeniably proves that Newport then possessed a Concert Hall where on "Tuesday Evening in Easter Week" The *St. Caecilia Society* granted to one of the members a benefit concert. Whether this society cultivated sacred vocal music only or both sacred and secular or instrumental music, does not appear. This possibly was the last concert of the century recorded by the press, unless we admit Mr. Tubbs' Concert and Reading at Mr. Penrose's Hall on May 2, 1797. It was called "*Oddities*, or a Certain cure for the spleen. After the manner of Dibdin consisting of singing and comic readings from eminent authors"[5]).

Newport's rival, Providence[6]), was not blessed with overly many concerts. To be sure, as early as August 1762 "Concerts of musick" were advertised in the Boston Evening Post (!) to take place there at the new School-house but these were daily performances of such tragedies as Cato and the pantomime of Harlequin Collector, the acts separated by music,

---

1) Reprinted under the heading 'Music in Rhode Island, 1739' in the Publ. of the R. I. Hist. Soc., New Ser., VII. Jan. 1900. The organ had been presented by Dean Berkeley in 1733 and Mr. Jacobi was induced to come over from England in 1736 as organist. The expenses of his voyage, £ 18, 15 s. were paid, and he was given a salary of £ 25 per annum. The organ was set up with the assistance of Charles Theodore Pachelbel of Boston, who was also the first organist. (See Brooks, p. 52.)
2) Newport Mercury, April 27, 1772.
3) Newport Mercury, August 1, 1774.
4) This Mr. Knoetchel must have been a relative, perhaps the son of the John Ernest Knoetchel who was organist of Trinity Church in the sixties at a salary of £ 30 and who died in October 1769. (Mason's Annals of Trinity Church, Sec. Ser. 1894, p. 313.)
5) Newport Mercury, May 2, 1797.
6) Population: 1790—6380; 1800—?451 inhabitants.

called concerts merely to evade the restrictions against theatrical entertainments. The first concert proper seems to have been given at Providence early in August 1768 under the direction of a Mr. Dawson[1]). It was announced as a concert of instrumental music during which by particular desire Mr. Dawson "presented the company with a hornpipe and Mr. Tioli [was to] perform a tambourin dance in Italian taste". This was followed on September 26, 1768[2]) by a concert under the direction of Mr. Tioli at Mr. Hacker's Room. Shortly afterwards, business urged Mr. Tioli's immediate departure and he "quitted with reluctance a place, the inhabitants of which are justly remarked for their politeness and affability towards strangers". Then we notice a concert of vocal and instrumental music given by William Blodgett with the assistance of "a number of masters from Boston" on Sept. 2, 1772[3]).

Not until after the war did I run across another concert announcement, when on June 28, 1784[4]) wás to be given

A Concert of Instrumental Music (consisting of clarinetts, flutes, French horns, bassoons etc.) at the State House ... beginning at early candle light.

This evidently was a band concert and there is reason to believe that it was given by a Mr. Hewill who in April had informed the young ladies and gentlemen of Providence that he had opened "a school of instrumental music in College street — [where he taught] the German flute, clarinet, bassoon, French horn, etc."[5]). Presumably Mr. Hewill simply gave an exhibition of the abilities of his pupils acquired under his tutorship. During the last decade of the eighteenth century the inhabitants of Providence received a taste of legitimate opera and drama and naturally the members of Mr. Harper's company sought to add to their income by offering entertainments when not on duty at the theatre. Thus Mr. and Mrs. Harper gave an 'Attic Entertainment' in December 1794[6]) but real concerts none. In fact the only entertainment presented during this and the following years which might deserve the name of concert was the one held on April 27, 1797[7]) by Mrs. Tubbs at the theatre for her benefit prior to leaving town. On this evening "the best selection of the most popular songs and duets [were to] be sung by Mrs. Tubbs and Miss Arnold, a young lady of 10 years of age. The songs to be accompanied on the Forte Piano by Mr. Tubbs".

Now Mrs. Tubbs, odd as this may seem at first reading, was the mother of Miss Arnold for, when announcing in the Eastern Herald of Portland,

1) Providence Gazette, July 30 1732.
2) Providence Gaz. Sept. 11, 1768.
3) Providence Gaz. Aug. 22, 1712. Subsequently, in 1714, W. Blodgett proposed to open a dancing school.
4) Providence Gazette, June 26, 1784.
5) Providence Gazette, April 24, 1784.
6) Providence Gazette, Dec. 6, 1794.
7) United States Chronicle, April 27, 1797.

Maine, Nov. 17, 1796 her intention of having at the Assembly Room there on November 21 a concert "to consist of the most popular songs sung last season at Covent Garden", she called herself "Mrs. Tubbs, late Mrs. Arnold of the Theatre Royal Covent Garden, London" incidentally remarking that after the concert Mr. Tubbs intended setting up a theatre. Without prying to closely into her family relations, it is clear that Mr. Tubbs cannot have been the lucky husband of such an accomplished artist for very long as the Oracle of the Day, Portsmouth, N. H.[1]) informed its readers on July 21, 1796 that Mrs. Arnold would give a concert at the Assembly Room on August 3d. The following was to be part of the selection for the occasion[2]):

Song 'The Bonny Bold Soldier'	Mrs. Arnold
Song 'The Market Lass'	Mrs. Arnold
Song 'Ellen, or the Richmond primrose girl, as sung by Mrs. Arnold repeatedly at the Boston theatre, with universal applause, accompanied on the Forte Piano	Mrs. Arnold
Voluntary pieces.	
Song 'Henry's cottage maid'	Mrs. Arnold
Song 'By moonlight on the green'	Mrs. Arnold
Song 'The heaving of the lead'	Mrs. Arnold
Song 'O listen, listen to the voice of love'	Mrs. Arnold
Song 'Mary's dream, or Sandy's ghost, by particular desire, accompanied on the Forte Piano	Mrs. Arnold

But this song recital is not the first concert on record at Portsmouth as "the band of music belonging to Col. Crane's regiment of artillery" gave a Public Concert at the Assembly Room on February 17, 1783[3]). How erroneous the popular belief is that the bands in the Continental Army consisted merely of a few fifes and drums and were incapable of playing none but fife and drum music may again be seen as this artillery band performed on said occasion

"several overtures, simphonies, military music, several songs, and several duettos on the French horn"

as it did about the same time at Salem, when on furlough.

Between this and the concert of 1796 we further notice one for the benefit of Horatio Garnet, composer of an 'Ode for American Independence', on September 28, 1789[4]) at the Assembly Room. And as "the musick, entertainment, etc. [was to be] the same as the assemblies last winter" it must be inferred that Portsmouth had occasion to enjoy concerts also in 1788. Indeed, it is more than probable that concerts, though perhaps private and interspersed with readings, etc., were given at the singing schools and Assemblies of all the different small cities mentioned and elsewhere very much more frequently than an examination of the extant newspaper files would

---

1) Population: 1790 — 4720; 1800 — 5339 inhabitants.
2) Copied from Brooks, p. 162.
3) New Hampshire Gazette, February 15, 1783.
4) New Hampshire Gazette, Sept. 24, 1789.

allow us to prove. A fitting illustration of how perhaps such affairs looked, may be found in a communication to the Columbian Centinel, Boston, from Concord, N. H. on September 23, 1797:

MUSICAL SOCIETY

On Tuesday the 12th inst. was the anniversary meeting of *Concord Musical Society*. At 2 o'clock, the members of the Society met at the Town House; and at 3 o'clock they moved in procession to the Meeting House, preceded by a number of musical performers, belonging to the society, playing on instruments and accompanied by a numerous crowd of spectators belonging to this and adjacent towns. The Rev. Mr. Parker, of Canterbury, introduced the exercises of the day by a most ingenious, excellent and sublime prayer, perfectly adapted to the occasion, addressed to the throne of the great author of "Harmony Divine". Several pieces of music, vocal and instrumental, were performed. A really classical Oration on Music, neat in composition, ingenious in design, was delivered by Philip Carrigan, jun. A. M. in which he gave a brief but enlightening view of music in general, from the earliest ages to the present day; stated the general principles of the nature of the art; delightfully describing its pleasing captivating charms; tracing its astonishing and beneficial influence over the mind, and its various socialising effects upon the heart of man, both in his native ferocious and more civilized state, justly ascribing to the powers and influence of music, not a little of the glory of the triumphs of our veteran armies over the minions of tyrants, in our late contest for liberty with Great Gritain, in which Americans were made freemen, and led to glory and honor by a *Washington* — and attributing to it much of the unprecedented courage and bravery of the numerous legions of Bunaparte, whom he has conducted to immortal fame, rendered invulnerable by the extatic inspirations of this heavenly science, every nerve beating time to the music of 'Marseilles Hymn' and other popular songs. In the style and delivery of this oration we observed with pleasure those traces of genius and gesticulations characteristic of the refined orator, which truly deserve and must ever command respect; and which gained Carrigan the liveliest testimonials of public applause, from a most brilliant ,respectable and very numerous and learned audience. He closed with a moral apostrophe, addressed to the auditory, in which (after a neat comparison of the human frame to a musical instrument) he enchantly invited all so to attune their hearts and lives, that they might meet in unison in the great Musical Society above. This is but an inadequate Comment on the worth of this oration. We hope to see it soon in print, when it will gain from the lovers of the Belles Lettres the eulogiums it deserves.

Perhaps there were never seen so many people together in this town, where all appeared so well satisfied; and where such unanimous applause was given the performances — the tribute was warm, general and hearty. Great thanks are due Mr. *Flagg* for his attendance, and the complaisant Mr. *Maurice* and the obliging Messrs. *Longs* for their assistance in the musical exercises. All was harmony and a brilliant ball graced the evening of the festive day.

This letter affords a curious glimpse into the activity of these provincial musical societies and proves at least that they were sincere, enthusiastic exponents of the musical art, fully aware of its importance as a factor of civilisation — and not wholly addicted to psalmody. Nor were contests between the musical societies of neighboring towns missing, and as such contests must be classed with concerts, an opportunity arises to quote the delightful description Mr. Louis C. Elson gives of the one between the singers of the First Parish of Dorchester, Mass. and the famous Stoughton Musical Society, founded in 1786 and the first impetus towards which was given by the establishment of William Billings' singing class of forty-eight members at Stoughton in 1774. Says Mr. Elson in his History of American Music (p. 28):

Many clergymen, in following the good old fashion of "exchanging pulpits," had become familiar with the excellent church music of Stoughton, and sounded its praises abroad. The singers of the First Parish of Dorchester, Massachusetts, took umbrage at this, and challenged the Stoughton vocalists to a trial of skill. The gauntlet was at once taken up, and the contest took place in a large hall in Dorchester, many of the leading Bostonians coming out to witness it. The Dorchester choristers were male and female, and had the assistance of a bass viol. The Stoughton party consisted of twenty selected male voices, without instruments, led by the president of the Stoughton Musical Society, Elijah Dunbar, a man of dignified presence and of excellent voice. The Dorchester singers began with a new anthem. The Stoughtonians commenced with Jacob French's 'Heavenly Vision', the author of which was their fellow townsman. When they finally sang, without books, Handel's 'Hallelujah Chorus', the Dorchestrians gave up the contest, and gracefully acknowledged defeat."

Occasionally several societies would form an association in lieu of contests and to one at least we possess a tangible clue. The Boston Athenaeum possesses (in 12⁰, 12 p.):

The Constitution of the Essex Musical Association. Established 28th March, 1797. Newburyport. Printed by Edmund' M. Blunt. State Street — 1798.

The curious pamphlet is divided into twelve sections dealing mostly with the transaction of routine business, but a few articles are of interest in connection with my theme. Thus the association was to be limited to the County of Essex but an ink memorandum reads' "excepting the case of honorary members". The association was to meet quarterly, beginning from the foundation and after the first year a public musical exhibition was to be held annually. As "standard book" being mentioned Hans Gram's "Massachusetts Compiler" probably the association cultivated principally sacred music but it is expressly stated that the "Performances [were to be] vocal and instrumental" with "bass viols, violins and flutes" as "instruments used at present"! The annual meeting was held on the second Monday in September and quarterly meetings on the second Mondays in December, March and June at the "permanent" "place of meeting — Mr. Parker Spoffords, Boxford". Possibly this pretty obscure town was selected because about half of the forty-four members hailed from there, amongst them the "Director" Samuel Holyoke, born at Boxford in 1762, who also seems to have been the founder of the Essex Musical Association as he heads the list of "the names of the members in their order of admission".

If public concerts were given at New Haven, Conn. they must have escaped my attention, but the city was inhabited by at least one musician capable of giving concerts. Said John Rowe in his diary[1]) under January 5, 1768 that he spent the evening at Joseph Harrison's when

---

[1]) Edited in extracts by Edward L. Pierce in the Mass. Hist. Soc. Proc. 1895, X, p. 11—108.

"Mr. Mills of New Haven entertained us most agreeably on his violin; I think he plays the best of any performers I ever heard."

On the other hand I am in a position to submit at least the odd program of a concert performed by the "musical family of Mr. Salter, organist of New Haven, late from England" and who has already attracted our attention in New Jersey and South Carolina, on February 2, 1797[1]) at Mr. Poole's Hall in New London, Conn.:

Act I. Master Salter, a boy of 10 years old, will play several beautiful airs, marches, minuets, etc. on the piano forte, accompanied by Mr. Salter on the violin. Miss Salter, a child of seven years old, will sing the Waxen Doll.

Act II. Duett, by Master and Miss Salter on the pianoforte, accompanied by Mr. Salter. A Song by Miss Salter. Several airs on the piano forte by Mr. Salter. The Battle of Prague, a favourite musical piece on the same instrument. To conclude with a

Sea Engagement

Representing two fleets engaging, some sinking, others blowing up. Neptune drawn by two sea horses, emerging from the waves. — Old Charon in his boat — A mermaid and Delphin — Between the music, Master Salter will speak the three warnings.

To begin precisely at seven o'clock. — Tickets may be had at the door. Price 1 *s.* 6 *d.* for grown persons, children 9 *d.* — D. Salter having the misfortune to be afflicted with weakness of sight, will, he hopes, claim the attention of the public.

Finally Hartford, Conn., then little more than a village[2]), attracts our attention and it will be seen that the very few concerts given there during the last decade of the century were incidental to the energetic but ill-advised efforts of the Old American Company to include Hartford in their theatrical *circuit* from 1794 on. It would be interesting to know what the unsophisticated inhabitants thought when the vocalists and instrumentalists of the company forced the *heavy* music of those days on their ears on July 27, 1795[3]) at the Concert House, and on August 25, 1796[4]) at the theatre for the benefit of Mr. Relain. The programs of these two Grand Concerts of Vocal and Instrumental Music read:

JULY 27, 1795

PART I

Grand Overture	Haydn
By Messrs. Relain, Hodgkinson, Henri, Beranger, Laumont, Pelissier, Dupuis, Savarin, La Massue, and Rosindal	
Clarinet Concerto	Mr. Henri
Song — Hunting cantata 'Hark the sweet horn' .	Mr. Prigmore
Quartette. Messrs. Relain, Hodgkinson, Laumont, and Savarin	
Harp Solo	Mr. Relain
Grand Symphony .. ., ...	By Messrs. Relain, etc.

1) Connecticut Gazette, February 2, 1797.
2) Population in 1810 only 3955 inhabitants.
3) Connecticut Courant, July 27, 1795.
4) Connecticut Courant, Aug. 8, 1796.

Part II

Grand Chasse. By Messrs. Relain, etc.	Stamitz
Solo French horn	Mr. Pelissier
Song 'Tom Tackle'	Mr. Hodgkinson
Harp Solo	Mr. Relain
Clarinet Quartette, Mr. Henri, Relain, Laumont and Savarin	
Grand Symphony. By Messrs. Relain etc.	Pleyell

AUGUST 25, 1796

I Act.

Grand Symphony, composed by	Haydn
Hunting Song, by	Mr. Tyler
Harp Concerto, by	Mr. Relain
Song, accompanied by the harp	Mrs. Hodgkinson
Violin Quartette by Monsr's Relain, Henry, Siruo and Rosindal	
Song	Mr. Tyler
Grand Symphony, composed by	Pleyel

II Act.

Grand Overture	
Song, by	Mr. Hodgkinson
Clarinet Concerto by	Mr. Henry
Harp Solo, by	Mr. Relain
Song, by	Mrs. Hodgkinson
Quintette by Mons'rs Relain, Henry, Siruo, Abel and Rosindal	
The whole to conclude with that admirable Symphony	
La Chasse, composed by	Stamitz

That these were excellent programs, nobody with historical instincts will deny and if the inhabitants of Hartford did not journey home with the impression of having enjoyed "grand" concerts we should pardon them, knowing as we do that even to-day, at the beginning of the twentieth century, similar symphony programs if given in American cities of Hartford's size in 1796, would very probably cause some uneasiness. Indeed, it may be doubted whether an American manager of to-day would be bold enough even to attempt such a "heavy" symphony concert in a settlement of less than three thousand inhabitants.

CONCLUSION.

THOUGH the inferences and deductions from the data filling this book
have been drawn in their proper place, it will do no harm to recapitulate
the most salient points.

In the first place, I hope to have permanently crippled the current
notion that secular music had a Cinderella existence in the *curriculum* of
our musical life during the eighteenth century. In fact, the theory may
be advanced that sacred music was cultivated in America, New England
possibly excepted, neither so steadily no so intelligently and progressively
as secular music. Then the observation forced itself on us that America
joined the movement towards public concerts simultaneously with European
countries [1]). This would have gone without saying, had it not become customary to deny the fact, indeed, its possibility. To compare our achieve-
ments during the formative period of our musical history with the concert-
life at London, Paris, Berlin and other musical centers of the Old World
would be folly, yet, considering the vast difference in opportunities, population, travelling facilities, distances, etc. we may well feel proud of our record.
Music in America was provincial but not primitive.

Being an English colony, our country naturally took England as a model
in musical matters, whether they pertained to repertory, customs, or details
of management. The French Revolution interrupted this predominantly
English current and visibly infused French blood into the musical body.
With the tide of immigration, caused by the outcome of our War for Independence, the cosmopolitan channels gradually widened and soon sub-
merged Colonial traditions. While the tide of immigration added many
capable musicians to the ranks of performers, it also altered the character
of our population in general. The emigrants of about 1800 certainly did

---

1) To illustrate the point (p. 2, f. n.) that musical societies were founded in
Germany long before 1660 mention should have been made of W. Nagel's instruc-
tive article on 'Die Nürnberger Musikgesellschaft (1588—1629)' in the M. f. M., 1895.
Further data were brought to light by Sandberger in his essay on Hassler in the
Bavarian Musical Monuments, 1905.

not possess the refinement of the Colonials and our musical life suffered accordingly. This change in the character and attitude of the public together with the double-edged effects of the expansion of opera undoubtedly produced towards the end of the century a stagnation of the interest taken in concerts. How long this stagnation lasted, will have to concern the historian who attempts to span the bridge between the eighteenth and nineteenth centuries.

Examining our early concert-life closely, we noticed how instrumental music was cultivated to the exclusion almost of choral. Efforts were made to draw the latter forth from the church choirs and singing schools but they were successful only temporarily or failed entirely. On the whole, vocal music was represented on the programs of the eightheenth century only by airs, duets, etc. from oratorios and operas, by popular songs or by catches and glees. Thus the vocal stars in combination with the "capital" instrumentalists gradually gained the upperhand. The programs became more and more miscellaneous but what they won in variety they lost in solidity. Yet the symphonies of Haydn and Pleyel, his rival in popularity the world over, remained the pillars and it cannot be denied that the American public had ample opportunity to form an acquaintance with their works and those of the composers of the Mannheim school and many others once in vogue. Finally, if those musicians who shaped the destinies of our concert-life, were to be pointed out, we would probably select Francis Hopkinson, James Bremner, Andrew Adgate, John Bentley, William Tuckey, Alexander Reinagle, James Hewitt, Josiah Flagg and William Selby.

INDEX.

Hausdruckerei Dr. Martin Sändig oHG., Wiesbaden